Africans and the Exiled Life

African Governance and Development

Series Editor: Olayiwola Abegunrin, Howard University

African Governance and Development identifies and elaborates on the strategic place of governance and development within the African studies. Reflecting the fact that life in Africa continues to change; particularly in political, development, and socio-economic arenas; this series explores issues focusing on the ongoing mobilization for good governance and the search for sustainable and economic development. The *African Governance and Development* series address gaps and larger needs in the developing scholarship on Africa and the African Diaspora. This series provides scholarly monographs and edited collections in the humanities, social science, and social scientific traditions. Contributors are encouraged to submit book length manuscripts that encompass, besides the above named topics, those focusing on: Africa's political economy and economic development, Africa's place in world trade development, democratization of African countries, the inclusion and representation of ethnic minorities, and the role of gender in Africa's development. Works can be focused on a single African country, a region of African countries, or the African continent's place as a global player.

Recent Titles

Pan-Africanism in Modern Times: Challenges, Concerns, and Constraints, edited by Olayiwola Abegunrin and Sabelle Ogbobode Abidde

Nigeria, Africa, and the United States: Challenges of Governance, Development, and Security, by Olayiwola Abegunrin

Human Rights in Nigeria's External Relations: Building the Record of a Moral Superpower, by Philip C. Aka

Nigeria's Niger Delta: Militancy, Amnesty, and the Post-Amnesty Environment, by Sabella Ogbobode Abidde

Trade Unions and the Age of Information and Communication Technologies in Kenya, by Eric E. Otenyo

Africans and the Exiled Life: Migration, Culture, and Globalization edited by Sabella Ogbobode Abidde and Brenda Ingrid Gill

Africans and the Exiled Life

Sabella Ogbobode Abidde
and Brenda Ingrid Gill

LEXINGTON BOOKS
Lanham • Boulder • New York • London

Published by Lexington Books
An imprint of The Rowman & Littlefield Publishing Group, Inc.
4501 Forbes Boulevard, Suite 200, Lanham, Maryland 20706
www.rowman.com

Unit A, Whitacre Mews, 26-34 Stannary Street, London SE11 4AB

British Library Cataloguing in Publication Information Available

Library of Congress Cataloging-in-Publication Data Available

ISBN 978-1-4985-5088-8 (cloth : alk. paper)
ISBN 978-1-4985-5089-5 (electronic)

∞™ The paper used in this publication meets the minimum requirements of American National Standard for Information Sciences—Permanence of Paper for Printed Library Materials, ANSI/NISO Z39.48-1992.

Printed in the United States of America

This book is dedicated to all immigrants—men, women, and children—from all corners of the world who are crossing and crisscrossing national and international borders in search of safety, security, comfort, and possibilities. May your dreams come true...be well and be safe!

Contents

List of Figures

List of Tables

Abbreviations

ACBC	African Capacity Building Centre
ASUU	Academic Staff Union of Universities
AU	African Union
BBC	British Broadcasting Corporation
CANOWACAT	Cameroon North Westerners Association
CCMA	Commission for Conciliation, Mediation and Arbitration
CODESRIA	Council for the Development of Social Science Research in Africa
CoRMSA	Consortium for Refugees and Migrants South Africa
CPE	Cameroon Pidgin English
CSME	CARICOM Single Market Economy
DRC	Democratic Republic of Congo
ECLAC	Economic Commission for Latin America and the Caribbean
ECOWAS	Economic Community of West African States
EDF	European Development Fund
ESOL	English for Speakers of Other languages
FSMB	Federation of State Medical Boards
GBP	Ghanaian Business Promotion
GDP	Gross Domestic Product
GPA	Grade Point Average
HVRI	Hazards and Vulnerability Research Institute
IDMC	Internal Displacement Monitoring Centre
IDP	Internally Displaced Persons
IDRC	International Development Research Center
IOM	International Organization for Migration
ILO	International Labor Organization

IMF	International Monetary fund
INADI	Institute against Discrimination, Xenophobia and Racism
ISIS	Islamic State in Iraq and Syria
LAC	Latin America, and the Caribbean
LGBT	Lesbian, Gay, Bisexual, and Transgender
LIFE	Legal Immigration Family Equity
MIPEX	Migration Integration Policy Index III
MST	Migration Systems Theory
NEMA	National Emergency Management Agency
NRC	Norwegian Refugee Council
NBME	National Board of Medical Examiners
OAU	Organization of African Unity
OECD	Organization of Economic Cooperation and Development
RCCG	Redeemed Christian Church of God
SADC	Southern Africa Development Community
SAP	Structural Adjustment Program
SIJ	Special Immigrant Juvenile
TT	Trinidad and Tobago
UN	United Nations
UNDP	United Nations Development Program
UNECA	United Nations Economic Commission for Africa
UNESCO	United Nations Educational, Scientific and Cultural Organization
UNHCR	United Nations High Commission for Refugees
UNICEF	United Nations International Children's Emergency Fund
USMLE	United States Medical Licensing Examination
WMR	World Migration Report
WTO	World Trade Organization

Acknowledgments

This book is an offshoot of a general-purpose essay the lead editor wrote several years ago, when he was a graduate student at Howard University. In the intervening years, a lot has happened in the areas of globalization, migration, and culture. Public intellectuals, scholars, journalists, activists, policy- and decision-makers have been writing and debating these issues especially in terms of how they affect the global common.

Thirty contributors initially signed up for this project. However, the vagaries of life and the challenges of intellectual commitment made it difficult for many to come on board. Even so, we are grateful to the twelve who eventually made their contributions. We are also grateful to Professor Olayiwola Abegunrin for his words of encouragement, and to Kathryn Tafelski (a former Assistant Acquisitions Editor at Lexington Books), who thought this book was doable and gave her support.

We would also like to thank Madhu Koduvalli for her professionalism and timely responses. In addition, we are grateful to Emily Roderick for her insightful comments and suggestions. And to Courtney Morales, who assisted Emily in doing such a wonderful job. And a special mention and appreciation to Professor Mojubaolu Olufunke Okome of Brooklyn College New York. As the editor of *Ìrìnkèrindò: a Journal of African Migration*, she gave her consent to reproduce Professor Nyang's essay; and to Nyang himself who, within hours of asking, signed off on the idea.

We are immensely grateful to the anonymous reviewers for their generosity of time and intellectual commitment. Thank you! Other than being a dependable friend and contributor, Professor Elisha Jasper Dung spent countless hours on formatting and technical issues. He made the writing and editing process less difficult.

Sabella Ogbobode Abidde
Montgomery, Alabama
Brenda Ingrid Gill
Mobile, Alabama

Introduction

The Goings and Comings of Africans in a Globalizing World

Sabella Ogbobode Abidde and Brenda Ingrid Gill

There is the inclination, among non-Africans, to think that globalization is a new phenomenon in Africa. It is not. For several centuries, Africans have had contacts with societies across the Atlantic, the Indian Ocean and the Mediterranean Sea. For instance, empires of the fifteenth- to nineteenth-century sub-Saharan Africa had relationship with their European and Asian counterparts—and so did the Pre- and Islamic empires of North Africa and the various empires and kingdoms in the Horn of Africa. In addition, there was the transatlantic slave trade, the spread of the Abrahamic religions, colonization, the two world wars and the Cold War and, eventually, contacts with global organizations such as the World Bank and the World Trade Organization.

Although these connections and relationships have not always favored Africans, they are nonetheless ways and means through which Africans have engaged, and were involved, in the globalization process. While in many instances Africans maintained their distinct culture, they also influenced and were influenced by other cultures and traditions. Since the twentieth century, however—and as migration has become almost a one-way event (from Africa to the rest of the world)—the African culture and traditions are being altered in ways many had not imagined possible. As Africans travel to lands far and wide, they imbibe new ways of life. Even within Africa's large cities and metropolitan areas, the effects of foreign culture on the local culture and social mores are very apparent.

Within and outside of the continent, Africans have had to content themselves with cultural dilemmas. These dilemmas are greater among generations of older African immigrants in the United States, the United Kingdom, Canada, Germany and other parts of the industrialized society. For instance, should they practice sororate, levirate and plural marriages? Should they enforce female genital circumcision? Should they accept having children outside of marriage? What is to be the ubiquitous dating and premarital-sex among teenagers, and the separation-divorce rate among married adults? At home and abroad, Africans need not be afraid. As members of the global community, therefore, they must embrace cultural and social changes. Africans need not abandon their authenticity and originality, but must be willing to adapt.

Events in the first two decades of the twenty-first century seem to indicate that international migration will not abate anytime soon. Political, social, economic, cultural, geoclimatic and globalizing forces in the Middle East, Africa, Latin America and Asia are propelling the movements of people—several millions—around the world. And while much of the conversation has centered on self-migration, millions more are forced to leave. They involuntarily go into exile. Whether migration is forced or voluntary, international borders, especially in Europe and the United States, are being breached by those fleeing or being beckoned.

As Syria, Yemen, Iraq, Afghanistan, the Democratic Republic of the Congo and other countries descend into chaos and turn into killing fields, the need to escape maiming, death and/or destruction has pushed millions of their citizens into exile. As the economic and political conditions in several African countries become unbearable, it is the human instinct to survive that has forced untold numbers to risk their lives for a better future for themselves and for their children. Even for those whose local and domestic conditions are not calamitous, the thinking is that there is a better life out there. Therefore, the search for greener pastures in a foreign land is as compelling as the need to escape persecution, wars, violent conflicts and geoclimatic uncertainties.

While relocation to a foreign country—especially to the industrialized countries of the West—has mostly been fruitful and beneficial to many, it can be and has been painful and agonizing for others. For instance, there are the complexities of culture, religion, social mores, the rule of law, etc. Not minding the difficulties and challenges associated with relocation, most immigrants are happy and have no regret leaving their native country. However, those who have benefited the most are the younger generation or children of immigrants; they have generally fared better—going on to become an integral part of their new country within a decade or two.

In putting this book together, we have assembled disparate voices to interrogate the processes, experiences and consequences of migration. In chapter 1—"Why They Migrate: Empirical Evidence"—Leo Bombom and Paul Erhunmwunsee shed light on the empirical evidence of the many implicit and obvious factors that shape the nature, direction, magnitude and implications of African migration to other parts of the world in the last few decades. In chapter 2—"The Geography and the Patterns of Migration"—Elisha Dung explores several questions, including but not limited to the demographic characteristics of migrants, and the temporal and regional patterns of migration. In chapter 3, "Trekking Across The Sahara: A Long History, Troubled Past," Alecia Hoffman wants to know what influence North Africa, with its sub-Saharan connections, had on Africa and the world in the post-modern era, and how the historical disconnect between the North and the South can be resolved.

Chapter 4—"Nigerians and the Pursuit of the Golden Fleece"—is by Olayinka Oyegbile. He argues that in post-Colonial Nigeria, as in the colonial era, Nigerians still venture overseas in search of the "Golden Fleece": going abroad in search of educational and economic opportunities not readily available to them at home. He goes on to examine contemporary factors that continue to make migration attractive to Nigerians. In chapter 5, "Impact of Culture on Exiles," Bruce Ormond Grant explores the terms "exile" and "culture" without extending a specific space to "Africans." In chapter 6, "The Children of Immigrant," Sasha Drummond-Lewis untangles the "black" immigrant children with an examination of how the various modes of arrival among African and Afro-Caribbean children who are foreign and native born impact their lived experiences in the United States.

In chapter 7, "Relocation From Africa, Latin America, And The Caribbean: Issues And Challenges," Brenda Gill examines some of the issues and challenges emigrants face in the host countries. Further, she identifies the positive and negative effects on the natives, their families, and their home countries' economic development. In chapter 8—"Xenophobia in Africa, Latin America the Caribbean"—Brenda Gill and George K. Danns examine the issues of xenophobia in Africa, Latin America and the Caribbean. They explore not only the impact of such issues on the exiled, but also the role of globalization on xenophobic practices and awareness. Sulayman Nyang, in chapter 9—"The African Immigrant Family in The United States of America: Challenges And Opportunities"—methodically explores many of the challenges and prospects an immigrant family in the United States faces.

In chapter 10, "Multifaceted Identity Options: The Case of Two Immigrant Associations in South Africa," Magdaline Mai explores what she calls "immigrants' multifaceted identity options." For instance, she argues that, in Cameroon, there is a divide between Anglophone and Francophones, but in the Cameroonian diaspora in South Africa, this divide is not as strong as it is often portrayed in scholarly literature. The result is thus the fragmentation of political and social identities where an immigrant may identify with conflicting national and transnational identity options. In chapter 11, "Building Individual Future as an Unwanted African Migrant in Johannesburg: Vulnerability, Hope and Micro-entrepreneurship," Christal Oghogho Spel calls attention to how social exclusion shapes the socioeconomic life of the unwanted migrants. Among others, the author argues that immigration management should focus on developing the space for micro-entrepreneurship rather than criminalizing informal migration.

In chapter 12, "Representation, Immigration, Experience and Memory: A Study of representational dynamics of "the other" in post-Imperial Britain (1947–1990s)" Dollin Wilson Ovaroh-Holt assesses the proposition that the British media coverage of African and African Caribbean minority ethnic communities is permeated with "othering."

In chapter 13, "African Immigrants and the American Experience," Sabella Abidde argues that the United States is not (exactly) what many aspirant immigrants think it is: as personally and professionally satisfying as the American society can be for many African immigrants, many are conflicted by the cultures and traditions of a society that may be at variance with their own experiences and expectations. Finally, again Sabella Abidde, in chapter 14—"Nigerians in America: Interpersonal Relationships and the Pull of Globalization"—argues that interpersonal relationships are complicated, but it is more so for new immigrants trying to navigate the new cultures and social mores of their societies. He argues that for older Africans who migrate to the West, one of the conflicting questions is whether to culturally and socially remain African, and if so, to what extent? Or to westernize, and if so to what extent?

In totality, *Africans and the Exiled Life: Migration, Culture and Globalization* examined how the forces of migration, globalization, and culture have shaped, and continues to shape, the thinking, the worldview, and the everyday lives of Africans and African diaspora who relocated to the United States, Asia, Africa, Europe, Latin America and the Caribbean. Overwhelming, the material presented suggests that living in exile, whether forced or voluntary, is not an easy experience, but one that presents several challenges and in some instances, pain and anguish. Further, the discussion of "Africans" and their exiled lives show that similar to other groups, Africans continue to relocate from their homelands in substantial numbers.

Several questions have been answered throughout this book: What is the geography and pattern of migration? Why do some Africans find it difficult to adjust to their new home? Where do they go when they migrate from their homelands? Why do they migrate mainly to specific countries? What theories can be used to make sense of migration, culture and globalization? Why do they migrate? What is the empirical evidence? What impact does culture have on exiles? What are some issues and challenges immigrants face as a consequence of relocation? What role does xenophobia play in the relocation of African and Latin America and the Caribbean (LAC) nationals? What are the experiences of children whose parents immigrate? The answers to these questions can assist professionals, politicians, international agencies, academicians, religious leaders and all those concerned with refugees and those concerned with refugees and other persons who migrate better address the resultant problems and challenges such relocation presents.

In the end, what this book has done is to cross-examine some of the realities, challenges and opportunities associated with moving from one culture to another. This book is not a finality on the question of migration and the forces of globalization. Rather, what we have done is to, modestly, add to the ongoing discussions and understandings of a phenomenon that has continued to impact, negatively and positively, a process that has been ongoing long before modern humans began to reshape the society they live in.

Chapter 1

Why They Migrate

The Empirical Evidence

Leonard Sitji Bombom and Paul O. Erhunmwunsee

INTRODUCTION

Before the crystallization of human civilization, human beings have engaged in movement between places. In its basic form, migration is a simple process of movement from one location to another. It is the same process that has remained unchanged over time. However, this simple process manifests in several types of patterns, engages many different forms of processes and produces a complexity of implications in our modern world that has warranted both local and global attention. It is a process that involves human trafficking, resources flow and transfer of ideas, which are vital to human and societal development. Yet, there are also many unpalatable implications associated with migration, such as human trafficking, crime and violence, resource depletion, among others. The cause for concern is therefore genuine.

As nations maintain their independence, territorial integrity has, essentially, assumed significant proportions, first for the protection of national resources and eventually develop and later to forge a common identity for its occupants. This development has necessitated the demarcation, preservation and protection of national boundaries with the notorious idea of keeping others out. It is in this sense that migration has become a global issue of concern.

Though movement within a country may be regulated, such regulations are frequently unchallenged. In this context, movement from rural, impoverished parts of the country into the urban, more developed cities, known as rural-urban migration, is an important aspect of migration as it changes the human-development landscape and rearranges resource production, flow and control. Rural-rural and urban-urban migration are other types of the movement process that have engendered serious consideration as well. Governments all over the world have proposed and implemented policies to enhance the profits of the internal migration processes and minimize any negative effects that may arise because of the process. They also examine ways to maximize the benefits of allowing others to cross into their borders without risking the loss of their identity, and deterioration in resources and quality of life. It is this international migration, with its almost endless waves of human traffic, that has drawn deserved national and global attention because it has vast implications that reverberate forever.

It is estimated that over 1 billion people in the world are migrants.[1] Most of these people are internal migrants—those who moved from one part of a country to another, without necessarily crossing international boundaries. In 2009, the UN Development Program[2] estimated that over 740 million people were internal migrants. In 2013, there were an estimated 232 million international migrants, that is, 3.2 percent of the world's population. This increased to 3.3 percent in 2015, with an estimated 244 million international migrant population.[3]

Africa's migrant population has been on the increase as well. Zlotnik[4] computed from several sources including statistics from the United Nations that, in 1960, there were 9.4 million migrants from Africa to the rest of the world. This increased to 9.7 million in 1970 and leapfrogged to 14.4 million in 1980. The increase in the number of international African migrants slowed. In 1990, there were 15.5 million; 15.6 million in 2000; and, 17.1 million in 2010. In 2013, the migration stock from Africa was estimated at 18.6 million.[5] This seemingly large volume of African migrants has created an impression of Africa and Africans as being on the move. As in other parts of the world, especially Asia, Europe and America, which form some of the most important migration corridors of the world, Africa has produced a constant flow of migrants to various parts of the world but most importantly to the Western Hemisphere, especially Europe and America. The share of African migration to Asia, especially the Middle East, has also been on the increase in recent years. The reasons for these movements from the African continent to other parts of the world are varied and more complex than have hitherto been assumed.

This chapter examines some of the fundamental reasons for why Africans move, and is organized thus: First, the migration process is conceptualized through several extant theories and concepts of migration to provide a general understanding of the factors and conditions within which people, all over the world, migrate. Second, the spatial diversity of African migration is examined. Third, some of the reasons for African migration are discussed along with their implications. Finally, the chapter concludes with recommendations of the way forward.

CONCEPTUALIZING HUMAN MIGRATION

Generally, the early models of migration are simple and attempted to explain, in rudimentary terms, the nature of migration. Ravenstein's model[6] conceptualized migration as a function of distance. The farther away a destination is the lower the number of migrants that would move to it. The principle around which this model is constructed is known as the distance decay principle.

One of the classical and most popular models of migration is the push-pull model. It is probably the model that is most commonly used to explain why people move. The model considers the conditions at either or both the origin and destination ends as the driving force behind the decision to migrate. When conditions are negative, unbearable and unacceptable, people are pushed away from the origin point. When conditions are positive and potentially beneficial, people are pulled toward a destination point. Push factors include natural disasters such as floods, earthquakes and volcanic activities, poverty, violence, crime and wars, economic hardship, political and religious oppression, and general instability. These conditions create conducive atmosphere for emigration. On the other hand, economic prosperity, political and religious freedom and liberty, social justice and violent-free conditions are factors that may attract or pull immigrants into a region. Movement between two places is therefore premised on either or both conditions existing at the locations.

It is important to note that usually these conditions are relative, which requires each potential migrant to weigh to arrive at a decision. When the advantages of leaving an area outweigh the benefits of remaining, the migrant may choose to relocate. However, often there are intervening barriers, which would have to be overcome by the potential migrant. This may include restrictive laws (e.g., Visa), costs and risks that may be associated with the journey to the desired destination.[7] The World Migration Report[8] and the International Organization for Migration (IOM) report[9] have indicated that both the risks and restrictions on international migration, particularly for African migrants to their preferred destinations in Europe and North America, have significantly increased. This illustrates the additional burden that migrants would have to surmount in their decisions to emigrate from a "push location" to a "pull location."

Flahaux and De Haas[10] offered an interesting perspective on the push-pull factors debate, especially within the context of international migration. They argue that the artifacts of the push-pull model are predicated on the assumptions that emigration from an area would decrease with improved conditions. However, most international migrations emanate from middle-income rather than the very poor countries with much less income and larger "geographical opportunity gaps." This migration trend, they argue, is better understood within Wilbur Zelinsky's hypothesis of mobility transition,[11] which was initially proposed to explain rural-urban migration. The hypothesis postulated that the relationship between development and migration is nonlinear, but generally, increasing development in countries considered as poor is associated with increasing mobility and migration activities rather than the expected decrease even as conditions improve.

The push conditions, therefore, are not sufficient prerequisites for migration. People need to possess the capacity and capability to migrate. These additional resources are often provided by modern development and improved socio-economic and political conditions at the points of origin. Consequently, as societies become more developed, people come into possession of greater ambitions and the necessary economic power to translate that ambition into reality. The potential for migration become more potent. The cost burden of international migration is large and can only be afforded by those who have the means, especially when the friction of distance is equally burdensome. Even for people at the borders of desirable destinations, governments' migration restrictions would demand a certain degree of ambition to make the leap from staying back to crossing the borders.

There is no denying the fact that eventually net emigrant countries may transform into net immigrant countries as they become wealthy. However, before such a transformation, there is a transition period within which large-scale emigration is tempered by trickles of immigrant population into the area, the process which eventually reverses as nations attain wealthy statuses. This is known in the literature as the Migration Hump, the point at which emigration flow becomes a trickle and eventually reverses into a net migration.[12] The development of societies is therefore an important impetus for immigration because it enhances both the aspirations of their people to better living and their capabilities to effect these aspirations. Access to resources, networks, education, the media and communication are expanded and information flow, which is vital to feedbacks and processes necessary for effective immigration to become more available and accessible. People's capacities are therefore developed to such an extent that they become very much aware of opportunities for self-development and their capacities to achieve their aspirations. Development therefore drives modern migration processes, rather than stymieing it. According to Flahaux and De Haas[13] this should be the context within which current migration patterns, intensities and directions should be examined.

The immigration process is more complex than conceptualized by any one of these models. It is a potpourri of many intertwined factors that span across the spectrum of these individual models. Of course, as migration processes become more complex, new perspectives are demanded to shed more light on an otherwise mundane event. In this wise therefore it would be difficult to isolate any one model that fits all the scenarios of why people move. Suffice to indicate, however, that migration events are subject to deeper influences of certain portions of any one of these conceptualized realities. This is necessary to explain and understand the patterns of African migration and why the people move.

Patterns and Trends in African Migration

In absolute terms, the number of international African migrants has been on the increase since the 1960s. However, the rate of increase has slowed down over the years. Figure 1.1 shows a fantastic leap between 1970 and 1980, and an almost steady migration incidence between 1980 and 2000. Since 2000, however, international African migration is in a gentle but noticeable slope incline. As a percentage of the population of Africa, however, the trend fluctuates. Figure 1.2 shows a dip in 1970 and a deeper dip in 2000. Between a high in 1980 and the dip in 2000, there is a steady decline in international African migration relative to the population size of Africa. There is a consensus that intra-continental migration in Africa has traditionally been larger than inter-continental migration. Figure 1.3 amply demonstrates this fact.

Whereas inter and intra-continental migration has increased in absolute numbers since 1960, immigration into Africa from other parts of the world has steadily declined. Between 1960 and 1980, the number of international migrants into Africa decreased by about 67 percent. From a low in 1960,

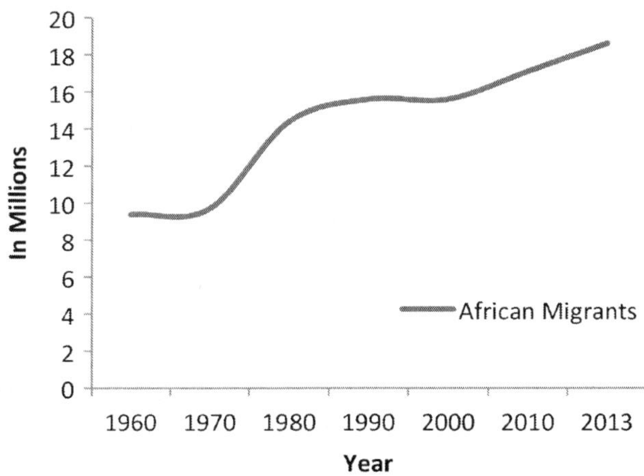

Figure 1.1 Trends in International African Migration.

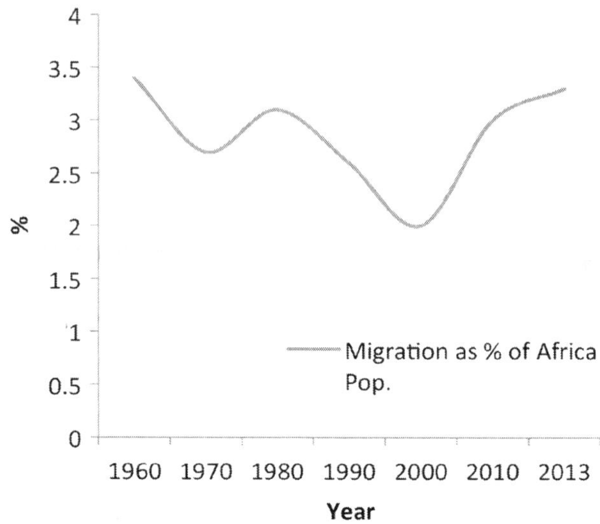

Figure 1.2 Trend in International African Migration as a Percentage of Population.

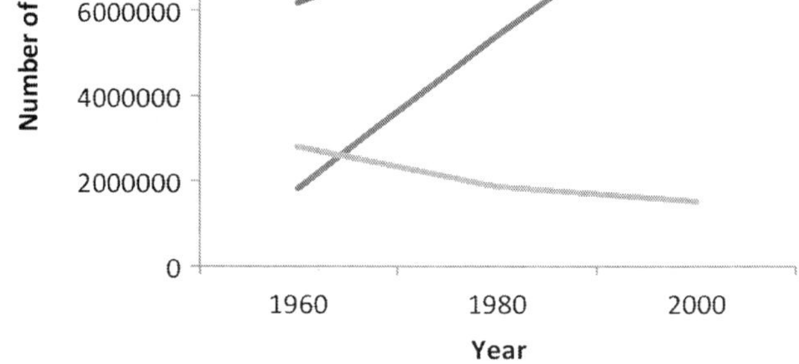

Figure 1.3 Africa International Migration Trends.

inter-continental migration has made a sharp increase, and so has intra-continental migration, though the figure suggests that the rates of increase for intercontinental are higher than intra-continental migration. In 1980, the gentle increase in internal migration took a sharper upward thrust. In fact, the only migration corridor among the top 20 in the world is the West African internal migration IOM.[14] The IOM asserts that over 70 percent of movements in West Africa take place within the region.

These trends are expected given the history of the African continent. For much of its recent history, Africa has experienced a lot of human activities and events that have had direct bearings on population movements. From empire to slavery to colonialism and postcolonialism, the African population has been a flow of humanity. Generally, 1960 is a seeming political watershed in Africa as most African countries in their new colonial composition attained independence at or shortly after this year. It may therefore not be inappropriate to examine migration patterns and trends starting from this point forward.

Pre-1960 international African migration was characterized by a small number of rich, political class Africans who were either in business or worked with government. A stream of college students were provided scholarship and training in Europe, the principal colonial governments in Africa, with the expressed intention that they become the new breed of politicians, government civil servants and bureaucrats designated to take over the running of the governments from the colonial administrations.

With independence around 1960 and new leaderships at the helm of Affairs of the new African countries, there was a rush of immigrants, largely from Europe and Asia into Africa hoping to reap the new found economic prosperity. The African continent was on the look up, and new governments were working to impress their people, gain international recognition and respect and create the utopias they had promised their countrymen during the struggles for independence. There were large contracts to be awarded and skilled labor, which was largely lacking or grossly inadequate at the time in most countries, to be gained by expatriate workers. Africa therefore was the attractive bride for many international immigrants from outside of the continent, who sought new beginnings or fortunes. The influx from other parts of the world was largely to fulfill the newly created opportunities that came with the creation of new countries.

The unfortunate economic realities of the 1980s that afflicted many African countries rendered many of them unfavorable for immigration. According to the World Migration Report former choice destinations in Africa, Nigeria and Cote D'Ivoire, are currently only transit countries for intended migrants from other parts of the continent. The number of immigrants into Africa therefore has experienced a reduction. Zlotnik[15] estimated that at least 42 percent of immigrants into Africa live in the West Africa region, 28 percent in East Africa, 12 percent in North Africa and only 9 percent in Central and Southern Africa. To further illustrate the dramatic turn of foreign migrants into Africa, Zlotnik[16] asserts that the percentage of international migrants in Africa in the 1960s, shortly after decolonization was 3.4 percent compared with the percentage of international migrants in Europe, which stood at 2.8 percent. In 2000, the statistics were 2 percent versus 7.7 percent, respectively.

Internal migration in Africa is far more significant in numbers and impact than intercontinental migration.[17,18] Shimeles[19] contends that it is the largest intra-continental migration movement in the world. The author estimates that intra-regional migration is highest in the West African region (90 percent), followed by Southern Africa (65 percent) and Central Africa (50 percent). East Africa has 47 percent while North Africa has only 20 percent. Most emigrants (more than 90 percent) from North Africa are involved in intercontinental movement. Those who choose to remain within the continent would more likely migrate to East or Central Africa rather than within the North African subregion. In West Africa, Nigeria is the primary migration destination of people from Benin, Ghana and Niger, while Cote D'Ivoire hosts migrants from Burkina Faso, Guinea Bissau and Mali. South Africa is the migration hub for people in the Southern Africa region especially Lesotho, Zimbabwe and Botswana. Eritreans, Ethiopians and Chadians favor Sudan while Kenya is the choice destination for migrants from Uganda and Tanzania.

Intercontinental migration of Africans has received more attention than intra-continental and immigration into Africa,[20] probably because it has a wider global implication for both Africa, which is the origin point, and the rest of the world, which constitute the destination areas. First, distances and economic costs are usually larger to cover in most instances than for most intra-continental migration. This migration process requires a large amount of resources to effect. Second, the restrictions on migration are much tighter in intercontinental migration than if it were intra-continental.

The World Migration Report[21] asserts that restrictions on African migrants have tightened in recent years, especially for Europe and North American destinations, which are the preferred places for most migrants. This means that alternative destinations are now becoming more attractive and the spread of African migrants is becoming more diversified. Third, a substantial amount of remittances sent back home to support families and local development projects come from intercontinental migrants. The IOM[22] reports that out of the USD550 billion sent in remittances over the world, more than USD60 billion flowed into Africa, mostly from Europe and North America. In Liberia, remittances amount to more than a quarter (25 percent) of the Gross Domestic Product (GDP) of the country. This is significant in alleviating poverty and contributing to the development of the economy of such countries. Nigeria, South Africa, Kenya, Senegal and Sudan are the important recipients of substantial sums in remittances from migrants. Finally, there are issues of international crime and violence that may be consequences of migration, which needs to be tackled at the global scale. Issues surrounding child labor, forced labor, human trafficking, sexual exploitation, terrorism and drugs have been associated with migration and countries have adopted stringent measures to curtail migration as a means to minimizing the incidences and consequences of these criminal activities.

As may be glimpsed from the aforementioned, there are several implications to migration, many of which stem from the factors that have initiated the need to move in the first place. These include displacement because of natural and anthropogenic causes, labor and commerce, and educational pursuits.

WHY THEY MIGRATE

The reasons for migration are as varied as there are migrants. It is difficult to place any one factor as the sole reason for the decision to migrate. Migration from one location to another is a complex human activity that demands effort, energy and, in many instances, exertions. There are psychological, sociological, geographical and economic factors to consider. Being uprooted from a place, especially one that has been considered home for quite some time involves a lot of emotions and sentiments. On the other side of the migration process, the destination, getting into the groove of a new environment and culture could be unsettling. It requires great flexibility in learning, adopting and adapting to the new environment. Migration is therefore not a fleeting decision and action in most situations. It requires deliberations and preparations. Usually the final act of moving is a culmination of much earlier decisions already made in anticipation of certain scenarios and especially opportunities that may present themselves.

In its basic form, migration may be forced or voluntary, either of which still subjects itself to the process of contemplation, decision, preparation and finally migration. Either forced or voluntary, the process is typically similar. It varies in intensity and in the amount of time to take the leap and to depart the place of origin.

Forced Migration

The IOM[23] defines forced migration as "a migratory movement in which there is an element of coercion, including threats to life and livelihood, whether arising from natural or from man-made causes." These include movements of refugees and internally displaced persons, as well as people displaced by natural/environmental disasters, chemical or nuclear disasters, and famine or development projects.

In some respects, forced migration is the "face" of migration from Africa. Flahaux and De Haas[24] observe that Africa is commonly regarded as a continent of mass displacement and migration that have resulted from poverty and violent conflict. Refugees and internally displaced persons (IDPs) in make-shift camps across the African plains, and boatloads of migrants across the Mediterranean Sea, are popular conceptions of migration in Africa, with which the global audience has been assailed by the media and online journalism.

Armed Conflict

Africa has had its share, probably more than enough, of forced migration occasioned by wars, famine, poverty, terrorism and natural disasters. According to Rwamatwara[25] the best-known form of forced migration in Africa was the slave trade that resulted into forced labor in the New World. This was followed by forced displacement of natives from their indigenous and ancestral lands by colonial administrators in search of new lands to settle. Since independence, African countries have undergone series of armed conflicts caused by a complex retinue of causative agents that range from political to socio-ethno-cultural factors. These essentially represent push factors that have forced people out of their home regions. These factors have since transmogrified but have not changed much in their substances. For example, the struggles for global political domination between the West and East at the height of the Cold War led to several proxy wars in African countries as each side propped up opposing leaderships in the countries. Angola, Mozambique and Ethiopia were turned into conflict zones of unending bloodshed that resulted into massive movements of people.[26,27] The Nigerian civil war between 1967 and 1970 also caused great movements across the West African subregion.

Globally, 65.3 million people were forced out of their habitations in 2015 because of wars, natural disasters and human rights violations.[28] This is an increase of 8.5 million people from the 56.8 million forcefully displaced in 2014.[29] This consisted of 21.3 million refugees and 40.8 million IDPs and 3.2 million asylum seekers. Added to this would be 19.2 million people who were displaced by natural disasters.

In 2014, Africa's contribution to the refugee crisis was 3.5 million and 7 million IDPs. Most of these are people fleeing from current or recent conflict zones in Somalia, South Sudan, Chad, and Central African Republic, Libya and Northeastern Nigeria and several other theaters of conflicts in Africa.

The East-Central African axis was a prolific zone of human refugee activity since the 1970s. The Ugandan civil war lasted for more than 20 years, forcing hundreds of thousands of people to move to neighboring countries especially Tanzania, Kenya and Rwanda. Incidentally, Uganda became host to large numbers of Congolese escaping the cycles of war (1996–97 and 1998–2003) armed conflict in the Democratic Republic of Congo. Though officially over, the violence continues to be perpetrated by several armed rebel groups who cause havoc and displace thousands of people. By 2014, it was estimated that over half a million Congolese refugees were camped in the surrounding countries of Uganda, Tanzania, Rwanda, Burundi, Zambia, Malawi and the Republic of Congo. More than 10,000 other refugees have been settled in the United States of America between 2008 and 2013.[30]

Rwanda has been a constant source of refugees to other states in the region as well. The Rwandan genocide of 1994 generated an estimated 2 million refugees and IDPs within a few months of its occurrence. The ripple effect of the refugee problem was felt globally as countries in Europe and North America attempted to absorb the spillover of the displaced persons.

South Sudan has joined Syria, Afghanistan and Somalia as one of the worst humanitarian crises in the world as over 2 million refugees have been generated since 2013. By December 2014, IOM[31] reports that over 1.4 million IDPs are scattered all over South Sudan and an additional half a million are found in neighboring countries.

The West African region accounts for about 20 percent of the refugees in Africa.[32] Liberia, Sierra Leone and Nigeria are major contributors to the number of IDPs in the region. It is estimated that more than 1.5 million people were displaced in 2014 in Northern Nigeria from the Boko Haram insurgency, which has wrecked the peace of the area since 2011.[33]

The State of Environmental Migration acknowledges the difficulty in collecting reliable data on refugees and IDPs as many of the internally displaced persons, especially these within the same country, seek refuge and accommodation with relations and social and ethnic network partners rather than in IDP Camps. These are people who easily slip through the cracks and are unaccounted for. Consequently, it is safe to assume that IDPs and refugee data are usually underestimated.

Environmental and Natural Disasters

Similarly, IDPs resulting from environmental and natural disasters could be easily unaccounted for. The Internal Displacement Monitoring Centre reports that, globally,[34] 19.3 million people were displaced in 2014 because of natural disasters. Weather hazards such as floods and typhoons were responsible for the displacement of 17.5 million people while geophysical hazards such as volcanic and earthquake activities accounted for the remaining 1.7 million people.

In Africa, it may be difficult to isolate long-term environmental migration process from the violence that appears seemingly ubiquitous in the region. Ethiopia has been the case study for this seeming interaction between violence on the one hand and environmental disasters on the other. Since the 1960s, Ethiopia has experienced drought which had caused famines and displacement of people all over the country. The worst hit case was the famine of 1983–1985, in which an estimated 400,000 lives were lost to famine and millions of people were displaced. The Hazards and Vulnerability Research Institute[35] of the University of North Carolina claims that the environmental disaster, which is thought, in the final analysis, to have caused more than a million lives was exacerbated by Ethiopia's civil war.[36]

In 2011, the Horn of African region came under severe famine conditions due to droughts. An estimated 50,000 to 100,000 people died from famine and more than a million people were displaced. Somalia, Ethiopia, Djibouti and Kenya were the countries most affected.[37] Similarly, the war in Somalia was reported to have hindered effective aid delivery to IDPs and vulnerable populations in some parts of the region.

In Northern Nigeria, Rizzo[38] links the environmental problems and displacement of the local population due to the drying up of most of the Lake Chad to the Boko Haram insurgency. The general idea is that the poverty engendered by this environmental problem has rendered the local population vulnerable to the entreaties and actions of the Boko Haram terrorist group. An environmental disaster, which has caused the displacement and economically disenfranchised thousands of farmers and fishermen who had relied on the lake for livelihoods for generations, has been taken advantage of by armed insurgents to perpetrate a humanitarian crisis of worse dimension than it possibly may have been. The IOM and National Emergency Management Agency (NEMA) report[39] that the number of IDPs in Nigeria alone was at least 2.2 million in 2014, not counting the spillover into the neighboring states of Cameroon, Chad and Niger.

The floods in Southern Africa (Mozambique in 2010 and South Africa in 2011) left scores of dead and hundreds of thousands of displaced persons all over the region. These and many other natural disasters have colluded to provide an image of Africa that is disaster-prone and with a fluidity of human movement derived from these uncanny realities.

It may be admitted that the scenario painted by the media, and even on these pages, are not attractive or worthy of news. Most of these forced migrations are internal, short-distanced and region-based and may contribute to the massive internal migration processes that Africa is known for. However, United Nations High Commission for Refugees (UNHCR)[40] declares that these movements, seemingly large as they may appear account for only 14 percent of the internal migration in Africa. This translates to 86 percent of the intra-continental migration being voluntary and unforced.[41] Probably the global attention is because most of these people forcefully displaced come from some of the poorest countries of the world. However, there are large waves of voluntary migration that are beneficial to, and have significantly positive implications for, individuals, communities and countries.

Voluntary Migration

The history of African migration has been painted as one driven by violence, natural disasters such as droughts and famine, and other agents of forced movement of a mass of people. Several studies have indicated that this impression is false. According to Flahaux and De Haas, most international African migration is embarked by people through proper processes and using valid passports, visas and documentation. This is in contradistinction to the image of the continent being moved involuntarily. Labor and commercial migration, education and social opportunities are some of the driving forces behind the decisions to migrate.[42]

Labor

According to the International Labor Organization (ILO)[43] more than 150 million international migrants in 2013 were migrant workers. This is an important driver of migration. About 39 percent of governments worldwide by 2011 have enacted policies to encourage skilled workers' migration. Within Africa, favorite work hubs include South Africa for the Southern African countries. About 27 percent of East African migrants also head to South Africa in search of job opportunities. The oil in Central African Republic has made the country an attractive hub for migrants from all over Africa and beyond.[44] Nigeria, Cote D'Ivoire and Libya have also been important hubs for job-seeking migrants in Africa.

Intercontinentally, both skilled and unskilled labor from Africa has fed the employment markets in many developed economies. A few examples may drive home the point that most migrants outside the continent are both skilled and unskilled.[45] Akinrinade and Ogen[46] recall that Nigeria's migration link with the United States started long before independence but the pace and intensity picked up after. Initially, most Nigerian migrants to the United States went for educational and business opportunities with the intention of returning home. Eventually, about 59 percent of skilled migrants from Nigeria have the United States as their preferred destination. Nigeria now comprises 19 percent of the total black African migrant population in the United States[47] and 59 percent of its skilled workers chooses the United States as their preferred destination, followed by the United Kingdom.[48] The International Organization for Migrants[49] indicates that about 78 percent of Nigerian migrants in the United States are employed, with a significant number of them in highly skilled employment. More than 60 percent have degrees and are therefore highly educated. This is true of many Africans involved in intercontinental migration.

For example, in 2000, 4400 physicians emigrated from South Africa, mostly to the United Kingdom. Out of about 45,000 physicians in South Africa, 12,000 have emigrated and practiced in one of the Organization of Economic Cooperation and Development (OECD) countries (this is a collection of 34 countries in Europe plus the United States and Australia). In the late 1990s, about 20 percent of the nursing professionals in the country (South Africa) also emigrated.[50] More than 20,000 Nigerian physicians have also migrated to one of the OECD countries.[51] Angola, Burundi, Ghana, Kenya, Mauritius, Mozambique, Nigeria, Sierra Leone, Uganda and Tanzania have also lost about 33 to 50 percent of their people with higher education who have left for employment in OECD countries.

Generally, these migrant workers have been important source of remittances to their home countries, helping with family and community development. Between 2004 and 2007, more than USD37 billion was remitted to Nigeria from the United States by migrant workers. By 2012, more than USD21 Billion was sent back home.[52] According to Labonté et al.[53] South Africa receives the second highest amount of remittances (USD1 billion) after Kenya (USD1.8 billion). Another important component of this, according to the authors, is the range of new skills that migrants bring back to the countries when they return. Then there is also the brain drain that such emigration creates. The argument here though is that most of these migrations are legal and valid, and usually precipitated more by aspirations and ambitions than by forceful evictions from origin countries.

Countries of North Africa are also important contributors to the intercontinental migration flow from Africa. Europe and the Middle East are the most important hosts of migrants from this region. Remittances from migrant workers from Egypt and Morocco are estimated at USD1.3 billion and USD1.7 billion, respectively. These amounts indicate a large migrant base, most of which are legal and validated.

Adepoju[54] asserts that commercial migration is fast replacing labor migration. Data from United Nations Economic Commission for Africa (UNECA)[55] show that 23.9 percent of African migrants into India, in 2013, were on business or commercial trips. Most of these are from Egypt, Nigeria and South Africa, three of the more emerging countries in Africa. This speaks to the relationship that development has with migration.[56]

Education

France is the largest recipient of African students with 29 percent of all African international students being hosted by the country. South Africa is second with 15 percent. The United Kingdom and the United States (9.7 percent each) are third, followed by Germany (4.7 percent).[57] Other emerging countries include Canada, Italy and Morocco.

One in every nine tertiary educated persons born in Africa resides in OECD countries. For Latin America and the Caribbean, it is one in 13; for Europe, it is one in 20; and, for Asia it is one in 30. The number of tertiary educated migrants originating from Africa increased to reach 2.9 million in 2010/11. The number of tertiary educated African migrants who arrived in the past five years (450,000) even exceeded that of Chinese migrants (375,000).[58]

Asian countries of India and China are becoming important host countries to students from Africa. About 8.7 percent of African migrants in 2013 to India are students.[59] The number of African students in China is on a steep increase. In 2005, there were only 2,757 African students in China. This increased to 3,737 in 2006 and rose sharply to 12,436 in 2009.[60]

Kigotho[61]estimates that students from sub-Sahara Africa represent 4 percent of all international students studying in the United States. Most of the 31,113 students originate from Nigeria, Ghana, Cameroon, South Africa, Kenya and Ethiopia. Hyams-Ssekasi estimates that there were 34,160 African students in colleges in 2012 in the United Kingdom, most of them seeking college degrees at different levels (undergraduate and graduate levels).[62]

These migrations are also aspirational as understanding of opportunities in destination countries creates the desire to reach them. Often the migration becomes permanent when the student eventually graduates and gets employed. In other instances, there is a return migration process, whereby the emigrant returns to the home country to contribute the new knowledge and skill to developing the self and the country.

Irregular Migration

Irregular migration principally refers to illegal migration. Several factors contribute to the incidences of irregular migration, which include formal and informal restrictions on migration. Formal restrictions are those imposed by government such as the requirement for a passport and visa, and certain processes and procedures of formalizing the act of migration. Informal restrictions are those imposed by the individual's capacity and capabilities, the ability or otherwise to harness the necessary resources for a regular migration process, and the knowledge, and opportunities to follow through with this process. Generally, it is the inability to follow through with the legal, formal process of migration documentation and validation that leads to the decision to engage in irregular migration. This decision may be occasioned by unattractive conditions at the origin or the perception of a desired destination as more attractive and promising.

Most irregular migration is undertaken for employment purposes, especially when the destination is an advanced country where documentation is required for educational and other purposes. Labor shortages in many developed countries contribute to the perpetuation of irregular migration as employers seek, admit and employ labor without much regards to the proper documentation, especially for jobs that the locals do not want to take.[63] Human trafficking, exploitation and smuggling therefore become means by which such demand by employers for labor may be supplied. There are incidents of extortion, abuse and exploitation of migrants as both legal and illegal migration became commercialized.[64,65]

The most popular irregular migration route in Africa is the infamous Mediterranean Sea crossing, which has claimed thousands of lives and drawn international attention to migration-related issues in Africa. Data by IOM indicate that in the first half of 2016 alone, one in every 23 migrants on this route has died.[66] The data further shows that between January 2014 and May 2016 alone, an estimated 9, 492 people have died on the route. Boatloads of people have sunk in the Mediterranean Sea enroute to destinations in Europe, especially Italy and Spain. These shipwrecks are perceived as products of overloading of the vessels by greedy human smugglers and apparently desperate migrants who are vulnerable to taking unnecessary and uncalculated risks by joining already crowded boats on such a perilous journey. In 2015, more than 3,770 people are believed to have lost their lives on the fatal journey across the Mediterranean to destinations in Europe. Conservative estimates place the number of deaths on this route at 60,000 since 1996.[67] In the first half of 2016, 3,100 deaths have already been recorded.

There are many reasons why people choose to make the fatal journeys that are associated with most irregular migration process. Crossing the Sahara and eventually the Mediterranean on the way to Europe or the barren Mexican deserts into the United States has claimed many lives. These are no secrets yet people keep making the journey. The secret may lie in both the origin and intended destination points.

Rizzo[68] asserts that weak governance and institutions have impoverished people at source countries, which have pushed them into desperate acts of dangerous migration. Also, the pull of the intended destinations with promises of fulfillment for aspirations and ambitions of migrants is an important attraction. Developments at the origin countries provide the resources to migrate but not enough to meet the ambitions of intended migrants. The feedback mechanism made possible by these developments allows the intended migrant to obtain and sieve information and weigh the probabilities of achieving set goals either at the source point or at the intended destination point. When the weight of the intended destination is favored, the decision to migrate is taken and set into action. The risks are usually generally known but the lure of achieving an ambition considered beyond the source area appears to tamper the need for caution. The result for many migrants is history.

Conclusion

There is a complexity of factors that mold the decision to migrate from Africa to other parts of the world. In large measures, migration is a conscious decision to leave an origin point for another, the destination. The logistics of this movement depends on nature of the process. Forced migration leaves people with little choice and alternative other than to stay or move. Yet the final action to migrate even in the face of threat to lives is usually a product of a decision waiting for opportunity. Africa has had its share of these push factors that have kept its population on the move. In other instances, the pull, rather than the push of source regions may be accountable for the decision to migrate. Ambitions and aspirations are important components of the decision-making process. This coupled with the capability to overcome the costs of distance between the origin and destination locations may decide in favor of a destination where the ambitions and aspirations may be achieved. In this case, the migrant needs certain infrastructure to be provided by the source location through development to enable them to acquire the needed resources and information necessary to migrate.

This chapter has demonstrated that rather than the classical and simplified push and pull model of migration, African migration is more complex and may be a reaction to several stages of development that Africa has achieved, which have been documented as correlated with increased migration. This is evidenced by the fact that most migration from Africa is legal, valid, voluntary and unforced.

NOTES

1. IOM, IOMSNAPSHOT, September 2016.
2. United Nations. "Human Development Report 2009: Overcoming Barriers, Human Mobility and Development." 2009. Accessed October 10, 2016. http://hdr.undp.org/en/content/human-development-report-2009.
3. IOM (2016), If We Leave We Are Killed: Lessons Learned from South Sudan: Protection of Civilian Sites 2013–2016, International Organization for Migration South Sudan.
4. Zlotnik, H. (2014), International Migration in Africa: An Analysis based on Estimates of the Migrant Stock, Migration Information.http://hww.Migrationpolicy.Org/Article/Internationalmigrationafricaanalysisbasedestimatesmigrantstock
5. United Nations (2013), *Trends In International Migrant Stock: The 2013 Revision.*
6. Ravenstein E. G, The Laws of Migration. *Journal of the Royal Statistical Society* 52, 2 (June 1889), pp. 241–305. Blackwell publishing.
7. E. S. Lee, A theory of migration. *Demography* 3, 1 (1966). pp. 47–57.
8. Lee, June H.H. and Guadagno, Lorenzo. "World Migration Report: Migrants and Cities: New Partnerships to Manage Mobility." International Organization for

Migration (IOM). Last modified October 9, 2017. http://publications.iom.int/system/files/wmr2015_en.pdf

9. International Organization for Migration (IOM) (2016), If We Leave We Are Killed: Lessons Learned from South Sudan: Protection of Civilian Sites 2013–2016, International Organization for Migration South Sudan.

10. Flahaux, M.-L. and De Haas, H. (2016), "African Migration: Trends, Patterns, Drivers," *Comparative Migration Studies* 4 (2016), 1, doi: 10.1186/S40878-015-0015-6.

11. Wilbur Zelinsky, "The Hypothesis of the Mobility Transition" *Geographical Review* 61, 2 (Apr., 1971), 219–249, Published by: American Geographical Society Stable URL: http://www.jstor.org/stable/213996.

12. Shimeles, A. (2010), Migration Patterns, Trends and Policy Issues In Africa, African Development Bank Group, Working Paper Series. Http:/Www.Afdb.Org/

13. Flahaux, M-L. and De Haas, H. (2016), African Migration: Trends, Patterns, Drivers, *Comparative Migration Studies* 4 (2016), 1, doi: 10.1186/S40878-015-0015-6.

14. IOM (2016), If We Leave We Are Killed: Lessons Learned from South Sudan: Protection of Civilian Sites 2013–2016, International Organization for Migration South Sudan.

15. Zlotnik, H. (2014), International Migration in Africa: An Analysis based on Estimates of he Migrant Stock, Migration Information Source. http://www.migrationpolicy.Org/Article/Internationalmigrationafricaanalysisbasedestimatesmigrantstock

16. Zlotnik, H. (2014), International Migration in Africa: An Analysis based on Esti mates of the Migrant Stock, Migration Information Source, Sept. http://www.Migrationpolicy.Org/Article/Internationalmigrationafricaanalysisbasedestimatesmigrantstock

17. United Nations. "Human Development Report 2009: Overcoming Barriers, Human Mobility and Development." 2009. Accessed October 10, 2016. http://hdr.undp.org/en/content/human-development-report-2009.

18. Awumbila, M. (2014), Linkages Between Urbanization, Rural–Urban Migration and Poverty Outcomes in Africa, International Organization for Migration (Iom), Background Paper.

19. Shimeles, A. (2010), Migration Patterns, Trends and Policy Issues in Africa, African Development Bank Group, Working Paper Series. Http:/Www.Afdb.Org/

20. United Nations. "Human Development Report 2009: Overcoming Barriers, Human Mobility and Development." 2009. Accessed October 10, 2016. http://hdr.undp.org/en/content/human-development-report-2009.

21. Lee, June H.H. and Guadagno, Lorenzo. "World Migration Report: Migrants and Cities: New Partnerships to Manage Mobility." International Organization for Migration (IOM). Last modified October 9, 2017. http://publications.iom.int/system/files/wmr2015_en.pdf

22. IOM: Promoting Better Management of Migration in Nigeria: Mapping of Nigerian Health and Education Professionals in the United States of America, July (2014).

23. Lee, June H.H. and Guadagno, Lorenzo. "World Migration Report: Migrants and Cities: New Partnerships to Manage Mobility." International Organization for Migration (IOM). Last modified October 9, 2017. http://publications.iom.int/system/files/wmr2015_en.pdf

24. Flahaux, M-L. and De Haas, H. (2016) African Migration: Trends, Patterns, Drivers, *Comparative Migration Studies* 4 (2016), 1, Doi 10.1186/S40878-015-0015-6.

25. Rwamatwara, E. (2005), Forced Migration in Africa: A Challenge to Development Stichproben. Wiener Zeitschrift Für Kritische Afrikastudien Nr.8/2005, 5. Jg.

26. Castles, S., De Haas, H., Miller, M. (2014), *The Age of Migration: International Population Movements in the Modern World* (Fifth Edition). New York: Guilford Press.

27. Flahaux, M-L. and De Haas, H. (2016), African Migration: Trends, Patterns, Drivers, *Comparative Migration Studies* 4 (2016), 1, doi: 10.1186/S40878-015-0015-6.

28. IOM (2016), If We Leave We Are Killed: Lessons Learned from South Sudan: Protection of Civilian Sites 2013–2016, International Organization For Migration South Sudan.

29. Lee, June H.H. and Guadagno, Lorenzo. "World Migration Report: Migrants and Cities: New Partnerships to Manage Mobility." International Organization for Migration (IOM). Last modified October 9, 2017. http://publications.iom.int/system/files/wmr2015_en.pdf

30. Centers For Disease Control And Prevention (2016), Congolese Refugee Health Profile, U.S. Department of Health and Human Services, March.

31. IOM (2016), If We Leave We Are Killed: Lessons Learned from South Sudan: Protection of Civilian Sites 2013–2016, International Organization for Migration South Sudan.

32. Zlotnik, H. (2014), International Migration in Africa: An Analysis based on Estimates of the Migrant Stock, Migration Information Source.http://www.Migrationpolicy.Org/Article/Internationalmigrationafricaanalysisbasedestimatesmigrantstock

33. The State of Environmental Migration, 2015. http://www.environmentalmigration.iom.int/projects/state-environmental-migration

34. Internal Displacement Monitoring Centre Worldwide coverage of internally displaced persons with country profiles and weekly news, publications, and links. DMOZ.

35. Hazards and Vulnerability Research Institute (2014), The 1983–1985 Ethiopian famine, Hazards and Vulnerability Research Institute, Department of Geography, University of South Carolina, Columbia, South Carolina. Accessed October 19, 2016. http://webra.cas.sc.edu/hvri/feature/oct2013.dom.aspx.

36. Human Rights Watch—Evil Days: Concerning famine, Africa Watch 1991. https://www.hrw.org/sites/default/files/reports/Ethiopia919.pdf

37. IFRC (2011), Drought in the Horn of Africa: Preventing the Next Disaste, R International Federation of Red Cross and Red Crescent Societies, Geneva, 2011.

38. Rizzo, J. (2015) A Shrinking Lake and a Rising Insurgency Migratory Responses to Environmental Degradation and Violence in the Lake Chad Basin. In Gemenne, Zickgraf and Ionesco (Eds) (2015) The State of Environmental Migration 2015, A Publication of the International Organization for Migration (IOM)

39. Lee, June H.H. and Guadagno, Lorenzo. "World Migration Report: Migrants and Cities: New Partnerships to Manage Mobility." International Organization for Migration (IOM). Last modified October 9, 2017. http://publications.iom.int/system/files/wmr2015_en.pdf

40. Ambroso, Guido, and Zuefle, Jeanette. "UNHCR Statistical Yearbook 2009. Trends in Displacement Protection and Solutions." The United Nations High Commission for Refugees, October 2010. Accessed October 20, 2016. http://www.unhcr.org/en-us/statistics/country/4ce532ff9/unhcr-statistical-yearbook-2009.html

41. Flahaux, M-L. and De Haas, H. (2016), African Migration: Trends, Patterns, Drivers, *Comparative Migration Studies* 4 (2016), 1, doi: 10.1186/S40878-015-0015-6

42. Bakewell, O. and Jonsson, G. (2011), Migration, Mobility and the African City, Synthesis Report on the African Perspectives on Human Mobility Research Programme, August. ILO Global estimates of migrant workers and migrant domestic workers: results and methodology / International Labour Office—Geneva: ILO, 2015.

43. Shimeles, A. (2010), Migration Patterns, Trends and Policy Issues in Africa, African Development Bank Group, Working Paper Series. Http:/Www.Afdb.Org/

44. Shimeles, A. (2010) Migration Patterns, Trends And Policy Issues in Africa, African Development Bank Group, Working Paper Series. Http:/Www.Afdb.Org/

45. Capps, R., Mccabe, K. And Fix, M. (2012), "Diverse Streams: African Migration to the United States" (Washington, DC, Migration Policy Institute). www.Migrationpolicy.Org/Research/Cbi-African-Migration-United-States?Pdf=Africanmigrationus.Pdf

46. Akinrinade, S. And Ogen, O. (2011), Historicising The Nigerian Diaspora: Nigerian Migrants And Homeland Relations, *Turkish Journal Of Politics* 2 (2), 71–85.*United Nations Development Programme, Human Development Report 2009. See Http://Hdr.Undp.Org/En/Content/Human-Development-Report-2009.*

47. Capps, R., Mccabe, K. And Fix, M. (2012) "Diverse Streams: African Migration to the United States" (Washington, DC, Migration Policy Institute). Www.Migrationpolicy.Org/Research/Cbi-African-Migration-United-States?Pdf=Africanmigrationus.Pdf

48. Mberu, B. and Pongou, R. (2010), "Nigeria: Multiple Forms of Mobility in Africa's Demographic Giant" (Washington, DC, Migration Policy Institute, 2010). www.Migrationpolicy.Org/Article/Nigeria-Multiple-Forms-Mobility-Africas-Demographic-Giant

49. Lee, June H.H. and Guadagno, Lorenzo. "World Migration Report: Migrants and Cities: New Partnerships to Manage Mobility." International Organization for Migration (IOM). Last modified October 9, 2017. http://publications.iom.int/system/files/wmr2015_en.pdf

50. Labonté, Ronald, David Sanders, Thubelihle Mathole, Jonathan Crush, Abel Chikanda, Yoswa Dambisya, Vivien Runnels, Corinne Packer, Adrian Mackenzie, Gail Tomblin Murphy, and Ivy Lynn Bourgeault. "Health Worker Migration from South Africa: Causes, Consequences and Policy Responses." *Human Resources for Health* 13, no. 92 (2015). https://human-resources-health.biomedcentral.com/track/pdf/10.1186/s12960-015-0093-4?site=human-resources-health.biomedcentral.com.

51. Kohnert, D. (2007), African Migration to Europe: Obscured Responsibilities and Common Misconception, GIGA Research Programme: Transformation in the Process of Globalisation

52. Lee, June H.H. and Guadagno, Lorenzo. "World Migration Report: Migrants and Cities: New Partnerships to Manage Mobility." International Organization for Migration (IOM). Last modified October 9, 2017. http://publications.iom.int/system/files/wmr2015_en.pdf

53. Labonté, Ronald, David Sanders, Thubelihle Mathole, Jonathan Crush, Abel Chikanda, Yoswa Dambisya, Vivien Runnels, Corinne Packer, Adrian Mackenzie,

Gail Tomblin Murphy, and Ivy Lynn Bourgeault. "Health Worker Migration from South Africa: Causes, Consequences and Policy Responses." *Human Resources for Health* 13, no. 92 (2015). https://human-resources-health.biomedcentral.com/track/pdf/10.1186/s12960-015-0093-4?site=human-resources-health.biomedcentral.com.

54. Adepoju, A. (2012) Trends in International Migration in and from Africa, doi: 10.1093/0199269009.003.0004

55. UNECA (2015) Africa-India: Facts and Figures, 2015, http://www.Uneca.Org/Sites/Default/Files/Publicationfiles/Africaindia_Ff_17oct_Rev4.Pdf

56. Flahaux, M-L. and De Haas, H. (2016), African Migration: Trends, Patterns, Drivers, *Comparative Migration Studies* 4 (2016), 1, doi: 10.1186/S40878-015-0015-6

57. ICEF Monitor (2013), A Closer Look At African Student Mobility, http://Monitor.Icef.Com/2013/07/A-Closer-Look-At-African-Student-Mobility/

58. United Nations (2013), *Trends In International Migrant Stock: The 2013 Revision.*

59. UNECA (2015), Africa-India: Facts And Figures, 2015 http://Www.Uneca.Org/Sites/Default/Files/Publicationfiles/Africaindia_Ff_17oct_Rev4.Pdf

60. Ferdjani, H. (2012), African Students In China An Exploration Of Increasing Numbers And Their Motivations In Beijing, *Centre For Chinese Studies, Stellenbosch, South Africa.*

61. Kigotho, W. (2015), A Profile Of Sub-Saharan African Students In America. Wachira Kigotho September 18, 2015, Issue No:382, University World News Issue 00429 http://Www.Universityworldnews.Com/Article.Php?Story=20150917132859939

62. Hyams-Ssekasi, D, Mushibwe, C.P & Caldwell, E.F (2014), International Education in the United Kingdom: The Challenges of the Golden Opportunity for Black-African Students, Sage Open. DOI: 10.1177/2158244014562386

63. Mutume, 2016, AfricanRenewal. www.un.org/africarenewal

64. Lucas E. B.Robert, CARNEGIE Papers; International Labor Migration in a Globalizing Economy

65. Shaw William, 2007, Migration in Africa: A Review of the Economic Literature on International Migration in 10 Countries. Development Projects Group, The World Bank, Washington, DC.

66. Brian T. and Laczko F., Fatal Journeys Vol. 2, Identification and Tracing of Dead and Missing Migrants. IOM's Global Migration Data Analysis Center.

67. Brian T. and Laczko F., Fatal Journeys Vol. 2, Identification and Tracing of Dead and Missing Migrants. IOM's Global Migration Data Analysis Center.

68. Jason Rizzo, A Shrinking Lake and a Rising Insurgency: Migratory Responses to Environmental Degradation and Violence in the Lake Chad Basin. In Francois Gemenne, Caroline Zickgraf and Dina Ionesco (Eds): *The State of Environmental Migration* 2015: A Review of 2014, SciencesPo. (2015).

Chapter 2

The Geography and the Patterns of Migration

Elisha Jasper Dung

INTRODUCTION

The last two centuries have brought far-reaching changes that have profound impacts on the geography and complexity of the world. In recent times, globalization has increased the interdependence of different regions and countries of the world. Increasingly, the global link of the world's economy has encouraged the movement of human capital and the flow of goods and services from one region of the world to another. In fact, the waves of globalization have left a legacy. Just as waves sweeping onto a shore affect the topography of the beach, which in turn shapes the flow of subsequent waves, so also have the tides of globalization impacted places and their appeal, which have affected the ensuing flows of global contact. In this wise, we can imagine the world as a series of places in a continual process of globalization and reglobalization.[1]

Perhaps, no other continent has been more impacted by this wave of human migration (voluntary and involuntary) than Africa. Migration involves the movement of people from one geographic location to another. This migratory process may take several forms ranging from domestic to international migration. Since migration involves the movement of people from their place of abode to another location, it may occur within the boundaries of a country in which case we refer to it as internal or domestic migration. It may also occur between one country and another, which we refer to as international migration. Typically, a desire for a better life in the wealthier regions of the developed world is the driving force of international migration. However, it is imperative to not lose sight of the millions of migrants who are refugees from civil unrest, political persecution, and environmental disasters that are part of this group.[2]

Due to its vastness in terms of area and the general lack of empirical data (which is an expensive endeavor by any metric), migration discussions and analyses regarding the African continent heavily relies on UN data, which is based on census stocks. Although the UN data is grossly inadequate in terms of overall quality of detailed demographic information, it is, nevertheless, our best option of obtaining and providing any numerical information with respect to migration from the African continent to Europe and North America. The discussion in this chapter focuses on international migration with emphasis on the movement of African nationals from countries south of the Sahara to Europe and North America. In this context, the chapter will attempt to examine the people who have relocated to Europe and North America to find a second "home."

The chapter assesses the historical and contemporary patterns of migration of people from Africa to the different parts of the world based on numerous geographic elements. This analysis is urgent and important for understanding some of the possible social ramifications of the recent migration wave within the context of economic and political developments of the African continent in the twenty-first century and beyond. To achieve this objective, the following questions are explored. What is the demographic characteristics of those who choose to migrate? What are the temporal patterns of migration? What are the regional patterns? What factors drive the observed temporal and geographic patterns and what are some of the implications of the observed patterns of migration for Africa on the one hand and the host countries on the other? The chapter concludes by examining the future directions of migration in the African continent.

THE GEOGRAPHY OF AFRICAN MIGRATION

Geographers like to think in terms of place (location) in space, with each space maintaining numerous attributes. Distance and direction for instance, tell us about its relationship with other places in space; thereby creating spatial variation between such places. Because of these variations, movements such as migration and diffusion occur from place to place in space.[3] Africans have always demonstrated the propensity for geographical movement, a trend that appears to be intensifying in contemporary times.[4] The movement of people among geographic regions has resulted into population changes in terms of distribution and size. It may lead to an increase in the number of people at the destination and depopulation in the origin. Migration may not only affect the scope, composition, and concentration of population, but can also restructure the ethnic/racial physiognomies of places; introduce new languages, religions, life-styles, and philosophies; and in some cases, rapidly enhance the process of cultural diffusion.[5]

The movement of people has been and will certainly continue due to differentials in certain phenomena based on geographic location. In many cases, the differences between the "haves" and the "haves-not" boil down to geography. If you have the misfortune of being at a location in which the conditions are extreme, chances are that you will be compelled to relocate to a more conducive or moderate location. This is because you would want to avoid or at least minimize the physical geographic barriers of such extreme conditions. These physical conditions are not in isolation because they drive the cultural (human) geographic conditions that lead to economic and social differences that exist among locations. These differences create pressure gradients where people who live in geographic locations that experience extreme negative conditions are forced to move to locations with conducive or moderate geographic conditions. In the context of our discussion, African countries are synonymous with regions of high environmental and social pressure necessitating the pull of people to destinations in Europe and North America where such environmental and social pressures are comparatively moderate. This is consistent with the push and pull factors as well as with the origin-destination concept of migration. As illustrated in Figure 2.1, African countries are depicted as the origin (location of the push factors) and Europe and North America considered as the destination (location of the pull factors).

Figure 2.1, presents information on African migrants to twenty-three European countries and North America in the last 25 years (1990–2015). This origin-destination map shows that the highest number of migrants from Africa to North America is coming from Southern and Northern Africa. These two

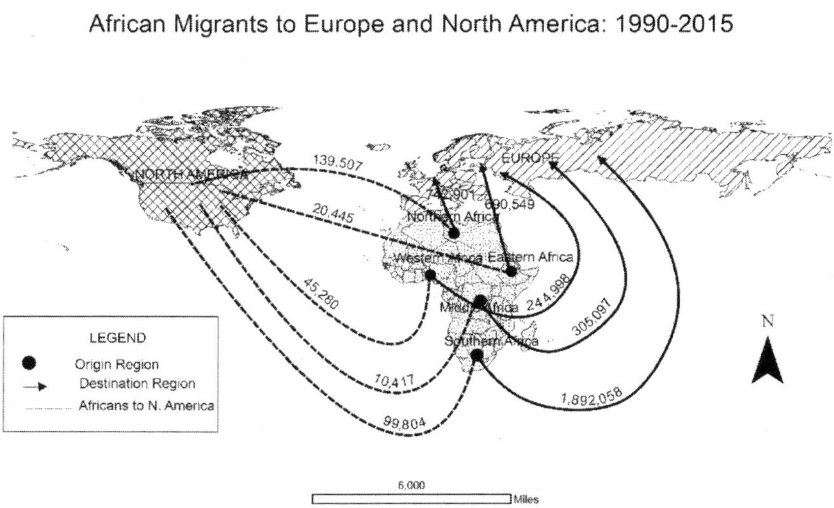

Figure 2.1 African Migrants to Europe and North America.

regions account for 75.86 percent of all African migrants to North America, while the remaining three regions (East, Middle, and West) makes up only 24.14 percent of the migrants to this region (North America). This means that there are fewer migrants from Eastern and Middle Africa moving to North America, and the number of migrants from Western Africa to North America appears to be surprisingly low. The data in Figure 2.1 also reveals that most Africans (92.8 percent) migrate to Europe with North America accounting for only 7.2 percent of all migrants from Africa in the last 25 years. These observed trends could be attributable to geographic distance (proximity) and the cultural element of language, linked to colonial legacies.

DEMOGRAPHIC CHARACTERISTICS OF THE MIGRANTS

An analysis of the demographic characteristics of migrants is important in understanding the possible ramifications of recent and future implications of transnational migration between African countries on the one hand and Europe and North America on the other. In aggregate terms, people in the productive range (18–45) of the population of most African countries tend to migrate more. Nevertheless, the percentage may vary from one country to another based on the main causative mechanism of the migration. In countries where migration is largely driven by voluntary impetus, this may be the case as opposed to countries where political conflicts and natural disasters force migration.[6] In such cases, selective migration may not be an option because the mass of the affected population will seek opportunity to flee from the political conflict. Thus, as observed in recent years, international migration from African countries is on the rise.[7] The number of international migrants increased about 33 percent within a span of 13 years from 2000 to 2013.[8] The composition of most of these African migrants across the Mediterranean tends to largely involve entire families including the old and the young.[9] In cumulative terms Table 2.1 indicates that 53.4 percent of African migrants to Europe and North America between 1990 and 2015 were males, while 46.6 percent were females. The pattern at the country level mirrors that of the entire continent, albeit with a wide variation in some countries. Several countries—Angola, Burkina Faso, Burundi, Chad, Comoros, DR Congo, Guinea. Malawi, Mauritius, Mayotte, and Niger—clearly go against this general trend noted for this period of analysis. For instance, in Chad, 53 percent of females migrated compared to 47 percent of males and Malawi and Niger had 52 percent females and 48 percent males each. This trend reversal may be attributable to, among other things, political instability such as war that may have led the women to flee while the males remain in the battle fields.

Table 2.1 Percentage of Male versus Female Migrants from Africa 1990–2015

Country	*Total Male*	*Total female*	*Tot mf*	*Percent M*	*Percent F*
Algeria	834105	686883	1520988	54.83963	45.1602
Angola	181078	183083	364161	49.72471	50.2759
Benin	515257	425821	941078	54.75175	45.2482
Botswana	277282	217845	495127	56.00217	43.9978
Burkina Faso	156896	1711190	3280096	47.8311	52.1689
Burundi	690465	718069	1408534	49.02016	50.9798
Cabo Verde	36636	35298	71934	50.93009	49.0698
Cameroon	894402	776001	1670403	53.54405	46.4552
Central African Republic	297439	262549	559988	53.11525	46.8845
Chad	729522	825183	1554705	46.9235	53.0765
Comoros	38259	41940	80199	47.70504	52.2942
Congo	927780	826337	1754117	52.89159	47.1083
Côte d'Ivoire	674561	5422732	12168363	55.435813	44.56419
Democratic Republic of the Congo	2480567	2592490	5073057	48.896888	51.10311
Djibouti	333329	295190	628519	53.034037	46.96596
Egypt	862080	713393	1575473	54.718805	45.28119
Equatorial Guinea	20067	16890	36957	54.298238	45.70176
Eritrea	44791	38340	83131	53.880021	46.11998
Ethiopia	2467941	2260648	4728589	52.191912	47.80809
Gabon	686855	516167	1203022	57.094135	42.90587
Gambia	541309	470426	1011735	53.503042	46.49696
Ghana	866097	784158	1650255	52.482616	47.51738
Guinea	1192179	1209157	2401336	49.646488	50.35351
Guinea-Bissau	63108	64801	127909	49.338201	50.6618
Kenya	2223932	2159454	4383386	50.735482	49.26452
Lesotho	21909	18978	40887	53.584269	46.41573
Liberia	420647	334844	755491	55.67865	44.32138
Libya	239700	1215858	3612908	66.34682	33.6537
Madagascar	87949	67724	155673	56.49598	43.5041
Malawi	108652	1169917	2256509	48.15365	51.8463
Mali	761906	721041	1482947	51.37781	48.6227
Mauritania	297170	242368	539538	55.07864	44.9214
Mauritius	48659	51058	99717	48.79706	51.2029
Mayotte	148492	151452	299944	49.50655	50.4933
Morocco	190192	181896	372088	51.11479	48.8851
Mozambique	575576	553084	1128660	50.99643	49.0036
Namibia	360342	312641	672983	53.54397	46.456
Niger	392099	431804	823903	47.59042	52.4097
Nigeria	230643	1868281	4174754	55.24818	44.7518
Réunion	310138	290223	600361	51.65855	48.3411
Rwanda	102975	1021479	2051254	50.20228	49.7978
Saint Helena	1565	1277	2842	55.06684	44.9335
Sao Tome and Principe	11989	11421	23410	51.21317	48.7864
Senegal	807919	739678	1547597	52.20471	47.7956

(Continued)

Table 2.1 Percentage of Male versus Female Migrants from Africa 1990–2015 (*Continued*)

Country	*Total Male*	*Total female*	*Tot mf*	*Percent M*	*Percent F*
Seychelles	31640	17011	48651	65.03464	34.9657
Sierra Leone	420214	343923	764137	54.99191	45.0083
Somalia	302826	285038	587864	51.51295	48.4877
South Africa	565873	3807338	9466061	59.77908	40.2203
South Sudan	553642	528385	1082027	51.16715	48.8328
Sudan	245031	2431648	4882009	50.19163	49.8085
Swaziland	113421	95702	209123	54.23652	45.7635
Togo	534166	525637	1059803	50.40236	49.5971
Tunisia	126055	121155	247210	50.99106	49.0084
Uganda	188424	1874955	3759229	50.12398	49.8765
United Republic of Tanzania	207263	1876313	3948916	52.48536	47.5143
Western Sahara	12848	9681	22529	57.02879	42.9718
Zambia	700596	674239	1374835	50.95851	49.0415
Zimbabwe	151019	1147339	2657538	56.82696	43.173
Total	531477	4637743	9952440	53.40097	46.5993

Source: United Nations, Department of Economic and Social Affairs (2015). Trends in International Migrant Stock: Migrants by Destination and Origin (United Nations database, POP/DB/MIG/Stock/Rev.2015).

Natural disasters such as drought and famine may also be a contributing factor to this seeming anomaly. Percentages vary slightly by African country of origin and by time. For example, the difference between male and female migrants appears to be greater for African countries south of the Sahara (Table 2.1). Some countries with wide gender gap in the migrant characteristic in favor of males: Benin (55 percent, 45 percent), Nigeria (55 percent, 45 percent), Botswana (56 percent, 44 percent), Cote D'Ivoire (55 percent, 45 percent), Liberia (56 percent, 44 percent), South Africa (60 percent, 40 percent) and Zimbabwe (57 percent, 43 percent). Many of the countries with higher female migrants than males appear to coincide with periods of political instabilities generated mainly by war. During periods of calm, though, African migrants tend to largely be male dominated.

As revealed in Figure 2.1 the most active migration age across regions in Africa within a span of 10 years (1990–2000) was the 0–4 to 30–34 age cohorts, but between 2005 and 2015 (Figure 2.3), the age bracket representing the most active migrants from the region expanded all the way to the 40–49 age group. The large number of migrants in the age groups of 0–4 to 10–14 will seem to reaffirm the suggestion of large movements of households with young children. The age bracket of 15–19 and 20–24 represents mostly undergraduate students who leave the shores of Africa in search of better educational opportunities abroad.

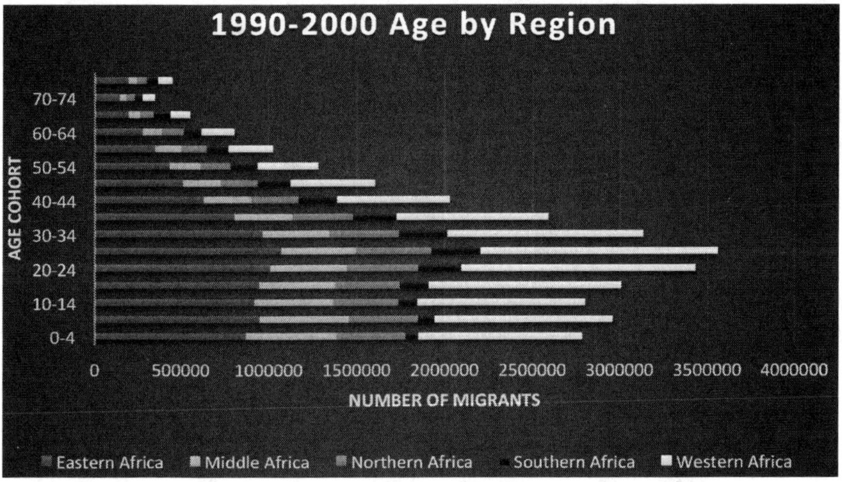

Figure 2.2 Age of Migrant by Region, 1990–2000.

Most of the economically active population (25–39) departs in search of greener pastures that offer greater employment chances, religious and social freedom, and an overall better quality of life. The data show that far fewer senior citizens (65+) migrate from the region. This is predictable and most of the ones that move are either tourists or people that are avoiding political, religious, and cultural persecution and prosecution. This is more so true in war torn and politically unstable areas of the African Region. A small percentage of the 65+ cohort that migrate are those that have medical needs and are brought in by their children who have become naturalized citizens in their respective origin countries.[10] Figures 2.1 and 2.2 also indicate that Eastern Africa and Western Africa have the highest migrants across all age spectrums in comparison to the remaining three regions (Middle, Northern and Southern Africa). These age disparities by region underscore the notion that migration is age dependent, a dependence that seem to largely favor the younger population.

TEMPORAL PATTERNS AND WAVES OF MIGRATION

Studies of migration generally show that temporal pattern may exist. In studies of internal migration, such temporal patterns may be related to occupational seasonality or changes in weather patterns that encourages migrant labor to move from one region to another. Temporal patterns in international migration may be driven by national and transnational events with far-reaching ramifications.

The oil boom era of the 1970s in Nigeria, for example, while serving as a magnet for attracting migrants from the entire African region (although a majority came from Ghana, Benin, Togo and Cameroon),[11] it also created a wave of out-migration from the region during the oil glut era. While the boom afforded the government much needed revenue, it also created serious structural problems in the economy. This occurred because the economy heavily depended on oil (the so-called black gold) as the main source of revenue by relegating agriculture which was the mainstay of the economy to the background. Consequently, Nigeria which was hitherto, self-sufficient in food production, became a net importer of food. Thus, food shortages and high costs encouraged people to move. This wave of migration also coincided with the Sahelian droughts of the 1960s, 1970s and 1980s,[12] as well as the Ethiopian civil war that lasted from 1975–1991.

The structural adjustment program (SAP) of the 1980s, which was imposed on African countries by the International Monetary fund (IMF) as a condition to obtain loans, created another wave of migration from the continent. This program created economic hardships that led to massive movements of people from the region. SAP did not consider the peculiarity of the independent countries in the region based on their specific economic needs and cultural differences, rather the program was designed as a "one size fits all" for the entire African continent. As expected, SAP was a total failure in more than 95 percent of the African countries. Only a handful of countries such as Ghana appeared to be successful under SAP.

In the 1990s, Africa was bedeviled by military coups and military takeovers that resulted in another wave of migration as political woes escaped persecution and prosecution. In this context, it is safe to say that the migration from Africa to Europe and North America indicates the existence of a temporal pattern which may be related to major political, economic, and natural environmental disaster events on the continent.

REGIONAL PATTERNS OF AFRICAN MIGRATION

An attempt has been made in this chapter to classify African countries into high potential, medium potential and low potential migrant countries. This grouping was done as a convenience to identify specific regions in Africa where migration is prevalent. As it turns out, this categorization is clearly indicative of a tale of two sides. On the one hand, some countries that are considered as high potential migrant countries based on just the total number of migrants (Figure 2.4) fall in a completely different class when we look at the number of migrants as a percentage of the country's total population (Figure 2.5). A case in point is a country like South Africa, which is classified as a high potential migrant country in absolute terms but becomes a low potential migrant country when it is considered as a percentage of the total population (See Figures 2.4 and 2.5).

It is useful to examine the magnitude of migration from African countries to Europe to understand countries with high migration potential. For simplicity, three levels of migration potentials have been identified; namely, countries with low (less than 1 million migrants), medium (1–2 million migrants), and high (2 million and above) potential for migration. Figures 2.4 and 2.5 show the cluster of countries within these three classes with some notable patterns. For example, five of the countries in West Africa show high potential for migration. This includes countries such as Nigeria and Cote D'Ivoire. Several countries in East Africa such as Kenya and Ethiopia also record high potential for migration. Overall, majority of the countries fall into the middle and low potential migration classes (see Figure 2.4). These same countries fall in the low potential category when considered as a proportion of total population. The only exception is Cote D'Ivoire, which falls in the medium potential class (see Figure 2.5). From these observed patterns, any meaningful discussions pertaining to potential migrant countries in Africa must be done within the appropriate context; otherwise, any derived conclusions from such discussions will either be grossly exaggerated or underestimated.

For this discussion, twenty-three European countries (some of the major ones include the United Kingdom, Germany, France, Russian Federation, Italy, Spain, Portugal, Belgium) and two north American countries (the United States and Canada) were identified as destination regions. In this

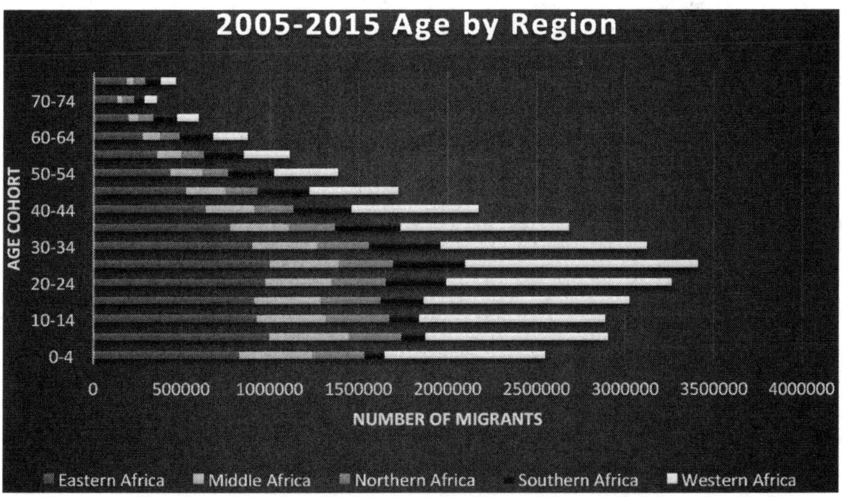

Figure 2.3 Age of Migrant by Region, 2005–2015.

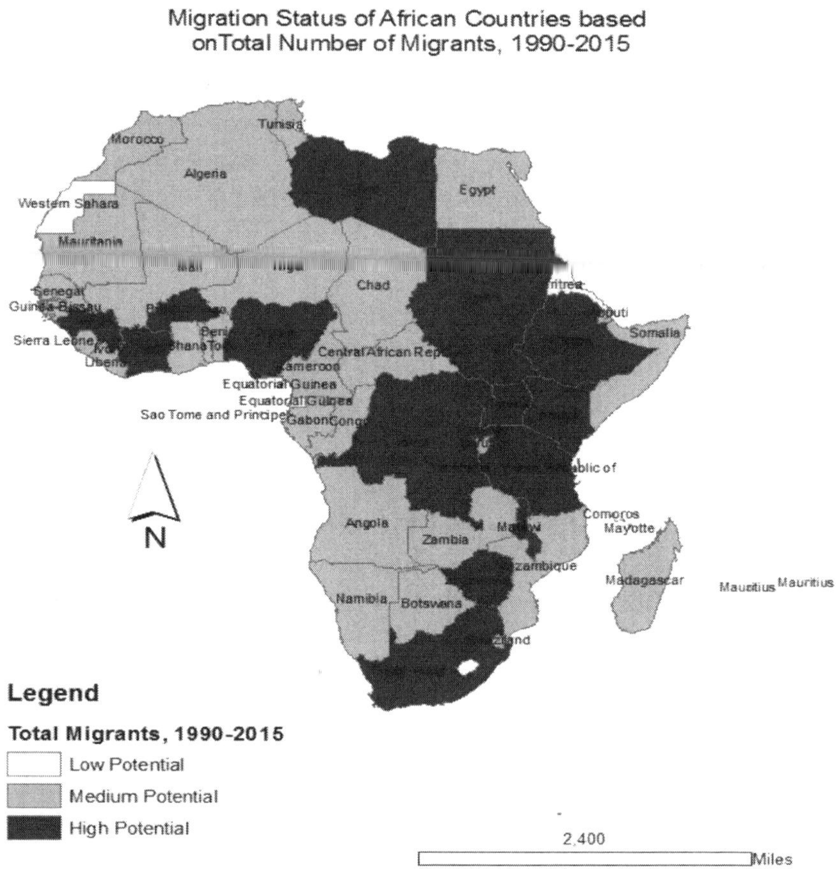

Figure 2.4 Migration Status of African Countries Based on Total Number of Migrants, 1990–2015.

regard, Europe appears to be a major destination for African migrants. Together, the United Kingdom, France, Germany, Russia, and Portugal account for 75 percent of the total number of migrants between 1990 and 2015. In North America, the US and Canada are the major destination countries (see Tables 2.2 and 2.3).

The country-level analysis suggests the influence of past colonial legacies (affiliation) in the choice of migrant destination countries. For example, migrants from Anglophone African countries tend to relocate to the United Kingdom, the United States, and Canada. A similar relationship can be observed between migrants from Francophone countries and France. These patterns are not surprising, given the linguistic, and to some extent the economic and cultural ties that were developed during colonial and postcolonial periods. Several studies tend to support these arguments. For example, while

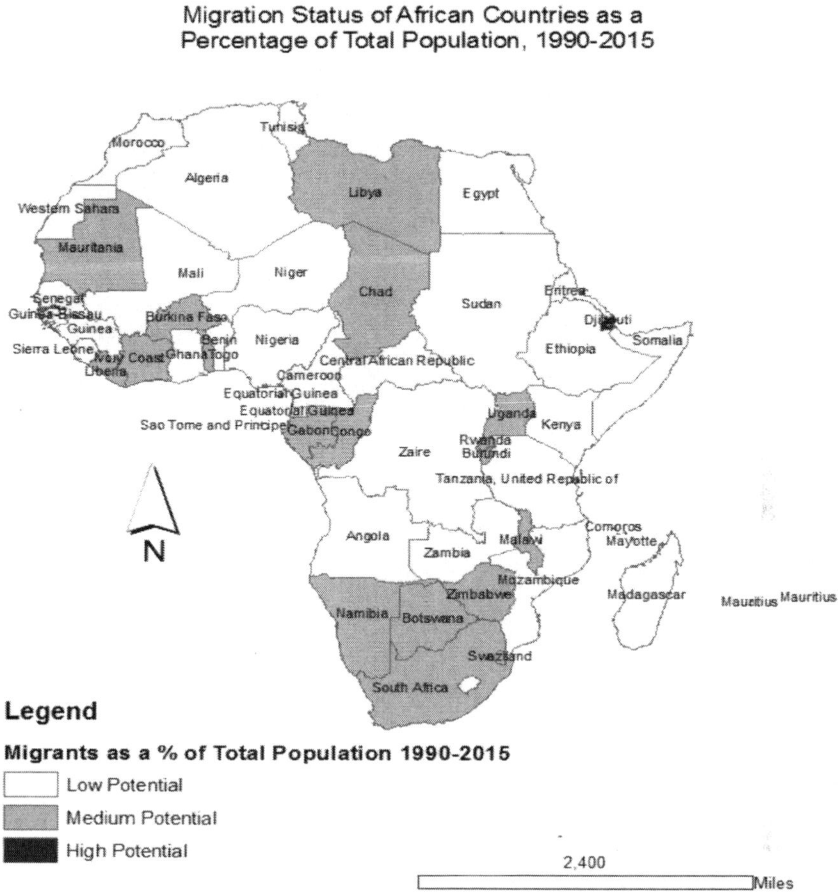

Figure 2.5 Migration Status of African Countries as a Percentage of Total Population, 1990–2015.

looking at African migration—trends, patterns, and drivers—Flahaux and De Hass demonstrated that intercontinental migrants from Africa tend to follow colonial lines.[13] The key driver here appears to be language. This is to be expected because when moving to a new country, the first thing you want to do is the ability to communicate.

CAUSATIVE MECHANISMS OF MIGRATION

Several causative mechanisms of migration have been identified in the migration studies literature relating to poverty and income gap.[14] Opinions based on the classical school of thought contend that economic consideration is a major

Table 2.2 Origin-Destination of African Migrants to Europe and North America 1990–2000

	Origin				
Destination	*Eastern Africa*	*Middle Africa*	*Northern Africa*	*Southern Africa*	*Western Africa*
Total	15 831 568	5 863 325	6 370 490	3 806 255	14 972 105
Austria	5 253	79	5 601	10 838	0
Belgium	2 078	574	7 981	13 938	1 018
Bulgaria	0	0	179	7 987	0
Canada	1 814	793	5 730	8 661	2 653
Cyprus	0	24	238	4 283	0
Czech Republic	0	0	589	2 878	0
Denmark	533	6	2 778	3 692	0
Finland	0	0	2 267	1 545	0
France	189 814	116 778	86 706	14 827	56 315
Germany	3 977	773	88 506	121 667	8 522
Hungary	0	0	1 223	0	0
Iceland	0	0	0	43	0
Ireland	50	26	268	16 333	0
Italy	2 814	164	53 080	33 144	2 384
Latvia	0	0	0	536	0
Norway	0	0	1 108	2 000	0
Poland	0	0	3 500	8 908	106
Portugal	20 853	20 773	116	56 716	5 930
Romania	0	0	2 217	2 203	0
Russian Federation	1 161	3 546	80 279	5 648	3 102
Spain	240	1 287	11 911	3 015	1 403
Sweden	0	43	3 265	1 122	3 289
Switzerland	109	563	12 716	9 111	829
United Kingdom	77 692	0	35 594	360 676	9 087
United States	6 416	2 813	68 584	29 562	18 394
Total	312 804	148 242	474 436	719 333	113 032

Source: United Nations, Department of Economic and Social Affairs (2015). Trends in International Migrant Stock: Migrants by Destination and Origin (United Nations database, POP/DB/MIG/Stock/Rev.2015).

driver of national and international migration.[15] This claim has been used to explain the phenomenon of rural-urban migration within national boundaries. In the same vein, international migration is motivated by people moving for better economic prospects for themselves and family back home, compelled in most cases by push and pull factors.[16] From this perspective, it is argued that if an origin location is substantially developed, this will stem the flow of out-migration. However, there has been a counterargument that, when poor societies develop, migration increases rather than decreases.[17] This is because the economic situation in the origin location will provide the necessary

Table 2.3 Origin-Destination, 2005–2015

			Origin		
Destination	*Eastern Africa*	*Middle Africa*	*Northern Africa*	*Southern Africa*	*Western Africa*
Total	15 531 968	6 376 495	5 862 715	7 077 926	17 831 613
Austria	0	69	3 797	14 236	0
Belgium	2 082	878	6 905	19 307	2 374
Bulgaria	0	0	202	9 374	0
Canada	2 383	1 585	9 544	14 988	4 341
Cyprus	0	23	252	11 600	0
Czech Republic	0	0	591	4 931	0
Denmark	545	6	2 961	7 194	0
Finland	0	0	2 969	1 762	0
France	301 900	106 653	116 218	19 457	107 878
Germany	4 979	2 111	52 565	143 527	12 338
Hungary	0	0	1 304	0	0
Iceland	0	0	0	74	0
Ireland	118	34	280	30 374	0
Italy	3 614	1 527	44 114	58 911	3 073
Latvia	0	0	0	967	0
Norway	0	0	1 259	3 740	0
Poland	0	0	2 941	23 241	138
Portugal	14 364	39 126	134	109 530	7 998
Romania	0	0	2 317	3 909	0
Russian Federation	1 315	5 778	45 485	9 356	8 723
Spain	315	3 081	13 224	4 456	1 424
Sweden	0	40	3 053	1 987	771
Switzerland	248	479	6 505	5 905	593
United Kingdom	56 495	656	35 703	727 110	7 703
United States	9 832	5 226	55 649	46 593	19 892
Total	398 190	167 272	407 972	1 272 529	177 246

Source: United Nations, Department of Economic and Social Affairs (2015). Trends in International Migrant Stock: Migrants by Destination and Origin (United Nations database, POP/DB/MIG/Stock/Rev.2015).

resources to offset the financial cost of relocation. On the other hand, the economic benefit of migration is evidenced by the remittances migrants from African countries send back to their home countries.[18] Globalization has undoubtedly complicated this debate in several different ways. Some of these causative considerations are dealt with below.

Economic and Political Factors

Other than economic forces, Political factors also play a major role in the international migration process. Political instability in many African countries leading to ethnic clashes, internal civil war, and international disputes has contributed to the displacement of large numbers of people, formation of refugees, and international migrants. This is evident from mass movements of people from Algeria, Angola, the Congo, Cote D'Ivoire, Liberia, Sierra Leone, and Sudan due to civil wars, which have also accounted for the death of about 15 million people from these countries in the last 25 years (1991–2016).[19] Political instability in some African countries has been compounded by the emergence of terrorist organizations (e.g., Nigeria, Mali, and Somalia). The feeling of insecurity amid these political upheavals has no doubt contributed to the mass exodus of people from African countries in recent years.[20]

Environmental Factors Associated with Natural Causes

The relationship between environmental problems and forced migration has been well documented.[21] In some instances, these relationships are direct, while indirect in others. Although many of the environmental problems wind up as natural disasters in the end, some of them (such as desertification, land degradation, soil erosion, floods and in some instances, drought) are human-induced. This occurs because of, among other things, farming practices, grazing intensities, and settlement patterns. Usually, these practices revolve around marginal lands that windup accelerating and/or exacerbating these environmental problems. The frequency and magnitude of these problems are increasingly becoming security issues and assuming social and economic problems of alarming proportions for a lot of countries of the world, including several African countries.

In the last decade alone, these environmental issues which include floods, earthquakes, soil erosion, desertification, deforestation, land degradation, hurricanes, cyclones, tornadoes, and drought have forced millions of people worldwide to relocate each year. Several international organizations have reported astounding numbers of people who have effectively become refugees because of these environmental inconveniencies. For instance, the Norwegian Refugee council (NRC) observed that about 36 million people fled their homes owing to natural disasters in 2008 alone. The number declined in 2009 with 16 million people displaced. However, in 2010, a whopping 42 million people were dislocated due to these natural disasters.[22]

Although Africa is a relatively stable continent devoid of many of the tectonic upheavals such as earthquakes, volcanoes, tsunamis, and hurricanes encountered in other parts of the world, the region does experience its own share of environmental challenges and natural disasters. In the first place, many African countries' land mass falls within the Sahelian zone where intense drought and desertification has occurred in the last two decades. Land degradation accompanied with this natural phenomenon has put the livelihood of many millions of people in this region in jeopardy. It has increased the difficulties of eking out a living in a region of Africa where the conditions were already marginal. In fact, prolonged droughts over several years have been a major cause of food shortage and famine in many Sahelian zone countries encouraging, rural to urban migration and ultimately contributing to international migration across the continent and between Europe and North America.

Educational Opportunities and Specialized Skills

People also migrate to Europe and North America for educational reasons. This subgroup of migrants often moves to Europe in pursuit of graduate studies although a sizable undergraduate population has been on the rise in the past decade. While the original intention of this group is to acquire advanced skills and knowledge in specialized disciplines such as engineering, medicine, information technology and return to their home countries to apply those skills for the development of African countries, that is not always the case, because many of them end up staying behind as immigrants. This practice was evident during the colonial period when early African students in Europe and North America helped to galvanize the clamor for political independence even though the number of African students studying abroad at the time was relatively few.

Post-independence, the need to produce technocrats for the newly independent governments of various African countries led many of these countries to encourage their citizens to study abroad, in most cases with government financial assistance. Indeed, most of these early "migrants" came back home to participate in the process of nation building after completing their studies. In recent times, however, most graduate students from African countries are seeking employment in Europe and North America after completing their studies because of better economic prospects. Those who go back to Africa often come back to Europe and North America after one or two years because of a combination of reasons including political instability, the inability to readjust to life back home after several years of study abroad, poor economic prospects, and the lack of facilities and institutional framework to harness their specialized skills and training. Accordingly, the proportion of permanent migrants contributed by students whose initial goal was to return to their country has been on the rise.[23]

Sociocultural Considerations

A variety of cultural factors also contribute to the process of international migration. In general, most African countries are still considerably socially conservative. In most cases, such conservative traditions, customs, and social norms often create opportunity gaps and inequalities that are usually gender biased. This gender gap in opportunity creates obstacles for educational and economic advancement of women in many African countries. Although many other minority groups such as gays and lesbians have been part of the fabric of the African culture for generations, they have operated clandestinely as about 80 percent of Nigerians, Ghanaians Kenyans, and Ugandans, among many other African countries believe that homosexuality is immoral;[24] thus, it is considered a taboo for one to openly declare such sexuality. As such, most of these minority groups operate out of the public eye for fear of humiliation, persecution and/or prosecution.

The identification of such persons in the community carries a cultural stigma (shame) that discriminates against such people making them look like, and treated as second class citizens. This factor provides the added incentive for migrating to Europe and North America where societal norms are comparatively progressive and offer opportunities for economic and social advancement of women and other minority groups such as Lesbian, Gay, Bisexual, and Transgender (LGBT). In many Western advanced countries, at least, minority rights (including women, children, gays, and lesbians) are increasingly considered as human rights.

These rights are either not recognized or deliberately violated by many African countries. In some cases, the violation of the rights of these minority groups have been legitimized by enacting and passing laws that criminalize gays and lesbians to deny or suppress such rights. Nigeria and Uganda are classical examples. In Nigeria, the former president Goodluck Jonathan signed into law a measure that punishes same-sex unions with 14-year prison sentences and 10-year terms for those guilty of "promoting" homosexuality.[25] Such draconian laws will surely disenfranchise members of the LGBT community. The appearance of a more conducive/tolerated environment for gays, lesbians and others in Europe and North America, arguably, serve as pull factors to such countries, thereby encouraging international migration.

Other cultural practices such as female circumcision that are still prevalent in sections (some cultures) of the African continent is another potential push factor that encourages women and other families that seek to ensure that their daughters avoid these practices to leave the continent and move to Europe and North America, where such practices are nonexistent or have been completely banned.

Religious Persecution/Freedom

In religious terms, although many African countries are officially secular, there is no denying the fact that religion plays a significant role in the political and social occasions of Africans, especially in many sub-Saharan countries where a sizable population of the different ethnic groups practice different religions. This is particularly true for West African countries such as Nigeria, Ghana, and Ivory Coast, where a North-South religious dichotomy of people who practice Islam and Christianity (also true for North and South Sudan) is evident.

This situation is often exploited by political parties and/or politicians for personal political gains. The result is that incidences of religious intolerance have been on the rise in countries like Nigeria and Mali, leading to frequent conflicts with religious undertones. Some of the religious crises have given rise to the emergence of terror groups on the African continent. Some of these terror groups include: Al Qaeda in the Islamic Maghreb (Mali), Boko Haram (Nigeria, also active in Chad, Niger, and Cameroon), Al-Shabab (Somalia) and the Lord's Resistance Army (Uganda). As people feel threatened, the prospects of international migration are guaranteed to be accelerated.[26]

IMPLICATIONS OF MIGRATORY PATTERNS ON AFRICA AND THE HOST COUNTRIES

Immigration has recently become a contentious issue in many industrialized nations of the world. The immigration debate has a particularly interesting and intriguing twist in countries where most of its residents are descendants of immigrants.[27] Many intended migrants to the United States, for example, see the Statue of Liberty as an open invitation to people who long for freedom. Yet, there has always been tautness between this open-door philosophy and anxiety of the economic and social impact of the next wave of immigrants to the country. Thus, those who are nervous about immigrants have been less thoughtful to the possible benefits of immigration in general.[28] The current wave of migration from African countries to Europe and North America has multidimensional implications for the origin countries of Africa and their host countries in Europe and North America. An analysis of this implication is imperative for regional economic planning and development in Africa. Some of the implications are examined in this section.

Brain Drain on the Origin Country

Although data on the educational attainment of the composition of African migrants to Europe and North America is not readily available, a cursory observation of information available on the numbers of African associations based in North America and Europe suggests that an important cohort of migrants from Africa include people with advanced degrees and technical skills in science, medicine, engineering and social sciences and the humanities. The outflow of these highly skilled and competent persons from Africa is well recognized in the literature in the so-called "brain drain" phenomenon. Rather than serving as a catalyst of innovation and development through the application of their advanced skills in African countries, this crop of highly trained migrants become agents of economic development in their "adopted" countries of Europe and North America.[29] This action further complicates the manpower shortage experienced by many African countries in specific sectors, especially education, health, technology, and engineering. It is worth noting, however, that the brunt of the brain drain on sub-Saharan Africa is multifaceted.

There is a well-known fact of the migration of highly educated Africans from the continent to other parts of the developed world.[30] There is also substantial movement of skilled Africans within sub-Saharan Africa. As a rule, the migration is assumed to be from poor, politically unstable, and/or conflict-prone countries to those that have stronger economies, are politically stable, and offer good security. This being the case, brain drain will have a negative impact on the origin countries. The brain drain does have a positive aspect for the African countries. In some cases, the diasporas have become significant sources of financial remittances back to the home country. Other Africans in the diaspora are finding ways to make their technical expertise available by networking and some return to help for short periods of time. Even so, the issue of brain drain is still generally damaging to the African continent, especially sub-Saharan Africa.

People have always wondered about the wealth disparities among countries of the world and why some are getting richer and others poorer. Answers to such questions may appear to be farfetched, but classical economic theory has always underscored differences in the educational levels of countries an important part of the answer. These economic theories assert that improved educational opportunities are interrelated to rising incomes in developing countries. Yet, while there is little doubt that highly skilled workers in many developing countries are scarce, it is also accurate to note that many scientists, engineers, physicians, and other specialists from developing countries work in Canada, the United States, and Western Europe. The complexity of this issue was put succinctly by the IMF:

> This phenomenon, often referred to as the "brain drain," was noticed as early as the 1960s and has been a contentious issue in the North-South debate ever since. One important implication of the brain drain is that investment in education in a developing country may not lead to faster economic growth if many of its highly educated people leave the country. Also, efforts to reduce specific skill shortages through improved educational opportunities may be

largely futile unless measures are taken to offset existing incentives for highly educated people to emigrate. But how extensive is the brain drain? Which countries and regions are especially affected? Do highly educated professionals from developing countries living abroad represent a sizable proportion of the pool of skilled workers in their countries of origin or too small a number to worry about? Unfortunately, attempts to answer these important questions quickly come up against a formidable barrier: there is no uniform system of statistics on the number and characteristics of international migrants. Also, source countries typically do not keep track of emigrants' characteristics, and, although some receiving countries do, their definitions of immigration differ. Thus, it is difficult to measure precisely the flow and levels of education of immigrants. Further, it has only recently become possible to measure the stock of educated workers in each source country—the pool from which brainpower is drained.[31]

Remittances from the Host Countries to the Origin Countries

Although outward migration from Africa often leads to brain drain, migrants from Africa do bring to bear positive economic contributions to their home countries. An aspect of this contribution is through income remittances. Income remittances have become a main source of foreign exchange earnings to some African countries. For example, in 2014 alone, six African countries (Cameroon, Côte d'Ivoire, Kenya, Ghana, Ethiopia, and Nigeria) remitted about 13.3 billion US dollars from six industrialized countries of Europe and North America.[32]

In recent years, most African countries have experienced difficulties paying for imports because of limited foreign currency to pay for them. The lack of available foreign exchange to pay for imports not only has impacted the public sector but has also led to difficulties in the industrial and manufacturing sectors where critical equipment and machinery becomes very challenging to be acquired. This is further compounded by the fact that most African countries' currencies are devalued relative to the US dollar, British pound and the Euro. In theory, the devaluation of African currency should make African exports cheaper and thus encourage inflow of foreign incomes. The reality is that most African countries have low volume of export to Europe and North America. Thus, they are not able to reap the reward that is associated with the boost in export. Hence, income remittances from African migrants in North America and Europe become a vital foreign exchange source for the region (Africa). Remittances not only aids in the balance of payments of African countries, but also helps to boost social and economic development at the community level in most African countries where these remittances are substantial.

Technological/Intellectual Transfer to the Origin Countries

Migration of highly trained Africans to Europe and North America has contributed to the pool of African intellectual and technological diaspora. There is evidence to show that African diaspora have been involved in various initiatives to foster social and economic development in Africa through technological and intellectual transfer at personal level and by institutional collaborations. For example, the Carnegie Mellon Foundation working with the Council for the Development of Social Science Research in Africa (CODESRIA) has supported the collaboration between African-born academics in North America with their counterparts in Africa through academic exchange funding.[33] Many African diaspora professional organizations have also engaged in direct technological transfer to their motherland. Nevertheless, it is obvious that more needs to be done. The pool of African diaspora technocrats provides enormous potential that has not been fully exploited by African countries.[34]

Skilled l\Labor Force to the Host Countries

African migrants have positive impacts on their host countries. African migrants contribute to the skilled and semiskilled labor force to their host countries. Many highly trained African migrants with advanced degrees in the sciences, medicine and the humanities reside in Europe and North America. Some of these highly trained Africans had previously completed their training in North America and Europe, returned to their countries only to find that political, social, and economic problems preclude them from being fully useful to their home countries. They are forced to return to Europe and North America, where their previous training and experience makes it easier for them to secure employment and get integrated into the economy. In recent years, due to political instability, many unskilled African migrants have been crossing the Mediterranean to swell the ranks of migrants in Europe.

Unskilled African migrants also contribute to their host's economy by providing cheap labor as they participate in low wage labor force that people in their host countries may not partake in. These migrants face enormous challenges, though, because when migrants settle in a new country, they are often faced with a "damned if they do, damned if they don't" predicament. If they are economically successful, they are accused of taking jobs or opportunities away from local people; if they are not successful, they are considered a liability on the system. Refugees and asylum seekers are especially likely to be treated with hostility as most are perceived as "takers" and not "givers." As evident from common themes in the media and radio talk shows—including claims that asylum seekers are "bogus" and associated with criminals, terrorists, and disease—these misinformation leads to dehumanization. This discernment allows some in the host nations to justify the unfair and inhumane treatment of refugees.[35]

These reactions by host nations are very fluid depending on the mood or condition of the country. If the economy in such a country is doing well, immigrants are tolerated, but during difficult times, host communities become agitated and anxious as uncertainty sets in. This anxiety and the fear of the unknown sometimes lead people to challenge the status quo. Economic recession, natural disasters and demands for equal rights for migrants can also aggravate perceptions of zero-sum competition and threat from outsiders. These debates take center stage even when issues are not mutually exclusive. The Ebola outbreak, for example, helped to fan the firestorms of anti-immigration feeling against Hispanics in the United States, despite the fact that Ebola was in a few West African countries and cases of Ebola did not exist in Latin American countries.[36]

Social and Cultural Diversity Challenges and Adaptation to Host Country

Despite some of the positive impacts that African migrants may have on the economy of their European and North American countries, migrants, as expected, also pose significant challenges to their host countries.[37] In the first place, African migrants must undergo social and cultural adaptation to their new country. The process of social and cultural adaptation and assimilation often takes time creating significant challenges to both the migrants and their host communities. African migrants and migrants from Eastern Europe and Latin America to the more affluent western European countries such as Britain, Italy, Germany, and the Scandinavian countries have led to cultural diversity in those countries while at the same time posing significant problems to the host countries. Among other cultural and social issues, resentment of the formation of cultural enclaves such as "little Africa" coupled with the economic challenges of many developed countries in recent years has contributed to the emergence of nationalistic feelings in political dialogues and discussions in many of these advanced countries.

Anti-immigrant sentiments and sensitivity has further been boosted by the massive arrival of migrants from the Middle East especially refugees from Syria, Iraq, and the rise in acts of terrorism in the United Kingdom, Germany, and France. Such Anti-immigrant feelings have started to emerge in the United States and Canada to a lesser extent. Formal political parties based on nationalistic doctrines that had hitherto remained on the political fringes are now assuming significance and/or taking center stage in the political space. This is exemplified in the vote of the British people to break away from the

European Union (BREXIT), which was championed by political parties with nationalistic learnings.[38]

Germany, Belgium, France, and the Scandinavian countries have also experienced the emergence of nationalistic political parties partly based on anti-immigration sentiments. In the current political environment in the United States, echoes and the reemergence of nationalism can be heard especially in the presidential election campaigns, with slogans such as, "America first" and "we want our country back." Opposition to immigration is widespread in many Western nations. Anti-immigration activists, the media and political elites have created a crisis mentality in which immigrants are portrayed as "enemies at the gate." Immigrants—particularly nonwhites—are held responsible for all of society's calamities.[39] Such portrayals encourage support for more extreme political platforms.

Nonetheless, as has been argued by many scholars, researchers and commentators, immigration is not a zero-sum game.[40] The idea of a zero-sum game surfaced due to the perception of competition in intergroup relations, even when none exists.[41] The notion that successes by immigrants is at the expense of prosperity of the host communities is simply not accurate because the two are not mutually exclusive. This perceived role of rivalry, as it turns out, is very relevant in the context of immigration today. Victoria puts it this way:

> As a rule, members of socially dominant groups tend to believe that their group is superior, in what geographers call cultural imperialism and hence feel entitled to resources and privileges. To maintain their dominance, they must fend off "invading" groups who are seen as competing with them for finite resources including jobs, political power and cultural and religious influence. This can occur irrespective of whether there are indeed limited resources and whether or not there is actual competition over them. This belief in zero-sum competition is central to attitudes about immigration. There is a widespread belief that any gains immigrants make must be at the expense of members of the host society. This belief is deeply embedded in Western society, even though it is seldom justified.[42]

These zero-sum game arguments certainly become more difficult to dispel since some of the migrants struggle to assimilate into the host community by making the adjustments necessary to succeed either culturally, economically, or socially. When such situations occur, these migrants form part of the urban poor in their respective communities since most migrants tend to settle in urban areas, especially those that are undocumented. The situation is also more pronounced in urban areas because such migrants can easily hide in high population concentrations and most job opportunities are found in the urban areas. Such failures only fan the anti-immigrant flames because they are perceived to be a burden on the government even if they are not benefiting from any government programs, as is the case with most immigrants.

The issue of cultural diversity is considered as an asset by some communities and as a contamination of culture by others. For example, gateway cities (main ports of entry) would be readier to accommodate foreigners because they see them on a regular basis than other cities that see them as intruders. These experiences may compound the challenges that many immigrants already struggle to cope with.

Future Directions

The advent of globalization has increased the economic and political linkages and interdependence of countries of the world. The movement of capital and human resources across national and transnational borders is likely going to be the norm for the near future despite the rise of anti-immigrant sentiments and nationalistic feelings in the advanced countries of Western Europe and North America. This appears to be a feasible trend given the ever increasing economic and technological gap between the rich and poor nations of Africa and other developing regions of the world. There is also a digital divide between Africa and the developed regions of Europe and North America. Although communication has improved in the region, facilities are still grossly inadequate and only a handful of people have access to internet services. Even the few that have internet access, the service is poor, unpredictable, and expensive. This is very important and central to any realistic chance of development in the region because the world is trending in the digital direction, and Africa must keep pace or else would be left behind again.

There must be a change in thinking in this direction in Africa, and migration might just be the catalyst that will ignite this change. Perhaps, African countries should focus on how to maximize the current spate of migration for the social and economic development of the region (Africa). Any feasible prospects of Africans returning home in large numbers from Europe and North America to help in the development of the region seems to be a dream, at best and unrealistic, to say the least. Governments in Africa should rather make conscious efforts to harness the potentials of African migrants living abroad. Generous incentives to encourage migrant to invest in the local economy may be one way to attract technology and technical knowledge that will contribute meaningfully to the advancement and development of the continent.

The philosophy and policy relating to African migration needs to be focused on the region (looking inward), rather than the Eurocentric posture that is the current norm. Other ideas that have formed the core of the characteristics of African migrants need some appraisal due to global events.

Globalization in its current form does not seem to be sustainable overall because its outcome has winners and losers. The winners are the top 1 percent in the industrialized capitalist countries, while the working class in those countries and all developing countries are the losers. Again, the general contention among scholars is that African migrants tend to be young, educated, and from households with above average income.[43] However, increases in natural disasters and political instabilities that have increased the number of asylum seekers from the African continent to countries in Europe and North America have profoundly changed this dynamic.[44]

The distance decay function had been a major determinant of how frequently and how far people were willing to travel.[45] In this respect, the rate of migration almost always declines with the distance from the area of origin to the destination, although the distance migrated increases with educational level. Most studies have concluded that economic motives are the primary determinant of the quantity and direction of migratory flows. However, this approach is limited in explaining the direction and rate of migration and in isolating the relevant economic variables in the decision-making process to migrate. Theoretical problems in measuring the relevant regional income differential compound this situation, although studies have shown that there is a significant and widening regional income disparity between developed and developing countries. Various noneconomic motives may also affect migration and factors such as family ties and the fear of the unknown may explain the large numbers who do not migrate. Distortions in the factor markets, the transfer of capital associated with migration, and externalities associated with migration have implications for migration policy in the region.

Future research should be directed toward 1) improving the basis of migration in the region, 2) improving the approach for studying migration in the African environment, and 3) integrating the results of this research into meaningful policy evaluation. Primary data should be generated through sample survey methods, with extensive interviewing of migrants, potential migrants, and return migrants over time. Since the private and social costs of migration may diverge, the effect on migration should be considered in policy analysis. Finally, since migration is selective with regard to education, research on migration should be linked with research on education for policy analysis and African Governments should invest toward this venture.

Conclusions and Recommendations

Although migration has its drawbacks both on the origin and destination locations, there are also a lot of positives that are derivable from the process. Some of the negatives will include depopulation and economic stagnation on the part of the origin nations since many of the migrants tend to be mostly able-bodied men and women. So when people migrate, it creates a vacuum because those who migrate are also in the productive (fertile) age cohorts. On the other hand, the positives come from the contribution of Africans in diaspora to the economy of the region, both in cash and in kind, individually and collectively. These involvements paint a very positive picture for the region. The host nations should embrace African migrants because of their economic contributions as well as the cultural diversity that they add to these communities.

From the current trends in migration, despite increasing opposition from host countries, we can speculate that immigration and asylum-seeking are not going away anytime soon. Countries that integrate immigrants successfully are less likely to feel the stress and more likely to reap the benefits of migration. Those countries that simply try to slam the door on immigrants by erecting barriers are simply kicking the can down the road. One of the ways to curb migration from Africa is to collaborate with African countries for capacity building toward economic prosperity and political and social stability. On the destination front, countries must come up with comprehensive immigration policies that will recognize the rights of immigrants as members of the international community consistent with international human rights laws.

Although, African migration to Europe is commonly seen as a tidal wave of desperate people fleeing poverty and warfare at home, reasons for migration are much wider and complicated. Typical "solutions" proposed by politicians usually include increasing border controls or boosting African "stay-at-home" development. However, these restrictive immigration policies have invariably failed to stop migration. Despite lip service being paid to "combating illegal migration" for political and diplomatic reasons, I will argue that neither European nor African states have enough genuine interest in stopping migration.

NOTES

1. John Rennie Short. *Human Geography: A short Introduction*. Oxford, NY: Oxford University Press, 2015.

2. Rowntree, L, Lewis, M, Price, M and Wyckoff, W. *Globalization and Diversity: Geography of a Changing World*, 5th edition, Upper Saddle River, NJ: Prentice Hall, 2015.

3. George O. Carney. 1995. Culture: a working definition. In *Fast Food, Stock Cars and Rock-n-Roll: Place and Space in American Pop Culture*. Carney, G.O. (Ed.). pp. 1–14, Lanham, MD: Rowman & Littlefield.

4. Richard Grant. *Africa: Geographies of change*. Oxford, New York: Oxford University Press, 2015.

5. Paul Erhunmwunsee, Sunita George, David Iyegha and Paul Tribble. *Fundamentals of World Geography*, 2nd edition. Boston, MA: Pearson Publishing, 2009

6. Lessault, D. & Flahaux, ML. Regards statistiques sur l'histoire de l'émigration internationale au Sénégal [Statistical Views on the History of International Migration from Senegal]. *Revue Européenne des Migrations Internationales* 29, 4(2013), 59–88.

7. Richard Grant. *Africa: Geographies of change*. Oxford, NY: Oxford University Press, 2015

8. United Nations, Department of Economic and Social Affairs (2013). Trends in International Migrant Stock: Migrants by Destination and Origin (United Nations database, POP/DB/MIG/Stock/Rev.2013).

9. Schoumaker, B., Flahaux, ML., Schans, D., Beauchemin, C., Mazzucato, V. & Sakho, P. "Changing patterns of African Migration: A Comparative Analysis." *In C Beauchemin (Ed.), Migration between Africa and Europe: Trends, Factors and Effects*. New York: Springer-Verlag & INED Population Studies series, 2015.

10. The Author's personal discussions with friends involved with this issue over the years.

11. Emmanuel Yenshu Vubo and Humphrey Ngala Ndi. Cross-border Migrations, Regional International and Conviviality in the Gulf of Guinea: Reality and Prospects. In *Environment, Agriculture and Cross-border Migration*, Emmanuel Yenshu Vubo (Ed.). Dakar, CODESRIA, 2015, 172 P.

12. Simon Batterbury. 2001. The Sahel region; assessing progress twenty-five years after the great drought. *Global Environmental Change* (2001) 11, no. 1, 1–95.

13. Marie-Laurence Flahaux and Hein De Haas. African migration: trends, patterns, drivers. *Comparative Migration Studies* (2016) 4, no. 1. DOI: 10.1186/s40878-015-0015-6

14. Collier, P. *Exodus: How Migration Is Changing Our World*. Oxford: Oxford University Press, 2013

15. Myers, N. (2005) Environmental Refugees: An Emergent Security Issue. Organisation for Security and Cooperation in Europe. http://www.osce.org/eea/14851 (Accessed on the Sep 28, 2016).

16. Schoumaker, B., Flahaux, ML., Schans, D., Beauchemin, C., Mazzucato, V. & Sakho, P. Changing patterns of African Migration: A Comparative Analysis. In C Beauchemin (Ed.), *Migration between Africa and Europe : Trends, Factors and Effects*. New York: Springer-Verlag & INED Population Studies series, 2015.

17. Clemens, MA. *Does Development Reduce Migration?*. Washington, DC: Center for Global Development, 2014.

18. Dung, E. J. and Paul E. Pan-Africanism and the African Diaspora: A geographic Perspective. In Pan-Africanism In *Modern Times: Challenges, Concerns and Constraints*. Olayiola Abegunrin and Sabella O. Abidde (Eds.). Lanham, Boulder, New York, London: Lexington Books, 2016.

19. William Mark Habeeb. *Civil Wars in Africa*. Philadelphia: Mason Crest, 2014.

20. Berriane, M. & De Haas, H. *African Migrations Research: Innovative Methods and Methodologies*. Trenton: Africa World Press, 2012.

21. Terminski, Bogumil. Towards Recognition and Protection of Forced Environmental Migrants in the Public International Law: Refugee or IDPs Umbrella, Policy Studies Organization Summit Proceedings, Washington, 2011.

22. NRC. 2011. Displacements due to natural hazard-induced disasters. Internal Displacement Monitoring Center (iDMC), Global estimates for 2009 and 2010.

23. Muzaffar Chishti and Stephen Yale-Loehr. The Immigration Act of 1990: Unfinished Business a Quarter-century later. MPI (Migration Policy Institute), Policy Briefs, July 2016.

24. Pew Research Center. The Global Divide on Homosexuality: Greater Acceptance in more secular and affluent countries, June 2013. http://www.pewglobal.org/2013/06/04/the-global-divide-on-homosexuality/. Accessed August 6, 2016

25. Tierney Sneed and Teresa Welsh. *What's Driving Homophobia in Africa?* U.S. News and World Report, October 16, 2014. http://www.usnews.com/news/articles/2014/10/16/how-anti-lgbt-legislation-in-uganda-nigeria-and-gambia-is-shaping-africa. Accessed September 8, 2016.

26. Onuoha, Freedom (2014). "Boko Haram and the evolving Salafi Jihadist threat in Nigeria." In Pérouse de Montclos, Marc-Antoine. *Boko Haram: Islamism, politics, security and the state in Nigeria*. Leiden: African Studies Centre. pp. 158–191.

27. Rachel M, Friedberg and Jennifer Hunt. The impact of immigrants on Host country wages, employment and growth. *Journal of Economic Perspectives*, 9, 2 (Spring 1995), pp. 23–44

28. Ibid

29. Gibson, John, and David McKenzie. 2010. "The Economic Consequences of "Brain Drain" of the Best and Brightest: Microeconomic Evidence from Five Countries." World Bank Policy Research Working Paper 5394, Washington, DC.

30. Benedict, O.H and Ukpere, W. I. Brain Drain and African Development: Any possible gain from the Drain? *African Journal of Business Management* 6, 7 (2011), pp. 2421–2428.

31. International Monetary Fund. *World Economic and Financial Surveys: Regional Economic Outlook: Sub-Saharan Africa*, Washington, DC: IMF, 2008.

32. Dung, E. J. and Paul E. Pan-Africanism and the African Diaspora: AZ geographic Perspective. In *Pan-Africanism In Modern Times: Challenges, Concerns and Constraints*. Olayiola Abegunrin and Sabella O. Abidde (Eds.). Lanham, Boulder, New York, London: Lexington Books, 2016.

33. Ibid.

34. CODESRIA. The Council for the Development of Social Science Research in Africa (CODESRIA) publications program has been designed to disseminate the results and ideas generated by networks of research institutions, seminars, conferences and other scientific activities. www.codesria.org. Accessed August 26, 2016.

35. Castles, S., De Haas, H., & Miller, MJ. *The Age of Migration: International Population Movements in the Modern World*. Houndmills, Basingstoke, Hampshire: Palgrave Macmillan Higher Education, 2014.

36. Victoria Esses. Siege Mentality. New Scientist Magazine Issue 3011, Published 7 march, 2015 by the Center for Research on Migration and Ethnic Relations at the University of Western Ontario in London, Canada, 2015.

37. Castles, S., De Haas, H., & Miller, MJ. *The Age of Migration: International Population Movements in the Modern World*. Houndmills, Basingstoke, Hampshire: Palgrave Macmillan Higher Education, 2014.

38. David Frum. Why Britain Left. The Atlantic, June 24, 2016. http://www.theatlantic.com/international/archive/2016/06/brexit-eu/488597/. Accessed September 26, 2016.

39. Stanford Encyclopedia of Philosophy. Immigration. Stanford Center for the Study of Language and Information (CSLI), Stanford University, 2015.

40. Victoria Esses. Siege Mentality. New Scientist Magazine Issue 3011, Published 7 march, 2015 by the Center for Research on Migration and Ethnic Relations at the University of Western Ontario in London, Canada, 2015.

41. Ibid.

42. Ibid.

43. Cati Coe. Child circulation and West African Migration. *Movement, Mobilities and Journeys, Vol 6 of the series, Geographies of Children and Young People*, pp. 389–407, 2016.

44. United Nations Children's Fund (UNICEF). Uprooted: The growing crisis for refugee and migrant children. Division of data, research and policy, *UNICEF* 3, United Nations Plaza, New York, USA, 2016.

45. James Hooper. A destination too far? Modeling destination accessibility and distance decay in toursm. *GeoJournal* 80 (1), pp. 33–46, 2015.

Chapter 3

Trekking Across the Sahara

A Long History, Troubled Past, and Hopes for the Future

Alecia D. Hoffman

INTRODUCTION

The history of Africa cannot be denied by those who study the continents of the world. Africa is the home of civilization, and scholars have concluded that some of the oldest remains of human ancestors were discovered in Africa. With a great deal of conclusive evidence discovered by anthropologist about the phenotypes and the study of mitochondrial DNA of the early persons who inhabited the eastern and northern parts of Africa, it is necessary to examine the trajectory of those persons who originated in sub-Saharan Africa, yet found their place in the northernmost part of the continent. This idea of "two Africa" was one that did not always exist. Rather, the creation of a separated continent is directly correlated to the vestiges of colonialism and the residual effects of independence. Prior to the development of this "two Africa" paradigm, relationship linkages existed, connecting the North of the continent with the South. There were also linkages between Africa and Europe. To date, scholarship abounds with discussions of the historic trade routes developed between the kingdoms of West Africa and merchants from the Far East. These original routes zig-zagged their way across the Maghreb and the Sahara, where merchants and middlemen of differing ethnic, religious and cultural backgrounds traded goods such as salt, spices, gold, dyes, and a host of other precious commodities originating either in Africa or from some other part of the globe. Literature also asserts the connection of Africa to Europe prior to colonialism. During this early period people of early Iberia (modern-day Spain and Portugal) and the people indigenous to Africa traded with and traveled across the Mediterranean without the consequence of deportations and xenophobic policies that are now deemed acceptable and commonplace in a number of countries.

In this chapter, an examination of the modern-day route(s) of people from sub-Saharan Africa to North Africa and beyond will be examined. The major questions to be addressed within this chapter are: (1) What influence has Northern Africa, with its sub-Saharan connections, had on the continent of Africa and the world in general during the post-modern era? (2) How have Africans that comprise the Northern portion of the continent been viewed and received by much of Western society? and (3) How can this disconnect between the North and the South be resolved among Africans residing on the continent and by those who seek to re-imagine the Pangea? To shed light on these questions, several countries that comprise the Maghreb/Sahara region will be examined. There are nine countries that comprise the northernmost portion of Africa and are situated within the Sahara Desert. These countries include: Mauritania, Mali, Algeria, Niger, Tunisia, Libya, Chad, Egypt, and North Sudan. An analysis of the countries of Mauritania, Mali, and Algeria will examine the policies that emerge from the governmental institutions and actors to encourage or discourage immigration and emigration to points outside Africa, most notably Europe.

In order to understand the implications of migration from sub-Saharan Africa to the northernmost portion of the continent and beyond, and to understand the linkages that remain between the "two Africa," there is a need to understand why migration takes place. The consequences of migration for both the host and origin countries are of importance to this analysis. To gain some understanding of the impacts of migration, the theoretical postulations that have been offered by scholars in the field of development studies, international relations, and sociology are important. The recent surge in immigration from northern Africa to Europe in the past decade deserves some attention, particularly as it pertains to an appropriate theoretical paradigm to examine and explain some of the pertinent actions taken by the governments of host countries in Africa and beyond to curb the flow of immigrants to their borders. Therefore, it is important to find a theory that appropriately explicates the salient features of what has been witnessed in recent reports provided by news media outlets, multilateral institutions, and think tanks. Organizations such as the United Nations Commission on Human Rights, Organization for Economic Development and Cooperation, the International Migration Institute, etc., have all provided relevant research and data migration.

AN EXAMINATION OF THEORIES OF MIGRATION AND REVIEW OF LITERATURE

There are a myriad of theoretical postulations that have been developed to examine migration. Each of them focuses on the push/pull factors that are evident in the decision for persons to migrate. Furthermore, many of these traditional theories tend to focus on the economic aspects of immigration. Whether these economic forces are a result of the dynamics of the home country which lead to decisions being made on an "atomistic" or a structural level to migrate in search of better opportunities is nonetheless important to the examination of migratory studies.[1]

The varied theories of migration include those that are neo-liberal versus those that are state-centrist.[2] The viewpoints for these theories can be neatly categorized according to Haas.

The importance of these characteristics of migration from an optimist versus a pessimist view point, as emphasized by Haas, are further highlighted and characterized by other scholars who have examined immigration and the causes thereof. In fact, the theories of immigration are not of new origin, but date back to individuals such as Adam Smith, who in 1776 authored *An Inquiry into the Nature and Causes of the Wealth of Nations,* where he surmised that "migration is potentially a response to spatial disequilibrium in labor markets."[3] After Smith, E.G. Ravenstein offered "The Laws of Migration" in 1889. In Ravenstein's manuscript seven laws

Table 3.1 Hein de Haas: Opposing Viewpoints on Migration and Development

Migration Optimist		*Migration Pessimist*
Functionalist	↔	
Structuralist		
Neo-Classical	↔	
Neo-Marxist		
Modernization	↔	
Disintegration		
Net North-South Transfer	↔	Net South North
Transfer		
Brain Gain	↔	
Brain Drain		
More Equality	↔	More
Inequality		
Remittance Investment	↔	
Consumption		
Development	↔	
Dependency Less Migration	↔	More
	Migration	

Source: Hein de Haas, "Migration and Development: A Theoretical Perspective" *International Migration Review,* Vol. 44, Iss. 1 (Spring 2010): 229. Table 1.

are postulated to gain some insight and understanding on immigration. He states,

> (1) Most migrants only move a short distance and usually to large cities; (2) cities that grow rapidly tend to be populated by migrants from proximate rural areas, and gaps arising in the rural population generate migration from more distant areas; (3) out-migration is inversely related to in-migration; (4) a major migration wave will generate a compensating counter-wave; (5) Those migrating a long distance tend to move to large cities; (6) rural persons are more likely to migrate than urban persons; (7) women are more likely to migrate than men.[4]

Others have added to the literature pertaining to immigration. Arthur Lewis provided a synopsis of migration as part of the neo-classical school in the year 1954 where he developed the Lewis model or the dualistic model, which posits that migration occurs because of two sectors, the rural and the industrialized.[5] During the 1960s, Larry A. Sjaastad's economic model on migration was regarded as the leading explanation in understanding immigration.[6] Sjaastad proffered these two important questions as it pertains to migration. "(1) What is the direction and magnitude of the response of migrants to labor earnings differentials over space? (2) What is the connection between migration and these earnings, that is, how effective is migration in equalizing inter-regional earnings of comparable labor?"[7] These aforementioned questions posed by Sjaastad's paper in 1962 influenced Harvard economist George J. Borjas, to embark upon further study as it pertains to migration. Borjas added close derivatives in 1987 and 1991 to the original economic model first proposed by Sjaastad and noted that the theory of migration "treats the decision to migrate as an investment. Thus, a person makes the decision to migrate if the income gain exceeds the migration costs."[8] A formula proposed by Borjas highlights the decision-making process that determines whether migration will be beneficial and whether the overall outcome exceeds the costs of migration.

"$V_1 – V_0 > C$" where V_1 represents the value of earnings if one migrates; V_0 represents the value of earnings if one stays in country of origin; and C measures the cost of migration.[9] The ideas presented by Sjaastad and Borjas were followed with migration theses from Gustav Ranis and John C. H. Fei in 1961; Michael P. Todaro in 1969, 1976, and 1989; and a host of other scholars who have provided insight into the major theoretical propositions of migration and development. [10]

To understand the causes and effects of migration, it is not only beneficial to examine the numerous theories that pertain to migration studies, but also important to recognize the political-economic aspects of migration, not just on the receiving country or area of settlement, but also on the sending country.

The definition of political economy by the Department for International Development, is "bridging the traditional concerns of politics and economics. It focuses on how power and resources are distributed and contested in different contexts and the implications for the development of outcomes. It goes beneath the formal structures to reveal the underlying interests, incentives, and institutions that enable or frustrate change."[11] It is evident that the previous paragraph indicates that there is an economic basis that undergirds and supports migration studies. A great majority of these migration theories are grounded in neoclassical economics of both the micro and macro form. Of these postulations, it is believed that the migration systems theory best represents an appropriate lens to study migration to the Sahara, migration within the Sahara and migration outside of the Sahara. This theory considers several factors that may cause migration, thereby linking the political with the economic.

Migration systems theory (MST) was espoused by Akinlawon L. Mabogunje in 1970 in his paper entitled "Systems Approach to a Theory of Rural-Urban Migration." Mabogunje states:

> A system may be defined as a complex of interacting elements, together with their attributes and relationships. One of the major tasks in conceptualizing a phenomenon as a system, therefore, is to identify the basic interacting elements, their attributes, and their relationships. Once this is done, it soon becomes obvious that the system operates not in a void but in a special environment ... [A] system with its environment constitutes the universe of phenomena which is of interest in a given context.[12]

Mabogunje utilizes systems theory as the foundation for the development of MST. What is significant about Mabogunje's theory is the applicability of this lens to Africa, unlike many of the other neoclassical theories which were grounded and applicable mainly to the Western developed world. MST provides a suitable framework and it can be aptly applied to Africa and other parts of the globe, particularly areas that are more industrialized. Furthermore, Mabogunje's theory has a correlation to constructivism, a theory devised by Nicolas Onuf and made popular by Alexander Wendt. Wendt notes that "a fundamental principle of constructivist theory is that people act toward objects, including other actors, on the basis of the meanings that the objects have for them."[13] Mabogunje's theory of migration takes into account the interacting elements and how these elements relate to each other in the world and or region (systems), hence the tie in to part of Wendt's title, *Anarchy is What States Make of It.* This interaction of the varied components or elements do not take place in a vacuum, but rather in the environment that is of a particular "interest" to that given system. This too is how migration can be examined in Africa, particularly, North Africa. Therefore, MST puts forth the following propositions as highlighted by Douglass S. Massey et al.

1. Countries within a system need not be close since flows reflect political and economic relationships rather than physical ones. Proximity facilitates the formation of exchange relationships, it does not guarantee nor preclude them on account of distance;
2. Multipolar systems are possible, whereby a set of dispersed core countries receive immigrants from a set of overlapping sending countries;
3. Nations belong to more than one migration system, but multiple membership is more common among sending than receiving nations;
4. As political and economic conditions change, systems evolve, so that stability does not imply a fixed structure. Countries may join or drop out of a system in response to social change, economic fluctuation, or political upheaval.[14]

Africa is a large continent and, as stated from the onset of this chapter, migratory patterns between the countries that comprise the continent is not of new origin. The migrations commenced prior to Western colonialism and the creation of the modern-day nation-states. And it is appropriate for some analysis to be given to the connections on the continent and beyond utilizing MST.

A GLIMPSE OF AFRICA'S CONTRIBUTIONS TO THE WORLD DURING THE PRE-MODERN AND MODERN ERAS

Historically, the human resource and natural resource components originating from Africa are commonly known as important contributions to the world. These contributions, which were mentioned the chapter's beginning, had started before the modern era and post-modern era. Some examples include the rich history of Mansa Musa's sojourns across the Sahara carrying immense amounts of gold that at one time caused the economic market of Egypt to falter and not regain stability until nearly ten years later. There are varied stories of the trade in spices, salt and other goods with men from the East, where middlemen scattered throughout the Sahara helped to facilitate the great trade empires that existed during pre-modern times.

The advent of Islam and its spread throughout Northern, Eastern, and Western Africa was also facilitated by Arab traders, and others who came with a more forceful agenda and interacted with merchants and rulers on the continent. The Moors conquered Spain and introduced numerous advancements to Europe, some of these include scientific progress; modern city planning; education, universities, and libraries; musical instruments; paper and Arabic numbers; and new agricultural crops. It was by way of Africa that many of advancements of Asia reached Europe.

In addition to the cultural, educational, and scientific contributions of Africa to the world, there were contributions of the human element. The Indian Ocean slave trade commenced approximately around the same time of the spread of Islam during the late seventh century and introduced human chattel into Asia. Individuals who were transported to Asian lands served in armies, acted as religious officials in the capacity of eunuchs, and women were concubines who bore children,who would later add to the rich history of Africa, Asia, and the rest of the world. These are some of the examples that serve as a glimpse of the influence of African persons in the world system during the pre-modern era. Furthermore, each of these events could rightly be categorized as migrations, some voluntary and some forced, across the Sahara Desert. And with each of these came implications for the regions, peoples and cultures in both political and social economic ways. More importantly, these migrations and cross-cultural exchanges pre-date the European imperialist era, which did not commence until the end of the pre-modern era during the late 1400s.

During the modern era, there is still much to be said about Africa and her contributions. Although this time period is most commonly associated with the period of European colonialism on the continent, the contributions of the African people and the resources of the continent were of great importance to the maintenance and growth of the metropoles of Europe. During the modern era, the transatlantic slave trade commenced and this resulted in the displacement of millions of Africans through patterns of forced migration. Just as contributions were made to Europe during the time of the Dark Ages by the Moors who conquered Spain, the continuation of African influence now stretched beyond Europe and Asia. Africans were transported to the new colonies in North and South America where they worked in capacities that are now considered as inhumane.

During the Great War, Africans played a vital part of serving in the military ranks and fighting with the European powers to defeat the Germans. In the Northern French and West African colonies, over 65,000 men died fighting in World War I. Although a great number of battles occurred in the Southern, Eastern, and Western portion of the continent, one of the main goals was the protection of the Suez Canal. During World War II the Saharan countries were considered a major theater where battles were fought to stop German advancements. These events highlight just a few of important contributions provided by Africa during the modern era.

Both World Wars I and II led to calls of solidarity among African people in the diaspora and led to the establishment of Pan Africanism and the subsequent conferences held around the world to address the problems that people of color endured around the globe. Although the first conference was held in 1919 and several additional meetings were held thereafter, the creation of the Organization of African Unity (OAU)—now the African Union—was a derivative of these meetings which occurred in cities such as London, Paris, Brussels, and New York. The founding of this organization in 1963 brought together some of the most powerful leaders of Africa, which included leadership from sub-Saharan and the Saharan regions of the continent. This synthesis of ideas and efforts to establish a trajectory for the path and future of the continent by the member states of the predecessor of the AU provides a semblance of the idea of "one Africa."

During the pre-modern and modern eras, there is evidence of the vast contributions of the continent in a plethora of events and areas. Commencing with great kingdoms that existed in what is now considered the sub-Saharan regions of the continent and the connections that were made with leaders and kingdoms in Asia and the paths forged across the Sahara to establish these relationships; the movement of people from the sub-Saharan area to points East and West during the spread of Islam during the late seventh century and later the transatlantic slave trade during the fifteenth century; the two world wars where the Sahara served as a major theater for the allied troops against the Germans; and the establishment of a multinational organization on the continent to bring some semblance of hope and the establishment of goals for the future, where all Africans could take part are evidence of Africa's contributions to the world. This background of Africa's contributions and the forging of relationships across the Sahara and the Sahel help to shape the discussion about the current trajectory of movements across the Sahara.

WESTERN PERCEPTIONS OF AFRICAN MIGRANTS AND AN EXAMINATION OF THE "THRESHOLD AREAS" OF THE SAHARA

MST provides a useful lens to examine the patterns of migration on the African continent today. It considers the political-economic aspects of migration which has implications on the sending countries, threshold countries, and receiving countries. To place this analysis in its proper context, the definition of "threshold" as espoused by Jocelyne Streiff-Fenart and Aurelia Segatti will be utilized to explain the role of those areas in the Saharan region of Africa that must contend with the consequences of immigration and emigration. Furthermore, the policies enacted by these host governments typically are a result of international pressure from the major powers, particularly those within the European Union. According to Streiff-Fenart and Segatti, threshold encompasses multiple scopes when discussing varied groups that are in transit. Utilizing Victor Turner's ideas regarding liminality, which is a concept that refers to a state of being between something or being in a state of passage, Streiff-Fenart and Segatti utilize an evolutionary approach to this original concept of liminality and apply multiple dimensions to what they call "threshold." These dimensions include:

> The discursive and conceptual frameworks that constitute the backbone of threshold policies aiming to keep undesirables beyond borders; the constitution of stopping places, intermediate areas, and relay towns, which all represent threshold spaces that challenge local urban equilibriums; the experience of liminality, in which individuals caught for a time between two states experience the ambiguous situations characteristic of threshold people.[15]

Turner, Streiff-Fenart, and Segatti's utilization of threshold allows for a more detailed understanding of MST and its applicability in Northern Africa. This approach allows for an understanding of the policy dynamics of the threshold spaces and how these policies affect those that are in the liminal phases of immigration and emigration.

MAURITANIA

The Islamic Republic of Mauritania is in northwest Africa. The population of the country is approximately 4,180,798 persons, and according to the International Organization for Migration, in 2015, the immigrant population of the country of Mauritania was 3.40 percent of the resident population with 138,162 migrants in the country. Within the past ten years, the country has seen an increase in the amount of immigrants that have made their way into its borders. The number of immigrants in the country in 2005 registered at 66,053 and just 2.2 percent of the total population of the country.[16] This increased 1.2 percentage points over the past ten years and numerically the country has seen a rise in the number of immigrants to 72,109 migrants in the country. Those arriving in the country come from a variety of other countries in Africa and outside of the continent. These areas outside of Africa include the United States, China, Russia, Canada, Belgium, Spain, and South Korea, just to name a few. The African continent also provides large numbers of persons immigrating to Mauritania. The countries of Egypt, Mali, Guinea, Algeria, Tunisia, Guinea Bissau, Morocco, and the Congo are just a few of the many countries on the continent where persons have migrated from their home of origin to one of the countries located in the northwest quadrant of Africa. Women comprised 41.9 percent of immigrants to the country in 2015. The reasons for these numerical increases deserves some attention and the push and pull factors that lead to the migratory patterns to Mauritania are also worth noting.

Returning to the theories of migration, Mabogunje, Massey, and some of the other neoclassical theorist have provided the link between the decision to move and the economic factor, or the need for work. Mabogunje's seminal work addressed this particular issue of rural to urban migration utilizing the systems theory. Studies have shown that Mauritania's pull factors that lead to a number of migrants choosing the country are indeed employment related, and hence, these pull factors would translate into push factors, such as the need for better employment, which would cause an exodus from the country of origin. The Migration Policy Centre and the International Organization for Migration note that, during the year 2000, a large portion of emigres come from the countries of Senegal and Mali found Mauritania as a suitable place to seek refugee or call home. Approximately 38 percent of the migrants were from Senegal and 28 percent from Mali.[17] Studies show that many individuals who have migrated to Mali from the two aforementioned countries have found employment in the cities of Nouakchott, Nouadhibou, and Rosso. In these cities, a 2010 report showed that 87 percent worked in the service sector and nearly 6 percent worked in the engineering and public works sectors where they were involved in unskilled labor.[18] Studies have further shown that many of the migrants to Mauritania are males with low levels of education.

Although the traditional migration patterns that occur in the country center on the movement of individuals from rural sectors to urban sectors or the movement of individuals to seek a better way of life for themselves and their families in their home countries, the outcomes are not always bright. The State Department of the United States notes that Mauritania is "a source and destination country for men, women, and children subjected to forced labor and sex trafficking." This forced labor is evidenced in varied communities in the country which include those that are indigenous communities such as the Afro-Mauritanians and the Black-Moors who are subjected to forms of forced labor. There are also reports of forced labor and trafficking among the women of some sub-Saharan countries. Many of these young women immigrate to Mauritania and would be shipped to Saudi Arabia. The hopes of finding a better way of life in respectable professions are not always realized after the false stories and dreams are sold to them by the recruiters and middlemen. Instead, many receive a raw deal.[19]

Mauritania as a "Threshold" Country

Utilizing the definition of "threshold" that was alluded to at the onset of this section, it is evident that during the twenty-first century, the country became the place of temporary stops for those seeking to cross the Mediterranean to Europe. Outward migration from Mauritania accounted for 119,334 persons in 2015 and 2.85 percent of Mauritania's population lived abroad, with approximately the highest recorded numbers in France registering 17,768; the second largest destination area being Spain, with a number of 8,606; and the third largest destination country being one on the African soil, Morocco, registering 1,619.[20] Mauritania became the destination place for sub-Saharan Africans who used the country as a temporary stopping place before traveling to the Canary Islands and later to Europe. Due to the many lives lost during the early part of the twenty-first century by those who attempted to make this perilous journey, the country of Mauritania passed a law in 2007. This law made it a criminal offense to participate in trafficking migrants. According to the African Capacity Building Centre (ACBC), the European Union provided support to Mauritania through its ninth European Development Fund, which sought to assist the country with its migratory woes. Various aspects of the project included training judges and law officials on immigration legislation and the creation and broadcast of a documentary that detailed the dangers of migration. The project and the support of the Mauritanian government has ensured that there is border security through the provisions of equipment, training of officers, and secure communication between border posts and command stations.[21]

In addition to the European Union, the country of Japan has made overtures to ensure that Mauritania and Mali can control its border issues. In 2015 the Organization for International Migration received financing from Japan to assist Mauritania with shoring up its border security for the time frame of March 2015 to March 2017. The Organization for International Migration also instituted new strategies in July of 2015 to support the Sahel regions' G5 countries of Mauritania, Mali, Niger, Burkina Faso, and Chad that aimed at "enhancing regional security in the Sahel by strengthening operational and strategic capacities, and developing regional approaches for immigration and border management." The country also launched assisted return and reintegration programs for those migrants who have existed in this "threshold state" of Mauritania and wish to return to their countries of origin.[22]

In the discussions pertaining to immigration and emigration, one of the main purposes of leaving one country and moving to another typically centers on better opportunities. As the theoretical frameworks of migration have noted, relocating from agrarian centers to more urban centers tend to be a common theme throughout much of the literature on migration theories. Furthermore, the notion of the availability of opportunities happens to be a factor which causes many to migrate. One of the common occurrences with those who move abroad is the use of remittances to the home country to assist family members who are dealing with economic disparity. The World Bank provides statistics relative to the amount of inflow remittances that Mauritania receives because of those who have decided to emigrate abroad. The chart below highlights the amounts between the years 1978 and 2015.

As indicated in Table 3.2, the amount of remittance inflow into Mauritania is not very large except for 1992 which registers a number of 50 billion according to World Bank statistical data. And, for the years 1999 through

Table 3.2 Remittance Inflows to Mauritania in Millions of US Dollars

1978	1979	1980	1981	1982	1983	1984	1985	1986	1987
1	*2*	*6*	*4*	*2*	*1*	*1*	*1*	*2*	*7*
1988	**1989**	**1990**	**1991**	**1992**	**1993**	**1994**	**1995**	**1996**	**1997**
9	*5*	*14*	*12*	*50*	*2*	*5*	*5*	*4*	*3*
1998	**1999**	**2000**	**2001**	**2002**	**2003**	**2004**	**2005**	**2006**	**2007**
2	*Nd*	*Nd*	*Nd*	*Nd*	*Nd*	*Nd*	*Nd*	*Nd*	*Nd*
2008	**2009**	**2010**	**2011**	**2012**	**2013**	**2014**	**2015**		
Nd	*Nd*	*Nd*	*Nd*	*Nd*	*Nd*	*Nd*	*Nd*		

Note: Nd denotes "no data"
Source: World Bank. "Migration and Remittance Data [XLS]" (Update April 2016). Accessed 15 August 2016. Available from: http://www.worldbank.org/en/topic/migrationremittancesdiasporaissues/brief/migration-remittances-data.

2015, there is no data recorded in addition to how remittances affect the Gross Domestic Product of the country.

In conclusion, the main theoretical paradigm utilized to study migration states that the distance factor is not something of great importance when studying migration. Mabogunje's theory is applicable in the case of Mauritania because a large swath of migrants are from Senegal and Mali, two border-countries of Mauritania. Mabogunje notes in his seminal work "Systems Approach to a Theory of Rural-Urban Migration" that in many of the traditional neoclassical theories, one of the many factors is distance when it comes to the decision to migrate. For Mabogunje, this is not the case. Furthermore, he notes the lack of consistency in examining rural to urban migration, a factor that has been historically prevalent in Africa. To this end, we find that during the twenty-first century many of the migratory patterns that exist that would cause individuals to migrate from sub-Saharan Africa to Mauritania is the fact that Mauritania has served as a "threshold country." Also, Mabogunje's theory highlights the environment in which those who chose to migrate live and operate. This system is one that consists of institutions. Therefore, the institutional element of migration cannot be ignored when dealing with the change of the "basic modal structure of a society," where people move from rural areas to more urban areas.[23]

The World Bank notes that the Gross Domestic Product (GDP) of Mauritania is one that is not very high and the country is predominately a poor country. The government has been taking increased measures to reduce the amount of poverty within the country through partnerships with the international community and instituting domestic policies. It is with this point that there is a need to understand how the former colonial structures and the independence movements shaped many rural societies, thus transforming them from isolated villages to systems that were connected to larger systems and institutions. So, to this end, we find the use of systems theory applicable to the study of migratory patterns to Mauritania and those who migrate to other parts of the world.

MALI

The second country of examination is that of the Republic of Mali, a landlocked country situated in Northwest Africa. Mali was discussed earlier in the section pertaining to the migratory patterns to Mauritania. According to the International Organization for Migration, there are approximately 17,189 Mauritanians who have immigrated to Mali juxtaposed to 56,557 emigres from Mali to Mauritania.[24] Some additional African countries that have emigres to Mali include Nigeria with 11,840; 33,225 from Gabon; 29,972 from the Republic of Congo; 20,144 from the Ivory Coast; 23,922 from Burkina Faso; and 18,561 from Ghana. The country has an inward migration figure of approximately 363,145 registered at 2.06 percent of the Malian population in 2015.[25] Outward migration from Mali registers the highest numbers on the African continent. There are approximately 1,005,397 Malians living abroad or outside of the country. There are approximately 356,019 residing in the Ivory Coast and 160,967 in Nigeria. Outside of the continent, a large portion of emigres are found in France, registering at 75,555. According to the International Organization of Migration 5.40 percent of Malians live abroad.[26]

The inward and outward flows to Mali provides a similar story to that of Mauritania. Furthermore, the utilization of Mabogunje's application of systems theory is useful. First, there are a large swath of emigres from the country moving to other points south of the Sahara. To understand the patterns of Malians leaving the country it is important to recognize the varied events that are occurring within the country which would cause individuals to relocate. Mali has a long history of emigres from the country seeking a better way of life abroad. These patterns of migration commenced as early as the fourth century and continued well into the period of colonialism and independence from France. During the colonial period, Malians migrated for the purpose of working on plantations to maintain the French colonial structure and bolster the imperial structure of France. After the end of colonialism, the migration continued, but this time with migratory patterns caused by other "push" factors such as weather patterns—which has always been a factor that affected the agricultural output and thus the economic standing of families and the country. In addition, World War II served as both a push and pull factor that led to many Malians leaving the country and settling in the land of the former metropole, France. According to the Migration Policy Institute, between the years or 1992–1993, a national migration survey found that 91 percent of the rural population was living in the district of their birth. Moreover, 47 percent of rural households had at least one member of the family emigrate in or out of the district. The typical family members who usually migrate in and out based on whether it is a good season or dry season are usually young males looking for employment opportunities.[27]

The factor of institutions also plays a role in the movement of Malians across borders due to the country's membership in the Economic Community of West African States (ECOWAS). On January 5, 1979, ECOWAS adopted the policy of Free Movement of Persons, Residence and Establishment (Protocol A/P 1/5/79) that allows for persons who are from member states of ECOWAS to freely move across borders of the member states, thereby creating a community of citizenship.[28] This regional institutional policy undoubtedly assisted many who sought refuge in other countries on the continent during the 2012–2013 domestic institutional fiasco when Islamic militants seized the northern portion of the country and the government of Mali faced a crisis as a result of this. With the return to normalization, other institutions outside of the continent have also worked to assist the country with the number of migrants or internationally displaced persons (IDPs). The European Union is one such example along with the Organization for International Migration (IOM), the African Union, and the United Nations. The European Union pledged 1.28 billion Euros to Mali during the Mali Conference held in Brussels in May of 2013 with a total of 3.285 billion Euros pledged overall by the donor nations. An additional 615 million Euros has been pledged by an arm of the European Union called the European Development Fund for the time frame of 2014–2020 to assist the Malian government with bolstering its security and the re-stabilization of its governmental institutions following the breakdown of civil order during the 2012–2013 crisis. Adding to the funding coming from the European Union, an additional amount of 1.88 billion Euros was provided by an emergency trust fund to tackle the migrations problems of the country.[29] Overall, Mali receives a great deal of support from the international community to assist with the myriad of issues that plague the country. The economic, weather, and internal conflict have exacerbated the burden on Malian government institutions to provide collective goods and solve collective action problems within the country, hence the large swaths of persons migrating from the country.

A negative aspect of migration in Mali pertains to the number of persons who are trafficked in the country and throughout the Sahara. The U.S. State Department has placed Mali in "tier 2" on its watch list for international trafficking. Just as there are forms of modern-day slavery that existed in Mauritania, we also find this to be the case in Mali, particularly among Black Tuaregs, who serve in salt mines in the northern part of the country. However, it must be noted that the Tuaregs have been in protracted conflicts with the central government of Mali in attempts to gain autonomy in the region.

It was in 2012–2013 that the Islamic uprising occurred and the Tuaregs long struggle with the government somewhat helped to fuel the disruption which led to the near weakening of government institutions by the Islamic militants. There are also reports of trafficking among Africans who are emigres from other countries where Mali simply serves as a "threshold" country as they attempt to make their way to Europe. Women and girls are noted by the U.S. State Department as the unlikely group that faces the harsh realities of the criminal syndicate world of trafficking and exploitation.[30] This negative side of migration undoubtedly reached levels of high proportion during the 2012–2013 crisis in the country. However, the international community is making attempts to counteract the negative sides of migration through the provision of funds from multilateral organizations and institutions.

One of the caveats of those who choose to emigrate is the remittances that may help those who are still residing in the country. Table 3.3 highlights the amount of funds that are sent to Mali from those living abroad in the form of remittances. Remittances accounted for 7.4 percent of the GDP of Mali for the year 2014.[31]

In conclusion, Mali has a protracted history as it pertains to migration. Commencing during the fourth century with patterns of movement across the Sahara led by individuals such as Mansa Musa, who is probably one of the most well-known figures of Malian history, who ruled during the height of Mali's glory when the country was renowned for its wealth in gold. During the period of colonialism Mali became a French fiefdom where indigenous persons were forced to migrate to varied plantations to maintain the wealth and power of the colonial state. Therefore, the juxtaposition of Mali placed it in one of the major theaters of the world ward. It allowed men to join the ranks of the French armed forces as part of their allied efforts in the battle against German forces. Thereafter, some men took up residence in the metropole, France. And lastly, the post-modern era where Mali witnessed its independence and the struggles to maintain

Table 3.3 Remittance Inflows to Mali in Millions of US Dollars

1978	**1979**	**1980**	**1981**	**1982**	**1983**	**1984**	**1985**	**1986**	**1987**
44	*54*	*59*	*48*	*39*	*36*	*32*	*67*	*68*	*88*
1988	**1989**	**1990**	**1991**	**1992**	**1993**	**1994**	**1995**	**1996**	**1997**
73	*76*	*107*	*93*	*117*	*126*	*103*	*112*	*110*	*92*
1998	**1999**	**2000**	**2001**	**2002**	**2003**	**2004**	**2005**	**2006**	**2007**
84	*86*	*73*	*88*	*138*	*154*	*155*	*177*	*212*	*344*
2008	**2009**	**2010**	**2011**	**2012**	**2013**	**2014**	**2015**		
431	*454*	*473*	*784*	*827*	*895*	*895*	*895*		

Source: World Bank. "Migration and Remittance Data [XLS]" (Update April 2016). Accessed 15 August 2016. Available from: http://www.worldbank.org/en/topic/migrationremittancesdiasporaissues/brief/migration-remittances-data.

its institutions, markets, and economy also led to many persons to emigrate and seek a better life on new soil. Those who seek a better way of life are not always welcomed in other countries due to the xenophobic tendencies and waves of nationalism, which tend to isolate Malians seeking work on foreign soil, as was the case in the Ivory Coast. Mabogunje's application of systems theory is one applicable to the state of Mali, for the rural aspects and weather patterns have caused many to relocate to urban areas within and outside of the country in search of better economic opportunities. This rural-urban pattern of migration is also coupled with recent conflicts and the near collapse of institutions that is not necessarily covered by Mabogunje, but nonetheless just as important when seeking to understand the patterns of migration in the twenty-first century. Also, multilateral Western institutions have played a vital role in attempting to mitigate the crises that are occurring in Mali's borders which have deleterious implications for its neighbors in the region and the world in general. By providing funds to deal with the migration and IDP issue, the international community hopes to assist the country in its efforts of fostering peace and security in the global system.

ALGERIA

The People's Democratic Republic of Algeria (Al Jumhuriyah al Jaza'iriyah ad Dimuqratiya ash Shabiya) is in the North of Africa bordered by the Mediterranean Sea to its north, the countries of Morocco to the west, Tunisia and Libya to the east and Niger, Mali and Mauritania to the south. Due to a large portion of the Sahara Desert being in the country, many of the populations reside in the coastal areas, with the most populous being Algiers. The IOM provides statistics highlight the numbers of Algerians living abroad. There is a total of 1,763,430 emigres that have left the country and a large proportion of them reside outside of Africa. There are 1,430,656 Algerians in France; 55,306 in Spain; and 45,680 in Israel whose intention is to migration to other non-African countries. Within Africa, the largest immigrant Algerian populations are few, but some large numbers are registered in the countries of Morocco with 13,664; Tunisia has 10,443; and Senegal, located in sub-Saharan Africa, boasts the third largest number registered at 4,050.[32] Inward migration to Algeria is not as large as the number of individuals who have left the country. However, the Western Sahara has approximately 90,939 persons who have emigrated to Algeria.[33] The internal and external issues are centered on the autonomy of the Western Sahara and its ongoing dispute with Morocco will likely account for the large number of emigres from its quasi-borders to Algeria.

Algeria has been recognized as that of a transit country or "threshold" region due to the large number of persons who travel through the country with the hopes of crossing the Mediterranean. As previously mentioned, several Western Saharans have found refuge in Algeria due to the protracted disputes between the indigenous and the Moroccan government. In addition to those from Western Sahara who emigrated to Algeria, the U.S. State Department also notes that there are numbers of people arriving from sub-Saharan Africa and the country serves as a transit country and also that of a "threshold" as previously stated. Mali, Niger, Cameroon, Ivory Coast, and Nigeria are countries from where emigres originate. Many men and women make the trek to Algeria with the hopes of reaching Europe. Those who are unsuccessful stay behind in Algeria and work in varied service sector jobs.[34] The policies that have been forged between Algeria and some of the migrant countries—with international backing—have included practices of repatriating immigrants to their home countries. The IOM highlights one such story where during the spring of 2016 approximately 9,273 migrants were returned to Niger due to an agreement forged between the two countries.[35]

Historically, the migratory patterns of Algerians have been based on the colonial relationship with France. During the colonial period, many left Algeria and relocated in Europe. However, in recent years the patterns have changed with the paths of migration centered on lack of suitable employment opportunities for the burgeoning highly educated and the political climate of the country.[36] The growth of *Harragas*, meaning those who burn their documents in the hopes of leaving Algeria to reach Europe, increased during the twenty-first century. There are many young educated Algerians who have attempted to make the journey across the Mediterranean in hopes of a better life. However, there are consequences associated for those who choose to embark upon this journey. Some do not make it across the Mediterranean and perish, while others face penalties and jail time if caught by authorities. For those who are successful, the risks still exist. If one is considered to be an illegal migrant, he/she may face exploitation by middlemen, have no place to live and work odd jobs, or even risk deportation. To combat the high levels of emigration from Algeria, the government has instituted policies to curb illegal immigration. For irregular entry or exit of a foreign resident or national citizen, a 6-month to 2-year prison penalty was imposed by the government. Furthermore, those who act as collaborators and assist foreigners with entrance, exit, or lodging in the country are subject to a 2 to 5-year prison sentence. There have also been some penalties enacted to curb human trafficking within the country and the neighboring nation-states through the implementation of agreements with all of Algeria's neighbors except for Morocco.[37]

Outside of the continent, Algeria has entered into agreements with multinational institutions such as the European Union, forming the EU-Algerian

Association Agreement which was entered effect in 2005. This agreement not only fosters cooperation in the areas of trade and economics, but also serves to control irregular migration patterns from Algeria to Europe.[38] Also, the countries of France and Germany have instituted protocols and agreements with the Algerian government to curb immigration from the country of origin to the host countries. France and Algeria entered into an agreement entitled Decree 2008—373 in April 2008 calls for cooperation between both countries to fight against irregular migration. Prior to the implementation of this agreement, the policies that have been instituted by the French government can be described as "exclusionary." The Migration Integration Policy Index notes, as it pertains to France, "newcomers encounter the least favorable and most contradictory integration policies of all major countries of immigration."[39] To this extent, many jobs are not made available to the immigrants due to contradictory policies that make it difficult for the unemployed. The Hortefeux Law was implemented in November 2007 and one of the law's purposes was to create better job opportunities. Additionally, the naturalization process in France exercises a bit more discretion than the naturalization processes in other places that are considered to be immigrant countries. Local voting rights are not extended to those who have undergone the naturalization process. The Migration Integration Policy Index III (MIPEX) also notes that French policy does not allow non-EU residents more opportunities to access labor than other countries of the European Union and "French eligibility provisions are the 2nd least favorable of all countries" after Cyprus and Slovakia.[40] The measures that are in place in France are considered to be protectionist to say the least. These policies that attempt to protect the labor market have been in place since the 1930s and MIPEX notes that these policies have a negative impact on the country by way of not taking full advantage of the economic potential that immigrants can offer to the country's economy.[41]

Germany has announced that Algeria will be designated as one of its "safe countries of origin" which will assist with the number of migrants attempting to emigrate from Algeria to Germany. This designation of "safe countries" means that Germany will not grant asylum to any migrants seeking refuge within its borders from the countries of Algeria, Tunisia, and Morocco. This agreement with Algeria will call for the Algerian government to repatriate those found emigrating to Germany.[42]

For those who successfully emigrate from Algeria, live abroad and can find steady employment, there is an expectation that funds will be sent home to assist the families. These monies that are earned in destination countries and sent back to the countries of origin tend to have an impact on the GDP of many developing nation-states. The amount of remittance inflows to Algeria are worth examining and are highlighted in Table 3.4. These inflows for the years 1978–2015 as provided by the World Bank are registered in millions of dollars.

Table 3.4 Remittance Inflows to Algeria in Millions of US Dollars

1978	**1979**	**1980**	**1981**	**1982**	**1983**	**1984**	**1985**	**1986**	**1987**
393	*417*	*406*	*447*	*507*	*392*	*329*	*313*	*358*	*487*
1988	**1989**	**1990**	**1991**	**1992**	**1993**	**1994**	**1995**	**1996**	**1997**
379	*345*	*352*	*1,290*	*1,390*	*1,140*	*1,395*	*1,120*	*880*	*1,060*
1998	**1999**	**2000**	**2001**	**2002**	**2003**	**2004**	**2005**	**2006**	**2007**
1,060	*790*	*790*	*670*	*1,070*	*1,750*	*2,460*	*2,060*	*1,610*	*2,120*
2008	**2009**	**2010**	**2011**	**2012**	**2013**	**2014**	**2015**		
2,202	*2,059*	*2,044*	*1,942*	*1,942*	*2,000*	*2,000*	*2,000*		

Source: World Bank. "Migration and Remittance Data [XLS]" (Update April 2016). Accessed 15 August 2016. Available from: http://www.worldbank.org/en/topic/migrationremittancesdiasporaissues/brief/migration-remittances-data.[44]

Although the numbers shown in Table 3.4 highlight remittance payments that are much higher than the previously examined countries of Mauritania and Mali, remittances were only 0.9 percent of the Algerian GDP in 2014. The fact that Algeria can be classified as a rentier state, rich with oil and natural gas, this has allowed the government to provide a good amount of the basic services to its citizenry over the years. However institutional constraints, corruption, lack of a private sector in the market economy and the over-reliance on oil receipts during a time of slumping oil prices has led to economic woes in the country. Coupled with these aforementioned areas are the border issues and the need of the Algerian government to show the international community that government policies are aimed at combating international terrorism and Islamic fundamentalism.

In conclusion, the country of Algeria has served as a transit and "threshold" country for those seeking to cross the Mediterranean to reach Europe. Furthermore, the lack of opportunities for many young educated people in the country has led to migrants leaving the country in search of better opportunities in recent years. The governmental policies, elitism and the lack of redistribution of wealth or the opportunities to obtain wealth have all served as contributory factors to the crises that have arisen in Algeria. The events of the Arab Spring, which had massive ramifications for many North African countries, serve as a reminder of the role of the system at the national and regional level and how policies, or lack thereof, can lead to regional destabilization and result in migration from the affected areas.

CONCLUDING STATEMENTS

This examination of the nation-states of Mauritania, Mali and Algeria reveals some of the complex realities facing emigres from other countries and those who immigrate from the countries of these case studies to points south of the

Sahara and to other parts of the globe, particularly Europe. Government, multilateral, and international institutions have implemented policies to mitigate the high levels of irregular migration with the intent of protecting migrants and international security. There are many reasons for migration. In some instances persons may be forced to do so due to conflict, economics, weather patterns or exclusionary policies in their countries of origin.

With the growing concerns of the international community regarding the high level of migrations that have taken place due to the reasons many North African countries, at the behest of the European Union, have instituted measures to limit the number of individuals leaving their borders and strengthening their borders with neighbors in the region. These policies make it difficult for migrants to leave both their states of origin and their "threshold" or transit states. For those who can successfully leave the Africa, it may be difficult to become fully integrated into the society of the receiving nation once they reach their final destination, specifically some nations in Europe. This is true for those who are undocumented and also for some who are documented. The European Union and other multinational institutions have entered into agreements and enacted policies with a number of North African nations and some sub-Saharan nations to repatriate large numbers of irregular immigrants. In addition, some Western nations have supplemented North African states with billions of Euros to strengthen border protection, train security forces, and assist the governments with the creation and provision of opportunities and training for those who are likely to migrate due to a lack of prospects in the countries of origin.

The theoretical framework of systems theory as explained and applied by Akin Mabogunje was utilized to examine the movement of people to the Sahara region and to points North and South. Although there are a myriad of neo-classical macro and micro theories on migration, Mabogunje's theory is one that examines the migratory patterns from an African perspective. Due to the history of colonialism and the independence movements that occurred in Africa, the salient features of migration provide a more nuanced background than many of the migratory patterns that occurred in the Western world. To this end, when studying migration in and across Africa, Mabogunje highlights a theoretical aspect of Africa—that of self-sustaining isolated areas that existed prior to colonization. However, after independence the continent witnessed the growth of urban areas and the decline—to some extent—of the agricultural sector. This new integration into the system within the nation-state eventually developed into an incorporation into the world system leading to more migration in search of better opportunities. When the integration between the rural and the urban occurs, it leads to changes in the market and economic structures of the nation-state. The structures of the nation-state may be a result of governmental policies which also have implications for those former rural societies and people who now become part of the system.[43]

The migratory patterns that lead to persons leaving the continent, and more importantly across the Sahara to Europe, are patterns that are a result of world systems also. The need to adapt to the changing system leads to emigration in search of better opportunities that are not available in the place of origin due to the impediments that may have been instituted by the system itself. This system includes the governing institutions of the nation-states that experience large emigrant populations leaving their borders and the government institutions that must contend with the immigrants arriving at their borders. For those countries that witness large numbers of emigres, it is important to examine the policies which emanate from the government institutions that may exclude certain groups and not allow these groups to develop to their full potential. Therefore, governing structures that do not provide or create opportunities can lead to systemic issues that if not addressed properly with new policies (or new rational actors) will lead to either a breakdown of order as witnessed with the Arab Spring and other internal crises in some countries in North Africa. This absence of effective policy pronouncements will lead to the exodus of citizens in search of better opportunities.

Within the international system, immigrants also may face exclusionary policies that are implemented by governing structures. These institutions within the international system may employ protectionist measures. Additionally, agreements have been erected between origin countries and receiving countries to repatriate those who migrate, thus dashing hopes of achieving hopes and dreams.

It is important to find solutions to these present day systems issues pertaining to migration. The allocation of funding form the international community to alleviate and combat some of the factors that lead to migration is just a piece of the puzzle. For those countries that are experiencing the mass exodus of people from its borders that contribute to brain drain, and those countries that serve as "threshold" and transit countries, there needs to be stronger governments to enact policies that will create the employment, economic, and market opportunities that are desired by those new graduates from their universities. There is a need to hold multinational corporations and firms accountable in hiring practices to ensure that young educated citizens are trained and employed to work in supervisory positions. Governments must also hold those groups and persons accountable who participate in illegal activities and not turn a blind eye to actions such as trafficking. Only by employing the appropriate measures and policies at the state, regional, and international levels, and by ensuring that those who are responsible for such crimes face justice, will the countries then be able to realize more secure borders and a decline in activities that cause international instability and may lead to acts of terrorism. These prescriptions will then bring about a more sustainable path in a globalized world—the new Pangea.

NOTES

1. Douglass A. Massey et. al., "Theories of International Migration: A Review and Appraisal." *Population and Development Review,* Vol. 19, no. 3 (September 1993): 431–466, 455.

2. Hein de. Haas, "Migration and Development: A Theoretical Perspective." *International Migration Review*, Vol. 44, no. 1 (Spring 2010): 227–264, 229.

3. O.B. Bodvarsson and H. Van den Berg. *The Economics of Immigration: Theory and Policy* (New York, N.Y.: Springer Science Business and Media, 2013), 29.

4. Ibid., 30. These seven principles were initially summarized by Michael J. Greenwood. "Internal Migration in Developed Countries," in Mark Rosenzweig and Oded Stark, eds. *Handbook of Population and Family Economics* (Amsterdam: Elsevier Publishers, 1997).

5. Gustav Ranis, "Arthur Lewis' Contribution to Development Thinking and Policy." *Yale University Economic Growth Center Discussion Paper no. 891*, (August 2004). Accessed 5 August 2016. Available from http://ssrn.com/abstract=583302.

6. For more information on Larry A. Sjaastad's economic model of migration see, "The Cost and Returns of Human Migration." *The Journal of Political Economy* Vol. 7, no. 5, Part 2 (October 1962): 80–93.

7. George J. Borjas, "Self-Selection and the Economics of Migration," accessed 4 August 2016. Available from: http://cream-migration.org/files/G_Borjas_Self-Selection_SOLE_Jun_10.pdf.

8. Ibid.

9. Ibid.

10. Gustav Ranis and John H.C. Fei, "A Theory of Economic Development." *The American Economic Review* Vol. 51, no. 4 (Sept. 1961): 533–565. JSTOR 1812785; Michael P. Todaro, "A Model of Labor Migration and Urban Unemployment in Less Developed Countries." *American Economic Review* Vol. 59, no. 1 (1969): 138–148.; Michael P. Todaro, *Migration and Economic Development: A Review of Theory, Evidence, Methodology, and Research Priorities, Occasional Paper 18* (Nairobi: Institute for Development Studies University of Nairobi, 1976. Accessed 12 August 2016. Available from mobile.opendocs.ids.ac.uk/opendocs/handle/1233456789/791; Michael P. Todaro, *Economic Development in the Third World* (London: Longman Publishers, 1989).

11. Alecia Dionne Hoffman, "The Influence of China's Foreign Aid Policies on the Political Economy of Nigeria, 1979–2010." (Ph.D. Diss., Clark Atlanta University, 2015), 27–28.

12. Akin L. Mabogunje, "Systems Approach to a Theory of Rural-Urban Migration." *Geographical Analysis* Vol. 2, no. 1 (Jan. 1970): 1–18, 3; Also see Oliver Bakewell, Hein de Haas, and Agnieszka Kubal, "Migration Systems, Pioneers, and the Role of Agency." *University of Oxford International Migration Institute Working Papers* No. 48 (Nov. 2011): 1–26, 4.

13. Alexander Wendt, "Anarchy is What States Make of It," in Robert Art and Robert Jervis, *International Politics: Enduring Concepts and Contemporary Issues* (New York: Pearson Longman Publishers, 2005), 61.

14. Douglass S. Massey et.al., 454.

15. Jocelyne Streiff-Fenart and Aurelia Segatti eds. *The Challenge of the Threshold: Border Closures and Migration Movements in Africa* (Plymouth, UK: Lexington Books, 2014), xiv.

16. "Global Migration Flows (IN)" *The International Organization for Migration.* Accessed 15 August 2016. Available from www.iom.int/countries/mauritania; "Immigration in Mauritania." *International Organization for Migration.* Accessed 15 August, 2016. http://www/iomdakar.org/profiles/print/21.

17. Ibid., 1; MPC Team, "MPC Migration Profile." *MPC Migration Policy Centre.* Accessed 15 August 2016. Available from www.migrationpolicycentre.eu/docs/migration-profiles/Mauritania.pdf.

18. "Immigration in Mauritania." *International Organization for Migration.* 1–2. Accessed 15 August, 2016. http://www/iomdakar.org/profiles/print/21.

19. U.S. State Department. *2015 Trafficking in Human Persons Report.* Accessed 15 August 2016. Available from: www.state.gov/documents/organizations/258880.pdf.

20. "Global Migration Flows (OUT)" *The International Organization for Migration.* Accessed 15 August 2016. Available from www.iom.int/countries/mauritania.

21. ACBC. "Support for Migration and Border Management in Mauritania." *The African Capacity Building Centre (ACBC): International Organization for Migration.* Accessed 15 August 2016. Available from: acbc.iom.int/where-we-work/ffeatured-iom-projects/37-support-for-migration-and-border-management-in-mauritania.

22. "IOM-Japan Project Implemented in Mauritania and Mali." *IOM Quarterly Newsletter: IOM Mauritania.* No. 1 (June 16, 2015). Accessed 15 August 2016. Available from: iom.int/news/iom-japan-project-implemented-mauritania-and-mali; IOM Mauritania. Accessed 15 August 2016. Available from: http://www.iom.int/sites/default/files/country/docs/mauritania/IOM-Mauritania-Newsletter-June-August-2015-EN.pdf

23. Akin Mabogunje, "Systems Approach to a theory of Rural-Urban Migration." 3.

24. "Global Migration Flows (IN)" *The International Organization for Migration.* Accessed 19 August 2016. Available from www.iom.int/countries/mali.

25. Ibid.

26. "Global Migration Flows (OUT)" *The International Organization for Migration.* Accessed 19 August 2016. Available from www. Iom.int/countries/mali.

27. Sally E. Findley. "Mali: Seeking Opportunity Abroad." *Migration Policy Institute* (1 September 2004). Accessed 19 August 2016. Available from: www.migrationpolicy.org/article/mali-seeking-opportunity-abroad.

28. "Free Movement of Persons, Residence and Establishment." (Protocol A/P 1/5/79). *ECOWAS,* Accessed 20 August 2016. Available from: http://documentation.ecowas.int/download/en/legal_documentation/protocols/PROTOCOL%20RELATING%20TO%20%20FREE%20MOVEMENT%20OF520PERSONS.pdf.

29. "EU Relations with Mali" *European Union External Action.* Accessed 20 August 2016. Available from: eeas.europa.eu/mali/index_en.htm.

30. U.S. State Department. *2015 Trafficking in Human Persons Report.* Accessed 15 August 2016. Available from: www.state.gov/documents/organizations/258880.pdf.

31. *World Bank.* "Migration and Remittance Data [XLS]." Accessed 15 August 2016. Available from: http://www.worldbank.org/en/topic/migrationremittancesdiasporaissues/brief/migration-remittances-data.xxxvi Ibid.

32. "Global Migration Flows (OUT)" *The International Organization for Migration.* Accessed 15 August 2016. Available from www.iom.int/countries/algeria.

33. "Global Migration Flows (IN)" *The International Organization for Migration.* Accessed 15 August 2016. Available from www.iom.int/countries/algeria.

34. U.S. State Department. *2015 Trafficking in Human Persons Report.* Accessed 15 August 2016. Available from: www.state.gov/documents/organizations/258878.pdf.

35. "International Organization for Migration. Niger Assists 30th Convoy of Repatriated Migrants from Algeria." *International Organization for Migration* (18 March, 2016). Accessed 20 August, 2016. www.iom.int/news/iom-niger-assists-30th-convoy-repatriated-migrants-algeria.

36. "Migration Facts Algeria" *Robert Schuman Center for Advanced Studies: Migration Policy Centre* (April 2013). Accessed 20 August 2016. Available from: migration policycentre.eu/docs/fact_sheet/Factsheet%20Algeria.pdf.

37. Ibid.

38. Ibid.

39. Ibid.; Thomas Huddleston, Jan Niesson, Eadaoin Ni Chaoimh and Emile White. *Migration Integration Policy Index III.* Brussels, Belgium: British Council and Migration Policy Group, 2011. Accessed 20 August 2016. Available from: http://www.mipex.eu/sites/default/files/downloads/migrant_integration_policy_index_mipexiii_2011.pdf.

40. Ibid., 82.

41. Ibid.

42. "MHUB Mixed Migration Trend Report for January 2016 Covering Mixed Migration Events in: Algeria, Egypt, Libya, Mali, Morocco, Niger, Sudan, Tunisia, Greece, and Italy." *Mixed Migration Hub*, (January 2016). Accessed 20 August 2016. Available from www.mixedmigrationhub.org/wp_context/uploads/2016/02/MHub-Trend-Bulletin-January-2016.pdf.xlviii *World Bank.* "Migration and Remittance Data [XLS]." Accessed 15 August 2016. Available from: http://www.worldbank.org/en/topic/migrationremittancesdiasporaissues/brief/migration-remittances-data.

43. Akin Mabogunje, 4.

Chapter 4

Nigerians and the Pursuit of the Golden Fleece

Olayinka Oyegbile

INTRODUCTION

Millions of Nigerians have responded to the Push-Pull factors of migration. During the colonial era, for instance, a select number of Nigerians traveled (mostly to Britain) to acquire and to advance their education. This trend did not abate in post-colonial Nigeria, as many traveled in search of the "Golden Fleece": they went in search of educational and economic opportunities that were not readily available to them at home.[1] Many who left the shores of Nigeria eventually returned to contribute their quota to the growth and development of their new nation.

Those who returned—qualified as lawyers, medical doctors, pharmacists, nurses, accountants, economists, etc.—readily found employment in the public and or private sector. While many ended up in the civil service, others, especially the lawyers and medical doctors, went into private practice—eventually becoming noted members of the elite cadre.[2] As was expected, the standard of living of these groups was higher than those who trained at home, and in most cases, at par with the living standard of the colonialists and the expatriate community.

But then, there was a gradual shift: as the social, economic and political conditions of the country worsened in the mid-90s, many Nigerians who traveled overseas refused to come back home. This was the era when many Nigerian universities and other institutions of higher learning became nothing but glorified "secondary schools"; and hitherto quality hospitals and medical centers became "mere consulting clinics." Today, Nigerians still migrate in large numbers. And while many can secure traveling visa through legitimate means, others risk their lives traveling through the tortuous Sahara Desert and other illegal routes.

In the process of illegal migration, many have lost their lives; and an untold number are lost in refugee camps in Europe and elsewhere. Almost two decades after the rejection of military authoritarianism—and the return to democratic rule—mitigating factors seem not to have taken hold. It is in light of these that this chapter examined contemporary factors that make migration attractive to Nigerians.

NIGERIANS AND THE OUTWARD MOVEMENT

At the dawn of independence in 1960, Nigeria had only two higher institutions of learning: Yaba Higher College, which later became Yaba College of Technology, was founded in Lagos in 1932. It was to teach mainly subjects that were vocational and meant to fill some colonial middle-level vacancies.[3] The school produced what many believed were *inferior manpower* that were unable to compete adequately and fill senior-level vacancies in the colonial administration. After sometime, nationalists were dissatisfied with the educational system and the kind of graduates produced because they felt it had not given them the sort of education that would satisfy the needs of the country. They began to agitate for better education that would cut the cord that had joined them to the garment of the colonial master. Thus, for anyone who desired education beyond what could be offered by the higher college, such a person had to go to London or make do with correspondence courses; this they felt was not good enough.

This led to agitations by the nationalists and the colonial master had no choice but to establish a real institution that would take care of the education of its subjects. This led to the establishment of the University College of Ibadan in 1948.[4] The establishment of the university fulfilled the desire of many who were in search of higher education that would place them on a better pedestal to compete with the colonial masters. Due to the limited space for admissions, many looked abroad for ways to satisfy their thirst for education and technical skills.

Many students were sent abroad by their rich parents; while some communities contributed money to send a few of their brilliant ones and thus became a sort of "communal investment."[5] This formed the theme of several novels written by African writers who examined the impact of getting foreign education on the elite. The lure for foreign education continued unabated and most Nigerians went to Europe, especially Britain. It was a time many scorned the American system of education; this was largely due to the belief then that the British education system, perhaps because it was the country's former colonial master, was better than any other.

However, by the seventies and eighties when the prospect of getting admitted to British schools became dimmer and tougher, many turned to the United States of America. In addition to the ease of admission, many perceived its liberal approach to education to be better suited to the African condition; moreover, its contents were deemed to be superior and appropriate to a globalizing world. Furthermore, tuition rate, fees and related expense were thought to be more reasonable. It is precisely for these reasons that Africans, especially Nigerians, have continued to flock to the United States, and increasingly, to Canada.

One of the first Nigerians to take advantage of this opportunity was the late Dr. Nnamdi Azikiwe, a journalist and nationalist who later became the first president of Nigeria at independence. He left his civil service job to travel as a stowaway in a ship that left Lagos for Liverpool on his way to the United States of America.[6] He had to stowaway because he did not have enough finance to pay for his trip and still have something left to pursue any meaningful educational quest in the new place to which he was going. His trip was perhaps one of the first kinds of encouragement for many Nigerians without government scholarship or communal support.

However, the first sets of Nigerians who moved abroad did this basically as a way of moving themselves up the ladder of life; they were in search of education for better life. Most of them traveled abroad and got the desired education and at times got married and returned home with their Caucasian wives.

THE NIGERIAN AND AFRICAN CONDITION

Going abroad in the sixties to early eighties, which was mainly driven by the search for education, suffered a setback in the nineties as the Nigerian currency, the Naira, began to be buffeted by military dictatorship, many citizens began to vote with their feet. Those who were fortunate to be admitted to foreign universities saw it as an opportunity not only to travel abroad but to stay in their host countries and look for greener pastures after their education. Many others left not because they gained admission but just to escape from the tough times at home. Nigeria became like the proverbial sinking ship in which the travelers began to jump out at the slightest opportunity to save them from the dreadful fate that awaits them if the ship capsized!

Majority of those who went abroad in the nineties have decided not to return home because of economic hardship and the fact that to secure jobs are becoming slimmer and more competitive while a few others feel that the *poor pay* at home does not adequately cater for their needs and pay for the investment on their education abroad.

The quantum of foreign exchange that the country also spends on payment for school fees abroad is enormous. According to Exam Ethics International,

Nigeria loses over N1.5 trillion ($3.3m) to foreign education annually, with neighboring Ghana alone getting about N160b. This is only for tuition less board, feeding and several other incidentals.[7]

Tertiary education in Nigeria and Africa in general has gained so much attention and many want to gain it because having education is viewed as having a foothold at the door of progress. Right from the days of the agitation for independence, the nationalists have discovered that it is the sure way to ensure that they have a say in the affairs of their various countries. From Dr. Nnamdi Azikiwe, Chief Obafemi Awolowo and to almost all the nationalists, education was emphasized and seen as the primary avenue through which one can climb the economic, social and political ladder. In East Africa, the late Jomo Kenyatta of Kenya and the Kwame Nkrumah of Ghana and many others also embraced Western education.

THE REALITY AND THE FANTASY OF MIGRATION

Right from time immemorial migration has been the prerogative of man. In fact, it was through migration that man from biblical times has been able to conquer his environment and make the world in his vision. The line separating migration and exile is usually very thin because sometimes migration might lead to exile or vice versa. According to Kole Odutola, a Nigerian professor in an American University, migration is natural to man and it is in his nature to move. In his word:

> Leaving one's country to another is just like leaving one's town to the city where there are better opportunities. If you read the story of immigration the world over you will notice that people move around for economic and environmental reasons…The desire to move away from home for most Nigerians was a political decision. In my case I left home to study and after my PhD found a job I could not resist. There are people who left during the Military era and needed space to organize or just hide from those after them. I did not run away from home. I just needed a change and a place I could be myself without too much distractions. I needed a place where my name means nothing to anyone or a place I could use my cultural beliefs as a weapon or a shield depending on the situation.[8]

On the other hand, Seun Akioye, a journalist who once moved to Britain to live and had to return home after a few years, said, "Nigerians want to leave the country to seek for a favorable environment abroad. Many are looking for better opportunities and or a better environment where they can best practice their art or further their career. Many are looking for the so-called greener pasture, security, health and secured future."[9] To him, the reason why many travels abroad is basically tied to economic reasons, the search for better alternatives to what obtains at home. Also, Pius Adesanmi, a Nigerian professor of African studies in Canada says the difference between migration and exile is a question of optics:

> Migration has a voluntary tack to it whereas exile connotes compulsion, a lack of any choice in the matter. Exile connotes being forced to leave as a consequence of persecution or other reasons. However, we now live in a world of global mobility and the distinction is blurry. In almost two decades, I have lived in France, the United States and Canada. There are times when I have felt like an exile and times when I have considered myself a skilled migrant.[10]

It is true that many Nigerians do not see moving away from their fatherland as anything strange because it has become their way of life. Those who don't travel abroad do so internally, moving from wherever their ancestral home is to other parts of the country: from the southern or eastern part to the northern or western part of the country—or from rural to urban centers.

The reason why many Nigerians move abroad is both economic and political. In the seventies through eighties and the late nineties when the military, a set of people Basil Davidson calls "pirates in power,"[11] held power in the country, most of the country's higher institutions became deserted as the government of the day sacked many university dons for "teaching what they were not paid to teach," meaning they were too radical and were teaching students to be "subversive." This was the beginning of the decline of university education in the country as many lecturers who could not stand the pressure or bear the brunt of being dictated to by the *pirates in power* left the university community and fled abroad.

The economy at this juncture had also taken a turn for the worse: it was on a tailspin with high inflation and rising cost of living. It was also a time when the umbrella body of the university teachers—the Academic Staff Union of Universities (ASUU)—adopted the moniker of "My take home pay cannot take me home."[12] This was to show that what they were being paid was not enough to take care of their needs, especially when the economy was in a free-fall. Many decided to go abroad in search of better deals. Hitherto, it was mainly students, especially those from rich homes or those on scholarships who traveled abroad to study and return home after their studies.

But with the situation the universities found themselves the teachers also began to look beyond the borders. They moved to the Americas, Caribbean and other far-fetched lands to engage in intellectual pursuits. The fact that universities at home have lost their attraction, and that many Nigerians seek to move abroad because of the economic decline at home, was confirmed by Adesanmi, who observed:

> If you look at what has been happening on the Mediterranean Sea in the last couple of years, you will have to conclude that economics plays a major role in why people leave...There is of course also the lure of education. You can see how badly Africa fares in various annual University rankings. The Universities of the First World are a huge attraction. In our own specific case in Nigeria, the leadership and the elite have simply abandoned our ruined educational institutions so their children are all over Europe and America. Even Ghana is a popular destination for education immigration by Nigerians.[13]

Ikheola Ikhide, another Nigerian who has been living in the United States for decades, agrees with Adesanmi, and states:

> Young people are giving up on the country as a source of progress and they see in other nations opportunities that they would like to take advantage of. They want good schools, jobs, and a good lifestyle, which to some is largely unavailable at home because of the atmosphere and poor administration of education institutions...virtually all institutions that should nurture young ones are broken. If you are young and still have energy, there is little motivation to stay behind.[14]

The observation and assertion of Ikhide and Adesanmi was further corroborated in a 2012 research by a nongovernmental organization, Exam Ethics International, which in a research it conducted concluded that the Nigerian craze for higher education abroad has subjected the country to loosing over N1.5 trillion annually to foreign education. Out of this Ghana, the country's West African neighbor gets N160b as tuition fees from the over 71,000 Nigerians registered in their various institutions.[15] Going abroad in search of better life is a common practice in Nigeria. Many subject themselves to so many terrible privations and denials to be able to save enough money to travel across the Sahara to the Eldorado they think lies abroad. Many travel through dangerous routes across the Sahara Desert where some die or are robbed by bandits.

In 2008 a Ghanaian, Freddy Kasseri, 23, told IRIN, a website that tracks human emergencies around the world that he was full of regrets for living his home country in search of better life in Europe. He was on his way to Libya when the vehicle he was traveling in was stopped in Agadez, Republic of Mali. According to him, "They made us undress and took everything of value." He added that the bandits who stopped the truck he was traveling in took five Ghanaian and Nigerian women along with them into the desert. Obviously to sexually abuse them, that was not all, he was also robbed of his dollars and clothing, I have lost everything enroute and am not sure how I will eat tonight."[16]

In the years since, things have not changed; they have instead gotten worse and desperate for immigrants from Nigeria, Mali, Ghana, and elsewhere in and from the continent. This long and tortuous with dangerous twists and bends along and when migrants get there they are tired, fagged and broke. To survive in their new environment and get money to move on they engage in any business to survive and make money. The women among them sometimes turn to prostitution and other demeaning things to survive. They meet smugglers who have a wide and impregnable network which works with some law enforcement agents to make them cross the borders or assist them to stowaway in ships that are headed toward Europe.

There have been reported cases of deaths, robbery and violence on migrants as they travel along the desert routes, even those who go by sea also do not often escape this too. Capsizing of boats when they are caught in the mighty waves of bigger ships are commonplace, leading, often, to death of hundreds on the high seas. In some cases, a few of the stranded migrants decide to stay put in North Africa rather than return home because they often believe it is shameful to return after announcing their departure from home with plump! Money is at the heart of the success of trips made by migrants, as those without enough money usually found themselves stranded.

According to de Haas, Migration from Africa to Europe is not a new phenomenon because crossing the Mediterranean by North Africans has been on since the 1990s, when Italy and Spain introduced visa requirements. Perhaps what is new is the fact that sub-Saharan Africans have since the 2000s overtaken North Africans as the largest category of irregular boat migrants. The movement of migrants to Europe is sometimes viewed in two different ways by those in authority—the migrants are sources of cheap labor when they get to their destinations while some after getting employed send money through remittances home to boost foreign exchange in their home countries.[17]

LIVING ABROAD

Before the advent of the internet and social media (which has mostly democratized the news and information space), some immigrants were wont to pose for pictures in front of exotics cars and homes they did not own, and then send such pictures home claiming it belonged to them. These helped to portray America, Britain and the rest of the industrialized society as some sort of El Dorado, as paradise: a place where fast cars, beautiful people, expensive taste and larger-than-life characters reign supreme. While such deceptions are no longer fashionable, many continue to be lured by fantasy and by what they see in the magazines and Hollywood movies.

The irony is that despite the realities that are sometimes portrayed in more realistic movies, books and magazines, many do not believe that things can be rough and tough in the United States and elsewhere in the Western society. And even if they did, the assumption is that things can never be as bad as they are in Nigeria or elsewhere in the continent. In the minds of many, it is better to be poor in Chicago, Texas or Boston than to be poor in Ibadan, Jos or Warri. Consequently, millions are willing to take the risk and bear whatever the cost might be in their trek through death-traps in North Africa until they arrive in Europe.

However, some of those who had lived abroad for years have bitter tales to tell. A recent deportee, Sadiq Ibrahim, has a bitter story to tell about his five-year sojourn in Los Angeles, United States of America. He said recently in an interview with *The Punch*, a newspaper published in Nigeria:

> I was at a friend's apartment in New York one afternoon when suddenly I heard a knock on the door. Two police officers had come to pick and hand me over to the immigration because, according to them, I was not permitted under the law to visit any other state yet aside from California where I lived. I had left Los Angeles two days earlier after some guys who racially abused and molested me threatened to kill me. Before I knew what was happening, I was already in a detention Centre. I was bundled into the next available flight to Nigeria after my appeal failed.[18]

CONCLUSION

In the final analysis, many Nigerians would still prefer to go abroad no matter the dangers and problems that lie ahead. This is because many still believe that the chances of making it abroad are better and faster than at home because, as Akioye puts it, "In Nigeria, we live on hope that suddenly we may hit it big and become wealthy overnight, it almost doesn't happen that way. But abroad, there is the assurance that even if you do not hit it big time, you will have a decent life for yourself and family. There is constant electricity, the roads are good."[19]

There are many reasons why migration—be it self-migration or forced migration—is not likely to abate anytime soon. There is the African landscape that is characterized by poor basic human needs, inequality and searing conditions that fuel the appetite for the Golden Fleece. Second, the geographical and political conditions are such that millions of Africans cannot avoid the constant search for safety and security. And of course, there are the globalizing factors that lure millions of people across the world to venture into societies where their skills and training are wanted and welcome and where there is a greater chance at political and economic successes, peace and the promises of human rights.

Because of poor record keeping, no one knows exactly how many Nigerians leave the country on a yearly basis to fulfill their dreams and aspirations. What we know is that they have been on the move since the colonial era. And since 1999, the collapsing economic conditions have severely affected the state of public infrastructure, social services, employment, and education.

These have in turned provided the rationale for Nigerians—especially the youths—to keep crossing national borders.

NOTES

1. Euphemistically, and especially within the Nigerian context, Golden Fleece refers to opportunities that are in abundance and readily available overseas, but cannot be attained within the country. Therefore, Nigerians go abroad to attain those things—that is, education and technical skills—that are hard to come by domestically.

2. Frederick Rotimi Williams (1920–2005); Adeyemo Alakija (1884–1952); Bode Thomas (1918–1953); Jaja Wachuku (1918–1996); Obafemi Awolowo (1909–1987); James Ajibola Idowu Ige (1930–2001); and Samuel Akintola (1910–1966) were some of those who went abroad and qualified as lawyers. As with many, before and after, they went on to become member of the ruling class.

3. R. Olufemi Ekundare. *An Economic History of Nigeria, 1860–1960.* New York: Africana Pub., 1973.

4. Kiluba L. Nkulu. *Serving the Common Good: A Postcolonial African Perspective on Higher Education*. New York: P. Lang, 2005.

5. Chinua Achebe. *No Longer at Ease*. London: Heinemann, 1960.

6. Nnamdi Azikiwe. *My Odyssey: An Autobiography*. London: C. Hurst, 1970.

7. Nigeria: The Madness of Foreign Education. Daily Trust, last modified February 14, 2016. http://allafrica.com/ stories/201602151753.html.

8. Odutola, Kole, interview by Olayinka Oyegbile (2016).

9. Ibid.

10. Adesanmi, Pius, interview by Olayinka Oyegbile (2016).

11. Basil Davidson. *The Black Man's Burden: Africa and the Curse of the Nation-state*. New York: Times Books, 1992.

12. Adebayo Olukoshi. "The Impact of IMF-World Bank Program in Nigeria." In *The IMF, the World Bank and the African Debt: The Economic Impact*, edited by Bade Onimode. London: Zed Books, 1989.

13. Adesanmi, 2016.

14. Ikhide Ikheola, interview by Olayinka Oyegbile (2016).

15. Nigeria: The Madness of Foreign Education. Daily Trust, last modified February 14, 2016. http://allafrica.com/ stories/201602151753.html.

16. "Freddy Kasseri, "Migrants Are Dying out Here." October 09, 2008. Accessed October 11, 2016. http://www.irinnews.org/report/80836/niger-freddy-kasseri-"migrants-are-dying-out-here".

17. Hein de Haas. *Irregular Migration from West Africa to the Maghreb and the European Union: An Overview of Recent Trends*. Publication. Geneva: International Organization for Migration, 2011.

18. "Humiliated Abroad, Rejected at Home: Pathetic, Painful World of Nigeria's Deportees—Punch Newspapers." *Punch Newspapers*. April 30, 2016. Accessed August 16, 2016. http://punchng.com/humiliated-abroad-rejected-home-pathetic-painful-world-nigerias-deportees/.

19. Segun Akioye, interview by Olayinka Oyegbile (2016).

Chapter 5

Impact of Culture on Exiles

Bruce Ormond Grant

INTRODUCTION

A critical reading of Edward Said's classic and globally reticulating essay "Reflections on Exile" (originally published in 1984) impels the reader to ruminate with logic about the centralities of culture in and on the lives of exiles. Said discussed many socio-emotional and cultural-political nuances around how the socio-emotional life of an exile is managed by the individual and group, but his central thesis was that the status of exile denoted a permanent stain of local, national and global emotional—and cultural dislocation. As such, for Said, the inhuman distancing of the modern world from the being of a human impels an incessant social direction of non-humanizing global exitism. The persistence of sadness, a need for belonging and a cry for home are core inhabitants within the human psyche of the exiled.

Issues around the limitations of the global human community are central to the theses of this chapter. Exiled persons and communities stand in concert, in opposition, and in a series of sophisticated matrixed relationships to other cultures. Culture, as a historical concept or thematically operationalized construct, has different meanings in time and space, and over epochs. As such, the title of this chapter is itself a broad and challenged pathos of social-scientific inquiry. The broad gravity of the title, however, allows for the introduction of intellectual thought on exile scholarship that is worthy of serious inquiry.

Intellectual curiosities have chosen to, throughout intellectual history; define culture in terms of structure, function, power, group membership and exclusion. From a Eurocentric and Non-Eurocentric series of definitional activities, this definitional trajectory represents an always evolving series of interpretational cosmological and ontological realities. Consequently, the global orientations around culture and the relationships among nodes of the exiled existence drive the ontological conversations among psychic and intrapsychic subsystems of the social and culturally defined human realities.

One major thesis of this chapter asserts that the terms "exile" and "culture," while they define, for some, operationalized domains of academic, political, other scientific and economic inquiry, these terms are not in any way definitional or operationally absolutist. This chapter will take a historic and thematic look at culture through the lens of Eurocentric and Non-Eurocentric lenses; this is important in order to provide non-linear interpretational gauges for readers. This chapter argues that the notion of culture is fluid, and can be matrixed through an unlimited series of interpretational lenses, thus making its definition illusive. Further, while scholars have provided specific environmental contexts to study subthemes of the term "exile," cultural interpretations of what is psychically and human-culturally relevant to individuals, groups and geospaces do and will vary over time, space and valence.

Further, while the notion of the exile is tied to many socio-emotional and culturally significant humanistic variables, the movement of the exile should also be analyzed within the economic contexts of human and national economic theories: The notion of the differential power dynamics among nation-states and global economic contexts, as well as the intrinsic movement of the rational toward human actualization, plays a huge role in the interpretational and experiential reality of the exile.

The exile furthest from the proximity power is subjugated at the social, cultural and most importantly, economical level—and, while the educated and further acclimated exiles are closer to the center of power (and may even frame it), they too are not exempt from the troubles that come with holistic human expressivity in a host state—given religion, cultural practices, political orientations and other human ends of social cooperation and human rights.

THE CONFLICT OF CULTURE

Culture, whether termed as a concept, theme, definition, aesthetic or anomaly, is overdetermined by context. Issues of cultural unity, diversity, and divisiveness are of critical importance as the concepts of culture are placed as definitional—within certain contexts and time. In the United States and some African nations, hate actions are quite common. Worldwide discussions about genocide, famine, governmental repression and terrorism, mostly rooted in culture and identity, consume people's everyday lives. Concurrently, culture exists at the center of many scholarly disputes, and at the forefront of many theoretical advances. The influence of culture is felt across all disciplines of intellectual inquiry, from anthropology to physics.

Interestingly, when any scholar discusses the concept of "culture" as a variable to explain some behavior, as a topic of academic discussion, or as a concept to explain some behavior, as a topic of academic discussion, or as a concept to help solve everyday problems, the introducing scholar(s) reflect diverse political, social and economic voices as they attempt to engage the populace in a discussion.

It would be easy enough to say that each scholar enunciates via her or his trained disciplinary rationality, but within and among disciplines, definitions proliferate. Analyses of the thematic definitional threads across the social sciences revealed that although it is still important to study the similar symbols and expectations that give rise to meaningful activity among a group, the actual term "culture" has so many definitions and facets that any overlap in this myriad of definitions might actually be absent. However, this analytic insight is not new. As early as 1945, Kluckhohn and Kelly described a discussion from the point of view of a tête-à-tête among a lawyer, a historian, an economist, a philosopher, a psychologist, a business professional, and three anthropologists, each defining culture in different ways. Consequently, a consensus among always-competing social science professionals has urged, and continues to urge, that the varied definitions of culture be re-evaluated considering the multifaceted nature of the concept's utilization and the inadequacy of historical approaches.

This debate surrounding the utilization of the term "culture" suggests that the term is a social-scientific enigma, an empty vessel waiting for people—both academicians and everyday communicators—to fill it with meaning. But, as a sign in the traditional semiotic sense, the connection between the signifier (the word "culture") and the signified (what it represents) shifts, making culture a moving target. No one questions that there are multitudinous definitions of culture. In fact, in a classic work on the subject, Kroeber and Kluckhohn collected some 150 definitions of the term and offered a critical summary, which has become the foundation upon which many writers from different disciplines have built their common understanding of culture.[1]

At the same time, much has transpired in the academic world in the past 65 years since that publication. Following a semiotic metaphor in this section, I will provide a diachronic (for historical) analysis, observing how culture as a sign has changed through times in the writings of various disciplines. Tracing the various etymologies of culture, we can develop a "tree of meaning" shown in Fig. 5.1. In this figure, readers can see the original roots of "culture" joined to the histories of "cult" and "cultivate." The word comes to Middle English ("a cultivated piece of land") through French "culture" and that from the Latin verb culturare ("to cultivate"). There is a kinship among the words, Cultus, for example (from which we get "cult") refers to religious worship, which might be seen as a way of bringing up ("cultivating") someone in a religious group. All versions of the word ultimately come from early Latin, colere, which means to till or cultivate the ground. Several authors outline the etymologic roots of the word, for example Kroeber and Kluckhohn.[2]

Williams traced the contemporary word to the contemporary Kultur, which refers to agricultural development. This yields, Williams suggested, three broad categories of usage in the history of the world. The first refers to the "cultivation" of individuals and groups of people in terms of the "general process of intellectual, spiritual, and aesthetic development," a usage beginning in the eighteenth century.[3] This last meaning, Williams contended, is the most widely used, and relates to literature, art, music, sculpture, theater, and other art forms.

Kroeber and Kluckhohn saw the term as first (in the 1700s) signifying a sort of general history. A second strain of meaning, running from Kant to Hegel (1700s–1800s) aligns the meaning with "enlightenment culture and improvement culture,"[4] a notion that gave way to the word "spirit" (Geist) as it moved away from the word "culture." The third and, for Kroeber and Kluckhohn, current strain, developing after 1850, treats culture as "the characteristic mode of human existence."[5] The authors argued that the Germanic usage of the term later became the conceptualization that anthropologists adopted. In England, one of the earliest definitions of culture noted was a "pursuit of total perfection by means of getting to know…the best which has been thought and said in the world."[6]

KROEBER AND KLUCKHOHN—THE CLASSICS

Kluckhohn's early writing on culture foreshadows William's definition noted earlier. Kluckhohn concluded that culture refers to the "total way of life of a people,"[7] "a way of thinking and believing,"[8] and a "storehouse of pooled learning."[9] Kluckhohn stated that a distinction needed to be made between people who shared a social space and mutual interaction, but not a way of life. This group of people, Kluckhohn called "society," which he distinguished from those sharing a way of life, which he labeled "culture." This hints at a deeper tension between the nexus of the terms "culture," "society," and civilization that has ripped into, and through, the social sciences.

Most of the authors in our list of definitions treat culture as some set of elements shared by people who have a social structure, with the latter referred to as "society." Winthrop echoed this distinction. "Culture," he noted "focuses attention on the products of social life (what individuals think and do), whereas social structure "stresses social life as such: individuals in their relations to others.[10] He delineated three definitions of civilization historically used in social science, each of which brought a different relationship to culture: (a) civilization as the more scientific and technical aspect of culture, (b) civilizations as a subclass of world cultures...characterized by complex systems of social inequality and state-level politics, and (c) the least useful relationship, culture as equal to society.[11]

Tylor's definition serves as an example of this last relationship to the terms. In summary, despite the relationship of culture to society or civilization, each culture serves to provide an orientation toward the world and its problems, such as suffering and death.[12] In addition, "every culture is designed to perpetuate the group and its solidarity, to meet the demands for an orderly way of life and for satisfaction of biological needs.[13] Kroeber and Kluckhohn devote most of their 1952 book to a critical review of definitions. They divide definitions into six groups, as follows: (1) Enumeratively descriptive—a list of the content of culture (2) Historical—emphasis on social heritage, tradition (3) Normative—focus on ideals or ideals plus behavior (4) Psychological—learning, habit, adjustment, problem-solving device (5) Structural—Focus on the pattern or organization of culture (6) Genetic—symbols, ideas, artifacts. After each set of definitions, they provide commentary, looking for the nuances of similarity and difference between the items under each category. The elements of definition focus on different aspects of culture: there is a set of elements, such as ideas, behavior, and so on, inherited or passed on among a group of people.[14]

These elements exist within a connected pattern, meeting purposes or solving problems for the group of people and making up part of the cultural learning of the behavior prescriptions and values that guide people in knowing how to behave in different cultural situations. Genetic definitions focus on the "genesis" or origins or culture. Such definitions address the questions: "How has culture come to be? What are the factors that have made culture possible or caused it to come into existence? Other properties of culture are often mentioned, but the stress is upon the genetic side."[15]

Finally, and after much deliberation, Kroeber and Kluckhohn synthesized the aspects or types of definitions into a single, complete, and useful definition:

> Culture consists of patterns, explicit and implicit, of and for behavior acquired and transmitted by symbols, constituting the distinctive achievements of human groups, including their embodiments in artifacts; the essential core of culture consists of traditional (i.e., historically derived and selected) ideas and especially their attached values; culture systems may, on one hand, be considered as products of action, on the other as conditioning elements of further action.[16]

These definitions are important because they shed some definitional orthodoxy on the state of culture within ones being. Limited as most of these operationalization's are, they attempt to control the defection of thought into an infinite, never ceasing latticed matrix of definitions. As culture impacts the quality of life circle of every inhabitant of the earth, the state of the exile must be expounded upon. But first, we must define who or what is an exile.

THE STATE OF EXILES

In the famous essay entitled "Reflections on Exiles," Said stated that "exile… is fundamentally a discontinuous state of being. Exiles are cut off from their roots, their land, and their past. They generally do not have armies or states, although they are often in search of them. Exiles feel, therefore, an urgent need to reconstitute themselves as part of a triumphant ideology or restored people. The crucial thing is that a state of exile free from this triumphant ideology—designed to reassemble an exile's broken history into a new hole—is virtually unbearable and virtually impossible in today's world."[17] He goes on, "Exile originated in the age-old practice of banishment. Once banished, the exile lives an anomalous and miserable life, with the stigma of being an outsider."[18]

As such, according to Said, an exile is one (or a group) that was banished from their homeland, with the homeland being the sole authentic cosmological space of intrinsic orientation where one's ontology is rooted, supplanted and supported. The state of the exile in the modern state of war, violence, permanent displacement across all nations of the world, especially for Africans, is one of establishing new worlds within and outside of the African continent. If, however, we are to assert primacy to Said's theological positionality around the socio-emotional content of exiles, many questions come to mind. For example, does one who chooses to be banished ever long for their romantic homeland, or do they forge new identities in new cultures in new homelands?

Does culture, a concept so adaptive and so fluid, intellectually and spatially compensate, at least in intellectual writings, adapt itself to simultaneously conflict with and accommodate all humans? And do African exiles face particular culture challenges as exiles, given their unique cosmological, ideological and ontological worldviews?

The philosophical interplay among terms like estrangement, longing for home, forced migration and mass displacement have triggered cannons of literature across disciplines, as the twenty-first century has seen unprecedented population displacement. But, the state of the African exile has been one that has been explored by numerous scholars across multiple disciplines across the globe. Without naming scholars, the themes of loneliness, adaptiveness, isolation, longing for home and displacement are themes that are congruent with scholars such as Said. This static displacement of the exile is what will be challenged in the next section of this chapter.

THE RESILIENCE OF THE EXILE

Surely, it has been argued by many scholars that the theme of exilism is one of estrangement, alienation, and cultural misalignment. But, in contrast to Said, this author takes a different approach: the argument of this author is that the intrinsic culture of the exile is itself self-reinforcing, providing for many a healthy mental health and cultural framework that allows for cultural adaptation and, even cultural domination and appropriation in host nations. For many, the notion of being an exile is not one confined to socio-emotional domains of alienation and estrangement—The notion, indeed, means many things to many people, and the experiences of those individuals termed exiles vary vastly.

Exiles thread many lines in multiple societies—as do children of exiles born in host nations or societies. For example, continental Africans that have been exiled within and outside of the continent may experience no feelings of longing and familiarity with their born nation or society, as that born nation or society may have been culpable in perpetrating violence and human instability in generations of lives lived within that nation or society. In essence, those who may have willingly or unwillingly been forced to migrate may not have any feelings of continuous dislocation and longing for their homeland. Further, they do not apologize psychically or sociologically for being in what they may consider a furthered human state. They willingly adapt to their host nation or society, and work diligently to incorporate their values and morals into the host environment within which they are charged to persist with. For some, the temporary homelessness is a necessary human condition as they forward to self-sufficiency and independence—a transitory construction of reality that aids their journey toward the future. As such, the impact of culture is quite important, in that culture of host and non-host must be in moral congruence about the holistic human movement toward human actualization.

THE ECONOMIC ECOLOGY OF AFRICAN EXILES

While most intellectual excursions about the African exile notate the aforementioned historic longing for "home," experiences of discrimination and hostility in foreign lands, brain drains and human resource depletion of their homelands, the dominant prevailing theme in the academic literature of exiles (forced migration, voluntary migration, and banishment) is the consistent desire for self-actualization. The quest for human betterment is an individual, a group and a globalist human phenomenon that has marked the upward movement of mankind since the inception of civilizations.

However, a contemporary exile humanistic conversation is one that espouses and endorses the principles of distributive justice, fairness, accountability, intrinsic humanity, participation and family-hood. It also cuts across economic theories that have dominated human history, as some within the historical and contemporary exile lexicon have argued that exilism, and particularly, the notion of brain drain that has been attributed to the best and most resilient leaving or being banished from African and non-continental nations, or willingly emigrating, to other neighborhoods, nations or religions, for example, has harmed the prior non-custodial state, broadly defined.

The literature on exile is increasingly looking to economics and utilizing its multivariate explanatory patterns of human ecological engagement in order to revise and extend its assertions about how and why people willingly and unwillingly are exiled. Scholarship by African scholars like Falola and others trace the historic patterns of the exilic movements of African disbursements from the 1500s, where Africans were deposited across the globe in efforts to economically and culturally impact the developing economies. Whether exile status was impelled or not, the overall theme from the research denotes a desire of the exiled to maximize the ideals of self-actualization. Correspondingly, however, the impact and relevance of economic theory that dominated and dominates the global purview concerns power, domination, subjugation, and accommodation.[19] In a nutshell, what we are talking about is global economic culture and its multivariate relationships to African exiles. The assertion here is that the political and cultural economies of the global economic culture subjugate and dictate the cultural expression of African exiles, especially in the West.

Embedded in the literature on exiles are themes of banishment, estrangement, a series of describable but disrupted relationships between one's physical home space and oneself. It is, for many scholars, a series of physical and geographical disruptions which are, in some instances, designed to prevent the banished and dislocated from enacting or effecting change in one's homeland. Those banished could be classed as the important, the elite, or the most vulnerable of any population. Buried within these discussions are a multitude of exile distinctions. For example, an individual or group of individuals can be exiles within their homelands, cut off from proximal and distal resources that are constitutive elements of holistic self-actualization; that is, a nation may deem an individual or group as a threat to the state, and take steps to deprive individuals and groups from civic participation, targeting them for retribution or in extreme manners, death. This exclusion from civic discourse and participation is reinforced by legal and illegal apparatuses, though individuals and groups may not be prime targets of the apparatuses themselves.

These noted designations and demarcations (chosen exilism, transculturalism, brain drain, etc). All occur within the econosphere culture of prevailing and dominant global economic cultures. In looking at the themes within African exile literature across disciplines over the past 40 years, whether one looks at the multitude of representations of the varied and complex African representations across the globe and within the intellectual rubric, one prevailing theme is of the African as being exiled to find a better life. Now, the term 'better' is indeed a complex and overdetermined construct, and it is operationalized within this discussion to connote increased cultural, political, social, environmental, militaristic and economic security. It is with the increased desire for economic security that this author rests the precipice of a central thesis of this chapter, as it is stated that the most impact of culture on exiles, irrespective of the stated geospace where one may be exiled to, is within the global economic culture of the time.

Okeke remarked that "Worsening economic conditions in many African countries have uprooted many of its people from their home countries, voluntarily and involuntarily, in search of their 'golden fleece' abroad. This has led to brain drain, brain gain and brain circulation."[20] Following this line of thinking, I trace the culture of contemporary economic theory to demonstrate the validity of this statement, in that the culture of the global economy is directly contributory to the migratory patterns of exiled self-actualization seekers, and as such, it is, the argument goes, this desire to seek self-actualization as an exile in a dominant economic culture that moderates the interpretations and expressions of the exile. Essentially, the exile is subjugated to the economy of the economic culture, which seeks to, among other things, exploit or leverage any positive additive capital of the exile. This link to capitalism is overt and additive to the host nation, when leveraged correctly.

The gap between the rich and the poor on this planet is larger than ever before and still growing—at least by most methods of measuring. Even after massive economic transfers during three 'development decades' that began in the 1970s, and trillions of dollars of development assistance, the situation remains dismal and getting worse in many places. About one half of the world's population lives on less than $3 a day, and in a number of countries, real wages peaked as long ago as the 1970s. It has been estimated that in 1750, the gap between the richest and poorest nations was at a ratio of 2:1; since then it has only increased.

Consequently, the human cost of poverty is enormous; the number of people who die from infant and child mortalities, preventable diseases, and a general low life expectancy is quite extreme. Civil wars and conflicts over scarce resources cause pain and suffering that in wealthy nations, are somewhat avoidable. To this list may be added the likely impact of environmental degradation on the poor. In poor societies, such vicious circles are easily created, where the only way to meet demands from an increasing population is to intensify the exploitation of nature.

Since the fall of the Berlin Wall in 1989, our economic order has—in a more fundamental way than before—been based on an economic theory which supposedly 'proves' the opposite of what in fact can be observed. World free trade is supposed to level out any differences in wages among rich and poor countries. If humankind does not interfere with the 'natural forces' of the market, if we apply the principle of laissez-faire, progress and economic harmony will reign.

As early as 1926 John Maynard Keynes (1883–1946), the English economist who diagnosed the depression of the 1930s, wrote a book entitled *The End of Laissez-Faire*. However, by 1989 the collapse of the Berlin Wall triggered an almost messianic euphoria about a world economy that would finally conform to the expectations of economic theory. The World Trade Organization's (WTO's) first secretary general, Renato Ruggiero, declared that we should unleash 'the borderless economy's potential to equalize relations between countries and regions.' This belief is at the core of the ideology of the International Monetary Fund and the World Bank, and from the early 1990s, for all practical purposes, these Washington institutions took over the management of the economic and political systems of most poor countries in Africa and beyond. For those countries, the result has been a colossal disaster for the people.

An abyss now separates the third-world reality from the vision of the WTO and other Washington institutions. Where the prophets of the new world order predicted harmony, we see famine, war, and progressive environmental collapse. The alternative and authentic reality evidenced is a bottom-up reality theory, based on a reality that is lived by the most vulnerable of people on the African continent and beyond.

The most vulnerable need not be the most educated or most outspoken only, as they may be any person or group in need of suitable human and safety options for increased or optimal subsistence. This reality-based analysis is in opposition to the prevailing Washington-based orthodoxy, as this interpretation extols the imperatives of removing the obstacles to human prosperity, as development must and should be it is—The conscious, deliberate and intentional motives of human beings developing policy and initiatives to advance humankind.

As evidenced in the global arena, an uncountable amount of African exiles lost their lives, households, wives, husbands, and children. Those who survive suffer from exploitation and hostility in their new homes, in their new countries, so that their relatives, in some instances, can be saved from human destruction. Further, another feature of the Washington consensus is that harmony is the natural state of any given society—in fact, it may be the opposite.

As such, the historical economic analyses denote that capitalism, or the need to expand production via the increase in productive labor pools drive the impetus behind chattel slavery in the United States and beyond, and as such, the economic culture impelled, for some, the movement of humans from continental Africa to the Americas, South America, the Caribbean, Asia, and to other parts of continental Africa in search of a better life. The desire for optimal self-actualization sustained the historical movements of Africans that were exiled within the African continent, and beyond. As such, it was the macro-conditions of the global economic climate that dictated where the exiles chose to migrate to; they did not choose environments where they did not stand a realistic chance for optimal self-sufficiency and independence.

It was this rational choice of the African exiled actors that I account for here. In the aims of human betterment and self-sufficiency, humans have always 'moved' with the intent of doing better; implicit in this analytic point is the notion that human betterment is an intrinsic component of humanness—at least for the rational human, whose motivation, as some instrumentalists may argue, is manifested by sole self-interest.

Since the beginning of time, human beings on earth have lived simple lives, in actual poverty, in an often-fragile balance between population size and physical resources available to them by ways of food, for example. Migrations and exilism have been created, for some, by the domain of what is called 'diminishing returns.' This is, by notes, an increasing population density that is challenged by an unchanged availability of natural resources and unchanged technology.

Consequently, in such a world, wealth and poverty become a zero-sum game; wealth was basically acquired by already existing riches changing owners. In essence, one man's loss is another man's benefit. As such, for the exile, the city became the focus of acquiring wealth and prosperity. As such, it was very clear to African people early on that most wealth was to be found in the cities, and particularly in certain cities. These cities, however, were the home of free citizens; in the countryside, people were generally poor and indentured, belonging to the land and landowners. Arising from these observations were investigations into an understanding of the factors that made cities so much wealthier than the countryside. Gradually, the wealth of the cities was perceived to be a result of collaboration: people of many different trades and professions sharing a community.

As manufacturing impacted African nations and beyond, the notion of "diminishing returns" gave way to "increasing returns." What his meant was that increased production yielded increased returns, which meant lower production costs. When you apply this economic idea to the patterns of economic development over the past 200 years or so, you come up with the same human-centered premise that simply utilizes humans: The additive effects of exiles, for example, with their increased intrinsic tools for production are themselves an increased return. The educated exile, for example, or a plethora of them, could increase production of, for example, Object A—all the while driving down production costs due to wage competition.

The summative effect of highly skilled or even slightly skilled exiles in a capitalist nation or society that has utility for their skill sets is a net economic and production gain for the host nation or society. This is not 'brain drain', as what is being described here is an example to the importance of the power positionality of the exiled for the host nation or society, as the intent of the host is to leverage and exploit the positive additive assets of the exiled. If, for example, the exiled individual or groups are at the center of the power periphery; if they are highly educated, speak Wall Street English, have a high income, etc., these individuals are more likely to occupy and control the center of the power periphery in their host nation or society. The corresponding exploitation of these persons by the economic culture of the global arena is less impactful and likely as compared to the exile that is not educated, older, ill, and overall less able to protect themselves and their families from the vicissitudes of life.

CONCLUSION

Exiles will always have the multiple streams of identities to shift among: mother, father, son, daughter, religious, doctor, lawyer—the list of identifiers may be infinite. As such, the impact on culture on each of these identity types would require, over time, cross-discipline studies that tap into the social-psychological dimensions of culture measurement. This, however, is quite possible with all the psychometric tools that scholars have within their current and future employ.

The impact of culture on exiles is a sophisticated question that will continue to a source of social, intellectual, cultural and economic inquiry over time. How culture impacts an exile depends on one's social class, educational background, gender, religious views, etc. Also, how does culture impact the individual in a host nation or society? Exiles may enjoy broader freedoms in the United States of America as opposed to Saudi Arabia, for example, where attitudes toward women and sexual orientation differ drastically. Some African exiles in France, for example, may enjoy broader freedoms as opposed to being in their native nation—the point being is that, culture itself, as a construct and series of practices, is reflexive, dynamic and interstitial. Culture is practice, culture is a way of thinking, culture is a set of accepted ideas—and its impact on exiles, in their multiple variants and parsed identities is robust.

The culture of global economics, however, directly drives the exiled into, and in some cases, contested and subjugated relationships between human expression and desired basic freedoms. For example, for the African who doesn't speak Wall Street English, they may experience discrimination in hiring, or even on the job due to their language barrier. Or, religious freedoms may be compromised when living in certain societies as an exile precludes practicing certain spiritual and/or religious exercises.

Nonetheless, the outflow of the African exiles is global in reach. Africans, armed with extremely high levels of formal education and high IQs tend to leave their home nations and live abroad. The developed world, with its perverse understanding of this quest for human betterment, leverages all the additive aptitudes of its incoming exiles for the betterment of host nations and societies. What you evidence in these human transactions is the flowing of skilled intellect, labor and human capital from poor African nations to rich nations, as opposed to the other way around. As such, the economic and cultural appropriation of the technical aptitudes and other abilities of the exiles keep rich countries rich and poor countries poor. Thus, this is an example of uneven development, which is predicated upon the exile seeking optimal self-actualization and a host nation's ability to leverage and exploit that human quest into economic gains for the host nation, which is typically richer. It is this impact on exiles that is most concerning, as it will continue to drive the disparate hemispheric economic divides between the North and South.

NOTES

1. A. Kroeber and C. Kluckhohn, *Culture: A Critical Review of Concepts and Definitions*. Massachusetts: Harvard University Press, 1952.
2. Ibid.
3. R. Williams, Keywords: *A Vocabulary of Culture and Society* (Rev. ed.). New York: Oxford University Press, 1983, pp. 90.
4. A. Kroeber and C. Kluckhohn, *Culture: A Critical Review of Concepts and Definition*. p. 23.
5. Ibid., p. 27.
6. Ibid., p. 29.
7. C. Kluckhohn, *Mirror for Man*. New York: McGraw-Hill, 1949, p. 17.
8. Ibid., p. 23
9. Ibid., p. 24
10. R. H. Winthrop, *Dictionary of Concepts in Cultural Anthropology*. New York: Greenwood, 1991, p. 261.
11. Ibid., p. 34.

12. E.B. Tylor, *Primitive Culture*. London: Murray, 1871.

13. C. Kluckhohn, *Mirror for Man*. pp. 25–25.

14. A. Kroeber and C. Kluckhohn, *Culture: A Critical Review of Concepts and Definition.*

15. Ibid., p. 65.

16. Ibid., p. 181.

17. Edward W Said, *Culture and Imperialism*. New York: Alfred A. Knopf, 1993, p. 177.

18. Ibid., p. 181.

19. Toyin Falola A. Usman (Eds.), *Movements, Borders and Identities in Africa.* New York: University of Rochester Press, 2009; Toyin Falola, *The African Diaspora: Slavery, Modernity and Globalization.* New York: University of Rochester Press, 2013.

20. Godwin S. Okeke, "The Uprooted Emigrant: The Impact of Brain Drain, Brain Gain, and Brain Circulation on Africa's Development." In Falola, Toyin and N. Afolabi (Eds.), *Trans-Atlantic Migration: The Paradoxes of Exile*. New York and London: Routledge, 2008, p. 119.

Chapter 6

The Children of Immigrants

Sasha Drummond-Lewis

Examinations of the rates of immigration and ability to assimilate for children of black immigrants are a relatively new focus within literature on immigrants to the United States. The experiences of migrating black children were assumed to be the same, if not less important, than that of their parental units while their rates of migration were overlooked altogether by scholars. The recent dramatic increase in numbers of black immigrants and noticeable presence of their families has finally rendered black immigrant children's invisibility visible and sparked interest not only on their circumstances of arrival but also on how they have successfully achieved social integration within American societies.

For instance, with regard to education scholars have noted that foreign-born black children have higher numbers of enrollments, are doing better in academically, graduating at higher rates, and attending college in larger numbers than US-born African American children. Black immigrant children are also faring as well as, if not better than, other immigrant children in the process of assimilation, leading some scholars to suggest that black immigrants may be the new "model immigrant," a title previously held by Asian-born immigrants. The intersections of their statuses as children, black, and immigrants qualify the experiences of these children as decidedly different from their native-born African American counterparts. In addition, the avenues by which black children become children of immigrants vary, as the children may or may not necessarily have migrated with their parents at the time of parental departure from their country and instead may have been born to immigrant parentage. Consequently, the need to understand and address the unique experiences of children of black foreign-born immigrants is being recognized and examined by academics.

Based on the Census 2010, the rates of "blacks" in the United States has risen from 12 percent to 13 percent over the last two decades but it is estimated that between 1990 and 2000 about 25 percent of the growth of the black population in the United States was due to the immigration of Africans and persons from the Caribbean.[1] Thus the largest numbers of immigrants are emigrating from overpopulated and under-resourced regions of the African-continent and the Caribbean islands, demonstrating that their ability to successfully assimilate occurs despite the circumstances that existed at the time of departure from their homelands.

Children of black immigrants from these regions are an important paradox but clearly the attention paid to them does not coincide with their rapidly growing numbers within the United States and their ability to rise above hurdles typically difficult for native African Americans to overcome. Extant literature identifies issues related to education, identity, health, physical activity, conduct, and school readiness as appropriate areas for assessing the ability of children of black immigrants to successfully assimilate and thrive. Though many of these areas are beyond the scope of this chapter some will be touched on as this chapter completes its endeavor to untangle the "black" immigrant child experience with a summary of current research of the rates of immigration, the various modes of arrival among African and Afro-Caribbean-born children, and issues related to assimilation (e.g., education, cultural expectations, etc). In an attempt to give voice to an often-unheard part of US population.

RATES OF BLACK IMMIGRANTS AND THEIR CHILDREN

The foreign-born population includes anyone born outside the United States who was not a citizen at birth.[2] As of 2010 foreign-born immigrants comprised 13 percent of the population of the United States.[3] With good reason, much of the research on foreign-born immigrants focuses heavily on the greatest proportion of immigrants who are from Latin America (53 percent) and Asia (28 percent).[4] Current research has turned its attention to foreign-born black immigrants recognizing that they are "now one of the fastest growing immigrant groups."[5] Logan and Deane estimate that the non-Hispanic black population grew by a rate of 21 percent between the 1990 and 2000 Census.[6] Among black immigrants, the largest numbers are emigrating from the Caribbean (9 percent), a region consisting of approximately 50 inhabited islands and stretching 2,000 miles,[7] and from Africa (4 percent),[8] a continent containing almost 52 countries.[9] The rates of immigration for children of black immigrants from these regions are problematic to ascertain from the literature as they are often unreported or are regionally unspecified within the homogenous term of "black child immigrant."[10]

According to Kent, "the number of black immigrants is growing at a remarkable rate"[11] as black immigrants of Caribbean and African heritage are entering the United States in unprecedented numbers. Black immigrants from the Caribbean are by far the largest group within black immigrants, with the highest percentages within this group emigrating from Jamaica and Haiti, at 18 percent and 15 percent respectively.[12] However, black immigrants from Africa are also a relatively large group within foreign-born blacks, as they have been experiencing rapid growth in numbers over the last 40 years."[13] In fact, while the number of Caribbean immigrants increased by over 60 percent, the number of African immigrants tripled during the 1990s.[14] The largest number of African immigrants comes from Nigeria and Ethiopia but when those from Egypt and Ghana are included, these four countries constitute 41 percent of the African-born total within the United States.[15] Rates such as these contain the frequency of both adult and child entrance into the United States and often the rates of entrance for black foreign-born children are not isolated or afforded independence in their count. Thus, unlike their adult parental counterparts, children of black immigrants receive less attention within research despite that they too are a rapidly growing part of the US population.[16]

Children of immigrants are children with at least one foreign-born parent, and these children, age 18 or under, account for nearly a quarter of all children (24–25 percent) in the United States.[17] When native- and foreign-born children of immigrants are compared 21 percent of children are native-born children with at least one foreign-born parent while 3 percent are foreign-born with at least one foreign-born parent.[18] The percentage of all children living in the United States with at least one foreign-born parent rose dramatically from 15 percent in 1994 to its present rate of 24–25 percent in 2014.[19] Given that more than one in five children in the United States has one or more foreign-born parents, children of immigrants, especially children of black immigrants, can no longer be ignored within literature on immigrant experiences.

Until recently, documented experiences of black immigrants frequently subsumed children within or even superseded experiences of parental guardians above those of their children despite that every member of the immigrant family encounters hurdles related to migration and assimilation when settling in another country. Non-Hispanic foreign-born black children are not a large portion of children in the United States, comprising just over eight percent of immigrant children (8.5 percent)[20] in 2014, but their numbers are growing. Despite the relatively small number of black children contending with immigrant-related issues, these children have specific and unique issues unlike other immigrant children, which are likely due to a combination of factors related to their age, race, and immigrant status. Nevertheless, these children appear to be successful in both adjusting to and navigating the American culture, as evidenced by their reported stable household structures, higher education achievements, and their model-immigrant-like behavior identified within the literature.

The current body of literature on foreign-born black immigrant children includes examinations of several issues related to adjustment in the United States: health, identity, education, physical activity, conduct disorder, family structure, and school readiness. The remainder of this chapter describes the methods of migration for black children and summarizes some of the more prominent issues discussed within the literature related to their lived experiences upon arrival in the United States. Whenever possible, this chapter endeavors to differentiate between the Caribbean and African immigrant child's experience. Given their growing rates of immigration and their ability to navigate within the US population, it is important to stay abreast of issues related to the migration patterns and assimilation process for black immigrant children.

Reasons for the Migration of Foreign-Born Children

Children of black immigrants, or children of any immigrants for that matter, are rarely immigrants by choice. Typically, they are subjects of the parental guardians' whims, economic opportunities or geographic requirements to relocate. The decisions of where, when, why and how to emigrate are most often made by adult guardians, not the children. Instead, these decisions are imposed upon the child with very little input from them, given their age and sometimes as a result of existing cultural norms requiring deference to authority. There are many reasons why black immigrants, and by default their children, migrate to the United States. Takyi, states that "economic, political, historical processes, educational opportunities, and changes to immigration policies in the United States have [all] been alluded to as providing impetus for [black] population movements."[21] It is therefore not surprising that no single, all-encompassing explanation exists as to why black immigrants and their children migrate to the United States.[22] Trends related to black migration to the United States have been found however with respect to the areas from where these immigrants are migrating. Kent, noted that before 1990, the majority of black immigrant arrivals were from the Caribbean but between 2000 and 2005 41 percent more black Africans arrived in the United States than in the previous decade.[23]

Important political and social issues in both the home country and the United States explain why black immigrants and their children were leaving from the Caribbean and Africa to pursue a new life in the United States. For countless Africans, political instability and civil unrest in their home countries provided some of the push to migrate with their children. For example, the deteriorating socioeconomic and political conditions in Africa[24] led to a reduction in the standard of living for the average African, which increased motivations to emigrate.[25] This subsequently led to the "push" for intercontinental migration of Africans to the United States in unprecedented numbers. For Africans, emigration to the United States is especially noteworthy because it is a fairly new development with African immigrants historically gravitating to countries that had colonial and cultural links to the continent (e.g., Britain, France, Belgium, and Portugal).[26] Among Caribbean immigrants, much of the literature focuses on the exodus of Jamaicans who have been migrating in steady numbers despite the disadvantaged origins from which they come.[27] For them, "the steady decline in the Jamaican economy; unemployment and underemployment rates greater than 25 percent; and an unequal distribution of land within a primarily agricultural nation"[28] provided the impetus for departure.

Education, jobs, and laws that were more favorable to admitting the families of immigrants helped lure many black immigrants and their children to the United States. For example, the educational opportunities and availability of jobs in the United States were some of the "pulls" for Africans to come to the United States instead of elsewhere.[29] Similarly for Caribbean immigrants, the availability of jobs with potential for income, educational opportunities, and presence of relatives and friends made the United States an attractive migration site for many Jamaicans.[30] In addition, changes to immigration laws were an instrumental reason why the United States became a target destination for black immigrants. The relaxed visa stipulations for work and school as well as the ability for immigrants to bring with them, or send for, their children solidified the United States as a worthwhile destination for both African and Caribbean migrants.

The favorability of the United States was first improved with the 1965 Immigration and Nationality Act (also known as the Hart-Cellar Act) that granted four important reprieves to the benefit of many black immigrants. First, it abolished the national origin quota system that was in use.[31] Previous geographic restrictions by and large limited the entrance of non-whites, many of whom were not located in the regions afforded quota-based opportunities. Elimination of quota system opened American gates for black immigrants. Second, it removed the restrictions on immigration based on national origin.[32] The removal of these national restrictions also made it possible for black immigrants, namely Africans, to enter the United States. Third, the Act made family reunification a priority. In particular, this policy encouraged the many Caribbean persons who had been steadily migrating to the United States to send for family members like children and encouraged those abroad to come reunite with family that had already come ahead of them.

Lastly, the emphasis placed on professional qualifications created visas for study, which allowed for the entrance of highly educated, skilled, blacks to fill some heavily underpopulated professions within the US Following the Hart-Cellar Act, there was the passage of the 1990 Immigration Reforms Act; a concerted effort for diversification within the US foreign-born population.[33] Some of the attempts at diversification were accomplished with admissions based on skills needed for specific jobs but others were achieved with a diversity visa lottery aimed at encouraging immigration from areas with previously low immigration rates. Overall, efforts were made through law to increase the number and diversity of immigrants admitted to the United States, which has played an important role in increasing the immigration of black populations in the United States.[34]

Migration Patterns of Black Immigrant Children

There are numerous reasons for migration making it clear that there are no patterns of when and why children of black immigrants migrate especially in light of the fact that much of the decision is not their own. There are however trends in how black children become children of immigrants. The three most common routes to becoming a child of an immigrant include: through migration with parents, delayed migration following parental departure, or being born in a host country to one or both foreign-born parents. The means of arrival to the United States can greatly impact the challenges faced by children of immigrants, as those who migrate must physically journey, assimilate, and endure additional hardships related to settling in a new country compared to their native-born counterparts who have not journeyed but share with them the commonality of having foreign-born parents. According to Smith, Lalonde, and Johnson, "immigrating to a new country involves a number of transitions and adjustments."[35] However, these transitions and adjustments are often compounded with issues of race for black immigrant children, who must learn the connotations associated with race in the United States and come to terms with no longer being part of the dominant race as they may have once been in their homelands.

Migration is a common practice for Caribbean nationals. Pottinger, Stair and Brown regard Caribbean people as always having "been a migrant population and [who] historically have used migration as an economic tool for progressing."[36] Serial migration, also known as staggered migration, is frequently discussed within the literature on children of black immigrants, as it refers to the phenomenon of separation and delayed reunion between parents and their children while attempting to migrate.[37] Smith, Lalonde, and Johnson found that "a staggered pattern of immigration, or serial migration, is a common feature of the movement of Caribbean people around the world."[38] As it pertains to children of black immigrants, during serial migration the parental unit migrates abroad first and a period of separation ensues between the parent and their children, until a reuniting later of the parent and child.

Migratory separation is the term used in reference to the period of separation when parents and their children live separately. During this time, the parent attempts to set up the environment in the host country for the child who will join them at a later time. The parent secures employment, residence, and accumulates resources to smooth the transition of migration for the child. Often this entails sacrifices on the part of the parent as they maintain their own residence in the host country but also must provide financially and whenever possible, emotionally, for the children who remain in the homeland. The usage of this form of migration is well known throughout the Caribbean and often is viewed as an economic necessity. High levels of poverty and unemployment in the region leads to the outsourcing of much labor in the Caribbean in an attempt to find monetary provisions, which can later be funneled back to the family until such time that family members, like a spouse or children, may later join the worker abroad.

The rates of children with migrant parents abroad are believed to be high in the Caribbean even though there are no available data to support this general perception. Jones, Sharpe and Sogren, as well as Pottinger, report some of the few existing statistics on these trends. They found that prevalence rates for children who have parents who have migrated to be 10.5 percent and 35 percent respectively for children in Trinidad and Tobago and Jamaica.[39] Though unverified, it is also believed that serial migration is "prevalent throughout many other islands of the Caribbean, including Barbados, the Dominican Republic, and St. Lucia."[40] As the largest group within black immigrants[41] to the United States and given the standard and customary nature of serial migration of persons from the Caribbean, children of Caribbean heritage often arrive at a much later time to the United States than their parents, sometimes as long as 10 years after. This may be a result more of social-structure than happenstance. According to Crawford-Brown and Ratt, "Parent-child separation from migration occurs across differing socio-economic levels of society; however, it is more commonly observed in low-income families."[42] Fewer resources, financial or otherwise, prevent some parents from bringing their children with them at the time of departure and they must work to save money, as well as find the means by which to send for their children. In this sense, migrating as a family is a luxury afforded to those who have the economic means to afford to do it.

In spite of good intentions and unbeknownst to many of the parents who go abroad, children whose parents preceded them to the United States experienced greater difficulties adjusting [in America] than children who accompanied their parents.[43] A mixture of psychological issues ensues for many of the children left behind including “loneliness, anger, joy, sadness and strong feeling of abandonment.”[44] Additionally, psychosocial outcomes such as depression, suicidal ideation and poor self-esteem have been documented among children left behind.[45] Many of these psychological issues persist even though children know that the separation is a temporary state. Yearwood conducted ethnographic interviews of 16 participants of Jamaican descent living and attending a church in the suburbs of New York and found that some of them “recalled disappointment and anger in not being raised by their biological parent.”[46]

For some children, the phenomenon of being in the home country with a parent abroad is a loss, often referred to as parental loss in the literature, as they experience the migration of the parent as they would a death of a parent. Pottinger found that “many of these children report a sense of abandonment and immense loss as well as guilt for having such feelings.”[47] Some children experience a period of grieving during separation; however, “grieving for the loss of the parent can be confusing to the child and is often stymied by family and friends”[48] who believe the migration of the parent and eventual reunion are joyous occasions to be celebrated. These psychological issues experienced by children are eventually confronted when the family is finally reunited. In fact, Smith, Lalonde and Johnson state that upon reunification “the stress associated with separation and reunion may sometimes lead to the disintegration of the family unit.”[49]

The reunification of parents and children can pose several problems for child immigrants. First, when the time comes for the child to migrate and the parents and children are finally reunited, children tend to be much older and in a different phase of development than when the parent last lived with them. Frequently, reunifications of children and parents often occur during adolescent years.[50] The child's developmental stage therein becomes one hurdle to a smooth reunion. For instance, if the child is at an adolescent stage at the time of reunification then they are likely to be battling with all the challenges of adolescence like body changes, understanding identity of self and family, and achieving a sense of belonging[51] in addition to getting to know their parent again and trying to navigate within a new country. Relatedly then, age is a factor when determining the successful transition of children who migrate to live with parent abroad. Research generally however finds that, the younger the child, the less stressful the unification.[52] Second, the advanced age of the immigrant child also means that the parent will spend less time helping the child adjust as they are believed to be old enough to figure it out on their own.

According to Lashley, the Caribbean parent often has little time to assist the child with settling into a new environment. Often the parents are working more than one job or working and going to school themselves.[53] With less supervision and little support, the child can experience more difficulty in transitioning to a country unfamiliar to both themselves and their parents. Third, just as they suffered a period of grieving due to parental loss, upon migration children can suffer a period of guardian loss "as a result of having been fostered by another adult while their parents were away."[54] Yearwood's interviews of adult children who had experienced migration separation during their childhood years found that these respondents made a concerted effort to be involved in the raising of their own children.[55]

Black children of foreign-born parents become part of the American population by several different means: some arrive with the parents, others arrive years after their parents as a part of the serial migration process, and yet others are born in the United States to one or more foreign-born parents. For those children who migrate, arriving with their parents at the time of parental arrival is optimal, so whenever possible, immigrant parents attempt to bring their children with them. However, Pottinger, Stair and Brown found that the "family migrating together tends to be more of a 'middle-class' family,"[56] suggesting that socioeconomic factors play a large role in methods of migration for black children. Since the issues of serial or staggered migration were absent from literature for African-born children, it appears that majority of black African children migrate with their parents to the United States, while staggered migration is a more common trait of migration for children of Afro-Caribbean heritage. Irrespective of the means by which they arrive in the United States there are various issues common to black children of foreign-born parents including: assimilation, education, living arrangements and cultural expectations.

Assimilation

Generally speaking, assimilation is the ability of immigrants to absorb the culture of the host country and eventually accept it as their own. For children of black immigrants, assimilation is assessed as a measure of successful integration into American society. Level of schooling completed is an example of an area assessed for degree of assimilation, as schools are recognized as a major transformative agent in the assimilation process for immigrant children. Rong and Brown support the prominence of schooling measures when they state that "the children of immigrants, as second-generation Americans,[57] become educated and socialized into the mainstream society through schools and other U.S. institutions."[58] Thus, assimilation suggests that immigrant children's level of schooling as well as achievements within school assessments will improve as they assimilate and so will that of each successive generation. Critics of this perspective point to the one directional and linear direction assumed in the ability of immigrants to assimilate. Subsequent and longitudinal research has determined that the second generation does make educational progress over the first generation but the third and later generations exhibit a persistent pattern of lower educational attainment compared to the previous generations.[59]

In an effort to explain the inadequacies riddled within the conventional assimilation theory's application, a more staggered process of assimilation, known as selective or segmented assimilation theory, is realized for black immigrant children. Selective assimilation theory, "suggest[s] a segmented process through which different immigrant groups take different paths at different rates, as determined by characteristics of the group and of the larger social context receiving them."[60] The main tenet of this theory suggests that immigrant children benefit more from selectively assimilating while preserving some of their ethnic culture. "This theory proposes that for groups who are racialized as nonwhite in the United States, selectively assimilating, or preserving ethnic cultures and identities, can facilitate socioeconomic mobility."[61] According to Bennett and Lutz "segmented assimilation theory argues that children of immigrants benefit more from maintaining an "ethnic" orientation than from acculturating to the cultural norms of their African American neighbors."[62] This suggests that process of assimilation for black immigrant children is more partial and nonlinear as demonstrated in their successful integration.

Education

The socializing capabilities of education have been measured extensively among immigrants, although this examination is more recent for black immigrant children. Thomas contends that historically "studies have generally paid little attention to the schooling outcomes of the children born to black immigrants."[63] However, the ability of these children to excel scholastically has brought them under the purview of scholars. In fact, "most of [the recent] studies indicate that the children of black immigrants have higher levels of educational attainment than the children of U.S.-born blacks."[64] Specifically, these studies show that children of black immigrants, whether they are foreign- or native-born, have higher GPAs, graduate high school at higher rates, and are more likely to go on to post-secondary education institutions than their native counterparts.[65] The exceptionality of children of foreign-born blacks with regard to scholastic achievement has some researchers purporting that black immigrants may replace Asians as the "model minority" group.[66] The reasons for the academic flourishing of children of black immigrants are both structurally and culturally influenced.

Overpopulation and scarcity of resources throughout the Caribbean and African regions means that many children in these areas are unable to attend high school in their homelands.[67] In the Caribbean, for example, "only 30% to 40% of the student-age population scores high enough on the required exam to enter high school."[68] For this reason whenever migration is feasible, foreign-born parents from countries in these regions migrate to further the secondary-level educational opportunities of their children. Once they are abroad, immigrant parents discuss with their children the importance of education and encourage them to do well academically. As a result, at the secondary level, children born to black immigrants have higher levels of educational attainment, higher GPAs, have lower dropout rates, and are less likely to fall behind in school compared with those born to native-born blacks.[69] Surprisingly, the influence of foreign-born parents on schooling outcomes holds even in single-parent households. According to Thomas "children born to black immigrants do significantly better [in school] than those born to native-born blacks regardless of whether children of immigrants live in two-immigrant or single-immigrant-parent families."[70]

Entry into higher education institutions is another important indicator of the degree of assimilation for children of black immigrants in US societies.[71] Postsecondary schooling is a well-known stepping-stone for elevating occupational status, income, and standard of living within the United States. An appreciation for the availability of higher education and an understanding of the importance of utilizing the higher education system is cultivated by black immigrant parents when they strongly encourage their children to attend college. Parental influence is believed to lead to an advantage for children of black immigrants.

Studies like Bennett and Lutz have documented the higher levels of postsecondary enrollment of children of black immigrants over both African American children and white children. In their study, Bennett and Lutz found that 75 percent of all children from black immigrant families were enrolled in college and not only were they more likely to enroll at colleges and universities than native African American students, but they were also more likely to enroll than white high school graduates. Other researchers have also confirmed the "overrepresentation of immigrant blacks in postsecondary education, particularly in select colleges."[72] For instance, Kent found that 35 percent of black students at the most elite US colleges and universities are foreign-born children or children of foreign-born black immigrants.[73] Massey et al. found in his study of prestigious schools, like Harvard, that immigrant blacks are overrepresented among freshmen who attend the 28 selective colleges that experience domination of African and Afro-Caribbean immigrants within the black student population.[74]

Thomas identified several important caveats regarding schooling achievements for children of black immigrants are identified, including the presence of step-siblings, age, duration of residence and migration. First, the composition of the household can affect the educational outcomes of children of immigrants. Tillman found that "Living with step-siblings or half-siblings, for example, negatively affects schooling performance."[75] Second, the advantage of being foreign-born children may have an age limit. Rong and Brown suggest that the Caribbean advantage among black immigrants may be limited to the age range of 15–24 while other researchers center on adolescence through teen years up to the end of high school (ages13–19) as the periods for greatest academic potential for children of black immigrants. Third, "most studies on the schooling outcomes of children born to immigrants identify duration of residence in the United States as an important factor affecting school performance."[76]

The greatest advantage identified for immigrants occurs in the first and second generation of immigration, with subsequent generations noting a decline. Even among foreign-born children, there is a need to distinguish between those who recently arrived and those who have resided for many years. Thomas compared length of residence among first-generation immigrant children and determined a contrast between "recently-arrived first-generation children [who were] living in the U.S. 0–5 years [and] long-term first-generation children [who were] living in the U.S. more than 5 years."[77] Fourth, the advantage of children of black immigrants versus native-black children has been explored by Thomas, who was able to determine that the immigrant advantage is robust across both internal black migrants and international black immigrants. He found that "the children of U.S.-born internal immigrants also have schooling advantage over the children of U.S.-born nonimmigrants,"[78] which means that the advantage of migration persists across all black immigrant groups, whether they migrate nationally or internationally. An important take away is that migrants, whether internal or external, tend to be positively selected in that the most educated, skilled and resourceful individuals migrate, and these characteristics also set them up for success once they are abroad. Clearly then, migration attracts the most "able, motivated and skilled individuals."

Living arrangements

The myriad of living arrangements existing within American families encompass variations of married or cohabitating, homosexual or heterosexual, couples or singles, childless or living with children, children may be biological, adopted or step-children, and the household may even include pets or extended family members. Trends within the living arrangements of children living with foreign-born parents are consistent of patterns of a nuclear familial structure. Black foreign-born children with foreign-born parents typically live in a two-parent household but this is particularly true for children in families of African descent: "Census data from 2000 show that 76 percent of African immigrant children (whether born in the United States or abroad) lived in a two-parent family, compared with about 65 percent of Caribbean immigrant children and just 44 percent of African American children."[79] The pattern of two-parent families extends to native-born children as well, with US-born children, living with foreign-born parents, are also more likely to live in two-parent homes than US-born children who do not have a foreign-born parent. Overall it is found that, "Regardless of their own nativity status, children with a foreign-born parent more often lived in a household with two parents present than did children with no foreign-born parents. In 2014, about 82 percent of native children with a foreign-born parent lived with two parents, compared with 68 percent of native children with two native parents."[80] Indelibly then, the household structure of black children living with foreign-born parents are typically higher concentrations of two-parent, nuclear households.[81] Living with two married foreign-born parents is an important distinction for children of black immigrants because it "generally results in a higher standard of living and access to more opportunities."[82] Black children with foreign-born parents living in two-parent households therefore fare better than their native-born counterparts, especially in areas like education, and appear to have an immigrant advantage over native-born African American children. Thomas' previously mentioned study demonstrates how the "schooling advantage enjoyed by children born to black immigrants is driven by the outcomes of children born to two immigrant parents."[83]

Understandably, not all households of black children living with foreign-born parents have two parents as some of these children live within a single-parent household. Single parentage does not work to the disadvantage of black children. In fact, when black children of immigrant parents live in single-parent households, they still fare better than native US-born black children. For those born to immigrant parents, the difference between living in two-parent versus single-parent families is not as great [as for US-born blacks], especially in families headed by parents with some college education or an associate degree.[84]

Trends do show that black children of foreign-born parents living in single-parent homes tend to be children of Caribbean-born immigrants. For instance, Landale, Thomas, and Van Hook find that "Caribbean-origin children of immigrants, especially those from the English-speaking Caribbean, are more likely to live in female headed families."[85] The reasons for this trend result from a combination of factors such as the higher numbers of females than males who emigrate from the Caribbean, the continuance of the pre-migration prevalence of female-headed households as well as the dominance of single-parent households in the Caribbean. In many instances Caribbean females are first in their family to come abroad, often for work purposes, and once they are settled they begin to send for family members, often the children first, so that at times single-parent households are actually "temporary family arrangements associated with sequential patterns of family migration."[86] Although, stepparent households are not discussed here, an important nuance to note regarding the family structure of black children with foreign-born parents is that children living in families that include a stepparent have less favorable educational outcome even after other demographic and background characteristics are controlled.[87]

Cultural Expectations

Culturally, there are high expectations for children of black immigrants to excel scholastically irrespective of whether they migrate to the United States or are US-born and living with a foreign-born parent. This is especially true for African and Afro-Caribbean children. Mitchell and Bryan report that in Caribbean households "the parental expectation of achievement and appropriate behavior in school [are] extremely important, given the fact that most Caribbean people migrate to the United States for improved educational and economic opportunities."[88]

Many African and Afro-Caribbean immigrant parents retain traditional parenting values and practices from their country of origin,[89] which includes trying to retain control over their children. Control and guidance, with limited decision making on the part of the child are some of the parenting strategies used, which lead to high academic expectations. These high expectations account for some of the successful school outcomes[90] among black children of immigrants like high achievement in GPAs and graduation rates, and these findings are robust across children of immigrants born outside or within the United States. Children of black immigrants often feel parented from two cultures and must balance parental expectations to succeed in school with American adolescent cultural norms of rebellion to parents, all the while maintaining their culture and traditions.[91]

Summary

Black immigrants are a diverse group, and research often fails to detail the varied experiences of "blacks" once they land in the United States.[92] Until recently there was no distinction in the literature between foreign-born and US-born blacks. All blacks were considered African Americans and considered equally disadvantaged. Failure to consider between- and within-group differences among persons of African descent blurred the lines of progress and disadvantage among blacks living in America. It is now becoming apparent that intragroup variability does exist among black Americans and some blacks are more disadvantaged than others.

In addition to the oversight of group distinctions among blacks, there has been great neglect in the study of the children of black immigrants. The admittance of great numbers of black immigrants, the largest portions of whom come from the Caribbean and African regions, is a direct result of changes to laws regarding quota requirements and policies related to increasing the number of educated and skilled laborers entering the United States. Subsequently there has been an increase in the number of black immigrant children arriving in the United States. These children are a small but rapidly growing part of the child population in the United States. As of 2010, foreign-born children comprised nearly one quarter of children in the United States, with less than one tenth of these children being non-Hispanic blacks.

The situations children encounter upon arrival differ greatly from their parents, and the need to highlight their unique experiences cannot be overlooked. For instance, children of immigrants from African Diaspora and the Caribbean do not all arrive in the United States in the same way. Some arrive simultaneously with parental immigration, others arrive later as a result of chain migration, and still others are here by birth. The nuanced means of arrival can greatly impact the experiences of these children compared to their native-born counterparts. Overall, research has found that children of immigrants are more successful than their counterparts with native-born parents.

This chapter endeavored to explore rates of immigration for foreign-born black children and to expose potential issues related to assimilation for these children compared to native-born black children. The various modes by which children become children of black immigrants fail to provide many difficulties in the educational outcomes of foreign- and native-born children of African and Afro-Caribbean descent. In fact, it appears that the immigration status of parents is more influential than the immigration status of the child in predicting the academic success of the child, in that children with at least one foreign-born parent are more academically successful.

Overall rates show that children of black immigrants are surpassing native-born African American children here in the United States. Also important is the finding that the "immigrant advantage is driven by the outcomes of the children of African and West-Indian [Caribbean] non-Hispanic immigrants."[93] Not enough studies examine effects of immigration on black children. Thomas spoke of the apparent invisibility of black immigrant youths in the literature on the children of immigrants and now there is a call for more studies highlighting the achievements and struggles of children of black immigrants.

NOTES

1. John R. Logan and Glenn Deane, "Black Diversity in Metropolitan America," *Lewis Mumford Center for Comparative Urban and Regional Research*, University of Albany, 2003, p. 1.

2. Yesenia D. Acosta and G. Patricia De la Cruz. *The Foreign Born From Latin America and The Caribbean: 2010.* US Department of Commerce, Economics and Statistics Administration, US Census Bureau, September 2011.

3. U.S. Bureau of Census, 2010.

4. Yesenia D. Acosta and G. Patricia De la Cruz, *The Foreign Born From Latin America and The Caribbean: 2010.* US Department of Commerce, Economics and Statistics Administration, US Census Bureau, September 2011.

5. Mary M. Kent, "Immigration and America's Black Population." *Population Bulletin,* vol 62, no. 4, 2007; Nancy S. Landale, Kevin J. A. Thomas, and Jennifer Van Hook, "The living arrangements of children of immigrants." *The Future of Children/ Center for the Future of Children, the David and Lucile Packard Foundation*, volume 21, no. 1, 2011, p. 58.

6. John R. Logan and Glenn Deane, "Black Diversity in Metropolitan America," *Lewis Mumford Center for Comparative Urban and Regional Research*, University of Albany, 2003.

7. Natasha Mitchell and Julia Bryan, "School-family-community partnerships: Strategies for school counselors working with Caribbean immigrant families." *Professional School Counseling*, volume 10, no. 4, 2007, p. 400; 401.

8. Yesenia D. Acosta and G. Patricia De la Cruz, *The Foreign Born From Latin America and the Caribbean: 2010.* US Department of Commerce, Economics and Statistics Administration, US Census Bureau, September 2011.

9. Baffour Takyi, "The making of the second diaspora: On the recent African immigrant community in the United States of America." *The Journal of Black Studies,* volume 26, no. 1, 2002, p. 36.

10. Ibid.

11. Mary M. Kent, "Immigration and America's Black Population." *Population Bulletin,* volume 62, no. 4, 2007, p. 3.

12. Nancy S. Landale, Kevin J. A. Thomas, and Jennifer Van Hook, "The living arrangements of children of immigrants." *The Future of Children/Center for the Future of Children, the David and Lucile Packard Foundation*, volume 21, no.1, 2011, p. 44; John R. Logan and Glenn Deane, "Black Diversity in Metropolitan America," *Lewis Mumford Center for Comparative Urban and Regional Research*, University of Albany, 2003, p. 15.

13. Gambino, Christine P., Edward N. Trevelyan, and John Thomas Fitzwater. *The foreign-born population from Africa: 2008–2012.* US Department of Commerce, Economics and Statistics Administration, US Census Bureau, October 2014.

14. John R. Logan and Glenn Deane, "Black Diversity in Metropolitan America," *Lewis Mumford Center for Comparative Urban and Regional Research*, University of Albany, 2003, p. 1.

15. United States Census Bureau. "African-Born Population in U.S. Roughly Doubled Every Decade since 1970." Accessed September 29, 2016. http://www.census.gov/newsroom/press-releases/2014/cb14-184.html; Baffour Takyi, "The making of the second diaspora: On the recent African immigrant community in the United States of America." *The Journal of Black Studies* 2002, volume 26, no. 1, 2002, p. 36.

16. Nancy S. Landale, Kevin J. A. Thomas, and Jennifer Van Hook, "The living arrangements of children of immigrants." *The Future of Children/Center for the Future of Children, the David and Lucile Packard Foundation*, volume 21, no. 1, 2011, p. 43.

17. Nancy S. Landale, Kevin J. A. Thomas, and Jennifer Van Hook, "The living arrangements of children of immigrants." *The Future of Children/Center for the Future of Children, the David and Lucile Packard Foundation*, volume 21, no. 1, 2011, p. 44; Migration Policy Institute, "Frequently Requested Statistics on Immigrants and Immigration in the United States." Accessed September 29, 2016. http://www.migrationpolicy.org/article/frequently-requested-statistics-immigrants-and-immigration-united-states#Children with Immigrant.

18. ChildStats.gov: Forum on Child and Family Statistics, "FAM4 Children of at least one Foreign-Born Parent: Percentage of Children Ages 0–17 by Nativity of Child and Parents, Parent's Education, Poverty Status, and Other Characteristics, Selected Years 1994–2014." Accessed June 15, 2016. http://www.childstats.gov/americaschildren/family4.asp

19. Ibid.

20. Child Trends Data Bank. "Appendix 1—Of Children Younger than 18, Number and Percentage who are Immigrants, and Percentage of Immigrants and Non-Immigrants with Selected Characteristics: Selected Years, 1994–2014." Accessed September 29, 2016. http://www.childtrends.org/wp-content/uploads/2012/07/110_appendix1.pdf

21. Baffour Takyi, "The making of the second diaspora: On the recent African immigrant community in the United States of America." *The Journal of Black Studies,* volume 26, no. 1, 2002, p. 33.

22. Ibid.

23. Mary M. Kent, "Immigration and America's Black Population." *Population Bulletin,* volume 62, no. 4, 2007, p. 5.

24. A. Adepoju, "South-North migration: The African experience." *International migration*, volume 29, no. 2, 1991.

25. Margaret Peil, "Ghanian migrants abroad." *African Affairs*, volume 94, 1995.

26. Baffour Takyi, "The making of the second diaspora: On the recent African immigrant community in the United States of America." *The Journal of Black Studies,* volume 26, no. 1, 2002, p. 33.

27. Nancy S. Landale, Kevin J. A. Thomas, and Jennifer Van Hook, "The living arrangements of children of immigrants." *The Future of Children/Center for the Future of Children, the David and Lucile Packard Foundation*, volume 21, no.1, 2011, p. 58.

28. Edilma L. Yearwood, "'Growing Up' children: Current child-rearing practices among immigrant Jamaican families." *Journal of Child and Adolescent Psychiatric Nursing*, volume 14, no. 1, 2001.

29. Gambino, Trevelyan, and Fitzwater, *The foreign-born population from Africa: 2008–2012*. US Department of Commerce, Economics and Statistics Administration, US Census Bureau, October 2014; Mary M. Kent, "Immigration and America's Black Population." *Population Bulletin,* volume 62, no. 4, 2007, p. 6.

30. Ibid.

31. Leon F. Bouvier, "Peaceful invasions: Immigration and changing America." Washington, D.C: Center for Immigration Studies as cited in Baffour Takyi, "The making of the second diaspora: On the recent African immigrant community in the United States of America." *The Journal of Black Studies,* volume 26, no. 1, 2002, p. 35.

32. Pamela R. Bennett and Amy Lutz. "How African American is the net black advantage? Differences in college attendance among immigrant blacks, native blacks and whites." *Sociology of Education,* no. 82, 2009, p. 71.

33. Baffour Takyi, "The making of the second diaspora: On the recent African immigrant community in the United States of America." *The Journal of Black Studies,* volume 26, no. 1, 2002, p. 35.

34. Kwadwo Konadu-Agyemang and Baffour K. Takyi, "An Overview of African immigration to U.S. and Canada," as cited in Kevin T.A. Thomas, "Parental characteristics and the schooling progress of the children of immigrant and U.S.-born blacks." *Demography,* volume 46, no. 3, 2009, p. 513.

35. Andrea Smith, Richard N. Lalonde, and Simone Johnson, "Serial migration and its implications for the parent-child relationship: a retrospective analysis of the experiences of the children of Caribbean immigrants." *Cultural Diversity and Ethnic Minority Psychology*, volume 10, no. 2, 2004, p. 107.

36. Audrey M. Pottinger, Angela Gordon Stair, and Sharon Williams Brown. "A counselling framework for Caribbean children and families who have experienced migratory separation and reunion." *International Journal for the Advancement of Counselling*, volume 30, no. 1, 2008, p. 22.

37. Ibid, p. 16.

38. Andrea Smith, Richard N. Lalonde, and Simone Johnson, "Serial migration and its implications for the parent-child relationship: a retrospective analysis of the experiences of the children of Caribbean immigrants." *Cultural Diversity and Ethnic Minority Psychology*, volume 10, no. 2, 2004, p. 108.

39. Adele Jones, Jacqueline Sharpe and Michele Sogren, "Children's experiences of separation from parents as a consequence of migration." *Caribbean Journal of Social Work*, volume 3, no. 1 as cited in Audrey M. Pottinger, Angela Gordon Stair, and Sharon Williams Brown, "A counselling framework for Caribbean children and families who have experienced migratory separation and reunion." *International Journal for the Advancement of Counselling*, volume 30, no. 1, 2008, p. 16.

40. Audrey M. Pottinger, Angela Gordon Stair, and Sharon Williams Brown. "A counselling framework for Caribbean children and families who have experienced migratory separation and reunion." *International Journal for the Advancement of Counselling*, volume 30, no. 1, 2008, p. 16.

41. Nancy S. Landale, Kevin J. A. Thomas, and Jennifer Van Hook, "The living arrangements of children of immigrants." *The Future of Children/Center for the Future of Children, the David and Lucile Packard Foundation*, volume 21, no.1, 2011, p. 59.

42. Claudette P.J. Crawford-Brown and J. Melrose Rattray. "Parent-child relationships in Caribbean families." In Nancy Boyd Webb and Doman Lum (Eds) *Culturally Diverse parent-child and family relations*, pp. 107–30 as cited in Audrey M. Pottinger, Angela Gordon Stair, and Sharon Williams Brown. "A counselling framework for Caribbean children and families who have experienced migratory separation and reunion." *International Journal for the Advancement of Counselling*, volume 30, no. 1, 2008, p. 16.

43. David A. Baptiste, Kenneth V. Hardy and Laurie Lewis, "Family therapy with English Caribbean immigrant families in the United States: Issues of emigration, immigration, culture and race." *Contemporary Family Therapy*, volume 19, no. 3, 1997; Andrea Smith, Richard N. Lalonde, and Simone Johnson, "Serial migration and its implications for the parent-child relationship: a retrospective analysis of the experiences of the children of Caribbean immigrants." *Cultural Diversity and Ethnic Minority Psychology*, volume 10, no. 2, 2004.

44. Pottinger, Audrey M., Angela Gordon Stair, and Sharon Williams Brown. "A counselling framework for Caribbean children and families who have experienced migratory separation and reunion." *International Journal for the Advancement of Counselling*, volume 30, no. 1, 2008, p. 16.

45. Adele Jones, Jacqueline Sharpe and Michele Sogren, "Children's experiences of separation from parents as a consequence of migration." *Caribbean Journal of Social Work*, volume 3, no. 1 as cited in Audrey M. Pottinger, Angela Gordon Stair, and Sharon Williams Brown, "A counselling framework for Caribbean children and families who have experienced migratory separation and reunion." *International Journal for the Advancement of Counselling*, volume 30, no. 1, 2008; Andrea Smith, Richard N. Lalonde, and Simone Johnson. "Serial migration and its implications for the parent-child relationship: a retrospective analysis of the experiences of the children of Caribbean immigrants." *Cultural Diversity and Ethnic Minority Psychology*, volume 10, no. 2, 2004, pp. 107–122.

46. Edilma L. Yearwood, "'Growing Up' children: Current child-rearing practices among immigrant Jamaican families." *Journal of Child and Adolescent Psychiatric Nursing*, volume 14, no. 1, 2001, p. 13.

47. Pottinger, Audrey M., Angela Gordon Stair, and Sharon Williams Brown. "A counselling framework for Caribbean children and families who have experienced migratory separation and reunion." *International Journal for the Advancement of Counselling*, volume 30, no. 1, 2008, p. 17.

48. Ibid.

49. Andrea Smith, Richard N. Lalonde, and Simone Johnson, "Serial migration and its implications for the parent-child relationship: a retrospective analysis of the experiences of the children of Caribbean immigrants." *Cultural Diversity and Ethnic Minority Psychology*, volume 10, no. 2, 2004, p. 110.

50. Myrna Lashley, "The unrecognized social stressors of migration and reunification in Caribbean families." *Transcultural Psychiatry*, volume 37, no. 2, 2000, p. 203.

51. Myrna Lashley, "The unrecognized social stressors of migration and reunification in Caribbean families." *Transcultural Psychiatry*, volume 37, no. 2, 2000, p. 207; Pottinger, Audrey M., Angela Gordon Stair, and Sharon Williams Brown. "A counselling framework for Caribbean children and families who have experienced migratory

separation and reunion." *International Journal for the Advancement of Counselling*, volume 30, no. 1, 2008, p. 17.

52. David A. Baptiste, Kenneth V. Hardy and Laurie Lewis, "Family therapy with English Caribbean immigrant families in the United States: Issues of emigration, immigration, culture and race." *Contemporary Family Therapy*, volume 19, no. 3, 1997; Andrea Smith, Richard N. Lalonde, and Simone Johnson, "Serial migration and its implications for the parent-child relationship: a retrospective analysis of the experiences of the children of Caribbean immigrants." *Cultural Diversity and Ethnic Minority Psychology*, volume 10, no. 2, 2004.

53. Myrna Lashley, "The unrecognized social stressors of migration and reunification in Caribbean families." *Transcultural Psychiatry*, volume 37, no. 2, 2000, p. 206.

54. Edilma L. Yearwood, "'Growing Up' children: Current child-rearing practices among immigrant Jamaican families." *Journal of Child and Adolescent Psychiatric Nursing*, volume 14, no. 1, 2001, p. 14.

55. Ibid.

56. Audrey M. Pottinger, Angela Gordon Stair, and Sharon Williams Brown. "A counselling framework for Caribbean children and families who have experienced migratory separation and reunion." *International Journal for the Advancement of Counselling*, volume 30, no. 1, 2008, p. 16.

57. First generation are children born outside the United States. with at least one foreign-born parent, second generation are children born in the United States with two foreign-born parents, and third generation are children born in United States with two US-born parents (Landale, Thomas, and Van Hook 2011).

58. Rong, Xue Lan, and Frank Brown. "The effects of immigrant generation and ethnicity on educational attainment among young African and Caribbean Blacks in the United States." *Harvard Educational Review*, volume 71, no. 3, 2001, p. 539.

59. Ibid.

60. Ibid.

61. Margaret A. Gibson, *Accommodation without Assimilation: Sikh immigrants in an American High School*. Ithaca, NY: Cornell University Press; Cynthia Feliciano, "Education and ethnic identity formation among children of Latin American and Caribbean immigrants." *Sociological Perspectives*, volume 52, no. 2, 2009.

62. Pamela R. Bennett and Amy Lutz. "How African American is the net black advantage? Differences in college attendance among immigrant blacks, native blacks and whites." *Sociology of Education,* no. 82, 2009, p. 72.

63. Kevin T.A. Thomas, "Parental characteristics and the schooling progress of the children of immigrant and U.S.-born blacks." *Demography*, volume 46, no. 3, 2009, p. 529

64. Kevin T.A. Thomas, "Migration processes, familial characteristics, and schooling dropout among black youths." *Demography*, volume 49, no. 2, 2012, p. 478.

65. Grace Kao, "Parental influences on the educational outcomes of immigrant youth." The *International Migration Review,* volume 38, no. 2, 2004; Mary M. Kent, "Immigration and America's Black Population." *Population Bulletin,* volume 62, no. 4, 2007, p. 9.

66. Lance Freeman, "Does spatial assimilation work for black immigrants in the US?" *Urban Studies*, volume 39, no. 11, 2002 as cited in Kevin T.A. Thomas, "Migration processes, familial characteristics, and schooling dropout among black youths." *Demography,* volume 49, no. 2, 2012.

67. Natasha Mitchell and Julia Bryan, "School-family-community partnerships: Strategies for school counselors working with Caribbean immigrant families." *Professional School Counseling*, volume 10, no. 4, 2007, p. 400; 401.

68. Ibid.

69. Kevin T.A. Thomas, "Migration processes, familial characteristics, and schooling dropout among black youths." *Demography*, volume 49, no. 2, 2012.

70. Kevin T.A. Thomas, "Parental characteristics and the schooling progress of the children of immigrant and U.S.-born blacks." *Demography*, volume 46, no. 3, 2009, p. 521.

71. Cynthia Feliciano, "Education and ethnic identity formation among children of Latin American and Caribbean immigrants." *Sociological Perspectives*, volume 52, no. 2, 2009, p. 135.

72. Pamela R. Bennett and Amy Lutz. "How African American is the net black advantage? Differences in college attendance among immigrant blacks, native blacks and whites." *Sociology of Education,* no. 82, 2009, p. 88.

73. Mary M. Kent, "Immigration and America's Black Population." *Population Bulletin,* volume 62, no. 4, 2007, p. 9.

74. Douglas S. Massey, Margarita Mooney, Kimberly C. Torres and Camille Charles, "Black immigrants and black natives attending selective colleges and universities in the United States." *American Journal of Education*, volume 113, 2007 as cited in Kevin T.A Thomas, "Migration processes, familial characteristics, and schooling dropout among black youths." *Demography*, volume 49, no. 2, 2012, p. 513.

75. Kathryn Harker Tillman, "Coresident Sibling Composition and the academic ability, expectations, and performance of youth." *Sociological Perspectives*, volume 51, no. 4, 2008.

76. Kevin T.A. Thomas, "Parental characteristics and the schooling progress of the children of immigrant and U.S.-born blacks." *Demography*, volume 46, no. 3, 2009, p. 516.

77. Ibid, p. 518.

78. Ibid, p. 494.

79. Mary M. Kent, "Immigration and America's Black Population." *Population Bulletin,* volume 62, no. 4, 2007, p. 11.

80. ChildStats.gov: Forum on Child and Family Statistics. "FAM4 Children of at least one Foreign-Born Parent: Percentage of Children Ages 0–17 by Nativity of Child and Parents, Parent's Education, Poverty Status, and Other Characteristics, Selected Years 1994–2014." Accessed June 15, 2016. http://www.childstats.gov/americaschildren/family4.asp

81. Pamela R. Bennett and Amy Lutz. "How African American is the net black advantage? Differences in college attendance among immigrant blacks, native blacks and whites." *Sociology of Education,* no. 82, 2009, p. 89.

82. Nancy S. Landale, Kevin J. A. Thomas, and Jennifer Van Hook, "The living arrangements of children of immigrants." *The Future of Children/Center for the Future of Children, the David and Lucile Packard Foundation*, volume 21, no.1, 2011, p. 46.

83. Kevin T.A. Thomas, "Parental characteristics and the schooling progress of the children of immigrant and U.S.-born blacks." *Demography*, volume 46, no. 3, 2009, p. 530.

84. Ibid, p. 521.

85. Nancy S. Landale, Kevin J. A. Thomas, and Jennifer Van Hook, "The living arrangements of children of immigrants." *The Future of Children/Center for the Future of Children, the David and Lucile Packard Foundation*, volume 21, no.1, 2011, p. 59.

86. Ibid, p. 60.

87. Kevin T.A. Thomas, "Parental characteristics and the schooling progress of the children of immigrant and U.S.-born blacks." *Demography*, volume 46, no 3, 2009, p. 516.

88. Natasha Mitchell and Julia Bryan, "School-family-community partnerships: Strategies for school counselors working with Caribbean immigrant families." *Professional School Counseling*, volume 10, no. 4, 2007, p. 402.

89. Chamberlain, 2003; Stromquist and Monkman as cited in Bertranna Muruthi, J. Maria Bermúdez, Kevin R. Bush, Megan McCoy, and Morgan A. Stinson, "Afro-Caribbean Mothers in the US: An Exploratory Study from a Transnational Feminist Perspective." *Women & Therapy*, volume 39, no. 3–4, p. 415.

90. Grace Kao, "Parental influences on the educational outcomes of immigrant youth." *The International Migration Review,* volume 38, no. 2, 2004.

91. Bertranna Muruthi, J. Maria Bermúdez, Kevin R. Bush, Megan McCoy, and Morgan A. Stinson, "Afro-Caribbean Mothers in the US: An Exploratory Study from a Transnational Feminist Perspective." *Women & Therapy*, volume 39, no. 3–4, p. 424.

92. Yesenia D. Acosta and G. Patricia De la Cruz, *The foreign born from Latin America and the Caribbean: 2010*. US Department of Commerce, Economics and Statistics Administration, US Census Bureau, September 2011; Kevin T.A Thomas, "Migration processes, familial characteristics, and schooling dropout among black youths." *Demography*, volume 49, no. 2, 2012.

93. Kevin T.A Thomas, "Migration processes, familial characteristics, and schooling dropout among black youths." *Demography*, volume 49, no. 2, 2012, p. 494.

Chapter 7

Relocation from Africa, Latin America, and the Caribbean

Issues and Challenges

Brenda Ingrid Gill

INTRODUCTION

The rise of South-South migration is noted from research. Despite this growth, however, the United Nations report that in 2013 South-North migration flows accounted for the movement of 81.9 million persons, or 35 percent of all migration origin and destination flows.[1] Bearing this in mind, the focus of this chapter is on examining on examining relocation of citizens who move to countries outside the regions of Africa, Latin American, and the Caribbean. The United Nations identified twenty countries as the top destination for international migrants worldwide.

Of these twenty countries, United Nations report that nine countries are in Asia, seven in Europe, two in Northern America, and one each in Africa and Oceania.[2] Additionally, the United Nations in their assessment of international migration trends for 2015 further suggest, "Persons living in a country other than where they were born—reached 244 million in 2015 for the world, an increase of 71 million, or 41 per cent, compared to 2000."[3] This increased rate of international migration—especially that of persons from Africa, Latin America, and the Caribbean (LAC) countries—is of importance to this chapter.

More precisely, "recent" immigration (after 1945) to Europe, North America, and Asia are of relevance to this discussion. The impact of such relocation for the migrants, their families, and source countries is explored. The chapter traces migration trends and examines some of the issues and challenges emigrants face, challenges to family and family life, and the positive and negative effects on the natives' home countries' economic development. This chapter explores the social, temporal, and spatial influences of migration.

INTERNATIONAL MIGRATION FROM AFRICA, LAC REGIONS: ISSUES AND CHALLENGES

This discussion recognizes that international migration is not a new or unique phenomenon, rather an old practice captured and discussed by many authors.[4] For this discussion an international migrant is a person who is living in a country other than his or her country of birth.[5] That is, any person who changes his or her usual place of residence for any period of time for various reasons: refugees, displaced persons, economic migrants, and persons moving for other purposes.[6] The importance of this discussion is underscored by the United Nations report that suggests that the number of international migrants worldwide continues to climb. The report further advises that for 2015, of the 244 million international migrants worldwide, Latin American comprise the third largest birth place of immigrants (62 million) a quarter; while those born in Africa were fifth and accounted for 34 million, or 14 percent of all international migrants.[7]

Often migration outside of the areas of Africa and the LAC regions has been divided into broad periods.[8] Even so, this current discussion is only concerned with the relocation of persons from Africa and the LAC regions to areas outside of the two regions. More specifically, South-North immigration is under consideration here. First, relocation from Africa will be covered followed by that from the LAC region. After highlighting the relocation that occurred in the two regions focus shifts to some relocation issues and challenges.

Africa

Though some authors prefer to focus on what is termed "sub-Sahara" Africa, this discussion deviates to focus on the African continent in its entirety. The South-North movement of people from all 54 countries (Algeria, Angola, Benin, Botswana, Burkina Faso, Burundi, Cabo Verde, Cameroon, Central African Republic, Chad, Comoros, Democratic Republic of the Congo, Republic of the Congo, Cote d'Ivoire, Djibouti, Egypt, Equatorial Guinea, Eritrea, Ethiopia, Gabon, Gambia, Ghana, Guinea, Guinea-Bissau, Kenya, Lesotho, Liberia, Libya, Madagascar, Malawi, Mali, Mauritania, Mauritius, Morocco, Mozambique, Namibia, Niger, Nigeria, Rwanda, Sao Tome and Principe, Senegal, Seychelles, Sierra Leone, Somalia, South Africa, South Sudan, Sudan, Swaziland, Tanzania, Togo, Tunisia, Uganda, Zambia, Zimbabwe) is the polestar here. Interest is on relocation to countries outside of the African continent by people from the African region.

Africa is undisputedly a continent characterized by substantial migration influenced by demographic factors, political climate, economic challenges, political matters, conflict, poverty, access to resources and connections that facilitate migration, and security conditions. Other factors proffered include the pursuit of education, for work, and for family-related reasons.[9] Though debated by some, Ricca's description of Africa as a "Continent perpetually on the move" is relevant here.[10] The relevance of his description is underscored given the continuous and arguably persistent South-North international or out-migration of African-born nationals from the continent. Relocation of African population occurred mainly via three main periods. The first was the forced migration of Africans during the Transatlantic Slave trade of the sixteenth to the nineteenth century (and not of interest to the present discussion). Nonetheless, the second and third periods of migration are germane to this discussion.

The second period of migration from Africa was during the late-colonial, early period post-independence era from the 1950s. Africans enthusiastically left Africa to pursue better working, educational, and quality of life opportunities. This era was characterized as having mainly "voluntary migration" and witnessed increasing migration of African nationals mainly to Europe and North America.[11]

The third migratory epoch commenced during the 1980s because of political persecution, wars, poverty, broken states and several other factors. The migrants fit diverse sociological classifications such as age, occupation status, gender, educational level, social class, and family structures. In most cases migration to Europe was an elite affair due to cost. Those who migrated often had scant intention of returning to their native land.[12] The level of relocation from Africa is underlined by the 2015 International Migration Report which suggests that of the 244 million international migrants worldwide, 34 million, or 14 percent, were born in the African continent. It is estimated that most Africans migrate to Europe. This trend is impacted by geographic propinquity and involvement with colonization. This is evident from the importation of migrant workers from North Africa into European countries such as Spain, Portugal, Malta, and Italy during the late 1970s. Substantial numbers of these immigrant workers remained in the countries and their numbers grew significantly.[13] It is estimated that around about 30 percent of all immigrants in Europe are from African countries such as Algeria, Tunis, and Morocco.[14]

Apart from European countries, Africans immigrate to North America, especially the United States of America. The 2015 International Migration Report categorizes the United States as home to the largest number of international immigrants (47 million; 19 percent). African migration to Europe and the North America is well acknowledged.[15] Africa's role as an origin region for migrants to the United States is documented by numerous authors.[16] The pre-1965 US immigration restrictions considerably hampered immigration of Africans to the United States, though non-Black Africans who were not affected by the US immigration restrictions accounted for whatever migration occurred during this period. [17] Despite their small growth during the 70s and 80s, between 1980 and 2009 relocated Africa-born migrants increased from fewer than 200,000 to about 1.5 million. Most of these African immigrants were from Eastern and Western Africa with the top countries of origin being Nigeria, Ethiopia, Egypt, Ghana, and Kenya. More than one-third of all African immigrants live in New York, California, Texas and Maryland.[18] Recent research findings suggest that African-born immigrant population to the United States has one of the fastest growing rates.[19]

Further, the beginning of the twenty-first century has been described as one that witnessed even more significant levels of African emigration to the United States. [20] The 2015 International Migration Report specifies that migration of African nationals to the United States is rather high. This is supported by statistics that reveal that from 2001 to 2010 28.4 percent of refugees and those granted asylum were African nationals. Additionally, nearly half (48 percent; 23,903) of all who won the diversity visa lottery program in 2010 (49,763 persons) were born in Africa. Between 2001 and 2010 more than 860,000 African immigrants gained lawful permanent residence in the United States.[21]

Interestingly, unlike the LAC region, most immigrants from Africa tend to be males. The 2015 International Migration Report advises that between the years 2000 and 2015 there was a 5 percent difference in the rate of men who migrated from Africa compared to females (42 percent males compared to 37 percent of females).[22] Gender variances were noted among immigrants from different countries. More males reportedly immigrated from Senegal (63.7 percent), Morocco (59.0 percent), Tanzania (58.3 percent), Ghana (57.6 percent), and Guinea (57.6 percent). More women reportedly emigrated from Zimbabwe (51.7 percent), Somalia (51.3 percent), Sierra Leone (50.6 percent), and Cape Verde (50.2 percent).[23] Nonetheless, even though this disparity exists, some authors report that the feminization of migration is a phenomenon that currently affects migration from Africa.[24]

Another striking characteristic of relocated Africans is that African-born adults are more likely to have bachelor's degrees or higher level of education compared to US-born natives. The differences in reporting high educational levels vary by countries of origin. For example, immigrants from Uganda (66.5 percent), Egypt (61.1 percent), Algeria (61 percent), Nigeria (60 percent), Zimbabwe (57.5 percent), South Africa (55.3 percent), Cameroon (54.6 percent), and Tanzania (51.2 percent) report having a bachelor's degree or higher education compared to immigrants from Cape Verde (38.4 percent), Somalia (37.5 percent), and Guinea (35 percent) who reportedly lacked a high school diploma.[25] The entering of a foreign country with high levels of education has implications for relocation experiences for immigrants as well as potential benefits and losses to the sending country.

In addition to Europe and North America, African nationals also migrate to Asia. The 2015 International Migration Report advises that Asia is one of the fastest growing destinations for African migrants. Migration to the Middle East, China, the Maghreb countries, and Gulf States are also noted. Migration to Gulf States and Israel has increased since the 1980s as these countries rely on non-Arab labor from sub-Saharan countries. Moreover, due to fear of reliance on Arab labor, oil-rich countries such as Saudi Arabia and Libya attracted laborers from Egypt, Sudan, Somalia, Eritrea, and Ethiopia.[26]

While this discussion is a brief synopsis of relocation of African-born nationals, it provides some insight into the phenomenon and sets the stage for later examination. Let us now shift our focus on the LAC region and their relocation experiences.

LAC Region

This discussion of international migration in the LAC region is by no means a novel undertaking. Instead such a task has been completed by several more competent authorities.[27] For this discussion, the LAC region is comprised of thirty-three countries: Antigua and Barbuda, Argentina, Barbados, Belize, Bolivia, Brazil, Chile, Colombia, Costa Rica, Cuba, Dominica (Commonwealth of), Dominican Republic, Ecuador, El Salvador, Grenada, Guatemala, Guyana, Haiti, Honduras, Jamaica, Mexico, Nicaragua, Panama, Paraguay, Peru, Saint Kitts and Nevis, Saint Lucia, Saint Vincent and the Grenadines, Suriname, The Bahamas, Trinidad and Tobago, Uruguay, Venezuela (Bolivarian Republic of).[28]

Two broad phases of relocation may be applicable to the LAC region. Within these two broad phases, mainly three migratory patterns have been suggested in the literature. These are: overseas immigration to Latin America, intraregional migration, and emigration by LAC nationals to countries outside of the region.[29] While all the patterns are important, prominence is given to the third pattern: South-North migration from the LAC region is pertinent to the present discussion. Often when South-North migration is discussed, the literature tends to refer to the South as poor developing societies and the North as developed industrialized societies.[30]

South-North migration by LAC nationals is no new phenomenon. Instead, the flow of migrants to developed countries in the North has fluctuated over the years. Commenting on this, Lohrmann declares that the most prevailing type of migration in Latin America post 1945 was irregular in nature and unproblematic until the late 1960s.[31] It is important to note here that mostly South-North migration is discussed and measured within the context of domination, reliance, inequality, and the attraction for another country by LAC nationals. The attraction frequently stems from the perceptions of enhanced and easier access to opportunities, and ultimately a better quality of life.

The South-North migration by LAC nationals generally tend to flow mainly toward specific destinations. Increased numbers of persons from the region migrate mainly to various European countries, Canada, Japan, and the United States. The variations in emigration movement often are associated with changes in legislation in some receiving countries' immigration policies. For instance, though initially migrants were solicited from other European countries, after 1945 some Caribbean countries were a part of the New Commonwealth countries (former British colonies) and they became pivotal providers of immigrant workers for Britain.[32] Concerning this period, Thomas-Hope accounts that Caribbean migration during the 1950s and 60s involved mainly travel to the United Kingdom and the Netherlands.[33]

By the mid-1990s immigrants from other regions including Latin America and Caribbean destinations were common in Southern and Western Europe. More specifically, such migrants went to countries such as Spain, Ireland, and Italy. These migratory trends happen together with some European integration policies. Two such strategies were the establishment of the borderless Schengen zone, and the attendant reinforcement of border controls of the European Union's external borders.[34] The Economic Commission for Latin America and the Caribbean (ECLAC) in their 2014 report advise that Spain is the second most popular destination place for LAC nationals. The report shows that at least 2.4 million people (8 percent) migrated there.[35]

Emigration to Japan is also noteworthy here. Immigrants from Brazil and Peru who can trace direct Japanese descent tend to benefit more from such relocation. Temporary return migration to Japan by Brazilians commenced in the early 1980s (1980–84) with mainly first-generation Japanese who had some ties there and were familiar with the language. Their migration was a precursor to later substantial migration drifts to Japan by Brazilians. Thus, by 1985 because of Brazilian economic crisis and Japan economic boom that forced the acquisition of more workers. Japanese capitalized on Brazilians as a new source of such labor and engaged in massive advertisement campaigns in Brazil. Often the first-generation return Japanese migrants were instrumental in soliciting Japanese Brazilians for the Japan's workforce. Consequently, over one million Brazilians migrated after securing jobs in Japan between 1986 and 1990. This recruitment effort later extended to Argentina and Paraguay.[36]

The Canadian impartial "points system" for picking prospective migrants was one provision that gave impetus to immigration by LAC nationals to relocate to Canada. The "White Paper" policy of 1966 legitimated the mass exodus of LAC immigrants into Canada. During this period immigrants were perceived as settlers and future citizens and families were encouraged to migrate. Thus, by 1970 Jamaica and Trinidad were among the main sourcing countries for immigrants into Canada.[37] Though LAC nationals migrate to Europe, Asia, and Canada in record numbers, there is almost unanimous argument among migration authorities and researchers respectively that the United States is by far the prototypical South-North flow for LAC nationals.

Several LAC nationals relocate to the United States following World War II. The arrival of workers from the Bahamas, Jamaica, Barbados, Saint Vincent, Saint Lucia, and Dominica is documented. The large-scale migration of Puerto Ricans, Cubans, Dominicans, and persons from the Dominican Republic, is also noteworthy of mention here. Latin Americana nationals are often described as playing a major role in the foreign-born population growth of the United States. The most significant of such role is given to Mexico and Cuba, which are considered top sending countries.

The Bureau of Census suggests that for the 1990s 8,416,924 persons of LAC origin migrated to the United States. Mexico, Cuba, El Salvador, Guatemala, Nicaragua, Haiti, San Salvador are among the countries with the largest number of persons migrating to the United States. Such migration influenced by dependency, colonization, and agricultural labor and other relationships.[38] Supporting the above information is a 2014 report by the ECLAC. The report suggests that for LAC states about 28.5 million of LAC people live outside of the region with about 70 percent of them living in the United States with most being Mexicans (12 million).[39] It is evident from this discussion that relocation from Africa and LAC countries affects large numbers of persons. Exactly how such relocation influences the migrant, host countries, and source countries is the focus of the remainder of this chapter.

ISSUES AND CHALLENGES OF RELOCATION

We have noted from the earlier discussion that several African and LAC nationals have migrated or relocated to countries outside of their regions. The matter that now confronts us is determining the impact of such relocation on African and LAC countries and the migrants themselves. This section addresses some of the issues. Relocation of nationals from Africa and LAC countries has been shown to affect these societies in both negative and positive ways. It offers new opportunities, but also raises great concerns in some instances. Some of the areas affected by relocation include ethnic and cultural composition of the region, social and economic modernization, demographic transition, internal displacement of the population and their geographic distribution, the adoption of legal principles and the democratic institutional framework.[40]

Relocation of nationals from the two regions incurs several contradictory aspects that both benefit and harm migrants from the two regions under discussion. Using the sociological "eye" focus will be on presenting some of the sociopolitical positives and negatives outcomes of relocation. Examination will be at the micro and macro levels of society. At the micro level, the impact on the migrant him/herself will be explored. The effect on families, especially children, and the feminization of migration and rise of trafficking in human beings, especially girls and women will be presented. At the macro level the emigration of skilled health and other professionals from the region, huge remittance flows, and contributions to GDP will be exposed.

Issues and Challenges to the Immigrant

There is no denying that relocation to another country brings several positive and negative changes. The immigrant status, reason for migration, one's social class, educational level, duration of the migration, geographic destination, population composition, voluntary or forced nature of the relocation, all serve to influence the relocation experience in the host country. Those who relocate legally with all required documentation are apt to get settled into a job and some degree of normalcy quicker than those who migrate illegally or relocate as refugees or other asylum seekers. Nonetheless, regardless of the immigration status of those who relocate multiple stresses can be experienced.

These stresses can in some cases even impact one's well-being.[41] International migration whether permanent or semi-permanent could contribute to stress which may result from one or a combination of these stressors: loss of one's cultural norms, religious customs, climate changes, language differences, food choices, social support systems, adjustment to a new culture, changes in identity and self-concept, experiences with xenophobia, difficulties communicating, mobility issues, differences in educational setup and requirements, employment requirements, job recruitment procedures, are in no way an exhaustive list of stressors.

In compiling this chapter, two persons were arbitrarily asked about their relocation experiences. Each person was asked to share his/her experience as an immigrant and to pinpoint what they think was a great stressor he/she had to overcome. Mrs. Dexter [a pseudonym] reports that she along with her husband and three sons entered the United States as permanent residents. For her, the stress she faced was placing her oldest son in a high school. Though the child spoke only English, she was informed that the child must take English for speakers of other languages (ESOL) classes. Though she tried to explain to the principal of the local high school that though she was from South

America, her first and only language was English, this information was dismissed. After about four trips to the school board she was finally able to find one officer who was willing to listen. The officer looked on a map for Mrs. Dexter's home country and realized that English was the official language, and that there was no need for the child to take the ESOL exam or be placed in ESOL classes. This lack of knowledge of other cultures and by extension the school system contributed to stress and several expensive and unnecessary trips to the school board to sort things out. Bear in mind that Mrs. Dexter did not have a driver's license yet, did not own a car, did not really understand how the bus system worked, and generally was lost in a new system.[42] Her experience was not unique.

Mr. Mayfield [a pseudonym] joking related a few of the stressors he faced as an immigrant to the United States. He stated that his biggest anxiety was getting familiar with the language used in the United States. For example, he shared how the differences in the names of things sometimes cause confusion and even inconveniences. He recounted how on one lunch break he asked his coworkers to buy him some chips and two pieces of chicken from a renowned fast food restaurant. To his dismay, they returned with the chicken and a very small pack of potato chips in a packet. Mr. Mitchell really wanted some fries, but used the name "chips" which he knew previously to describe what he wanted. He also expressed how he had to learn the differences between biscuits and crackers; a pop versus a soda; boots versus tennis shoes or sneakers, windshield versus windscreen, dinner versus supper, and so many other things.[43]

In both cases above, the migrants were somewhat lost due to some things being different. This loss of the familiar Eisenbruch calls grief reaction. Grief may arise from loss of things that are familiar to the migrant such as social structures, cultural values, and self and group-identity. Eisenbruch suggests such grief reaction is a normal and healthy reaction to immigrants as long as such reactions are not prolonged to the point of affecting sleep and day-to-day interaction and functioning.[44] Similarly, Bhugra and Becker suggest that relocation may result in cultural bereavement and loss of one's cultural identity. In some instances, the migrant may relocate and leave his relatives behind. The absence of family members in dealing with stressful situations, celebrations of success and other matters cannot be overstated.[45]

In some instances, relocation to countries or states where the migrant has no cultural or ethnic connections may pose a great challenge. In some instances, the challenge is assimilating to the culture. Learning the correct terminologies and terms for items, foods and so on as expressed by Mr. Mayfield and Mrs. Dexter above. Our identities are formed as a consequence of and by our experiences with our culture. Hence, older persons who migrate to cultures that are significantly different from what they know often find it harder to assimilate.

Conversely, those who migrate to cultures and societies where there exists a migrant community often find it less challenging to assimilate. Despite the cultural enclaves that may buffer assimilation into the host country's culture, cultural changes in themselves are challenging to one's identify and sense of self. In some instances, the migrant may suffer from culture shock, cultural confusion, feelings of alienation, and depression.

In some instances, cultural changes such as language differences tend to make it even harder for successful relocation. One older migrant, for example, shared that upon his arrival he had to take time to first learn the language of his host country. Once he had successfully learned the language, he then spent several years studying for a career. By the time he became qualified and knew the new language sufficiently to seek employment however, he was quite near the host country's age of retirement and employers' hesitancy in employing older persons negatively impacted his acquisition of "suitable" employment.

With relocation often comes the anxiety of finding employment, in some cases acquiring higher education, achieving financially, and fitting into the host country as a productive member of society. The lack of opportunities for advancement coupled with racism, xenophobic experiences, legal concerns, poor housing, and other issues may all contribute to hardships and, in some cases, culminate in mental health problems for some migrants.[46] Several other issues may affect migrants who relocate.

On the more positive side, however, international migration may afford the migrant an opportunity to develop his/her independence. It may allow them approaches for refining their economic, educational, and overall well-being. In some cases, migrants tend to improve both their own economic circumstances as well as that of family members left behind. For some women migration allows them a chance to pursue education, manage their own affairs, take control of their lives and make decisions, which they could not do in their home country. In the case of refugees, relocation though challenging may afford them an opportunity to stay alive, provide a safe-haven for their families, allows them access to the necessities of life along with medical care, and in some cases, provides opportunities to start over in a new place.[47]

For children and youth who migrate from African and LAC countries several conflicting characteristics are noted. UNICEF notes that, on the positive side, children and youth migration tends to most likely afford these young people better educational opportunities than that which is available in their countries of origin. Migration could allow them a safe space away from violence, drug related crimes, gang involvement, and other social risk behaviors and environments.[48]

Issues and Challenges on Families

Similar to personal benefits, migration affects families both positively and negatively. Various types of relocation patterns involving families exist: accompanying or dependent family members may enter with the primary migrant; family reunification in which spouses or children or other relatives join an immigrant; family formation in which a citizen may marry a foreigner; families who migrate to escape some social ill such as war, natural disasters or persecution.[49] Regardless of how families relocate, the one constant fact is that migration of families is complex and influenced by socioeconomic, demographic and political factors.[50]

One challenge of family migration is the role of women in migration. Though previously it was noted that migration of women from African countries is less than that of men, the fact remains that the role of women as it relates to immigration is changing rapidly. The feminization of migration is a new trend that is steadily increasing. In the LAC context, more women migrate than men. In the wider scheme of things, migration of females is closely tied to the changing roles of women as providers in families. Some migrant women are forced to take jobs that may expose them to violence, sexual exploitation, human trafficking, drug abuse, and in extreme cases even death.

Supporting this view is the International Organization for Migration (IOM), which advises that a significant proportion of family migration involves female migrants. The IOM states that for 2013, 48 percent of all international migrants worldwide were comprised of women.[51] In several instances some women who migrate work and remit resources to support their male counterparts who may have been left behind, children, parents, and other relatives.

For some families when the mother is the migrant the family left behind may experience several positive and negative benefits. On the positive side of things, when the situation of children and elderly parents and other relatives are examined migration could be very accommodating. For those who are left behind, their living conditions may improve significantly due to remittances from the migrant family member(s). At times, they may be able to more readily access better services such as health care. Instead of going to a free public hospital in one of the African or LAC countries, persons with family members who have migrated to the North often can secure the funds to seek private medical care, which for most times is of a higher quality than that provided by the publicly run state facilities. In other cases, the family members left in the home country may also be able to access better quality education, and other goods.[52]

On the negative side, however, when the migrant parent is a mother, she may be forced to leave her children behind. Separation anxieties for both parents and children cannot be ruled out as a negative effect. Realizing family reunification sometimes is too expensive and drawn out for some families. At times while waiting for such processes to work, some families drift apart. Husbands and wives may separate and/or even divorce. Children may "age out," making it often impossible for the mother to sponsor them to the host country. This often leads to acts of delinquency, emotional stress, anger by the children, mistrust and loss of respect for the mother, truancy, early marriage for girls, increased risk of drug use and abuse, feelings of having been abandoned by the mother, and other issues. For the father who may be left to manage the family several socio-emotional issues may arise that may contribute to frustration for the father, lack of know-how in dealing with children of all genders may exacerbate the situation and intensify tensions and frustrations in the family as well. For the mother, this most likely increases her emotional stress and anxiety, which could negatively impact her day-to-day activities.

In other cases, families may experience problems finding the required fees, navigating the reunification process (especially in a society where language is a barrier), successfully completing required tests, showing sufficient income/financial thresholds to sponsor children and/or a spouse left behind is quite a bother and could delay the process of reunification. In some cases, such delays may result in poor parent-child relations developing.[53]

Relocation may affect families in other ways. In some instances, migration, may pose substantial socioeconomic challenges. Families who migrate illegally may face the risk of abuse, abandonment, and exploitation. Sometimes due to illegal migration the family may often be denied access to support and social services in the host country. This truly becomes an issue if one or more family members become sick and requires medical attention. The sometimes harsh and restrictive policies that migrant families must overcome often have negative consequences for their well-being. Such restrictive policies also do not really benefit the host country either. The frustrations, delays, restrictions, and delayed reunification of families often hinder the migrant's successfully contribution to the host country. More effort is spent trying to navigate the system than really assimilating and integrating into the new society.[54] These are but some of the challenges and issues the migrant family must navigate and transcend.

ECONOMIC ISSUES AND CHALLENGES ASSOCIATED WITH RELOCATION: FOCUS ON SOURCE COUNTRIES

One impact of international relocation on African and LAC countries is economic development. Hein De Haas suggests that migration should be considered a process that is naturally linked economic development. Though often contradictory, the general idea is that immigration is considered a means of positively improving the country of origin's economic growth and development. One way to measure such economic development is via remittances received from migrants. Though grossly underreported, both the LAC and African countries usually experience high flows of remittances. The World Bank suggests that the volume of remittances has substantial effects on the receiving countries. For, example, the World Bank proposes that for 2006 remittances back to developing countries equaled the amount of official assistance received by developing countries; US$221 billion.[55] The World Bank further suggests that remittances via informal channels could potentially contribute 50 percent to the globally recorded flows.[56] The World Bank reports that while remittances declined by 2.4 percent for 2016 for developing countries generally, for Latin America and the Caribbean, however, an increase of 6.9 percent was recorded in remittance flows to the region. This trend is projected to continue in 2017.[57]

Remittances is one of the most visible and apparent economic effect. In some instances, remittances can fund human capital investments such as education, health, private investment in physical capital when migrants establish businesses and provide new sources of employment in source countries.[58] These types of remittances are visible normally at the micro and macroeconomic levels of society. They usually influence the economy on a more permanent basis, and are counted as factors for development, which in the long run may reduce poverty and increase per capita incomes—a somewhat optimistic view of migration's contribution to source countries.[59] Taylor suggests that one [positive] way in which migrants' relocation affects the source country micro economics is by them remitting a portion of their income to household budgets of those who remain in the source country. Another way is by some of them investing in both the source and host countries.[60] For the LAC region, for example, Ratha et al state that for 2015 LAC countries experienced the most rapid growth rate of remittances, 4.8 percent.[61]

Conversely, a negative or more cynical view of relocation is its negative effect on the source country. This view is taken when the background of most immigrants is considered: mostly entrepreneurs, young, educated, highly skilled and qualified persons migrate. The exodus of these people out of the source country may lead to the conclusion that migration exacerbates poverty. [62] Further, some question the effectiveness of remittances when it is noted that only a small amount of remittances is used productively.

Some authors suggest that remittances merely help in the maintaining of a minimum standard of living at the micro level. Some direct that due to the poverty level extant in the source country, remittances in most cases are used for day-to-day expenses—for providing basic short-term goods and services for the emigrants' families. The potential issue with remittances is that they often encourage dependence and, in some cases, lead to structural dependence. That is, some families' structural dependence on financial assistance and their reduction in work aspirations while they wait for the emigrants' remittances. This type of dependency and incurred "laziness" leads some to conclude that remittances are not sufficient to promote any social mobility in the source countries.[63]

Empirical research findings related to the economic effects of remittances in LAC and African countries are mixed. While some studies show no evidence that remittances positively affect economic growth rate,[64]others suggest the opposite.[65] Interestingly, however, is the definition of "productive" and the debate about what is meant. Some authors suggest that remittances are used to buy luxury items. However, other researchers have found that often these luxury items are used in creative ways to create avenues to provide economic cushions to families in source countries.[66]

Spending much time in the LAC region has allowed the author to note the "productive" use of "luxury" items acquired from remittances in several LAC countries. For example, some families have used their remittances received from emigrants to purchase vehicles (maybe a car or in many instances mini-vans). These vehicles are often used as taxis or mini-buses. This provides jobs for family members and in several instances for others outside of the immediate family. Likewise, some persons have used television sets (acquired either directly from emigrants or from remitted cash), stereo sets, hair dryers, computers, cameras, and several other items remitted to them or bought with remitted cash as a means of income and job creation for themselves and others. In several instances, these items have been used to create small businesses which sustain families. So, the debate about how "productive" remittances are in reducing micro level economic hardships remains. While some studies have been conducted, more research in this area is required. The LAC and African regions provide much scope for such research.

Brain Drain and Development Concerns and Issues

The relationship between international migration, brain drain and economic development is no new one. Education has been cited as one of the paramount components of long-term economic growth. Bearing this in mind therefore, the archetypal argument that has arisen is that the international migration of people endowed with a high level of human capital is detrimental to source countries. It has been established that relocation from Africa and the LAC regions usually involves the movement of skilled, highly educated persons. This movement of highly educated and skilled persons from the society is often referred to as "brain drain" or the "International mobility of talent."[67]

The brain drain problem is one of the challenges facing source countries. Brain drain reflects the interaction between skills shortages in the First-World countries and the supply of highly educated individuals, who are trained in emerging economies and developing countries. It involves the willingness of these professionals to migrate internationally due to their professional ambitions.[68]

The seriousness of this problem for source countries in Africa is noted by the warning of the UN Economic Commission for Africa Dr. Lalla Ben Barka who states, "In 25 years, Africa will be empty of brains."[69] This warning comes amidst the recognition that the African continent is losing the personnel it needs most for economic, scientific, social and technological progress. For African countries brain drain due to immigration brings financial, institutional, and societal costs.[70] The International Development Research Center (IDRC) notes that since 1990 Africa loses 20,000 professionals annually with more than 30,000 professionals living outside of the continent. It is estimated that there are more African scientists and engineers in the United States than in the entire African continent.[71]

The challenge facing African countries are many. First, to satisfy the needs of the professional sectors, institutions are forced to solicit foreign expertise. In some cases, as much as 150,000 expatriate professionals are employed annually at a cost of US$4 billion.[72] Second, the international mobility of talent in the health and other social service fields has contributed to the erosion of the health and social services available. To this end, research suggest that 47 of the sub-Saharan countries fall short of the World Health Organization standard of 20 physicians per 100, 000 people.[73] Third, this affects the ability of the region to compete in the world education arena. UNESCO reports that the African continent is trying to augment their capabilities in science and technology. Though other reasons were proffered for the continent's poor performance in the two areas, one focal cause for their region's challenge was brain drain. The Report states that for 2009 at minimum, a third of African researchers lived abroad.[74] Additionally, in several instances its investment in education sees little return as either most graduates emigrate from the continent or those who are given scholarships to study abroad do not return home upon completion of their studies.[75]

For the LAC region, a similar trend is noted. The UN statistics for the region suggests that 83 percent of the LAC population who reside outside the region lives in North America. This is one reason for concern about the brain drain problem in this region. This is no new problem. As of 2000 for instance, over 80 percent of all college educated people from Haiti, Jamaica, and Guyana were living outside the region.[76]

Data from Özden's study show that about 3.5 percent of the LAC labor force lives in the United States. Nonetheless, when data for specific country were disaggregated in some cases countries had as much as 30 percent of its labor force living abroad. The data also reveal that for some LAC countries, large numbers of college-educated persons who had relocated to the United

States originated from smaller, poorer and some medium-sized countries in the LAC region (Jamaica, Haiti, Guyana, Belize, Grenada, El Salvador, Guatemala, Honduras, Nicaragua and Panama).[77] The social, economic, and political implication of such loss of educated persons from the LAC region cannot be overemphasized in terms of the argument for loss of highly trained and skilled human capital, resultant reduced productivity, competitiveness and loss in social welfare.[78]

On the more positive side of things, however, though the initial emigration of professional and technical personnel may result in brain drain for the source or origin country, both sending and receiving countries can benefit from access to new markets, new technologies and contacts established with the outflow of some entrepreneurs to developed countries. In other cases, source countries may benefit from the return of or the continued connection with scientists, entrepreneurs, university professors, and scholars who live abroad.

The phenomenon of brain drain may encourage educational growth and stimulate economic progress in source countries. In some instances, these benefits may be derived partially from remittances. Such remittances may include financial assistance and scholarship opportunities for others to access educational opportunities locally, joint teaching and research appointments, exchange of new and improved ideas for education, manufacture and other development areas, increased investment and entrepreneurship may all accrue for countries of origin.[79] The importance of addressing the brain drain issues and challenges in source countries is crucial. A number of workable policies should be enacted including those that encourage and provide stimuli for persons to remain in the source countries, improvement stimulating and competitive environments for educated persons, offering attractive remuneration packets to skilled and educated persons, establishing and maintaining links with diasporas who have migrated are but a few suggestions for restricting the flow of skilled and educated and hence reducing the hemorrhaging of the regions talents.

CONCLUSION

This chapter has examined the issues and challenges nationals born in Africa and the LAC regions face when they relocate. The role of migration in the development of the countries was also explored. The chapter clearly shows that the United States receives a greater portion of all migrants from Africa and the LAC region. The information presented reveals that relocation from the diaspora countries in LAC region and of persons from the African mainland continues to pose a threat to social and economic development of the two regions. While this chapter mainly focused on South-North migration, the growth of South-South migration and its resultant issues for the regions were obvious and worthy of attention in future discussions of migration. The need for countries of origin to devise policies to reduce the level of migration cannot be overlooked.

The importance of foster, fertilizing, and maintaining linkages and partnerships between and among diasporas and specific institutions in the source countries cannot be exaggerated. This is one sure way to retain lucrative connections with migrants. Such connections it is hoped will assist in the facilitation of research, social and economic investments as well as greater exchange of remittances. Though the earlier discussion highlighted some of the negative drawbacks from remittances to source countries, surely the reader also noted the preponderance of positive effects of such remittances back to the countries of origin. Such remittances can hopefully serve to enhance the acquisition of up-to-date technological devices and equipment, new technologies, virtual networks and even newer ideas geared at better political leadership in some countries.

NOTES

1. Andrés Solimano, Global Migration and International Development in Unstable Times. International Center for Globalization and Development, Working paper No. 25, June, 2016, p. 7.

2. United Nations, United Nations Recommendations on Statistics of International Migration, Revision 1 *in International Migration Flows to and From Selected Countries: The 2015 Revision Cd-Rom Documentation*, United Nations Economic and Social Affairs, Population Division, December, 2015, p. 1.

3. United Nations (nd). Sustainable Development Goals: 17 Goals to Transform our World. Accessed http://www.un.org/sustainabledevelopment/blog/2016/01/244-million-international-migrants-living-abroad-worldwide-new-un-statistics-reveal/

4. See Robin Cohen, Ed. *The Cambridge Survey of World Migration*, New York, NY. Cambridge University Press, 1995; Magnus Mörner and Harold Sims, *Adventurers and Proletarians, the Story of Migrants in Latin America.* Pittsburgh, PA: University of Pittsburgh Press, 1985; Stephen Castles, Hein de Haas, and Mark J. Miller, *The Age of Migration: International Population Movements in the Modern World* 5th Edition. New York, NY: Guilford Press, 2014, pp. 84–95.

5. UN Department of Economic and Social Affairs, International Migration Report 2015. United Nations New York, 2016, p. 5. Retrieved http://www.un.org/en/development/desa/population/migration/publications/migrationreport/docs/MigrationReport2015_Highlights.pdf.

6. United Nations, United Nations Recommendations on Statistics of International Migration, Revision 1 *in International Migration Flows to and from Selected*

Countries: The 2015 Revision Cd-Rom Documentation, United Nations Economic and Social Affairs, Population Division, December, 2015, p. 1.

7. Ibid., P. 5. Retrieved http://www.un.org/en/development/desa/population/migration/publications/migrationreport/docs/MigrationReport2015_Highlights.pdf.

8. Douglas S. Massey, "Patterns and Processes of International Migration in the 21st Century," Conference on African Migration in Comparative Perspective, Johannesburg, South Africa, 4–7 June, 2003. pp.1–41.

9. Oliver Bakewell, & Ayla Bonfiglio, Moving Beyond Conflict: Re-framing mobility in the African Great Lakes region. Working paper for the African Great Lakes Mobility Project, Volume IMI working paper 71. Oxford: International Migration Institutes, University of Oxford, 2013, p. 4.

10. Sergio Ricca, 1989 *International Migration in Africa: Legal and Administrative Aspects*. Geneva: International Labour Office, 1989. p. v.

11. The ICD, "Experience Africa" Program. The African Diaspora. Introduction to the African Diaspora Across the world. nd. Retrieved http://www.experience-africa.de/index.php?en_the-african-diaspora

12. Ibid.

13. Castles, Stephen, and Mark J. Miller, "The Age of Migration: International Population Movements in the Modern World," in Douglas S. Massey, *Patterns and Processes of International Migration in the 21st Century*, Paper prepared for Conference on African Migration in Comparative Perspective, Johannesburg, South Africa, 4–7 June, 2003, pp. 7.

14. Douglas S. Massey, *Patterns and Processes of International Migration in the 21st Century*, Paper prepared for Conference on African Migration in Comparative Perspective, Johannesburg, South Africa, 4–7 June, 2003, pp. 7.

15. David Van Moppes, *The African Migration Movement: Routes to Europe*. The Working Papers on Migration and Development, Report No. 5. Nijmegen, The Netherlands: Research Group on Migration and Development, Radboud University; Carling, Jorgen,Unauthorized Migration from Africa to Spain. *International Migration,* Volume 45, no. 4, 2007, pp. 3–37.

16. Kristen McCabe, African Immigrants in the United States. Migration Policy Institute, July 21, 2011. Retrieved http://www.migrationpolicy.org/article/african-immigrants-united-states; Randy Capps, Kristen McCabe, and Michael Fix, *New Streams: Black African Migration to the United States*. Washington, DC: Migration Policy Institute, 2011.

17. Yanyi K. Djamba, "African Immigrants in the United States: A Socio-demographic Profile in Comparison to Native Blacks." *Journal of Asian and African Studies*, Volume 34, 1999, pp. 210–215.

18. Kristen McCabe, African Immigrants in the United States, p?

19. Rubén. G. Rumbaut, "Origins and Destinies: Immigration to the United States since World War II." *Sociological Forum,* Volume 9, no. 4, 1994, pp.583–621.

20. Mary Mederios Kent, "Immigration and America's Black Population." *Population Bulletin,* Volume 62, no., 2007, pp.3–16.

21. Kristen McCabe, African Immigrants in the United States, p?

22. UN Department of Economic and Social Affairs, International Migration Report 2015, United Nations New York, 2016, pp.10–11.

23. Kristen McCabe, African Immigrants in the United States, p?

24. Catherine Cross, Derik Gelderblom, Niel Roux, and Jonathan Mafukidze, Editors, Views on Migration in Sub-Sahara Africa. *Proceedings of an African Migration Alliance Workshop*. Cape Town, South Africa, HSRC Press, 2006. p. 24.

25. Kristen McCabe, African Immigrants in the United States, p?

26. Stephen Castles, Hein de Haas, and Mark J. Miller, *The Age of Migration: International Population Movements in the Modern World*. New York, NY: Guilford Press, 2014, pp 172–197.

27. Jorge Martínez Pizarro and Miguel Villa, "International Migration In Latin America and the Caribbean: A Summary View of Trends and Patterns," United Nations Expert Group Meeting on International Migration and Development, Population Division Department of Economic and Social Affairs United Nations Secretariat. New York, July 6–8, 2005, pp. 1–6;

28. Jorge Martínez Pizarro and Miguel Villa, "Countries in Latin America and the Caribbean," *Worldometers*. Retrieved August 22, 2016. http://www.worldometers.info/geography/how-many-countries-in-latin-america/; Alvarado Iván González and Hilda Sánchez, "Trends in the Region—Migration in Latin America and the Caribbean: A view from the ICFTU/ORIT," n.d. Retrieved August 20, 2016. library.fes.de/pdf-files/gurn/00084.pdf. p.101. Baltica Cabieses, Helena Tunstall, Kate E. Pickett, and Jasmine Gideon, "Changing Patterns of Migration in Latin America: How can Research Develop Intelligence for Public Health?" *Rev Panam Salud Publica*, Volume 34, no.1, 2013, pp. 68–74.

29. Pizzaro and Villa, International Migration in Latin America, 1–10; Alvarado Iván Gonzálezand Hilda Sánchez, "Trends in the Region—Migration in Latin America and the Caribbean: A view from the ICFTU/ORIT," n.d. Retrieved August 20, 2016. library.fes.de/pdf-files/gurn/00084.pdf. p.101. Baltica Cabieses, Helena Tunstall, Kate E. Pickett, and Jasmine Gideon, "Changing Patterns of Migration in Latin America: How can Research Develop Intelligence for Public Health?" *Rev Panam Salud Publica*, Volume 34, no.1, 2013, pp. 68–74; Alvarado Iván Gonzálezand Hilda Sánchez, "Trends in the Region—Migration in Latin America and the Caribbean: A view from the ICFTU/ORIT," n.d. Retrieved August 20, 2016. library.fes.de/pdf-files/gurn/00084.pdf. p.101; Baltica Cabieses, Helena Tunstall, Kate E. Pickett, and Jasmine Gideon, "Changing Patterns of Migration in Latin America: How can Research Develop Intelligence for Public Health?" *Rev Panam Salud Publica*, Volume 34, no.1, 2013, pp. 68–74.

30. Pizarro, Jorge Martines, International migration in Latin América and the Caribbean: A summary view of trends and patterns. Santiago, Chile: Economic Commission for Latin America and Center for Latin American Research in Demography, 2005.

31. R. Lohrmann. "Irregular Migration: A Rising Issue in Developing Countries." *International Migration*, Volume 25, no. 3, 1987, pp. 253–266.

32. Migration in Europe since 1945. In Stephen Castles, Hein de Haas, and Mark J. Miller, *The Age of Migration: International Population Movements in the Modern World* 5th Edition. New York, NY: Guilford Press, 2014, pp. 102–125.

33. Elizabeth Thomas-Hope, Trends and Patterns of Migration to and from Caribbean Countries, 2014, pp. 1.2.5. Retrieved http://www.cepal.org/en/search?as_q=ECLAC%20immigration%20report%202014.

34. Ibid., 102–125.

35. ECLAC, "Around 28.5 Million Latin American and Caribbean People Live Outside their Native Countries," Intraregional migration flows have intensified in recent years, according to a new study by ECLAC. Retrieved http://www.cepal.org/en/pressreleases/around-285-million-latin-american-and-caribbean-people-live-outside-their-native.

36. Higuchi, Naoto, Brazilian Migration to Japan: Trends, Modalities and Impact. Expert Group Meeting on International Migration and Development in Latin America and the Caribbean Population Division Department of Economic and Social Affairs, United Nations Secretariat Mexico City, 30 November–2 December 2005, 2006, p. 3.

37. R. Breton, W.W Isajiw, W.E Kalbach, and J.G Reitz. *Ethnic identity and equality*. Toronto: Toronto University Press, 1990.

38. Rubén G. Rumbaut, *Origins and Destinies*, pp. 594–599.

39. ECLAC, "Around 28.5 Million Latin American and Caribbean People Live Outside their Native Countries," p?

40. Bárcena, Alicia. *Migration in Latin America and the Caribbean at the Service of Development and Human Rights.* Economic Commission for Latin America and the Caribbean (ECLAC), 2016. Retrieved December 6, 2016. http://www.cepal.org/en/articles/2016-migration-latin-america-and-caribbean-service-development-and-human-rights.

41. Dinesh Bhugra and Matthew A. Becker, Migration, Cultural Bereavement and Cultural Identity, *World Psychology*, Volume 4, no. 1, 2005, pp. 18–24.

42. Face- to-face discussion held November 11, 2016.

43. Telephone discussion held October 21, 2016.

44. M. Eisenbruch, "From Post-Traumatic Stress Disorder to Cultural Bereavement: Diagnosis of Southeast Asian Refugees." *Social Science and Medicine*, Volume 33, 1991, pp. 673–680.

45. Dinesh Bhugra and Matthew A. Becker, Migration, Cultural Bereavement and Cultural Identity, pp. 19–21.

46. Ibid., p. 21.

47. Rut Feuk, Nadine Perrault and Enrique Delamónica, *Children and International and the Caribbean Migration in Latin America.* ECLAC, United Nations, UNICEF. Challenges, Newsletter on progress toward the Millennium Development Goals from a child rights perspective. November 11, 2010.

48. Ibid.

49. World Bank, Migration and Families, International Dialogue on Migration (IDM), 2014: Human Mobility And Development: Emerging Trends and New Opportunities for Partnerships Intersessional Workshop, October 7 & 8, 2014. International Organization for Migration (IOM), Background paper. p. 2.

50. Ibid.

51. Ibid.

52. Ibid

53. Ibid.

54. Ibid., pp. 4–6.

55. World Bank, *Global Economic Prospects: Economic Implications of Remittances and Migration.* Washington, DC: World Bank, 2006.

56. Ibid.

57. *World Bank. Migration and Remittances. Recent Development and Outlook. Special Topic: Global Compact on Migration.* Brief 27, April 2017. P. V. Retrieved http://pubdocs.worldbank.org/en/992371492706371662/MigrationandDevelopmentBrief27.pdf.

58. Hein De Haas, *Migration Transitions: A Theoretical and Empirical Inquiry into the Developmental Drivers of International Migration.* In: XXVI IUSSP International Population Conference. Marrakech, Morocco. October 2, 2009, pp. 1–49.

59. Giuliano, P.; Ruiz-Arranz, M. Remittances, "Financial Development and Growth." *Journal of Development Economics*, Volume 90, 2009, pp. 144–152.

60. J.Edward Taylor, "International Migration, Remittances and Development: Myths and Facts." *International Migration*, Volume 37, no.1, 1999, pp. 63–88.

61. Dilip Ratha, et al. *Migration and Remittances Recent Developments and Outlook.* Migration and Development Brief 26, Global Knowledge Partnership on Migration and Development (KNOMAD), April 2016, p. 7.

62. Hein De Haas, "Migration and Development: A Theoretical Perspective." *International Migration Institute Working Papers*, University of Oxford, N.9, 2008, pp. 1–61.

63. Jan Brzozowski, "International Migration and Economic Development." *Estudos Avançados*, Volume 26, no. 75, 2012, pp. 137–156.

64. N. Spatafora, "Worker's remittances and development." *World Economic Outlook*, Washington, DC, IMF, April 2005, Chapter 2.

65. Acosta, P. et al., "Do Remittances Lower Poverty Levels in Latin America?" In: P. Fajnzylber and J. H. López, (Eds.) *Remittances and Development.* Lessons from Latin America. Washington, D.C.: World Bank, 2008, pp. 87–132; S. Grigolini, "When Houses Provide More Than Shelter. Analyzing the Uses of Remittances within their Sociocultural Context." In: Trager, L. (Ed.), *Migration and Economy. Global and Local Dynamics.* Oxford: Altamira Press, 2005, pp. 193–224.

66. Ibid.

67. Andrés Solimano, Editor, *The International Mobility of Talent: Types, Causes and Development Impact.* New York, NY: Oxford University Press, 2008.

68. Andrés Solimano, Global Migration and International Development in Unstable Times. pp. 1–5.

69. Ainalem Tebeje, "Brain drain and capacity building in Africa." *International Development Resource Center (IDRC).* Retrieved https://www.idrc.ca/en/article/brain-drain-and-capacity-building-africa

70. Ibid.

71. Ibid.

72. Ibid.

73. Ibid.

74. UNESCO, *The Current Status of Science Around the World.* UNESCO Science Report 2010. Retrieved www.unesco.org/new/.../HQ/.../SC_Facts-Figures_USR10_EN.pdf.

75. Ainalem Tebeje, Brain drain and capacity building in Africa. p?

76. Özden, Çağlar, *Brain Drain in Latin America*, Expert Group Meeting On International Migration And Development In Latin America and the Caribbean, 2006, pp. 1–17.

77. Ibid., pp. 5–8.

78. Lisdey Espinoza Pedraza, "Brain Drain Social and Political Effects in Latin American Countries." *Revista Grafía,* Volume 10, no. 2, 2013, pp. 29–48.

79. Andrés Solimano, "Global Migration and International Development in Unstable Times." pp. 13–22.

Chapter 8

Xenophobia in Africa, Latin America, and the Caribbean

Definitions, Theories, and Experiences

Brenda Ingrid Gill and George K. Danns

INTRODUCTION

This chapter examines the phenomenon of xenophobia in Africa, Latin America and the Caribbean. Georg Simmel's theoretical construct of the "The Stranger" is employed to provide analytic interpretation of xenophobia. Further, we postulate a seven-fold typology of xenophobia to account for the varied manifestations of this phenomenon in Africa, Latin America and the Caribbean (LAC). Case studies of selected countries in Africa and LAC provide revealing and practical insights into xenophobic practices and justification for theoretical constructs employed and conclusions drawn. The relationship between xenophobia and the exiled lives of Africans in the motherland and the diaspora is also explored.

XENOPHOBIA DEFINED

Xenophobia, translated from its Greek root words xénos' and phóbos, means the fear of a foreigner.[1] Accordingly, the Center for Human Rights defines xenophobia as the perceived fear, hatred or dislike of a non-native or foreigner in a particular country.[2] The United Nations Special Rapporteur on Contemporary Forms of Racism, Discrimination, Xenophobia and Related Intolerance (Rapporteur) states that xenophobia is "a rejection of outsiders." This definition therefore suggests that xenophobia involves citizenship, national identity, and a rejection of foreigners who belong to other states or nations.[3]

At the heart of the definition of xenophobia is a negative orientation toward and rejection of what Simmel calls "the stranger." Understanding the concept of the stranger is integral to an explanation of xenophobia. Simmel defines the stranger not as "the wanderer who comes today and goes tomorrow, but rather as the person who comes today and stays tomorrow." Yet, Simmel surmises the stranger is a "potential wanderer" who has not quite overcome the freedom of going and coming. "He is fixed within a particular spatial group, or within a group whose boundaries are similar to spatial boundaries. But his position in this group is determined, essentially, by the fact that he has not belonged to it from the beginning, that he imports qualities into it, which do not and cannot stem from the group itself."[4] The stranger occupies the common geography or space and as such is part of the larger group though not a member of the in-group. Yet, Simmel carefully noted that strangers are not really conceived as individuals, and "strangeness" means he who is also far, is actually near. Simmel concludes: "The stranger, like the poor and like sundry "inner enemies," is an element of the group itself. His position as a full-fledged member involves both being outside it and confronting it."[5]

It is the "strangeness" that is at the heart of a definition of xenophobia. Perceived strangers are members of a community or society in that they live there while at the same time being perceived of and treated like sundry "inner enemies." Immigrants, refugees, people of other races, ethnicities, nationalities, skin color and other biological and social markers are the perennial strangers in a society. Traders, foreign investors, imported and migrant labor, refugees, slaves, former slaves and the descendants of slaves are also strangers that are subjected to xenophobic treatment in a society. Xenophobia is always present in any society and can be either passive or latent or active or manifest. Once there are individuals or groups who are perceived as "strangers" there is xenophobia. Xenophobic markers such as race, ethnicity, tribe, color, religion and nationality may form the bases for the rejection of minorities by a majority group. Racism, nativism, genocide, prejudice and discrimination are all xenophobic responses to the "inner enemies" that the stranger perennially represents.

Economic and other crises in a society may lead to xenophobic responses. The strangeness of other ethnic groups often leads to them being negatively stereotyped and scapegoated for perceived ills in a society by its majority group(s). The stranger is often a minority and is subjected to disadvantageous treatment. Xenophobia is a conscious assertion of the pride and cultural and other similarities of the in-group triggered by socially constructed awareness of their differences with an out-group. It is articulated through the ethnocentric treatment of the stranger or the out-group. Xenophobia may include racism, but is by definition, a much broader notion of fear and rejection of outsiders.

Typology of Xenophobia

We offer a seven-fold typology of xenophobia: xenophobia of race, xenophobia of ethnicity, xenophobia of color, xenophobia of culture, xenophobia of nationality, political xenophobia, and economic xenophobia (See Figure 8.1). These xenophobia types are not mutually exclusive and may in fact overlap but are here made separable for the purpose of analysis.

Xenophobia of race refers the fear and/or rejection of strangers based on their race. Macionis defines race as a "a socially constructed category of people who share biologically transmitted traits that members of a society consider important."[6] Groups may be racialized based on characteristics such as skin color, eye color, facial features, hair texture, and body shape.[7] Racism is a powerful form of prejudice and the belief that one racial category is innately superior or inferior to another.[8] The physical markers of race form the bases for identifying one's own kind and differentiating the stranger or out-group. Racism is a negative response to the stranger and to groups characterized by such identifiable strangeness. Racism is the articulation of xenophobia and for some scholars has been treated as a type of xenophobia.

Xenophobia of color is an aspect of the xenophobia of race. It is here differentiated because of the importance of color as a conspicuous marker in promoting xenophobic and racist treatment of people of African descent. Skin color is a readily identifiable marker for pinpointing the stranger in the community. It is often used as a basis for justifying the stratification order in a society. In this schema white, yellow or brown skin take precedence over darker or black skin. In much of the diaspora and even in Africa itself whiteness and nearness to whiteness have resulted in privileged treatment and majority group identification. Blackness and nearness to blackness have been used as the bases for

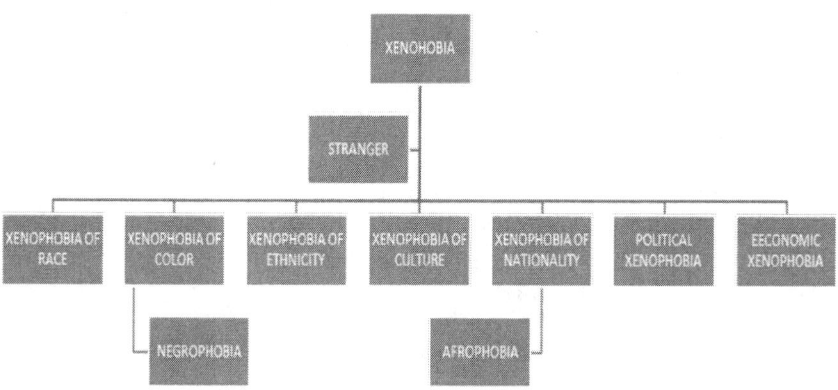

Figure 8.1 Typologies of Xenophobia.

negative social ranking, social marginality and rejection. White, mullato, and black are socially constructed color markers that cement identity and social ranking of individual and groups particularly in societies that would have experienced European colonization. In the United States, lighter complexioned Africans American males such as President Obama earn similar wages similar to white males, while dark skin African Americans earn appreciably less.

Xenophobia of ethnicity refers to the fear and or rejection of strangers based on shared cultural heritage such as their religion, language, common ancestry which enables others to define them as different or strange. Like race, perceived or socially constructed differences in ethnicity have formed the bases for more or less severe ethnic conflicts all over the world.

Xenophobia of culture is a derivative of the *xenophobia of ethnicity*. Culture involves both material and ideational aspects and these are seen as symbols of strangeness and of the markers of the enemies within. Religious xenophobia is a key aspect of cultural xenophobia. Religious identity in part defines ethnicity and cast a spotlight on the stranger as other. Radical Islamic rantings of the Islamic State in Iraq and Syria (ISIS) movement are the lenses through which terrorism is viewed. Radical Islam is being viewed globally as engendering terrorism and as the epitome of strangeness leading to the demonization of all Islam and Muslims.

Xenophobia of nationality is based on fear of and resentment toward immigrants or refugees from a country different from one's own. Nationality can form the bases for xenophobic treatment since the individual or group can be regarded as originating from another country and therefore not really belonging. The xenophobia of nationality may impact immigrants even beyond the first generation. Refugees are invariably subject to xenophobic treatment. Xenophobia of nationality involves not only a rejection of other nationalities in one's country, but also the colonial conquest of other territories and nations and the subordination of their peoples.

Political Xenophobia is the fear and rejection of the spread of political ideologies of another group or nation. The cold war between the West and the Soviet Bloc countries is an example of political xenophobia. The spread of socialism was an anathema to Western countries and the spread of capitalism induced a similar response. Political xenophobia is of course related to the xenophobia of nationalism.

Economic Xenophobia is the fear of and negative reaction to outsiders who are seen as competitors for jobs, resources and other economic goods. These outsiders may be immigrants, traders, migrant labor, slave and indentured labor, and investors from other countries and are often a virulent source for xenophobic treatment. These strangers are the first to be blamed for loss of jobs, privilege and downturn in the economy. They are scapegoated for social problems which they may or may not have caused.

Xenophobia as Negrophobia and Afrophobia

Negrophobia and Afrophobia are variants of xenophobia and have special importance for this chapter. Although the types of xenophobia previously discussed have explanatory value Negrophobia and Afrophobia are the primary prisms through which this chapter is analyzed.

Xenophobia toward black people or people of African descent is called *Negrophobia*. It is the xenophobia of color, a phobia toward people of dark pigmentation. It has been defined as the "Fear or contempt of black people and their culture. Behavior based on such an attitude or feeling."[9] Police in the United States who shoot unarmed black men are alleged to have displayed Negrophobia.[10] Negrophobia is the denial of the humanity of black people. It accords with Simmel's typification of the stranger as not really being an "individual."[11]

Simmel affirms that "strangers are not really conceived as individuals, but as strangers of a particular type."[12] This conclusion gives Simmel's construct of the "Stranger" much explanatory value in our definition of xenophobia and the interpretation of its conceptual derivatives such as Negrophobia and Afrophobia. Negrophobia has meaning in the fact that the offspring of miscegenous unions between blacks and other races are viewed and treated as Black. The US president Barack Obama, whose father was black and mother was white is an example insofar as he is viewed and treated as America's first black president.

It is of interest to note that there are physical gradations of color between black and white. And even among people of color. There are light-complexioned blacks and dark-complexioned blacks who may gravitate to their own kind with the lighter complexioned afforded more privilege and the darker complexioned treated as inferior. Negrophobia can subsequently result in self-hate and/or rejection of one's own kind among black people themselves. Negrophobia is not necessarily based on nationality or country of origin. It is the fear and rejection of blackness. It is related to but conceptually distinguished from Afrophobia. Other races such as Indians from Asian continent or Asian ancestry may also experience xenophobic treatment from other races and within their own race. Dark skin Indians are more likely to people the lower caste than light skin Indians and be the target for discriminatory treatment.

Xenophobia toward Africans and people of African heritage is called *Afrophobia*. Frsa defined Afrophobia as the ideology and practice of extreme hatred, hostility, prejudice, fear, dislike, disapproval and discrimination toward Africans, people of African ancestry, culture and the African continent.[13] Frsa further asserts that Afrophobia is essentially "Actions or inaction to cause havoc to and discrimination specifically directed at Africans, diaspora Africans and the African continent" [14] and argued that "The phenomenon of Afrophobia as an underlying ideology and distinct discrimination which drives sustained assault and entrenched erosion away of the fundamental human rights of Africans, people of African ancestry and perilously exposes the interests of the African continent to multiple-jeopardy."[15]

This scholar also concluded that Afrophobia "Is an extremist phenomenon with consequences of statistically-backed genocidal proportions of the trans-atlantic cartel slave trade, colonization, apartheid, neocolonialism, contemporary institutional racism and the African development conundrum etc."[16] He pinpointed the markers or what he called the diacritics of Afrophobia as xenophobia perpetrated specifically against people: located in, or whose immediate origin is, the African continent; of African physical appearance; of African name constructs; of African native languages; of African accents; of African nationalities; of African countries; of African cultures for example values, music, and dress; of African history; of African dietal regimes; of African traditions; who champion the cause of total emancipation of the African people; and who advocate for Africa's sustainable economic development and prosperity.

In the following section, we use the typologies and definitions above to discuss specific xenophobic experiences in Africa, LAC. While we are aware of the phenomenon existing in several countries in the regions the confines of this chapter do not allow for a comprehensive discussion. To this end a select number of countries are discussed; these selected with no specific bias by the authors.

Xenophobic Displays in Africa

Ghana: An Early Case

Xenophobic experiences in the African continent are noted as far back as the mid-twentieth century. During 1932, for example, there was agitation by Ghanaian citizens for deportation of "aliens" or "strangers" by Ghanaians when the Nigerian cocoa farmers in Akyem Abukwa opposed the king's holding up the cocoa from the European firms. At that time, there was a call for the "troublemakers" namely the migrants to be kept out of Akyem Abukwa. There was a direct call for punishment by deportation of all who opposed the customary laws of the various states. To support their resolution to deport foreigners, the town's residents formed the National Crusade for the Protection of Ghanaian Enterprise aimed at opposing foreign entrepreneurs.[17]

Ghana's consideration as the "Gold Coast" and the perceived affluence enticed several immigrants from West Africa, especially Nigeria.[18] Most of the foreigners in Ghana as early as 1930s were from other West African countries with most being from Nigerians. Other countries represented were

Burkina Faso, Ivory Coast, and Togo. This influx of migrants and the perceptions of their dominance and effect on the country's economy led to tensions. Politically motivated attempts to deport foreigners also occurred during 1957 and 1961 under the Nkrumah leadership via the Deportation Act. This Act allowed the government to legally deport any foreigners reckoned to be "a threat to the nation." This period saw several aliens from Mali, Burkina Faso and Nigeria were deported under the Act.

The Nigerians in Ghana were very successful business people in areas such as: traders, cocoa farmers, farm laborers and contractors, factory workers, and menial workers in construction sites. The success of Nigerians encouraged other Nigerians to move to Ghana for employment in existing Nigerian businesses, to set up their own businesses, or to seek other employment in Ghana. Note, however, that while the Nigerians were successful, the Ghanaians were experiencing poor socio-economic problems compounded by severe levels of unemployment. The belief among Ghanaians was that the foreigners were dominating trade and employment opportunities in their country and were held responsible for their economic and social plight.[19] The indigenous Ghanaian population wanted increased participation of native peoples in the commercial and industrial life of their country. They mounted tremendous pressure on the government which ultimately led to the introduction of policies.

First, the Aliens Compliance Order also called the "Aliens Order" of November 18, 1969, by the then prime minister Kofi Busia was passed. The aim of the Order was to get rid of all aliens who lacked work permits. They were given two weeks to leave the country.[20] Research suggests that though other aliens from other West African countries (Togo, Burkina Faso, and the Ivory Coast) were affected by the Aliens Order, a mass exodus of Nigerians (an estimated 191,000)[21] were mainly of Yoruba from Southwestern Nigeria (about 140,000) from Ghana occurred.[22] The second measure was the Ghanaian Business Promotion (GBP) initiative. The GBP allowed only Ghanaians to run certain businesses. Aliens were allowed to participate in certain economic activities only if they invested certain determined capital amounts.[23] In fact, the GBP initiative was praised by Ghanaians as a nationalistic initiative that ensured jobs for them.

While mainly economics played a great role in the deportation of several foreigners from Ghana, xenophobia can also be considered a contributing factor. It may be argued that the ways Ghanaians felt as they observed (mostly Nigerian) foreigners exhibiting their Ghana acquired wealth; wealth acquired from Ghana in front of locals could have added fuel to xenophobic actions. In several instances, Ghanaians felt deprived, displaced, hostile, discontented, and disillusioned. Further, they began to blame the foreigners for the increased crime rates along with their inability to find employment. These feelings are contributed to incidents of economic xenophobia. Since Nigerians seemed to have been targeted more for expulsion than other West African migrants, xenophobia of nationality may be applicable to their experience.

Uganda

Uganda is another African country that experienced xenophobic tensions. Forty-four years ago, Idi Amin ordered the deportation of all the 60,000 to 80,000 Asians in the population who were not Ugandan citizens. This was a serious order noting that several of the Indians had lived in Uganda for over 100 years and were contributing in positive ways to the economy. The order by the dictator leader was mainly fueled by worsening economic conditions in the country. Searcey reports that the Indians and Pakistani minorities were asked to leave because they were "accused of hoarding wealth and sabotaging the economy."[24] The BBC News reported Idi Amin as having stated that the Asians were "bloodsuckers" who milked the economy of its wealth.[25]

The Uganda Human Rights Commission Report for 2009 suggested that ethnic tension and xenophobia were threats that still plagued Uganda. The reported isolated intolerance as one of the leading causes of human rights violations in Uganda. It also places the blame of such intolerance on the doorsteps of leaders at national and local levels who are accused of being intolerant of others' views of ethnic, political, religious or other grounds.

The report also suggested that the level of hatred noted in Uganda often leads to persecution, hounding of those who belong to different ethnic groups, unfair distribution of public service jobs, heightened tension between Ugandan traders and Indian, Chinese, and Congolese traders. It is further proposed by the report that unfair competition for business and trade between the groups mentions previously. Unfair competition is also considered a likely contributor to xenophobia as is seen as having divided the country into "us" versus "them," and dehumanization whereby one group denies the humanity of the other group and classifies them more as animals and insects than humans. Furthermore, the report outlines several other xenophobic occurrences in the country one of which was the xenophobic clashes between the Banyoro and Non-Banyoro (Bafuruki). The tensions resulted from tensions over land and marginalization of indigenous communities.

Kenya: A New Type of Xenophobia?

While not neglecting Kenya's past experiences with xenophobia, the present focus is on the more recent, shocking, and very disturbing xenophobic attacks. Terrorist-based attacks have become a new kind of experience in that country. The various experiences with violent extremism in in the country have led to the stigmatization of the Somali Kenyan community by the ethnic

Kenyans and the Kenyan Somalis.[26] This is interesting when it is noted that the Somalis fled from Somalia to Kenya seeking asylum but instead they often face the same treatment in Kenya from which they originally tried to escape. One journalist for example who was arrested after the bombing of a Sunday school in which a child was killed stated, "We are suffering just like everyone else. We suffered the same fate in Somalia. This is where we thought we'd be safe and now we're not, is there no reprieve? I don't blame Kenyans for suspecting us—but they must not stereotype."[27]

The Somali al-Shabaab group's attacks and negative reactions to the Somalis by Kenyans have contributed to a new kind of xenophobia in Kenya. Most non-Somali residents seem to think that all Somalis are al-Shabaab fighters based on the infiltration and recruitment of Somalia refugee population residing in Kenya by al-Shabaab operatives. This situation has led to, among other things, a threat to Kenya's national security from the al-Shabaab—Somali armed faction. Therefore, even though Kenya wishes to accommodate refugees as has been the practice previously, it is now faced with the dilemma of a disproportionately growing refugee population. This contributes to several social, economic, and political problems for the country.[28]

Often the hatred of the Somalis is demonstrated in several ways. They are blamed for the attacks executed by al-Shabaab in Kenya. In the areas where they live such as Eastleigh, they are often subject to police pounces during which anyone who appears to be Somali is arrested. Often, they are beaten, their homes are vandalized, and in some cases, they are forced out of public service vehicles. In some cases, the clashes are deadly and result in deaths. One example was the grenade attack on a Sunday school that killed a child. Kenya government continues to battle with policies to enhance the security and maintain its national security while trying to confirm to international sanctions and expectations.

South Africa: A More Recent Case

Some of the xenophobic acts in South Africa involved attacks on persons and businesses. In several cases, the death of citizens from other African countries who previously had considered South Africa a safe haven for them. Some of the outbreaks occurred in Isipingo in the eThekwini metro south of Durban's Central Business District, in the northern township of KwaMasha, in Verulam, Durban, KwaZulu-Natal, Alexandra Township, Jeppestown and Cleveland, East Rand, and Soweto are noteworthy here. In several instances, large numbers of locals marched around the cities, blocked streets, looted foreign-owned businesses, burned tires, used aggression and assault toward foreigners and foreign-owned businesses all as a means to "drive the migrants" out of South Africa.[29] Sosibo, Wet, and Zwane also questioned the appropriateness of the term xenophobia and reported that large numbers of Pakistanis, Ethiopians, Somalis, and Bengalis were displaced. They account that six persons were also killed during the January 2015 looting turmoil in Soweto and other townships in Gauteng that targeted foreign-owned businesses and nationals.[30]

One underlying reason for the violent instances in South Africa may be what Kesting described above as the flexibility in labor and capital movement. A view also supported by Bekker, who questioned the appropriateness of applying the term xenophobia to the South African, clashes with African asylum-seekers from other African countries. He maintains that in the case of South Africa, other migrants who came to labor and invest capital fueled the assaults. The presence of foreigners in the society along with the perception and/or rumor of the migrants being hired to replace local workers was deemed the fuel that ignited the situation. He additionally suggests that the clashes that occurred during 2008 and 2015 resulted from unfulfilled expectations of what the South Africans perceived to be their fair entitlements.[31] In South Africa's case, arguably, this includes being considered first for an employment opportunity and having no fear of being replaced by foreigners.

Rydgen's explanation for xenophobic experiences is easily applicable to the case of South Africa when the various justifications for the attacks are examined. Though in most instances latent xenophobia may exist, manifestations are often combined with political rhetoric and nationalistic sentiments, self-perceived negative impact of immigration, perceptions of low amounts of cultural capital, status deprivation, minority issues, feelings of deprivation, growing discontent with political institutions, especially established political parties, and/or other issues can all contribute to the intensification of xenophobic episodes in a society.[32] Some of the reasons given by politicians for the actions of "locals" during the 2008 and 2015 xenophobic acts included: they were being squeezed out by foreign shop; township entrepreneurs felt demoralized, frustrated and could not thrive as business owners in their own communities; experiencing justifications for the violence perpetuated, and the common belief and assurance of protection from punishment (Bekker), Afrophobic attacks (Gqirana).[33]

From the preceding texts it is noted that some xenophobia in Mother Africa were impelled by economic considerations, politics, terrorism, and the rhetoric that foreigners were committing crimes. Regardless of the reasons that bolstered xenophobic reactions in the countries discussed, the bottom line is that xenophobia was not a new manifestation. The problem is not confined to Africa as we will discuss subsequently for Latin America and Caribbean region.

Latin America's Xenophobia

When asked about "Blacks" in Latin America, most persons tend to agree that there are no blacks in the region. Nonetheless, research shows that there are approximately 150 to 250 million people of African descent living in Latin America.[34] Despite their large numbers in the region their experiences with xenophobia is very much alive and frequently very disruptive. In Latin America, most instances of xenophobia originated from nationalist ideologies compounded by a colonial mentality that prefers whiteness and despises diversity, especially diversity associated with anything "Afro," "black" or "indigenous." In some occurrences, the transfer of new ideas to the region is hampered by suspicions coupled with nationalism that leads of hesitancy of accepting new ideas. Such hesitance noted especially from those who emanate from what Wallerstein called "core" or "first world" countries.[35]

In Argentina, for example, the homogenous and Europeanized definition of whiteness until rather recently was the normal way of thinking about the country. The level of xenophobia in Argentina influenced the Census for centuries such that the category Afro-descendant was non-existent. In fact, the majority of Argentines had lived believing that no blacks or indigenous peoples lived in Argentina. The country was tasked with raising awareness to the diversity in the country. This heightened awareness was to allow for easier acceptance of the projected 2010 Census findings. For the first time, the idea of different races was being introduced along with the concept of diversity. The Institute against Discrimination, Xenophobia and Racism (INADI) were impelled to promotion diversity sensitivity campaigns. These campaigns were intended to educate citizens to Afro-Argentines. To this end a video was created to first convince the citizens that these Afro-Argentine do exist, showcase images of how they look, and even some insight into their music genre.

Similar to Argentina, Peru also exhibits a clear case of both Negrophobia and Afrophobia as well as xenophobia of race and color. Mostly, Afro-Peruvians are treated as an invisible composition of the population. This invisibility evidenced by the absence of Afro-Peruvians from the Census since 1940. The World Bank reports that, in Peru, "Black is an invisible color."[36] This inconspicuousness often leads to them being overlooked for access to health, political office, employment, educational, and other opportunities.

Similar to Argentina, Peru has also initiated the Afro-Peru photography and video exhibit to raise awareness to this "invisible" population who compete for jobs. In some cases, some Afro-Peruvians refer to job advertisements that require "tall, fair skin" applicants. Our previous discussion of gradations within a single race becomes applicable. Though Afro-Peruvians are of several shades with some "brown" or "whiter" than others, they are all considered to be and treated as "Black." Some Afro-Peruvians state that they are treated as though Black is bad and this makes them feel invisible.[37] Chile, Brazil, Mexico, Venezuela, Cuba, Ecuador, and Columbia are other examples of countries in Latin America where xenophobia is a problem that is negatively impacting some segments of the population.

Xenophobia Experiences in Caribbean Countries

Caribbean Countries are part of the Caribbean Community (CARICOM) and Common Market.[38] As members of this regional integration movement they are signatories to the CARICOM Single Market Economy (CSME). The CSME provides for the unencumbered exchange and sharing of labor in the region through measures such as removing obstacles to intra-regional sharing of skills, labor and travel. Notwithstanding the commitment to regional integration, the Xenophobia of nationality and economic xenophobia are prevalent in the relations between Guyanese nationals and Antiguans, Trinidadians and African nationals, Haitians and Bahamians, Haitians and the Dominican Republic, Trinidadians and Tobagonians and Guyanese, Jamaicans and Caymanians, Barbadians and Guyanese, and the relationship between Jamaicans and Barbadians to mention a few. Often, such experiences result because the "locals" believe that the "foreigners" will affect their social and economic well-being. In several instances, there is the belief that foreigners over-populate a country, take away their locals' jobs, deplete their social services, increase the crime rates, and negatively impact the national budgets and political decisions.[39]

Bahamians Hatred of Haitians

The Bahamians treatment of Haitians in the Bahamas is a case of nationalistic xenophobia in the Caribbean. Though the similarities between the Bahamians and Haitians are many, the Bahamians often seek to separate themselves from the Haitians. This effort to appear different demonstrates itself as xenophobia. Sharing similarities in cultural heritage, music, and even physical appearance contributes to this need to really "be different" from the attitude displayed by the Bahamians. The hatred is often extant through marginalization and immigration policies geared to stop the flow of foreigners, more specifically, Haitians into the Bahamas. The fact is that so many Haitians live in the Bahamas that the Bahamians are afraid that the Haitians may eventually try to remap their country and claim a section for Haiti. Another fear is that the Bahamian culture will be watered-down to resemble that of the Haitians and the Bahamian identity may eventually be like that of the Haitians.[40]

Regional and international initiatives such as CSME and the World Trade Organization's quest to enhance and promote even more trade and free movement of people is somewhat counter to the Bahamas goals of keeping the Haitians out.[41] Instead, the Bahamian government as early as the 1980s had developed immigration policies geared to halt the influx of Haitians into the

Bahamas and had placed Haitian immigrants in the Bahamian Immigration Stop List. Despite these measures, however, the numbers of Haitians born in the Bahamas and those born to at least one Haitian parent continue to grow. Though such persons can apply for Bahamian citizenship the process is often difficult and often not realized.[42]

Despite the change in political leadership during 2007, Haiti maintained its anti-Haitian anti-immigration position. The idea of regionalism and cooperation with the tenets of CARICOM and the CSME continue to challenge the Baha-ma's nationalism. The opening of its border to allow free movement of people, culture, trade and labor continues to be a challenge to the country's identity in the region. This is compounded by the fact that the Bahamas' economy itself is supported by the entrance of "foreigners" into the country as a support to tourism, which is the backbone of the economy. Interestingly, however, is that generally Bahamians seem to be comfortable with other foreigners, but not those from Haiti who are often perceived as poor, lacking economic power.[43] Similar Xenophobia of nationality exists between Haitians and Dominicans.[44]

Guyanese: The Largest Ethnicity Targeted Regionally

Guyana is one CARICOM country whose residents often suffer xenophobic treatment in several countries in the region. It is also the country in CARICOM that experiences the most cases of deportation of its nationals. It is therefore fitting to examine the case of xenophobia between Barbados and Guyana. Most Bajans (native Barbadians) tend to accept as true that the foreigners (especially Guyanese) are the ones that contributed to their experiences with poverty and the increase in crimes. Nonetheless, the negative implications for regionalism, cooperation, and the economic advancement of Barbados cannot be exaggerated. This underscored by the contributions of Guyanese to the economy as in several instances Guyanese do jobs the Bajans refuse to do.[45]

Girvan addresses Caribbean xenophobia and its potential impact on "ordinary-level citizens" the Caribbean "family" and Barbados as the case of Barbados and Guyana was examined. The author discusses the move by Barbados' prime minister to enforce the country's migration policy to deport all foreigners. Girvan argues that such a deportation could have implications (if addressed by the other nations) on Barbados's trade and economy. Being a very small island dependent on mainly tourism and trade, especially regional trade and tourist with CARICOM countries were pinpointed as a crucial factor that could hurt Barbados because of its perceived xenophobic migration policy was implemented.[46] This move was allegedly due to the rise in crime rates and the poverty epidemic in Barbados. Several Guyanese had fled Guyana in search of employment opportunities, and to live in what they perceived as "greener pastures" in Barbados.

This problem was further discussed in the article "*Barbadian First" Policy Flogs Guyanese in Barbados*." The Council on Hemispheric Affairs discussed the spill-over effect the implementation of the law formulated by the Barbados Cabinet Subcommittee on Immigration that met in 2008. This law was made public by Barbados' prime minister's on May 5, 2009 and became effective on June 1, 2009. The law necessitated that all Guyanese who had entered Barbados prior to December 31, 1998, normalize their status of residency within 6 months from June 1, 2009 or face deportation. Next, it required that any Guyanese who entered Barbados after the 1998 date were to face compulsory deportation.[47] The law included additional stipulations.[48]

Trinidad and Tobago vs the "Africans"

Xenophobia in the Caribbean sometimes extends to include nationals from other regions. Take for example the case of 15 Ghanaian nationals who were living in Trinidad and Tobago (TT). While noting that most deportees from Trinidad and Guyana between 2010 and 2014 were Guyanese, the Attorney General disclosed that African nationals were number 7 on the list of nationals deported. For 2010 the Attorney General further specified that 70 African immigrants were deported from TT. The matter gained much coverage when the Trinidad and Tobago government decided to spend TT$ 2.6 million to charter a plane and deport the 15 illegal Ghana nationals back to Ghana though the foreigners through their lawyers made a great effort aimed at regularizing their status.

The argument, quite similar to others discussed before, was that illegal immigrants were draining the country's resources and contributing positively to the increase in crimes. Reference was also made to the presence of 66 rebel Nigerians. These Nigerians, though they had done nothing to indicate such, were projected to cause potential havoc in the country and were therefore placed under constant surveillance.[49] The behavior of TT was considered detrimental to CARICOM. In fact, it was considered a racist act and denounced as such.[50] We argue that this was not a racist act, but rather a xenophobic act.

CONCLUSION

This chapter shows quite clearly that Bilateral and multilateral cooperation between and among Africa, LAC is in trouble. The presence and practice of xenophobia is posing a serious threat to the survival of the required cooperation. Such cooperation is necessary to sanctioned trade agreements with the countries in the three regions.

Idi Amin Dada expelled all Asians from Uganda during his regime in 1970. Hitler subjected Jews in Nazi Germany to the Holocaust. The Dominican

Republic and the Bahamas have defined Haitians who have settled in those countries for generations as strangers and outsiders, depriving them of citizenship rights even though several of them were born there. Guyana is deporting Venezuelans who have fled their homeland because of economic hardships. TT and Barbados constantly conduct night raids and deport other nationals, especially Guyanese, despite regional agreements that support unencumbered travel and employment exchanges. Countries in Africa are experiencing xenophobic responses from their populace toward refugees fleeing for their lives from war-torn countries in the Middle East and Africa. Immigrants, refugees, migrant labor are the strangers about whom Simmel had written.

NOTES

1. Jamie Bordeau, *Xenophobia: The Violence of Fear and Hate.* New York: Rosen Publishing Group, 2010. p. 4.
2. Centre for Human Rights. *The Nature of South Africa's Legal Obligations to Combat Xenophobia.* Pretoria: Centre for Human Rights, 2009.
3. International Labour Organisation, "International Migration, Racism, Discrimination and Xenophobia," International Organization for Migration and Office of the United Nations High Commissioner for Human Rights, 2001.
4. Georg Simmel, "The Stranger," From Kurt Wolff (Trans.), "*The Sociology of Georg Simmel,*" New York: Free Press, 1950. pp. 402–408.
5. Ibid. pp. 402–408.
6. Macaulay, Ronald. Is Sociolinguistics Lacking in Style? Cuadernos de Filologia Inglesa R (1999): 9–33.
7. Francis B. Njamnjoh, *Insiders and Outsiders: Citizenship and Xenophobia in Contemporary Southern Africa.* London: Zed Books, 2006.
8. Ibid.
9. http://www.thefreedictionary.com/Negrophobia.
10. Brandon Hill, "Negrophobia: Michael Brown, Eric Garner, and America's Fear of Black People." *TIME*, August 29, 2014, http://time.com/3207307/negrophobia-michael-brown-eric-garner-and-americas-fear-of-black-people/ (Retrieved July 18, 2016).
11. Simmel, Georg, "The Stranger," in Kurt Wolff (Trans.), *The Sociology of Georg Simmel,* New York: Free Press, 1950. pp. 402–408.
12. Ibid.
13. Koko Adomdza Frsa, "Understanding Afrophobia, Afrophobism and Institutional Afrophobia." *Afrophobia Challenge*, 2010, Retrieved July 18, 2016. http://afrophobia.webs.com/understandingafrophobia.htm
14. Ibid.
15. Ibid.
16. Ibid.
17. Olaosebikan Aremu Johnson and adeyinka Theresa Ajayi, "Expulsion of Nigerian Immigrant Community from Ghana in 1969: Causes and Impact," *Developing Country Studies* 4, no. 10 (2014): pp. 176–186.

18. W.A. Cardinall, "The Gold Coast, (Accra, 1931)," cited in T. Antwi-Bosiakoh, "Understanding Migration Motivations in West Africa: The Case of Nigerians in Ghana," *Legon Journal of Sociology* 3, no. 2 (2009): p. 6. See also A. Adepoju, "Patterns of Migration in West Africa," in T. Manuh (Ed.), *At Home in the World?: International Migration and Development in Contemporary Ghana and West Africa.* Accra: Sub-Saharan Publishers, 2005. p. 32.

19. Johnson Olaosebikan Aremu, and adeyinka Theresa Ajayi, "Expulsion of Nigerian Immigrant Community from Ghana in 1969: Causes and Impact," *Developing Country Studies* 4, no. 10 (2014): pp. 176–186.

20. Roger S. Gocking, *The history of Ghana.* Westport: Greenwood Publishing Group (2005): p. 156.

21. WTS. Gould, "International Migration in Tropical Africa," *The International Migration Review* 8, no. 3 (1974): pp. 347–365.

22. M. Hundsalz, "The Migration of the Yoruba to Ghana and their Return to Nigeria," p. 218 Cited in Aremu, Johnson Olaosebikan and Ajayi, adeyinka, Theresa, "Expulsion of Nigerian Immigrant Community from Ghana in 1969: Causes and Impact," *Developing Country Studies* 4, no. 10 (2014): p. 176.

23. Obed Yao Asamoah, *The Political History of Ghana (1950–2013): The Experience of a Non-conformist.* Bloomington: AuthorHouse, 2014. p. 187.

24. Ian Searcey, "Immigration archive: Ugandan Asians in Leicester 1972," *4 News*, Wednesday April 24, 2013.

25. BBC News, "*1972:* Asians Given 90 days to Leave Uganda," *BBC News*, On This Day 1950–2005, Retrieved July 5, 2016. http://news.bbc.co.uk/onthisday/hi/dates/stories/august/7/newsid_2492000/2492333.stm.

26. Catherine Wambua-Soi, "Rising xenophobia against Somalis in Kenya," Al Jazeera Blog on Africa. http://www.aljazeera.com/blogs/africa/2012/11/50161.html.

27. Ibid. (np).

28. Avery Burns, "Feeling the Pinch: Kenya, Al-Shabaab, and East Africa's Refugee Crisis," *Refuge Canada's Journal for Refugees,* 27, no. 1 (2010): pp. 5–15.

29. Ibid., pp. 5–15.

30. Kwanele, Sobibo, Sobibo, Phillip de Wet, and Thuletho Zwane, "Township Politics Fuel the Attacks on 'Outsiders,'" *Mail & Guardian* January 30, 2015. (Johannesburg). Retrieved. http://mg.co.za/article/2015-01-29-township-politics-fuel-the-attacks-on-outsiders July 5, 2016.

31. Simon Bekker, "Violent Xenophobic Episodes in South Africa, 2008 and 2015," *African Human Mobility Review,* 1, no. 3 (2015): pp. 229–252.

32. Jens Rydgren, "Meso-level Reasons for Racism and Xenophobia: Some Converging and Diverging Effects of Radical Right Populism in France and Sweden," *European Journal of Social Theory,* 6, no. 1 (2003): pp. 48–50.

33. Kwanele Sobibo, Phillip, deWet, and Thuletho Zwane, "Township Politics Fuel the Attacks on 'Outsiders,'" *Mail & Guardian* January 30, 2015. (Johannesburg). Retrieved July 6, 2016. http://mg.co.za/article/2015-01-29-township-politics-fuel-the-attacks-on-outsiders.

34. Darién, J. Davis, "Latin America: Afro-descendants, State of the World's Minorities," 2006, Accessed July 27, 2016. www.refworld.org/pdfid/4795b32e1f.pdf.

35. Teresa Ko Chisu, "From Whiteness to Diversity: Crossing the Racial Threshold in Bicentennial Argentina," *Ethnic and Racial Studies* 37, no. 14 (2014): pp. 2529–2546.

36. World Bank, "In Peru, Back is an Invisible Color," Retrieved July 27, 2016, http://www.worldbank.org/en/news/feature/2013/10/14/Peru-negro-color-invisible.

37. Ibid.

38. CARICOM, "The CARICOM Single Market and Economy (CSME)", Secretariat Address: Turkeyen, Greater Georgetown, Guyana, South America, 2001–2016. Retrieved July 11, 2016. http://caricom.org/our-work/the-caricom-single-market-and-economy-csme/.

39. Council on Hemispheric Affairs, "Barbadian First Policy Flogs Guyanese in Barbados," August 5, 2009. Retrieved July 12, 2016. http://www.coha.org/barbadian-first-policy-flogs-guyanese-in-barbados/.

40. Ian A. Bethell Bennett, "Economy, Migration, Identity: Late Capitalist Reactions against Haitians and the CSME in the Bahamas," *Wadabagei, A Journal of the Caribbean and Its Diasporas* 13, no. 2 (2010): pp. 35–64.

41. Ibid., pp. 35–64.

42. Ibid., pp. 34–36.

43. Ibid., pp. 40–42.

44. Paulino, Edward, "Anti-Haitianism, Historical Memory, and the Potential for Genocidal Violence in the Dominican Republic," *Genocide Studies and Prevention: An International Journal*, 1, no. 3 (2006): 264–288 Article 5. Available at: http://scholarcommons.usf.edu/gsp/vol1/iss3/5.

45. Council on Hemispheric Affairs, "Barbadian First Policy Flogs Guyanese in Barbados," August 5, 2009. Retrieved July 12, 2016. http://www.coha.org/barbadian-first-policy-flogs-guyanese-in-barbados/.

46. Norman Girvan, "Caribbean Xenophobia: Where will it end?" *Caribbean Political Economy*, May 26, 2007. (np). Retrieved July 12, 2016. http://www.normangirvan.info/caribbean-xenophobia-where-will-it-end-norman-girvan/.

47. Council on Hemispheric Affairs, "Barbadian first policy flogs Guyanese in Barbados," August 5, 2009. Retrieved July 12, 2016. http://www.coha.org/barbadian-first-policy-flogs-guyanese-in-barbados/.

48. Ibid., n.p.

49. Wallerstein, Immanuel, "Trinidad Denies Racial Profiling Following Deportation of African Nationals," *Caribbean* 360, December 10, 2014. Retrieved July 12, 2016. http://www.caribbean360.com/news/trinidad-denies-racial-profiling-following-deportation-african-nationals.

50. Wallerstein, Immanuel, "US Group Condemns Trinidad's Deportation of Africans," *Jamaica Observer*, Friday, December 12, 2014. Retrieved July 12, 2016. http://www.jamaicaobserver.com/news/US-group-condemns-Trinidad-s-deportation-of-Africans.

Chapter 9

The African Immigrant Family in the United States of America

Challenges and Opportunities

Sulayman S. Nyang

INTRODUCTION

The Africans who migrated into the United States of America in the twentieth century came unencumbered by the strictures of enslavement and bondage. Unlike their predecessors who were enslaved, and came to the United States via the Middle Passage, these Africans came to the United States to some degree, voluntarily, being only compelled by unrelenting economic crisis, political turmoil and the deleterious effects of natural disasters. There were also a few who were not compelled by such dreadful strictures, and these immigrants had widely disparate motivations. Even without any reliable data from interviews of these men and women who left their homes in Africa in search of education, fortune, refuge or adventure, one can identify four categories among them. The first were the students who came in the late nineteenth century, sometimes with the support and assistance of American missionaries who hoped that they would later return to establish Christian missions, and collaborate with like-minded Christians to extend the message of Christ to their fellow Africans. This group of Africans went primarily to historically Black colleges and universities. Many came from West and Southern Africa.

There were also a few from East Africa. The second group was African students who came during the twentieth century for both secular and sacred education. Some entered into conjugal relationships with White American and African American women and decided to stay permanently in the country. The third group consists of seamen and stowaways who found their way to American seaports such as New York City or New Orleans, Louisiana. Many of these men who sailed on American or foreign ships settled in the New York-New Jersey area. Their activities in Harlem attracted the attention of some of their contemporaries. The fourth group of Africans who entered the history books, as part of the growing African immigrant community, are the political refugees. Most of these African immigrants are the victims of the civil wars fought, either as a result of the Cold War, in pursuit of national liberation, or in pursuit of national or sectional interest in border conflicts, or on the domestic front.

This chapter will address the challenges and opportunities facing the African immigrant community and the African immigrant family. Its first objective is to identify the building blocks that contribute to the development of the African immigrant community in the United States of America. The second is to explain how changing times, conditions, and circumstances have combined to define the nature of the relationship between the African immigrant and the larger American society. The third is to identify the main issues facing the African immigrant communities around the United States of America. Working on the assumption that the African immigrant community is not monolithic, and that cultural background has differential impact on immigrants, this chapter argues that African immigrants could either embrace or eschew assimilation. For those that desire it, the assimilation process would depend on several critical variables: the ease of functioning in a society that speaks an intelligible language, the social class, and the socio-cultural origins of the immigrant, the immigrant's political and psychological position, as well as the level of interest and dedication to the idea of settlement in a host country. Even where settlement is desired, increasingly, there is the realization that immigrants could be transnational and thus disinterested in assimilation. The fourth objective is to give a synthesized conclusion based on my assessment of the evidence gathered while investigating this subject matter.

THE MAKING OF THE AFRICAN IMMIGRANT COMMUNITY

African immigrants began coming to the United States of America voluntarily not long after the Civil War and the abolition of slavery. During the first thirty years after the Civil War, the number of free Africans who ventured to this part of the world was very small. The accounts of Africans from the continent who visited the United States during the last three decades of the nineteenth century show that many of these men and women were Liberians and other West Africans from other points along the coast. There were also African Americans who settled in Liberia and established linkages between the two African peoples (in the continent and the United States) and created travel opportunities for many continental Africans who previously had neither dared nor were welcome as free immigrants to this part of the Atlantic in the era of the slave trade.[1] One African immigrant, whose activities have now become a significant chapter in the history of Pan Africanism and African immigration to the United States, was Chief Sam from Ghana.

Professor Jabez Ayodele Langley's book on the Pan African movement in West Africa tells the story of how Chief Sam came to the United States in the late nineteenth century and settled in New York. His business ventures enabled him to prosper and to establish networks of friendship with African Americans. In the early part of the twentieth century, when race relations between blacks and whites in the United States were at their worst, and lynching was prevalent in the South, Chief Sam offered his services to black families in Oklahoma and Kansas, who wished to emigrate from the United States to the African continent. His efforts failed not because of his inability to organize and lead his followers into the Promised Land, but because the colonial authorities conspired to stymie his efforts. They saw as clear and present danger, this massive migration of New World blacks, into their newly pacified colonies.[2]

Although we do not know much about the lives and times of the other African contemporaries of Chief Sam in New York and in other spots within the borders of the United States, there is circumstantial evidence from the writings of others that point to an African immigrant presence in Harlem during the first three decades of this century. Ras Makonnen, a Trinidadian activist of the global Pan African movement, spoke of some African residents in New York during the inter-war period.[3] Many of these Africans were Somali men who reached this part of the United States, either as seamen or stowaways. Many settled in Harlem and started new lives. In my investigation of Islam among the African-Americans, data from my interviews with some of the earliest Muslim activists in Harlem, suggest some Moroccan, Somali, and West African presence among the blacks settling in New York. Moving Westwards from New York, we have records on the appearance in Pittsburgh, Pennsylvania, of Muhammad Majid, a Sudanese who came to the United States to work with African American converts to Islam. According to FBI records obtained under the Freedom of Liberation Act by Professor Robert Hill of UCLA, editor of the Marcus Garvey Papers, Muhammad Majid attracted the attention of the authorities who saw him as part of a Japanese propaganda campaign against the United States. He had to leave the United States in 1928.[4] Details about Muhammad Majid and his activities are presented to the scholarly community by Professor John Hunwick and a Sudanese collaborator. The two scholars stumbled upon a scholarly gold mine when they located a box of files relating to the life and times of this Sudanese immigrant who had settled in Pittsburgh some seventy years ago.[5]

Besides the records on these immigrants, there is also the story of Duse Muhanutiad Ali, a Sudano-Egyptian journalist, playwright, and activist who came to the United States of America in the 1920s and settled for some time in Detroit before his relocation to West Africa, where he founded newspapers and contributed to the Pan African discourse. Prior to his appearance in the United States, Duse Muhammad Ali was the editor and publisher of the *African Times* and *Orient Review* in England. Because of the nature of this publication and the manner in which it dealt with the events of the times, one can make the case that Duse was the doyen of Afro-Asian journalism in England. One of his protégés, who would later enter history as a great Pan Africanist, was Marcus Garvey. This Jamaican immigrant crossed paths with many Africans in Europe and in the United States of America.[6]

Besides the figures who made history, there were many unknown African immigrants who melted into the ocean of names and faces in America. Their stories are parts of anecdotes told by individual family members, and passed from one generation to the next. Today, modern families can reconstruct their past with the aid of official documents and even scientific innovation. However, those whose ancestors never experienced the horrors of degradation and humiliation of the Middle Passage, may be able to reconstruct their histories more easily.

The composition of the African immigrant community changed in the 1930s and 1940s, when a growing body of African students began to come to the United States for higher education. Among these men and women, those from former British colonies were breaking with tradition by choosing American schools over British ones. Majority of these students of the interwar period returned to Africa. Some of them made a significant impact on world history; others simply faded away into the mist of historical time. We learn much from the autobiographies of several of these men and women who wrote about their experiences in the United States. In many respects, they portrayed a picture of life in the United States as experienced by continental Africans. One early account came from the pen of Nnamdi Azikiwe of Nigeria, who had studied at Lincoln University and later became the first president of Nigeria.[7] Some of his contemporaries from West Africa who came to America remained in the United States. Of these, particularly remarkable is the saga of Dr. K. W. Aggrey of Ghana, whose activities in the United States are legendary. Married to an African American, and being one of the first generation of African professors in America, this educator from Ghana returned home to teach at Achimota College. He also straddled the continent and its Diaspora in his family relations. Aggrey's children, grandchildren, and great grandchildren are now a part of the African American community. One of his children rose to the rank of US ambassador in the State Department and served as the director of the Howard University Press in Washington, D.C., for many years.[8]

The generation of Kwame Nkrumah followed the first wave of Africans coming to the United States in the twentieth century. Like the earlier cohort, the students who came at the same time as Nkrumah, also witnessed the settling of some who decided to remain permanently in America.[9] The African students, who for one reason or the other, stayed on, became part of the Black community. Their descendants have now become an integral part of Black America. The composition of the African immigrant population has become more complex in the postcolonial period. Two factors were responsible. In the first instance, African independence opened the floodgates of Americanism in the continent, and African peoples saw this as a new opportunity to seek firsthand experience of the United States. Many belong to the category I have called elsewhere "The children of the Cold War." In essence, they were the beneficiaries of the ideological rivalry between the Soviet Union and the West. These two contending powers offered generous scholarships to young Africans for higher education. Chosen purposely, to serve as ideological proxies in the Cold War, most returned home to obtain lucrative jobs in their countries of origins.[10] However, a tiny faction decided to remain in the United States. This body of Africans gradually made up a significant building block in the house of "Samba Africa" in America.

The gradual but significant development of an African immigrant community, was due to the state of African governance in the postcolonial period. Although the arrival of political freedom in Africa spelled success for many of those with Western education, the political battles for a piece of the African pie soon led to political instability and conflict. The challenges of nation-building meant that many Africans found their countries transformed into battlegrounds, and their careers stymied by the political breakdown and chaos in their countries. Many of these men and women fled abroad, and some of them returned to the Western countries where they had received higher education, including the United States. Most of them have engaged the struggle to become acclaimed and as a result the African immigrant population became diversified, because those who had stayed behind due to marital ties were joined by refugees from political crises and conflicts.[11]

The diversity of the African immigrant community has been manifested in several ways, including gender, regional origin, and socioeconomic class. Until the postcolonial era, the African immigrants were overwhelmingly male and single. This distribution pattern changed with political independence. By the time Africa achieved her political freedom, a large and growing body of women had Western education. They were also beginning to compete with their male counterparts for opportunities to study in colleges and universities abroad. Some of these women returned home just like their male counterparts; others were married to African men who decided to remain in the United States; a small percentage also decided to stay due to marriage to American men.[12] The attainment of political independence also contributed to the diversification of the population of African immigrants.

Until the early 1960s, these men and women were mainly from the English-speaking African countries and were interested in navigating the stormy waters of American society. The post-independence period created many opportunities for Africans from other colonial territories to venture outside the continent, mostly in quest of higher education. Owing to the diversification process that resulted in increased settlement of migrant Africans in the United States, the African immigrant community now includes permanent residents from virtually every country in the continent regardless of the language inherited from their experience of colonization. The numbers vary from country to country. The African states that have experienced political stability since independence are less likely to have many permanent residents in the United States. When such African countries combine steady economic growth with political stability, the numbers of their indigenes that choose permanent migrant status in the United States is even more minuscule. Thus, the largest concentrations of Africans in the United States are the Nigerians, Ethiopians, Ghanaians, Sierra Leoneans, Liberians, South Africans, Somalis, Senegalese, and Kenyans (all citizens of countries that have experienced considerable political turmoil and/or conflict since their independence). There are also sizable numbers of Zairois, Sudanese, Egyptians, Eritreans, Ugandans, Cameroonians, Algerians, Moroccans, Libyans, Malians, and Cape Verdeans in the United States. The African immigrant population also includes immigrants from smaller states like the Gambia, Togo, Mauritius, and Lesotho. Many of these are students who initially came to study, but have decided to stay on in the United States. Some of these African immigrants had at some point returned home to take lucrative jobs, but because of changed political fortunes in their countries, relocated from their original home countries.[13]

The most recent additions to the growing list of African immigrants are the Somalis and Rwandans. The collapse of the Somali state and the much-televised bloodletting that followed the crisis attracted the attention of many Americans. Thousands of Somalis now live in the United States. They are scattered in various parts of the country. Some are in the Greater Washington area, especially in northern Virginia; others are in the West Coast, especially in San Diego, California; yet others are in the Midwest, particularly in Minnesota and parts of Illinois. In the northern Virginia region of the United States, according to figures from the Immigration and Naturalization Services, three thousand Somalis took up residence in the jurisdiction. Many of these are women and children seeking reunification with their husbands and fathers.[14]

As with the Somali case, the Rwandan genocide triggered a series of migrations to other countries. The Hutu were the largest number of migrants to flee Rwanda. Majority took refuge in other African countries, and a small fraction sought refuge in the United States. However, African refugees have not benefited from US immigration as much as refugees from other countries. The Rwandans who were in the United States at the time of the genocide managed to stay on in the United States because they made a case for their continued stay. In return, they received the US government's bureaucratic wink, rather than an open invitation to remain in country until the political situation improved in their home country. This was the same response given to the Ugandans and Liberians when their countries became embroiled in turmoil.

THE AFRICAN IMMIGRANT FAMILY: CHALLENGES AND OPPORTUNITIES

Several issues confront the scholar studying the African immigrant family in the United States. However, many such issues are not peculiar to Africans. Most immigrants contend with them. The first issue concerns identity and self-definition. Coming to a White and Christian majority society, how have African immigrants fared thus far? This question cannot be answered conclusively. There is need for more research on African immigrants from each of the continent's countries. There are already studies on the Nigerians, Ethiopians, and Senegalese living in various parts of the United States. These studies show that the new immigrants are juggling with multiple identities. Their American experience has made both the individual and family members take a hard look at their circumstances and conditions in American society. In a society where people define themselves racially, ethnically, economically, and linguistically, members of African families have multiple identities, and each is meaningful depending on the context in which they find themselves. At one level, she/he is a black person in a sea of whiteness. At another level, there are religious and denominational differences with other Africans and Americans. The same African may be in one instance, the only restaurant owner at the Parents/Teachers Association meeting, and in another instance, a parent from Ethiopia as opposed to Gambia or Ghana. Within the smaller universe of continental Africans, the immigrant may be one out of thousands of Nigerians, Sierra Leoneans, South Africans, or Kenyans living within a given city. Under these conditions, the African immigrant may find out that the process of splinterization of the original African community in that city, has reached what I have called elsewhere the "islandization" process. This is to say, at this juncture, the immigration now witnesses the clustering effects of culture, language, and the increase in the number of "homeboys" and "homegirls." This process of islandization may lead to the rediscovery of their ethnic, subethnic, and African high school affiliation as the bases of the identities they choose to embrace or reinforce as new immigrants.

Many African organizations were created because of such acts of self-definition among the African immigrants.

The process of self-definition can also take on a religious character. In their study of the Ethiopian communities in the United States of America, the husband and wife team, Professors Gactachew Metaseries and Margined Shifferew, demonstrated how the Ethiopian Coptic Church now plays an important role in the adjustment of Ethiopian immigrants to American society.[15] The Nigerian, Ghanaian, Sierra Leonean, and Liberian Christian churches are also playing similar roles in their communities. One of the African Protestant leaders that has received a lot of media attention is Rev. Dr. Darlingston Johnson from Liberia, who now serves as the Apostolic General Overseer of Bethel World Outreach Fellowship, with its headquarters in Liberia. Dr. Johnson is a founding senior pastor of the Bethel World Outreach Ministries in Silver Spring, Maryland. According to a piece written in the April 1998 issue of *The Christian Times International*, a monthly published by Nigerian-born journalist, Chuks Anyanwu, Rev. Dr. Johnson's Church in Washington was established in 1990 when the Liberian crisis forced some of the Christians to pray for peace and stability in their country. The Christian pastor told this Africa-oriented Christian publication that he and seventeen others gathered to set up this ministry among their people. They saw themselves not as refugees but as missionaries.

The African Christian communities include the highly organized Nigerian Catholics, whose organization has led to the offering of religious services in Igbo, and some Eastern African Catholics who have their services in Swahili. There are also various branches of the Christ Apostolic Church, Aladura and Celestial Church of Christ whose services are held in Yoruba. These steps are taken largely because, the congregations that introduced these innovations have reached critical mass as linguistic communities in the United States, and they are responsive to the demands of their congregation for worship in their indigenous languages.

Among the Protestant groups that are also organizing are the African Initiated Christian churches, which have also responded to the challenge of aiding African family adjustment to American life and culture. The Redeemed Christian Church of God (RCCG) was founded in Nigeria in 1952 by Pa Josiah Akindayomi, is now led by Pastor Enoch A. Adeboye, as the General Overseer. With over 6,000 parishes worldwide, 431 of them in the United States, the RCCG has its North American headquarters in Dallas, Texas.[16] The Brotherhood of the Cross, founded by Olumba Obu in Calabar, Nigeria (OOO), [17]now has a branch in several American localities. With about two million followers worldwide, this religious group caters to its African flocks in those US cities where sizable populations of Nigerians and Cameroonians live. The Cherubim and Seraphim Church, International House of Prayer for

All People also has a chapter in Washington, D.C. Founded by Reverend (Dr.) Fred O. Ogunfiditimi, this church now has followers all over the United States. According to Chike Anigboh, the church has staked a claim for itself in the realm of healing and spirituality. With the ever-growing challenges of daily stress and pain, many African immigrants, including those with limited financial and emotional means, are drawn to these churches. The churches are socializing agencies that respond to the material and spiritual needs of tormented humanity in the jaws of city life. For example, Reverend (Dr.) Ogunfiditimi's church states its mission as sheltering stranded Nigerians, and first-time Nigerian sojourners to the United States. These stranded Nigerians could stay at the church for two months, to enable them to sort out their problems. These efforts of the African Initiated Christian churches are also evident in the activities of the mainline Protestant African Christian

Churches.[18] The news report on Rev. Dr. Johnson of Liberia cited above stated that the "building hosting the church is concise and spiritually uplifting. The outside does not easily tell the hidden treasures inside. It has a day care center, a Bible College, Computer Learning Program, and Christian books and supplies." The chapter enumerates other agenda items of this African Christian Church in the Greater Washington area. Among the projects planned is the dream of establishing a Daily Bread Community Action Program to help the homeless and the needy and counseling programs to rehabilitate drug addicts and alcoholics. According to the newspaper article, they also plan to establish a cafeteria, and have set up a facility to handle the financial, immigration, legal and other problems of their members.

Muslim African immigrants have also embraced their religion to offer security and meaning to them in their new environment. There are Senegambian, Sierra Leonean, Ghanaian, Nigerian, Ethiopian, Somali, Sudanese, and various North African Muslim organizations. The African immigrant Islamic groups are inspired either by the traditional Sufi orders back home, or by the Islamic revivalism that presently hold sway in certain parts of the Muslim World. According to Sylvaine Diouf-Kamara, in an essay on Senegalese immigrants living in the United States, particularly in New York City, African immigrant women are increasingly independent. This she attributed to the influence of the prevalent gender relations in their new environment, part of which is due to the imperatives of the need for daily survival in an industrial society, which make it difficult for families to survive on one income. In addition, the number of highly educated women emigrating from Senegal to the United States has increased in recent years. There is evidence that African Muslim immigrants are changing their attitudes and perceptions. These changes and the manner in which they are received and perceived by African immigrant Muslims would have serious consequences in shaping family values among African immigrant Muslims.[19]

Another issue that confronts African immigrants is the "myth of return." All immigrants entertain the notion of leaving their home countries for countries of settlement, striking it rich, and then returning home with enough resources to live well in their countries of origin. Often, this does not happen. Instead the single immigrant marries a local woman or man and ends up with a family and children. The immigrant may then feel compelled to stay long enough to ensure those children's education and autonomy, but more often than not, the children establish their own families and what was originally meant to be short-term migration becomes permanent. Due to the myth of return among the African immigrants, there is a serious gap between ideals and realities. Most have grand ideas about what they would like to contribute to the transformation of their home countries. Because of their procrastination and ambivalence, they focus on their home countries, while neglecting to socialize their children to cope with life in their countries of origin. It is owing to this neglect that there is a growing body of young Africans who do not speak any African languages. Many thought that these languages would be acquired, as if by osmosis, through the child's interaction with members of the family. Given these challenges, it is appropriate to raise the question of socialization and the need for social and moral agency in the education of African immigrant children. There is a serious gap between the ideals of the first generation of African immigrants and the needs of the second and subsequent generations. However, the research data is still very limited, and more scholarly attention should be devoted to the study and understanding of this phenomenon.[20]

Connection with the embassies of their countries of origin in the United States is an avenue through which some support could be garnered in support of the efforts by African immigrant families, to cope both with the adjustment problems encountered in the United States, and with the linguistic and other cultural resources that could support them in the socialization of their children. It is not an exaggeration to say that most African immigrants have little or no contact with their embassies. The only time these immigrants visit their embassies is when they need to replace their expired passports. Otherwise they try their best to keep them out of their business. There are several reasons for this ambivalent relationship. The first is that the political conditions in the immigrant's home country may be such that he or she does not want to get too close to those in power. Sometimes this is because immigrants belong to a losing party, and the post-electoral political crisis and/or other related reasons decided to seek political asylum in the United States. Another possible reason is that African immigrants may feel that their countries' embassies do not have much to contribute to their welfare, and that the officers running it are ethnically or regionally biased against them. These ethnic or regional biases have often poisoned and muddied the waters of African solidarity abroad. Besides the myth of return, there is the issue of sending remittances to relatives back home. Because of the extended family system in Africa, the African immigrant families cannot think solely in terms of nuclear family arrangements. Since, on the average, the African immigrant hails from a large extended family, the opportunity to live in America is a boon or a bane, depending on the personal circumstances of the immigrant family. The African immigrants who have close social and familial ties back home have the constant ritual of going to American banks, money transfer agencies, African-managed foreign exchange bureau, and to returning compatriots to deposit monies intended for relatives back home.[21]

Another issue that increasingly affects African immigrant families is the spread of negative values into the African immigrant community. These include the rise of criminal activity and embrace of the drug culture by some African immigrants. The drug culture deserves proper historical treatment. There are many gaps in our knowledge about this phenomenon. New research is necessary. Some African immigrants are now confined to US jails and prisons as a consequence of involvement in the narcotic trade.[22] Some have become homeless due to complications from uncontrollable drug use, mental illness, alcoholism, and spiraling financial downturn. There remains such a dearth of information about the causes and consequences of homelessness among African immigrants that scholars must engage in research and share their findings. Data and information on African immigrants in the United States could also be useful in shaping public policies to better meet the needs of the homeless.

CONCLUSION

Five points are worth remembering about the new waves of African immigrants in the United States of America. First, Africans have now decided to settle in the United States voluntarily over one hundred years after the Civil War, and over two hundred years after the American abolition of the slave trade. This is a historical watershed in the sense that the diversity of Africa that characterized the first waves underwent transformation in the colonial era. Whereas the first wave of Africans came as citizens and subjects of ethnic nationalities, kingdoms, and empires, of the pre-colonial era, their brethren who came here during the last one hundred years arrived as citizens of nations that did not exist in 1619 or 1865. Secondly, the new Africans are transnational, and they carry multiple identities that will affect their relationships with African Americans, and other Americans, with fellow African immigrants and with persons living in their home countries. This is part of the new reality of globalization. The African immigrants who can successfully juggle these multiple identities effectively are qualified to call themselves transnational. Many are not only comfortable in their culture of origin, but able to operate meaningfully and effectively anywhere in the global environment. Thirdly, the African immigrant family faces the same difficulties as other immigrant families. The problems of identity and self-definition will remain issues that individuals and communities must address. Fourth, the role and place of religion in the lives of the African immigrants is of great consequence. The African tendency to hedge their metaphysical bets is most evident in the loving embrace of Abrahamic faiths, while simultaneously pouring libations at weddings, baby showers, public events, and funeral rites. Finally, African immigrants are now a part of American society, and their children and grandchildren will most likely be driven by similar impulses that have propelled other Americans.

NOTES

1. For some discussion on the founding of Liberia and the Post Bellum relations that existed between African Americans and Africa, see the following works (Magubane, 1987; Uya, 1971; Weissbord, 1973).

2. The story of Chief Sam is available in Langley, J. A. (1973). *Pan Africanism and Nationalism in West Africa 190* ("Growth of Islam in America," The Saudi Gazette, October 19, 1983) see also Adib Rashad, Islam, Black Nationalism & Slavery. A Detailed History (Beltsville, Maryland: Writer's Inc., 1995), pp. 141–142, *0–1945*. New York: Oxford University Press and Geiss, W. B. (1964). *The Longest Way Home: Chief Alfred Sam's Back to Africa Movement.* Detroit: Wayne State University.

3. Weissbord, R. G. (1973). *Ebony Kinship. Africa, Africans, and the Afro-American.* Westport, Connecticut: Greenwoord Press.

4. See Nyang, S. (1983, October 19). "Growth of Islam in America." *The Saudi Gazette,* and Rashad, A. (1995). *Islam, Black Nationalism & Slavery. A Detailed History.* Beltsville, Maryland: Writer's Inc.

5. Ahmed I. Abu Shouk, J. O. (1997). "A Sudanese Missionary to the United States: Satti Majid, 'Shaykh allslam in North America', and his Encounter with Noble Drew Ali, Prophet of the Moorish Science Temple Movement." *Sudanic Africa*, 8, pp. 137–191.

6. For more information on Duse Muhammad Ali, see Ian Duffield's dissertation on this African journalist and activist, Duffield, I. (1971). *Duse Mohamed Ali and the Development of Pan-Africanism, 1866–1945.* Ph.D. dissertation, Edinburgh University.

7. For some continental views on American society and culture, see Azikiwe, N. (1970). *My Odyssey: An Autobiography.* New York: Praeger. Also see Dosumu-Johnson, T. (1980). *Reflections of an African Nationalist* (chapters 3 and 4). New York: Vantage Press, and Nkrumah, K. (1957). *Ghana: The Autobiography of Kwame Nkrumah.* New York: International Publishers.

8. For some discussion on K. W. Aggrey, see the following: King, K. (1970, Fall). "James E.K. Aggrey: Collaborator, Nationalist, Pan African." *Canadian Journal of African Studies*, 3 (3), pp. 511–530.

9. Kwame Nkrumah gives some interesting analyses of American society. See his autobiography, *Ghana. The Autobiography of Kwame Nkrumah*, op.cit.

10. For some discussion on the Cold War and its impact on educational programs in the developing areas, see the following works: Rowe, R. W. (1961, June 22). "Strangers in Africa." *The Reporter*, pp. 34–35. Robert Weissbord, op. cit., chapter 6.

11. The factors leading to the brain drain are well known in the literature. For more details and analyses, see the following studies: Mutume, G. (2003, July). Reversing Africa's "brain drain." *Africa Recovery*, 17 (2); Tebeje, A. (2005, 2 22). *Brain Drain and Capacity Building in Africa.* Retrieved October 31, 2008, from International Development Research Centre: Science for Humanity: http://www.idrc.ca/en/ev-71249-201-1-DO_TOPIC.html For a comprehensive database of mostly online sources on the brain drain, also see: The Board of Trustees of the Leland Stanford Junior University. (1994–2005). *Topics: Education: African Brain Drain.* Retrieved October 31, 2008, from SULAIR: Africa South of the Sahara: http://wwwhttp://www-sul.stanford.edu/depts/ssrg/africa/africaneducation/africa-brain-drain.htmlsul.stanford.edu/depts/ssrg/africa/africaneducation/africa-brain-drain.html.

12. For some discussion on African students in the West, especially in the United States, see the following books: Kayira, L. (1965). *I will try.* New York: Doubleday. Nkrumah, K. (1957). *Ghana: The Autobiography of Kwame Nkrumah.* New York: International Publishers. Azikiwe, N. (1970). *My Odyssey: An Autobiography.* New York: Praeger. Dosumu-Johnson, T. (1980). *Reflections of an African Nationalist* (chapters 3 & 4 ed.). New York: Vantage Press.

13. For U. S. Immigration & Naturalization Service's statistics on African immigration since the late 1950s, see the annual reports from 1955–98*;* also see: Lennon, C. J. (1999, February). "Historical Census Statistics on the Foreign-born Population of the United States: 1850-1990." Retrieved October 31, 2008, from US Bureau of the Census, Population Division: http://www.census.gov/population/www/documentation/twps0029/twps0029.html ; United States Department of Homeland Security. (2004–2007). *Yearbook of immigration Statistics.* Retrieved October 31, 2008, from http://www.dhs.gov/ximgtn/statistics/publications/yearbook.shtm; Robinson, B. A. (1994, December). *US Bureau of the Census Population Division Working Paper No. 9.* Retrieved October 31, 2008, from ESTIMATES OF EMIGRATION OF THE FOREIGN-BORN POPULATION: 1980–1990 http://www.census.gov/population/www/documentation/twps0009/twps0009.html.

14. For some discussion on the Somali presence in the United States since the fall of ex-dictator Siad Barre, see: Condon, P. (2006, February 17). *Minnesota leads nation in Somali immigrants.* Retrieved October 31, 2008, from Minneapolis Public Radio: http://minnesota.publicradio.org/display/web/2006/02/17/somalipop/; Semple, K. (2008, October 15). *A Somali Influx Unsettles Latino Meatpackers.* Retrieved November 1, 2008, from New York Times: http://www.nytimes.com/2008/10/16/us/16immig.html?ref=us; Grieco, E. (2004, September). *The African Foreign Born in the United States.* Retrieved November 1, 2008, from Migration Policy Institute—Migration Information Source: US in Focus: http://www.migrationinformation.org/Usfocus/display.cfm?ID=250.

15. Husband and wife team, Getachew Metaferria and Maiginet Shifferew attest to the key role played by the Ethiopian Coptic Church as an agent of socialization. See: Haddad, Y. Y. (Ed.). (2002). *Muslims in the West: From Sojourners to Citizens.* New York: Oxford University Press, p. 256.

16. RCGG North America "Our Legacy." http://www.rccgna.org/mcm/rc/tgen.aspx?articleid=62&zoneid=1 Accessed January 15, 2011; Afe Adogame, "Contesting the ambivalences of modernity in a global context: The Redeemed Christian Church of God." *Studies in World Christianity*, Volume 10, pp. 25–48, 2004; Andrew Rice "Mission from Africa," *The New York Times*, April 8, 2009 http://www.nytimes.com/2009/04/12/magazine/12churches-t.html?pagewanted=all accessed January 17, 2011.

17. "Brotherhood of the Cross and Star. Christ Universal Spiritual School of Practical Christianity." http://www.ooo-bcs.org/ Accessed January 17, 2011

18. See Chike Anigboh on the role played by Nigerian immigrant churches, Ibid, p. 257.

19. Diouf-Kamara, S. "The Senegalese in New York: A Model Minority?/Senegalais De New York: Minorite Modele?" *Black Renaissance/Renaissance Noir, 1* (2).

20. There are limited studies on African immigrants regarding language maintenance. For some general discussion of the African immigrant situation, see the following works: Lamba K. Navjot, M. M. (2000). *Immigrants and Ethnic Minorities on the Prairies: A Statistical Compendium.* Edmonton, Alberta, Canada: Prairie Centre of Excellence for Research on Immigration and Integration.

21. Okome, M. O. (2006). "Spinning an African Academy into the World Wide Web: the Liberatory and Democratic Potential of African Scholarship in Cyberspace"; *The Bridging the North-South Divide in Scholarly Communication on Africa: Threats and Opportunities in the Digital Era Conference.* Leiden: The Netherlands Online <.PDF>. 2008-10-31 http://www.ascleiden.nl/Pdf/elecpublconfokome.pdf. 22 For some discussion on Africans and the narcotic trade, see Ebbe, O. N., 2003-08-16 "Drug trafficking, money laundering, and political-criminal nexus in Africa," *Paper presented at the annual meeting of the American Sociological Association, Atlanta Hilton Hotel, Atlanta, GA Online* <.PDF>. Accessed 2008-10.

22. Neal, Ronald V, "Merchants of Death Target Africa," *Africa Recovery*, 12, no. 1 (August 1998): p. 7.

Chapter 10

Multifaceted Identity Options

The Case of Two Immigrant Associations in South Africa

Magdaline Mbong Mai

INTRODUCTION

Anglophone and Francophone identities are the defining identity markers in Cameroon which seem rather irrelevant in South Africa. In Cameroon, various factors in terms of linguistic identification come into play, the most important of which is the geographical distribution of the country, with 80 percent of the regions being Francophone (French-speaking) and only 20 percent Anglophone (English-speaking). Nonetheless, with current globalization trends, the term "Anglophone," and being Anglophone is sometimes contradictory for it could be used to denote both the inferior and superior "stranger." For instance, unlike some Francophones who may scorn English, some Anglophones seem to take official bilingualism (of English and French) seriously by portraying some degree of fairness in mastery and usage of both languages in Cameroon. Yet, in order to gain the advantages of globalization often expressed in English, and to gain advantages of the Commonwealth, some Francophones also identify with English and Anglophones.[1] However, erudite literature continuously shows that it is the two official languages, and not the many national languages, which constitute a problem.[2]

Ultimately, the choice of using one language over the other is complex because it is not solely a linguistic choice. It is a choice that reflects issues of identity or belongingness as revealed in the social practices (or daily activities) of social actors. This complexity is captured in the notion of performative identities[3] complemented by notions of amalgams[4] captured in discursive practices which show how social agents talk about things using the *discourses* at their disposal.[5] This is tantamount to the notion of "language as a social practice, speakers as social actors and boundaries as products of social action[6] in times when many languages are fused together as in amalgams by focusing on the dynamic nature of place in order to capture what is in places and, how people move through them as in translocality.

Translocality here is defined as a variety of enduring, open and non-linear processes, which produce close interrelations between different places and people. These interrelations and various forms of exchange are created through migration flows and networks that are constantly questioned and reworked.[7] In fact, the usefulness of performative identities is seen in the shift of multilingualism away from completely bounded units of code and community to a more processual and material approaches where language is a social practice as discussed further on.

Like Cameroon, South Africa has also been colonized by different European powers, which variously shaped the dominance, "officialness" and importance of certain languages over others. Nevertheless, unlike Cameroon, the advent of democracy in 1994, paved the way for constitutional recognition of eleven official languages, including South African indigenous languages. However, in South Africa, English is the main lingua franca among speakers of different languages, and it is also preferred language in education and the media.[8] Given the complex multilingual diasporic landscape in which heterogeneous Cameroonian immigrants find themselves, it becomes interesting to investigate how they confirm and/or contest their Anglophone and Francophone identity options among others.

In the paragraphs that follow, I offer a brief review of the effects of demographic distribution, the concept of performative identities, the relocation of Cameroonians to, and transplantation in, South Africa, and a summary of orders of discourse. This chapter ends by arguing for disorder of discourse and other underlying notions of mobility and trans-(localization) and recommend further investigation on stylization and amalgams.

Performativity in Identities: Demographic and Socio-Economic Trends

In Cameroon, the relationship between language, identity, and demography is saliently reflected in the fact that Francophones occupy top-ranking positions in government and civil service. [9] Although not explicitly related to identity, the role of language in identity construction is widely acclaimed and its slippery nature is readily acknowledged.[10] Not unexpectedly, the dominance of French including the Francophone identity over all other linguistic groups becomes so visible that "one cannot travel in Cameroonian cities without gaining a sense of pervasiveness of French culture as an influence on Cameroon in terms of language, dress, food, items for sale in shops and stores, and in numerous other ways ..."[11] On the other hand, the feeling of unity is so strong that "being Anglophone" denotes a new ethnicity, transcending older ethnic ties. For[12] the plurality of Cameroon and its French-English official bilingualism has constituted various linguistic strata identification for Cameroonians for decades while the national languages remain inferior, and Cameroon Pidgin English (CPE, arguably a creole) is still treated with scorn despite its widespread use for over 500 years.[13]

Following from this, it can be said studies on identity constructions in postcolonial states often overlook the multilingual realities in such societies.[14] I argue that languages extend the performance of different identities.[15] Some authors contend that "we can make no sense of the emblematic function of *things* without first considering whether their emblematic functions are formulated through text-level or stereotypic principles of indexical effectiveness."[16] Agha's point here is that a person's "enregistered identities" depend on the context and topic of conversation ("text-in-context relations") "between signs that occur in their actual behaviours" in a particular encounter. The usefulness of the notion of performative identities' in this chapter stands in its ability to open new ways for arguments that question the hegemonic view of nation-states while simultaneously offering alternative accounts for the way speakers draw on available resources to perform different identities.[17]

Cameroonians have often demonstrated linguistic and emotional attachment to their many national languages that number up to 230, in addition to their two official languages, to the country's dominant lingua franca, CPE, which for many is a mother tongue) and the various regional lingua franca: Fulfulde, Ewondo, Basa'a, Douala, Hausa, Wandala, Kanuri, Arab Choa and Camfranglais, a new sociolinguistics phenomenon (also known as Franglais, or Francamglais).[18]

Cameroonians in South Africa: A Brief Sociolinguistic Context

With the collapse of apartheid, especially after the 1994 election, there was continuous influx of immigrants for various reasons. In Cape Town, some came in search of higher standards of living, and joined the world of commerce as business people (among whom are hotel managers, waiters, hawkers, and cyber café and shebeen (informal business) owners, others joined the entertainment industries as movie actors or attendants, other came for further education, and other came as refugees.[19] Yet there are others who came as highly skilled professionals, for example medical doctors.

Consequently, one finds Cameroonian immigrants in almost every sphere of life in Cape Town. In 2013, there were 108,711 immigrants in South Africa of which approximately 2,234 (2.9 percent) were Cameroonian immigrants. Given the rapid influx of this population every year together with its linguistic diversity and plethora of languages, this population became a compelling sample for this chapter. Cape Town, where the study is situated, is equally a multilingual environment with eleven official languages.

Following the Group Areas Act No 41 of 1950, which not only authorized rigid and forceful separation of people based on ethnolinguistic background but also restricted movement,[20] the sociolinguistic situation in South Africa like that of Cameroon also becomes emotive. For instance, the provincial languages of the Western Cape are Afrikaans, English and isiXhosa. But once in Cape Town, Afrikaans is still the most dominant language compared to isiXhosa in the Eastern Cape. In other words, there is an apparent lack of order on how the three-language *policy* is to be rationalized, practiced or implemented. Hence, Cameroonian immigrants tend to choose any available language depending on the contexts and the topic.[21]

Orders of Discourse: Disorders of Discourse in Cameroonian Meetings

Discourse is more than just ways of thinking and producing meaning. Rather, it constitutes social practices, forms of subjectivity and knowledge, and power relations.[22] The Foucauldian focus on orders of discourse clarifies how discourses shape and create meaningful systems, giving the appearance that these systems are given and natural. Once naturalized, these orders tend to dominate personal identity and social practices, often leading to the marginalization of other discourses. Foucault, looking specifically at the social construction of madness, punishment and sexuality, points out that alternative discourses which are subjugated can become sites of contestation and resistance to the hegemonic practices.

Disorders of discourse, on the other hand is a new approach to understanding communication and possible barriers to communication in various institutional contexts such as, clinics and schools. This theoretical approach identifies and describes certain mechanisms often embedded in contexts such as the media, hospitals, and so on, that affect communication by distinguishing between the outsider and the insider through familiar jargon that are inherent in structure of the various discourses themselves, that may result in some conflict between domains of knowledge.[23] In both CANOWACAT and Mifi formal meetings, what seems to be the case is that the people may appeal to both pure standard norms of doing business as in orders of discourse at one point, and/or to non-standard norms and preferred linguistic choices of mixing codes simultaneously.

Methodology and Research Design

Data were sourced from open-ended interviews, field notes, focus group, and participant observations. This multi-sited ethnography was suitable for interpretative naturalistic approaches.

The design was qualitative. Given the dense linguistic structures and actions explored, this research design relied on descriptive analysis.

Data Collection Strategies and Ethical Procedures

Data collection began with a three-month exploratory work followed by thirteen-month additional fieldwork. To access the daily affairs of Cameroonian immigrants during this period, the researcher participated in their leisure activities (e.g., soccer matches and family functions). Both purposeful and opportunities sampling techniques were used. Purposeful sampling targeted only those Cameroonians that had been identified by other Cameroonians as responsible and knowledgeable given the sensitivity on issues of identity and choice of language.

Forty key informants were selected for interviews depending on sociolinguistic factors namely Cameroon official languages[24] and other languages spoken by participants and their diasporic socio-economic activities. Each interview session lasted between 45 minutes and an hour depending on the responses of the participants. The focus group discussions lasted for at least one hour. The focus group discussions comprised four separate groups; two of which were made up of Anglophones and the other two Francophones. There were ten participant observation sessions of at least two hours. Each was recorded during meetings. Five of these observation sessions focused on the Cameroon North Westerners Association (CANOWACAT). The other five observation sessions focused on the Mifi Association. The length of time for recording depended on participants' willingness to continue an interview session, levels of noise, and other distractions at any given site. Permission was requested while soliciting free and unforced consent before audio recordings. Following from the level of familiarity with informants, they felt at ease both with researcher and research materials. The anonymity of all participants was maintained by the use of pseudonyms. Given the linguistic nobilities described herein, it was often difficult for the researcher to determine who was an Anglophone or a Francophone.

Research Participants

This consisted of two meetings: the Cameroon North Westerners Association (CANOWACAT), and the Mifi Association in Cape Town. Initially created for those immigrants from the North-West region CANOWACAT was suitable because it is relatively older than others group with a constituency of one and sixty members. In addition, both Anglophones and Francophones attend this meeting. The Mifi Association in Cape Town is made up of Francophones from the Mifi division of the Western region in Cameroon and, although relatively new, it is the Anglophone counterpart in Cape Town especially because people from both regions are called Grassfield people. People from this province and the languages they speak are generally referred to as Bameléké.[25]

Limitations

Some interviews and observation sessions took place in shebeens, which could be noisy and disorderly environments, contributing to a level of Geertzian descriptive "thickness" and "messiness" in the findings. Furthermore, for those recordings in national languages, the researcher depended only on the verbal interpretations from an interpreter who could not write the languages given the underdevelopment of some national languages. With these gaps, this chapter cannot claim to have provided a fully comprehensive ethnographic picture describing all the features and practices within Cameroonian meetings in Cape Town.

Data Analysis

The data were transcribed by the researcher and analyzed based on content analysis following the systematic procedure outlined by some scholars.[26] Given the researcher's translation background, the researcher was able to translate French, Camfranglsis and CPE to English. Translation was done in a literal manner to maintain originality. The data analysis was conducted using content analysis by first listing and coding all comments from research participants. Next, response patterns were identified and organized into coherent categories. Then, the recurrent ideas were grouped into themes. This was later classified into emergent categories. Both females and male participants were considered to address gender balance.

RESULTS AND DISCUSSION

Orders of Discourse in CANOWACAT Meetings

Like CANOWACAT, Mifi meetings use official languages too. It is expected that both *standard* norms and *pure* linguistic forms would be used during interactions in these official meetings. But, CANOWACAT and Mifi meetings seem to be observing both orders of discourse and disorders of discourse in the sense that some standard norms (the use of official languages, English or French) of conducting business and a combination of disorders of discourse in form of the use of a preferred linguistic form or the insertion localized informal aspects of language were observable. Code-mixing often occurred in just one word, a phrase, a sentence or other practices specific to Cameroonians.

Prayer, which was always first on the agenda, was said in stiltedly "biblical" English, as demonstrated below:

Samantha: Thank you lord [. . .]. Grant your travelling mercies to our brothers and sisters who are still on their way and bless our brother (name) [. . . .].

In the prayer above, the use of "Old" English was obvious. This was achieved by using highly "standardized" biblical forms of English "Grant your travelling mercies . . ." Even by British standards, such stilted English could be deemed outmoded. That is, the English themselves would rarely use such English nowadays. The question then is why is it still used here? It could be because the legacy of the influences of British colonialism which ensures that missionary-era diction still finds relevance for Cameroonians gathered at such meetings.

However, in terms of language use, there were a lot of amalgams and chat back at Cameroonian gatherings which is not the case in Western ones.[27] Even though meetings could start in English as shown above, it was not uncommon to start meetings with Cameroonian indigenous languages or with CPE as shown below:

Ursula: Papa God, you [. . .], wu beg say make you bless wa other brother and sister dem for reach here safe. Thank you, papa, [...]. /God our father, [. . .], we beg you to equally bless our brothers and sister still on their way and lord, thank you [...].

Ursula's prayer and message was similar to that of Samantha but was in CPE. Here, disorders/orders of discourse is implied in the sense that like a madman's discourse; CPE, Franglais and some Cameroonian national languages may be used even during Cameroonian *official* meetings in the diaspora. Whatever the language used, it was usually a formal traditional version full of meaning. The content of the prayers often circulated around safety/protection, guidance, and thanksgiving.

Also, there is a lot of flexibility with regard to time unlike in Western meetings.[28] The issue of a quorum was not necessary for a meeting could start whenever the chairperson was ready, and those early for the meeting thanked God for protecting them while requesting traveling mercies for the latecomers. Alluding to latecomers does not necessarily mean that those present were on time. It simply means those coming after prayers.

Normally, the people will come between half an hour to two hours late and then members begin to find out about personal wellbeing of others and if others had received text messages reminding them of the meeting. Whereas Western meetings always have set norms and people's contributions are judged as being related to the point,[29] in Cameroonian meetings, there is spontaneous multilingualism and some "talk" might appear irrelevant to proceedings from a Western perspective.

Even when meetings started in English and French, the issues of standard and non-standard did not seem to matter. What was evident from the outset was that interactional regime or the rules governing Cameroonian meetings are not as systematic as suggested in orders of indexicality. *Orders of indexicality* refers to a systematically reproduced stratified meanings often called norms or "rules" of language, like those found in "standard" forms versus *non-standard* forms.[30] Therefore, it can be said that language and socio-economic structure have not crystallized neatly into a package among Cameroonian immigrants. This means language choices and forms do not necessarily relate to socio-economic status[31] of the interactants or the formality of the meeting. In this regard, the researcher tends to condone researchers who have argued that standard norms in sociolinguistics have increasingly proven to be a fallacy.[32]

In African multilingual contexts, people use their linguistic repertoire to perform different identities, often unimpeded by Western restrictions of *formalities* on language usage.[33] Thus, as they used their linguistic repertoire to continuously redefine who they are and to position themselves and others in various ways, the two Cameroonian official languages may be articulated interchangeably within the two Cameroonian meetings in question without any inference about the divisive component attached to the official languages. Even when they used the *standard* or official languages English and French, they did so in a way that reflected their life experiences and every day practices (or social practices) by using them together with other languages as a singular linguistic repertoire.[34] Important here is the issue of transference of linguistic items from one language to another. This includes both code-mixing or intrasentential code-switching (i.e., the change from one language to the other in a single utterance) and code-switching (which is more or less the subconscious change into another language) by bilinguals. The Cameroonian immigrants' activities therefore represented "a reordering of the 'order of indexicalities.'"[35] This means, the Cameroonians assign a symbolic value to English and French as these languages alone neither carry any significant value nor helped them "climb the social ladder."[36]

Moreover, discourse among Cameroonian immigrants did not reflect the binary constructs of Anglophone or Francophone which is disseminated in many scholarly works.[37] Not only that, even when the meeting started in English or French variation, social stratification according to language or register based on centers and peripheries, was still blurred for the meeting continues in CPE and/or other national languages. Often, meeting activities and other announcements were circulated in CPE. For instance, Tommy a CANOWA-CAT member used the following short message service in CPE to announce pending elections:

Tommy: Tomorrow na CANOWACAT elections for 4pm [...]. Na (name) and (name) them di contest 4 that election [. . .]/The CANOWACAT elections shall be at 4pm tomorrow. Do not fail to come cast your votes. Those contesting are (name) and (name) [. . .].

The above excerpt is essentially a mixture of the global where both a localized form of language (CPE) and a global way of communicating—the internet is a norm.

On the contrary, sometimes the use of so-called Standard English at such gatherings was frowned upon. During most meetings, peoples' index hierarchy of identity[38] was contested if it was contrary to the group mode of solidarity. In one case, some meeting members expressed their displeasure in the linguistic choice of English-based codes only by screaming and disturbing. When someone insisted on using only Standard English, they were ostracized not because the audience did not actually understand as they claimed, but as a matter of social values, which dictated that "Standard" English was for people who wished to show off by speaking "Grammar" (note that "grammar" not just is Standard English in the real sense of the concept but represents high sounding English words). The extract below captures audience's response to a contributor at CANOWA-CAT meeting who spoke what they considered a "foreign" sounding English.

Audience: (?) wu no di hear because say ye di talk na grammar /we do not understand because he is speaking grammar (the word grammar among Cameroonians denotes standard English).

That meeting members showed their dislike for pure standard forms on one occasion corroborates the argument that in urban Africa, people do not just use English or French, often they use a *mix* of languages or amalgams.[39] This is also at the center of the disorders of discourse and it is the nature of urban language use in Africa as shown in an urban African city—Cape Town.

In another instance, Sammy who was to coordinate an American auction sale during a meeting performed many identities thus:

Sammy: I will first apologise for coming late. Make I try for dress like America-wander now, [turns his face cap in a way that the front is at the back],—I look now like yoh no bi so? / [. . .]. Let me try to dress like an American [. . .],—Now I resemble a stunning youth, don't I?

He first addressed the people in "standard" English then, switched to CPE combined with an African Americanism *Yoh* oscillating between the official languages (English), CPE African Americanism and even isiXhosa shows how social agents are able to claim multiple ownerships.

Yoh is commonly used by Cameroonian immigrants to refer to a trendy youth. The same explanation can be used to explain the compound the CPE *America-wander*. Americanisms have become part of the complex multilingual blend from which Cameroonians also draw their linguistic inspirations. Sammy's speech is "at least performance"[40] but in a heterogeneous situation where he uses available linguistic codes to signal hybrid and multiple identity affiliations. That both Cameroonian national languages and official languages may be spoken in one meeting house during one meeting session constitutes disorders of discourse.

Solo, who is from the North-West Region of Cameroon, preferred to identify more with Mifi of the Western region of Cameroon. Admittedly, Solo neither knew the name of the language attributed to him nor spoke the language of his assumed tribe. He was, however, fluent in the Bamiléké "dialect" of Baleng (a linguistic group of the Western province of Cameroon). In addition, he interacted with his parents in English and then used Camfranglais (mixture of French, English, national language phrases of Cameroon that varies between cities), English and French, and CPE, with friends. Since coming to South Africa, he has also added isiXhosa to his linguistic repertoire. This questions spatial boundedness and capture complex socio-spatial interactions with a focus on the social actor and hence provides translocal perspective for example translocality (or reterritorialization) that seeks to integrate notions of fluidity and disjointedness and associated nobilities. When asked about his national language Solo instead reveals a Mifi affiliation thus:

Solo: What language ah (laughs)? Actually, I don't know the name of my dialect. *Yeah, I actually understand a [...] bit of Baleng, Mifi—Bamiléké.*

Solo performs various identity options irrespective of ascribed identities. Such linguistic behavior, like that of other immigrants discussed elsewhere, questioned the validity of value of the indexical role played by language in relation to ethnic identity. Even though a member of CANOWACAT by birth, he is happy that people thought he was from the Mifi division. Solo actually claimed this Mifi identity during an interview. Through his social and cultural performances, he articulated ongoing acts of identity that are not always predetermined,[41] thus reconstructing and defamiliarizing the values behind monologic traditions or fixed discourses.[42]

It can be said that Cameroonian immigrants used an amalgam system[43] that is many languages at once to demonstrate the mobility of available identities options within dense multilingual settings[44] instead of mobility of (multilingualism and multiculturalism) across domains and contexts. This phenomenon of highly fused identities indicates multilingual and multicultural dispensation constitutes a way of life in postcolonial communities, and is not new.[45] It can be said different option have long been overlooked because of the predominance of monolingual bias in multilingual contexts.[46] What one sees among Cameroonian immigrants is the performativity of identities displayed in the usage of more than one code, a feature of language use which has been present since the onset of colonialists, and some cases, even before that.[47] Even the executive members of CANOWACAT for instance, the president are not insusceptible performing various multifaceted identities thus:

President: [The Secretary, whispering I no really know how wu go do with dis kitchen palava]. [to the general assembly] Thank you very much […] = =; [shouts at the noisy crowd seated in the kitchen] Eh kitchen […]. I really want beg for here say, [...] for those weh them di disturb [...].na meeting time. [...]. / [to Secretary in CPE] I do not really know what to do with this kitchen issue [then switches to English addressing general assembly] and shouts at the nosy crowd in the kitchen in CPE] Eh kitchen….] I really want to beg that […] for those disturbing, [...] now is meeting time. […].

It is noteworthy that before every meeting, there are always instructions from president for members to speak English only in order to accommodate South Africans. Yet, in the excerpt above, the president began using CPE, then addressed the general assembly in English and switched back to CPE to address those in the kitchen. Thereafter, he also spoke in what could be classified as neither English or CPE. That side talks mostly continued in CPE, other national languages and/or Camfranglais, which was never predetermined from the start in spite of the formal beginning in some meetings constitutes disorders of discourse.

Clearly, Cameroonian identities, are not only many but hybrid. Like in amalgams, their identities consist of a mixture of many languages and linguistic variations all of which form a communication code. There is no better demonstration of amalgams than Rico's speech, an active executive member of CANOWACAT:

Rico: In South Africa, Cameroonians do attend *crydie*, and *bornhouse*. [...] So once in a while, we put on these traditional clothes. […] and I go to dance mbaghalum [...].

Multilingualism among Cameroonians does not simply show them as language users. It reflects how they use language. Rico transliterates CPE and national language expressions into English by combining *crydie* (mourning for the deceased), *bornhouse* (celebrating new births), and *Mbaghalum* (one traditional dance practice). Code-mixing among Cameroonian immigrants is evident when they drew from various languages at their disposal even within one sentence to perform different identities. Before the formal start of their meetings, members may claim any identity suitable for them and this continued in side comments and even during meetings.

In essence, Cameroonian immigrants move between languages as a way to enhance meaning making and, in the process, signal various identities. Rico explains why he mixed codes:

Rico: You see, sometimes [. . .] when I'm speaking in English [...] I can better express myself with, those Pidgin words—[...].

What Rico is saying is that, in urban African contexts, a form of communication that is more than code-switching has developed. Though contradictory to his initial view of CPE as boring and unfit to be spoken outside of Cameroon, Rico draws from this language and other Cameroonian expressions to communicate and explicitly positions himself. He explains in the excerpt below why he uses this form of hybrid language that constitutes diverse elements from different sources. This is important in understanding the link between social contexts and languages use which simultaneously construct and constrains each other.

Rico: . . . sometimes, I feel that I really want to talk English but I feel that [. . .] the other people will think that it is like a show, [. . .] I try to also put in some of the pidgin words.

Ultimately, interactions and discourse practices by Cameroonians move away from dominant and political ideologies of pure and separate languages. Therefore, the Cameroonian discourses and social practices do not always reflect the binary constructs of either Anglophone or Francophone. Rico explained that all Cameroonians of both "Anglophone" and "Francophone" descent exploit their available linguistic resources to signal their various identities. He believed a Cameroonian can be Anglophone, Francophone, or both, depending on the circumstances.

Rico: It also depends on the individual, you and what situation that they are in that they will be able to say I am Anglophone, I am a Francophone.

Evidently, participants did not necessarily restrict themselves to a strict structural regime or orders of indexicality in terms of language use. They took control of language by positioning themselves in ways that enabled them to assert agency like Solo, president, Sammy and Rico did above. This form of language use shows that, among Cameroonian immigrants, the use of multiple codes is a norm, and English and French can be part of that code repertoire either separately or together as Victor explained further on.

In the same way as an individual was allowed to use an armory of languages to interact intelligibly, so too was it allowed to have multiple "tribal" and language affiliations with somewhat distinctive social practices or meeting agendas. Rico explains this.

Rico: [. . .] we have inter-tribal Associations. Like in South Africa, here I belong to CANOWACAT which is the mother association. I also belong to the Nkwen itself and the BFU [Banso Family Union] which is the Banso[Family] union.

Rico above belonged to three different socio-cultural groups, in addition to the Cameroon Association, which makes a total of four. The agendas of the different groups may overlap and sometimes appeared contradictory. An important complication occurred in the Cameroon soccer tournament of May 20, 2008 (May 20 is a public holiday in Cameroon commemorating the reunification of the two Cameroons) in the Maitland field—suburb of Cape Town. A goalkeeper was supposedly registered as member in two sub-associations within CANOWACAT and both wanted him to play on their side. For the goalkeeper choosing one group means relinquishing membership of the other social group. Sociolinguistically, this would also mean reproducing the socio-cultural structures built around ethnic classification at macro-social levels. The goalkeeper in this condition decided to play for CANOWACAT. As such, he successfully downplayed social structures by reminding the other groups of his belongingness to both through the parent association—CANOWACAT. Next, I explore proceeding of Mifi meeting together with its similarities or dissimilarities with CANOWACAT.

The Reconstruction of Great Mifi and Blurring of Linguistic and Social Structures in the Diaspora

This section highlights the tension between local and the transnational cultural flows as interaction of members within and across CANOWACAT and Mifi groups in Cape Town depict a localization (i.e., how multilinguals make sense of linguistic heteroglossia and multiple meaning that surrounds them) in Cape Town.

Although there may be some differences between CANOWACAT (Anglophone) group, and Mifi, the two groups, also have similarities as shown elsewhere. It is interesting to note that the kind of sociolinguistic behavior found at the CANOWACAT meetings also happens at Mifi meetings. Elianne, an active Mifi member illustrated this point:

> *Elaine:* Seigneur, Dieu tout-puissant, toi qui nous as permis de nous retrouver dans [...]. Que tu sois avec nous [...] et fait que ceux qui sont encore en chemin arrivent dans de bonnes conditions et que tous ensemble nous menons à bien l'évolution […]. / Lord God almighty who has made it possible that we meet in [...]may you be with us […] and make it possible for all those still on their way to arrive safely and that together we may […].

Mifi meetings also started in prayer but in French, and usually continued in French mixed with English and/or other national languages. Like Samantha, Elaine used an archaic language form (of French), triggered by the biblical references as follows: "Que tu sois avec nous...," and "que tous ensemble…." This form of French could be described as archaic even in France (as was the same with English in CANOWACAT). What is important here is how both forces of globalization and localization are at play during interaction. While minutes are mostly read in French or a blend of English, and French at Mifi; for instance, in CANOWACAT, successive secretaries have been noted for writing down minutes in English and read them in CPE. Such dense hybridity and mixing indicates there is re-ordering of discourse during these meetings, as the *normal* Western-style discourse order, and use of a *pure,* standard language from the start of a meeting until the end is reconfigured.

Oftentimes, the linguistic structuring is not along the numerous African languages, but along the colonial languages, French and English.[48] Just as was seen in CANOWACAT, Mifi did not always use French. The Mifi division (in the Western region of Cameroon) is a neighbor to the North-West province. Given their similarities in socio-cultural activities and sociolinguistic practices, indigenes of the Western region and North-West regions of Cameroon are referred to as grass fields people. Sammy's excerpt below substantiates this.

> *Sammy:* [...] you find that our traditions are virtually the same. [...] the Bamilékés for example; you know the North West traditional regalia [...]. You find the Bamiléké people having the same garment [...]. […] achu, the traditional dish in Mankon […]. […] their dead celebration. Is the same. Firing the guns, […].

The above extract shows the shared socio-cultural and sociolinguistic practices among Cameroonians. While Anglophones and Francophones are said to have different cultures because of their different colonial experiences,[49] data with respect to Sammy statement above emphasized identicalness among

Cameroonians through related socio-cultural practices, physical adornment and habitual cuisine across the grass fields. It is not surprising that some research participants seem to blame the colonial languages for the assumed and sometimes apparent division and tension. Sammy emphasizes this:

Sammy: It is only the language that separates us. But I still strongly believe that Africans are one ... in their culture.

Those of the Western region and the language varieties in this region are referred to as "Bamilékés"[50] by other Cameroonians and some indigenes of this province. Interestingly, most people of the Western Province prefer to specify a linguistic group especially when interacting with other Bamilékés. This classification into groups still subtly plays a role in the lives of the Cameroonian immigrants. The Western province of Cameroon consists of five other divisions, namely Nde, Haut Nkam, Bamboutos, Noun, and Menoua, with their respective capitals being Bangangté, Bafang, Mbouda, Foumban and Dschang. Today, the former Mifi division, known as the "great" Mifi division, has been divided into three more divisions following a government decision in the early 1990s. These include the following: Haut Plateaux, with Baham as its capital; Khoung-Khi, with Bandjoun as its capital; and (simply) Mifi, with its capital still at Bafoussam. Interestingly, the splitting up of the great Mifi division in 1990 has had no effect in Cape Town, since Mifi Association is still defined in relation to the boundaries of the great Mifi. The Mifi meeting are held every Monday, from about 2:00 clock until about 3:00 clock or 4:00 clock, at their president's residence in Goodwood (located in the northern suburbs of Cape Town).

Another form of disorders of discourse is perhaps the Cameroonian usage of the term "meeting" and its proceedings where many languages can be uttered in the same space and late coming acceptable. From the point of view of organization, the two Cameroonian meetings described in this chapter may not particularly fit into any of definitions or Western proceedings[51] since they are socio-cultural and/or socio-economic in form and late coming is not regarded as unhealthy. The Mifi meeting consisted of various segments, starting with *fond de caisse annuel* (annual contributions), and led up to *vente d'argent* (financial aid). Each segment was designed to perform separate tasks that together constituted the meeting but cannot be elaborate in this work given the limitation in space. However, practices during the *coup de cœur* (free-will donation) shows that a sacred and important Cameroonian ritual, namely incantation, was employed.

At this juncture, the person performing the task transcended social boundaries and drew from available resources at his disposal in this case a national language was employed, thereby portraying language as a social practice.

This instance directly counters the Focauldian structuralist approach in orders of discourse where language practices expected to be determined by specific discursive regimes or social structures.[52] That any Cameroonian language or language blend is used contributes to the disorders of discourse, the social nature of language and the performative nature of identities. Mifi also uses linguistic resources independently of the often prescribed or assumed identities of Anglophone, Francophone, Bamoun or whatever else. As such, these categories seem to represent mere social boundaries which really do not have an effect on the interactions of the immigrants in Cape Town.

Furthermore, in Mifi like CANOWACAT, multiple affiliation of participant is not a problem. The speaker in the case of incantation first spoke in one of the ten variants of the Bamiléké languages. It was evident from observations that such linguistic behavior is not planned from the start. Ultimately, great Mifi is both reconstructed and transformed while simultaneously reconfiguring, the Anglophone/Francophone discourses. The argument then is that the social stratification built around the constructs of Anglophone/Francophone are fluid. From the above practices, a new perspective of a world with cultural flux is proposed[53]

Admittedly, the *disorder of discourse* in the Cameroonian meetings is evident given that they neither fit into Western standard versus non-standard forms of discourses. This in turn blurs the notion of centers and peripheries[54] as Victor and Alain's excerpts elucidate below. Victor who claimed he did not enjoy speaking using amalgams, nevertheless explains how this works and why people use this *stylized* language form. In his opinion, this language exhibits the creativity of the people. Because they are able to draw several languages into one and make language attractive by talking in a nice way.

Victor: Actually [. . .]. I think that [. . .] they kind of make it as a jest (jest among Cameroonians means stylish) you know yeah. They want—may be put it in a funny style you know make it erhm attractive. They want to talk in a nice way, you want to put the French—to be creative [. . .]. To say no, I can still talk like this, and this man will understand me [...].

Evidently, when Cameroonians came together, they perform different identity options available in a "stylish" way which deliberately despises structural (monolingual) norms of communication and, simultaneously displays their creativity. For Alain, the importance of blending language helps in recognizing Cameroonians one has never seen before.

Alain: [..] en fait pour reconnaître que ça c'est un Camerounais n'est-ce pas, [. . .] c'est le pidgin. Il talk, il talk, bon je sais que ça c'est un frère. / in fact, to know this is a Cameroonian [. . .] it is pidgin. [here he explicitly uses Franglais to demonstrate how they sometimes speak] talks and talks, well I know this is a brother.

Essentially, the divisive nature of the colonial languages was mitigated by code-mixing or code blending[55] in the Cape Town Diaspora. Alain believed it was the use of CPE and Camfranglais as expressed in "il talk, il talk" that mattered in recognizing and embracing a Cameroonian and not English or French. Such preferences of one variation over others and, practices explored herein, may reveal diverse (metapragmatic) ideologies, attitudes and perceptions beyond the scope of this chapter. That there are constant traces of different languages in the speech of Cameroonians as exemplified in this chapter, means that they disregard "the expectation that languages will neatly correspond to separate domains, and stay put where they are meant to stay put."[56]

Even though this chapter presents language practices of both CANOWACAT and Mifi as a multilingual dispensation for social actors, the social roles these two groups play in Cape Town are not necessarily the same. In contrast to the Mifi transnational identities with their socio-economic structured meetings, CANOWACAT meetings are mostly socio-culturally based. Pierre, a forty-year-old registered member of Mifi Association and an active CANOWACAT registered member, explains the social functions of the two groups:

Pierre: They [Anglophones] are more sociable, they're—they think about people rather than money but the "Francophone" people most of their things are about money.

Pierre's statement shows how performative identities engender other perspectives for the processes of identification and language use. While still considering himself as a Francophone by referring to Anglophones as "they," his decision to use English deliberately downplays linguistic boundaries and signal his belongingness to CANOWACAT. Again, reference to Mifi as "the Francophone" neither includes nor excludes him from the group, clearly demonstrating the slippery nature of identities and accompanying identity options. As can be seen, he uses any available resources (linguistic or socio-cultural) at his disposal to simultaneously claim and contest his assumed Francophone identity.

Pierre estimates that CANOWACAT focuses on creating a sense of cultural awareness and sensitivity to the needs and well-being of its members unlike Mifi that concentrate more on monetary transactions and rarely entertain issues involving visiting the sick, new babies or whatever else. The onus is on members of Mifi Association to bring food and beverages to meeting sessions unlike in CANOWACAT where there are always ready volunteers to host a meeting. This notwithstanding the Mifi president or anyone celebrating a birth, thanking Mifi for some support or out of sheer goodwill may sometimes volunteer to host the meeting. These unpredictable actions problematize diasporic communities.

CONCLUSION

This chapter investigated fluidity and complexity of the Cameroonian identity options in relation to how they move across places. The author used disorders of discourse among Cameroonian immigrants in attempt to accomplish this goal. The linguistic diversity shown herein substantiated the argument that every word has its own social history imbued with social *localized* meaning.[57] This chapter also determines who Cameroonian immigrants are in the Cape Town sociolinguistic, socio-economic, and socio-cultural space. Above all, the chapter shows how national identity becomes increasingly deterritorialized from the context of territorial boundaries by reconfiguring homogenous concepts, showing the porous nature of boundaries, and cultural differentiation through the imperatives of heterogenizing and glocalizing conditions, through linguistic choices and social practices influenced by translocality. The fragmentations of social identities, for example, the reconstruction of the great Mifi division into three other divisions that has no impact in the diasporic space, serve as examples of the performative nature, social construction and fluidity of identities.

While considering the orders of discourse in Cameroonian meeting houses, the author is of the opinion that pluralistic mode of speaking which celebrate multiple cultures and complex identities through the usage of amalgams, is an asset, "… as it is able to withstand the totalising (and essentializing) tendencies of both centre and periphery agencies."[58] As a way forward, language scholars and sociolinguists may further explore the possibility of stylizing and maintaining the usage of amalgams.

NOTES

1. Eric A. Anchimbe, "Anglophonism and Francophonism: The stakes of (official) language identity in Cameroon," In Alizés: Revue Angliciste de la Réunion 25/26 (2005), 7–26.

2. George, Echu. "The Language question in Cameroon." Yaoundé (2004). http://www.linguistik-online.de/18 04/echu.html. Accessed, April 28, 2006. Anchimbe, "Anglophonism and Francophonism," 7–26. Nicodemus, F. Awasome, "Reunification question in Cameroon. Was the bride an enthusiastic or a reluctant one?" *Africa Today* 47 (2) (2005), 90 –119, Charles, Alobwed'Epie, The Concept of Anglophone Literature, in Lyonga, N., Bayreuth University: Eckhart Breitinger, 1993. Charles, Alobwed'Epie. The Concept of Anglophone Literature, in Lyonga, N., Bayreuth University: Eckhart Breitinger, 1993.

3. Asif, Agha. *Language and Social Relations*, Cambridge: Cambridge University Press, 2007.

4. Christina, Higgins. *English as a Local Language: Post-colonial Identities and Multilingual Practices*. Bristol: MPG Books Group, 2009.

5. Deborah, Cameron. Identity, difference and power: Locating social relations in talk. In D. Cameron (ed.) *Working with Spoken Discourse*. London: Sage (2001), 15.

6. Monica, Heller. *Bilingualism: A Social Approach*. New York: Palgrave Macmillan Ltd, 2007, 1.

7. Alexander, Peth. "What is translocality? A refined understanding of place and space in a globalized world 2014," Available, http://transre.org/en/blog/what-translocality/. Accessed, 11/9/2015.

8. Anne, M., Beukes. "The first ten years of democracy: Language policy in South Africa." Paper presented at the Xth Linguapax Congress on Linguistic Diversity, Sustainability and Peace, 20–23. May 2004, Barcelona, Spain.

9. Aloysius, Ngefac. "Linguistic Choices in Postcolonial Multilingual Cameroon University."

10. S. Erdmann. "A third space: discursive realizations of immigrant identity," *Language and Intercultural Communication* 15(4) (2015), 475–493.

11. Anchimbe, "Anglophonism and Francophonism," p. 5.

12. George, Echu. "The Language question in Cameroon," April 28, 2004, George, Echu, "Coping with multilingualism: Trends in evolution of language policy in Cameroon," (2003a). http://web.fu-berlin.de/phin/phin25/p25t2.htm Accessed September 7, 2007.

13. Aloysius, Ngefac. "Linguistic Choices in Postcolonial Multilingual Cameroon,"149–164. George, Echu. "Multilingualism as a resource: The lexical appropriation of Cameroon indigenous languages by English and French." Yaoundé, 2003b, 1–14. http://www.inst.at/trans/13Nr/echu13.htm. Accessed June 28, 2008

14. Felix, Banda. "Defying Monolingual Education: Alternative Bilingual Discourse Practices in Selected Cape Town Schools," *Journal of Multilingual and Multicultural Development*, 31(3) (2010), 223.

15. Asif, Agha. *Language and Social Relations*, 2007, 236.

16. Ibid.

17. Bailey 2007. Monica, Heller. *Bilingualism: A Social Approach*. New York: Palgrave Macmillan Ltd (2007).

18. Robert Young, Franglais or Camfranglais?

19. Magdaline M., Mai. "Negotiation of identities and language practices among Cameroonian immigrants in Cape Town," Unpublished PhD thesis, University of the Western Cape, Cape Town, 2011.

20. Kamwangamalu, M. Nkonko, "Ethnicity and Language Crossing in Post-Apartheid South Africa," *International Journal of Social Language 152*, (2001): 86–95.

21. George, Echu. "Multilingualism as a resource" Yaoundé, 2003a, 1–14.

22. Michael, Foucault. *The Order of Things: An Archaeology of the Human Sciences*, New York: Vintage Books, 1970.

23. R. Wodak. (1996). *Disorders of Discourse*, Longman: University of Michigan, 1996.

24. Aloysius, Ngefac. "Linguistic Choices," (2010), 49–164.

25. http://www.cameroonweb.com/CameroonHomePage/tribes/languages.php http://www.cameroonweb.com/CameroonHomePage/tribes/languages.php.

26. H.F, Hseih, and S.E. Shannon. "Three approaches to qualitative content analysis." *Qualitative Health Research* 15(9) (2005), 277–1288.

27. Magdaline M, Mai. An Analysis of the effects of space and territoriality on language use: A sociolinguistic analysis of a multilingual population in the Diaspora. Mannheim: LAP LAMBERT Publishing (2012). Magdaline M., Mai. "Negotiation of identities." Cape Town (2011). M. Doyle and D Straus. The new interaction method: How to make a meeting work. Chicago: Playboy Press (1993). M, Smith. Bringing Peace to the Workplace. Leona St: Oakland (1986).

28. Jan Blommaert, "Polycentricity and Interactional Regimes in 'Global Neighbourhoods'." *Ethnographer,* 2005 (5), 20–235.

29. M. Doyle, and D. Straus. *The New Interaction Method: How to Make a Meeting Work.* (Chicago: Playboy Press, 1993). Smith, M. Bringing Peace to the Workplace. Leona St: Oakland (1986).

30. Jan, Blommaert. *Polycentricity and Interactional Regimes* 73 (5) (2005), 20–235.

31. Cecile, Vigouroux. *"The Smuggling of La Francophonie": Francophone Africans in Anglophone Cape Town (South Africa). Language in Society* (37) (2008), 415–434.

32. S., Canagarajah, M. Jerskey, "Meeting the Needs of Advanced Multilingual Writers." In Roger Beard, Debra Myhill, Jeni Riley and Martin Nystrand (Eds.), *The Sage Handbook of Writing Development.* London: Routledge: 472–488 (2009). S, Canagarajah. "Constructing hybrid postcolonial Subjects: Codeswitching in Jaffna Classrooms." In M. Heller and M. Martin-Jones (eds). *Voices of Authority: Education and Linguistic Difference.* London: Ablex Publishing, 113–212 (2001). Monica, Heller. *Bilingualism: A Social Approach.* New York: Palgrave Macmillan Ltd (2007). A. Pavlenko and, and A. Blackledge, (eds). *Negotiation of Identities in Multilingual Contexts.* Toronto: Multilingual Matters 2004.

33. George, Echu. "The Language question in Cameroon," April 28, 2004.

34. Eric, Anchimbe, Multilingualism, postcolonialism, and linguistic identity: Towards a new vision of postcolonial spaces. In Anchimbe (ed). *Linguistic identity in postcolonial multilingual spaces.* Newcastle: Cambridge Scholars Publishing (2007).

35. Cecile, Vigouroux. "*The smuggling of La Francophonie*," 426.

36. Cecile, Vigouroux. "*The smuggling of La Francophonie*," 427.

37. Anchimbe, "Anglophonism and Francophonism," 7–26. Nicodemus, F. Awasome, Reunification question in Cameroon 47(2) (2005), 90–119. George, Echu, "The Language question in Cameroon," April 28, 2004 Alobwed'Epie. The Concept of Anglophone Literature, 1993.

38. T. Omoniyi, "Hierarchy of identities." In T. Omoniyi, & G. White (eds.). *Sociolinguistics of Identity, Australian Review of Applied Linguistics* 32(1) (2006), 195–208.

39. Christina, Higgins. *English as a Local Language,* 2009; F, Mc Laughlin (ed.) *Languages of Urban Africa.* London and New York: Continuum International Publishing Group, 2009.

40. Macaulay, Ronald, Is Sociolinguistics Lacking in Style? *Cuadernos de Filologia Inglesa R* (1999): 9–33.

41. A. Pavlenko and, and A. Blackledge, (eds). *Negotiation of Identities* (2004).

42. C. O'Connor and S, Michaels. *When is Dialogue Dialogic? Human Development* (50) (2007), 275–285.
43. Christina, Higgins. *English as a Local Language*, 2009.
44. George, Echu. "Multilingualism as a resource," 3002a, 1–14, Also see Bird, S. "Orthography and identity in Cameroon." *Written Language and Literacy,* 4(2) (2001), 131–162.
45. George, Echu. "The Language question in Cameroon," April 28, 2004.
46. Ellis, E. "Multilingualism: The unmarked case." *Estudios de Sociolingüística* 7 (2):173–196, 2006.
47. Mc Laughlin. (ed.) *Languages of urban Africa*, 2009, Bird, S. "Orthography and identity in Cameroon" (2001), 131–162. George, Echu. "The Language question in Cameroon," April 28, 2004.
48. George, Echu. "The Language question in Cameroon," April 28, 2004.
49. Aloysius, Ngefac. "Linguistic Choices," (2010), 49–164.
50. http://www.cameroonweb.com/CameroonHomePage/tribes/languages.php.
51. http://stevenmsmith.com/ar-waiting-for-people-who-arrive-late/.
52. Michael, Foucault. "The Order of Things," 1970.
53. Agha, A., *Language and Social Relations*, Cambridge: Cambridge University Press (2007).
54. Jan, Blommaert. *Polycentricity and Interactional Regimes* 235 (2005), 73.
55. Ruth, Wardhaugh. *An Introduction to Sociolinguistics,* 1992, pp. 106–107.
56. Monica, Heller. "Bilingualism: a social approach." 2007, p. 11.
57. Pennycook, A. *Language as a Local Practice*, New York: Routledge, 2010.
58. Canagarajah, S. *Constructing Hybrid Postcolonial Subjects,* 2001, p. 210.

Chapter 11

Building Individual Future as Unwanted African Migrants in Johannesburg

Vulnerability, Hope and Microentrepreneurship

Christal Oghogho Spel

INTRODUCTION

This chapter starts with an exploration of informal migration as unwanted migration. It then follows with a discussion of social exclusion as the product of the compelling power of the state, but also of ordinary individuals. Attention is then called to how different interests in South Africa interact to shape the vulnerability experienced by informal African migrants. Finally, it uses data from narrative interviews conducted in Johannesburg, South Africa, to discuss hope and microentrepreneurship as means through which informal migrants build their lives in a context of vulnerability.

MIGRATION AS AN ART OF UNWANTEDNESS

Art is a human activity consisting in this, that one man consciously, by means of certain external signs, hands on to other feelings he has lived through, and that other people are infected by these feelings and also experience them.[1]
Years ago, I remember walking into the art studio of Auchi Polytechnic, an institution of higher learning in Edo State, Nigeria. It was the studio for all forms of sculptures; I stepped into the room and I was captivated. Totally enthralled, I told my host I could stay there forever. My host looked around and laughingly suggested that the studio is thrash, because there was no completed artwork there. He advised me to visit the gallery where the completed artworks are displayed.

However, it was the "unfinishedness" of the sculptures that captivated me. There were few students in the room working on their pieces of sculptures; everywhere there were sculptures of various forms, at different stages of completion. It was like being in the presence of God during the biblical creation of the world, only not in the magical form reported in the bible, but as a process, a procedure. In this process, an ordinary piece of wood can be carved, chiseled and cut into a feminine, masculine, animal or even mystical piece. Until today, a finished piece of art easily bore me; it is still the process that reproduced the art that captivates me.

From that same captivation with the process of creating art, I have been fascinated with the contemporary political responses to migration, and more interesting, the response of the migrants to their socio-political context. In the political response, the migrant has been fashioned by several formal requirements and obligations, into different categories—economic, illegal, expatriate, refugees, etc. However, the general categorization of migrants as legal and illegal becomes intriguing, more so with the negative characterization of those categorized as illegal. According to Tolstoy, "Art begins when one person, with the object of joining another or others to himself in one and the same feeling, expresses that feeling by certain external indications."[2] He gave an example:

> a boy, having experienced, let us say, fear on encountering a wolf, relates that encounter; and, in order to evoke in others, the feeling he has experienced, describes himself, his condition before the encounter, the surroundings, the woods, his own lightheartedness, and then the wolf's appearance, its movements, the distance between himself and the wolf, etc. All this, if only the boy, when telling the story, again experiences the feelings he had lived through and infects the hearers and compels them to feel what the narrator had experienced is art. If even the boy had not seen a wolf but had frequently been afraid of one, and if, wishing to evoke in others the fear he had felt, he invented an encounter with a wolf and recounted it so as to make his hearers share the feelings he experienced when he feared the world, that also would be art.[3]

In conceiving of informal migration as an art of unwantedness, the characterization of informal migrants as dangerous and destabilizing, becomes a piece of art created by the political to coerce and convince the public to share in his opinion. It is created (and hence not real) and an opinion because before migration, every unwanted migrant was socio-politically perceived as viable, productive, and with potentials as a human, and then incorporated into the common social, political and economic rights as recognized by the home society. However, the act of migrating across international borders without the required documents legally obtained is judged to divest one of those positive qualities. However, the individual can still be seen as retaining the potential, productiveness and viability irrespective of the politically constructed characterization.

The potential and viability of the individual was initially based on the understanding of the potentiality of the human race and not tied to any economic or political acquisitions, gains or accord. Is that not why the birth of a baby is celebrated? It was a potentiality that was not conferred by any form of political institution; it is commonly upheld that the people of any nation are one of the vital resources for development or growth. Arendt cautions that to consider political action as 'making' something is dangerous.[4] Conovan also highlights Arendt's views when she charged, "To conceive of politics as making is to ignore human plurality in theory and to coerce individuals in practice."[5]

To not conceive of politics as making is to ask the rhetorical question of 'who is a migrant? Or the converse of 'who is not a migrant? Although rhetorical, yet, the relevance of that question 'who is not a migrant?' demand that any discussion of unwanted migration or informal migrant's lives starts with an engagement of the politics that created and characterized the informal migrant. It is worrisome to ponder over what causes the transformation and removal of the potentiality and viability of the migrating human or rather to wonder if the potentiality and viability was actually removed/destroyed or veiled and covered. If such human potentiality has been politically, socially and economically linked to the development of human society over the years, why shouldn't we hold complicit the agent or act that is responsible for the destruction or veiling of such potentiality? That is, complicit for attempting to deny or denying society the opportunity to benefit from the potentiality of that individual or group of individuals? In this vein, what agent should we hold as complicit; the act of mobility that is as old as man or the political agency that is an instrument of man? Several authors have poignantly explained informal migration as the result of state's intervention in migration. For political purposes, the state has steadily created a Frankenstein hologram of a social group of persons characterized as criminals and detrimental to everything positive in the society by their migratory decision. Politics have thus sort to fashion the social and economic experience of the informal migrant by the political characterization.[6]

Nordman (as translated in Torpey) noted that "The vagabond is by definition a suspect."[7] Thus, by politically labeling some migrants, the state coercively, tactically and strategically conditions the practices of the host society. By promoting images of migrants as threatening aliens, the state stealthily pushes the ethical boundaries of its citizens, provoking acts of abuse committed by ordinary citizens on migrants as seen in South Africa.[8] Theoretically, this action of the state to create the hologram of a Frankenstein migrant can be construed as a desperate effort to bring under control a group of people that have intentionally excluded themselves from what Torpey called the erfassen of the state. Traditionally, Mann argues that the "Unusual strength of the modern state is infrastructural."[9]

Torpey expounded this argument by highlighting how the state exercises such power to compel and nurture its citizens to carry out its aims. Through a system of registration and identification, the state carries out activities for the purposes of surveillance, administration and regulations in order to "successfully embrace their populations and thus to acquire from them the resources they need to survive, as well as to exclude from among the beneficiaries of state largesse those groups deemed ineligible for benefits."[10] However, unwanted immigrants that reside and survive within the state irrespective of the state's permission are consequently considered threatening to the state's self-appropriated hegemonic power not only over legitimate means of movement but also over access to societal resources. This suggests that the unwanted migrants by definition are criminals and socio-economic usurpers through political labeling.

Furthermore, Torpey argued that the idea of belonging that the state has painstakingly crafted in order to penetrate or embrace its society, is threatened when people move across international borders; "leaving spaces where they "belong" and entering those where they do not."[11] In the face of infrastructural or institutional failure to aptly control the immigration of those deemed unwanted, the state is increasingly employing its private citizens in the control of those unwanted, through its relentless propaganda of the migrants as 'dangerous others'. Effectively, attempting to condition the individuals and private agents that migrants as dangerous is not a political construct but a social-cultural reality that threatens the economic stability of the society, notwithstanding contrary findings. Several studies are highlighting how states are moving the efforts at migration control from the border to internal society, subtly relying on its citizens and private agents that have zealously bought into the construction of the migrant as the threatening other for immigration control.[12]

Arguably the state has been forced to share its hegemonic control of surveillance and regulation of people with private agents and individuals, unintentionally sharing the power of monopolizing movement with others. Although such private agents and individuals are thought to be acting on behalf of the government, yet their personal inclinations are wont to affect how they carry out such responsibilities. This, could mean, private citizens could disagree with the political labeling and exclusion of the migrants and provide access to services and resources denied them or else act over zealously in enforcing such exclusions and reinstating such labeling.

In South Africa, the actions of these individuals often has the possibility to become violent and abusive as in the murder of migrants and wanton destruction of their properties as forms of informal migration control.[13] The state becomes implicit in fomenting the context where individuals with impunity can appropriate unto themselves the power to act on behalf of the state on issues of migration control, and possibly on any other issue. By extension, the state thus simultaneously creates situations of underutilization of the potential and ability of a large number of abled individuals because of its preoccupation with surveillance and regulation instead of innovation and creativity as fundamental to societal building.

Decades ago, economists have argued that a nation's economic growth is based on new opportunities through entrepreneurship and job creation among other factors.[14] The point is that beyond the arguments of 'pro' and 'against' migration and the complicity of government or not in creating illegality in migration there is a human angle—a human resource angle to this phenomenon of strategically and tactically reducing the capability of people based on their migration status and promoting a context where their humiliation, victimization and consequently abuse is pervasive and accorded the norm in society.

THE COMPELLING POWER OF POLITICS: SOCIAL EXCLUSION OF INFORMAL MIGRANTS

Sen argues that the concept of social exclusion is better understood when placed in the broader context of poverty as capability deprivation.[15] Sen's seminal work, Development as Freedom, discusses poverty in forms of "unfreedom," which he characterized as lack of social, economic and political means or opportunities to live the life that is valued by the individual. He thus emphasized poverty as the deprivation of the capabilities to achieve the life that is valued. Critically, therefore, poverty is emphasized in "terms of poor living, rather than just as lowness of incomes."[16] Notwithstanding the conceptual connections between poverty, deprivation and social exclusion, social exclusion contributes to our understanding of poverty by "its focus on the relational features in the deprivation of capability and thus in the experience of poverty."[17]

The informal migrant is by definition a candidate for social exclusion in the host society. This means that beyond the often-visible forms of vulnerability in the lives of informal migrants, there is also a non-material aspect that calls attention to prevailing policies in the host society. Although the experience of poverty and vulnerability are shared both by informal migrants and by some citizens in a context of high incidence of poverty, high unemployment and limited presence of government in terms of economic and social infrastructures, such as in South Africa.

Nevertheless, social exclusion calls attention to the vulnerability of informal migrants by not focusing on the level of income they generate but by "looking at the impoverished lives."[18] That is, examining the experiences of informal migrants in their host society as the deprivation of relevant capabilities that is accepted as contributing to a 'meaningful' life. [19] In that sense, the experience of the informal migrant is expatiated from the perspective of its relational connections.[20] From that understanding, the relational conditions that create and sustain the exclusion of informal migrants can be seen as couched in an interaction that is dynamic. Examining the relational connections of informal migrant experiences in the host society is not new.

Indeed, Neocosmos in exploring African migrants' experiences in South Africa calls attention to the relationship between the state and society. In his discussion, he argues that the process of exclusion is a political process that is lodged in the politics of statism, traced to colonialism and its socio-political aftermath.[21] Neocosmos examination of the connectedness of the politics of the state to African migrants' experiences in South Africa highlights three important points: firstly, the political relationship of citizenship; secondly, the conception of belonging or not belonging to a community; and thirdly, the social connectedness of the political. In that vein, the platform of social exclusion becomes a ground of struggle between political interests and the interests of various agents in the society.

In order for the state to effectively prevail in that struggle, it creates its own political discourses and benefits that are promoted as pivotal to the survival of the other party, that is, the social. Thus, the fundamental power of the state has come to rest more on 'governmentality,"[22] through which it appropriates the benefits of coercion and conviction to itself. In this sense, the compelling power of the state solidly rests on the political propagation of its ability and dedication to providing security (in its broadest form) for those that identifies with it. It is important to point out here that although the provision of resources by the state for the welfare of its population has been used to discuss states legitimacy, the legitimacy of the state is not in dispute in migration discuss.

Notwithstanding, it is the same 'trusteeship' of the welfare of its population that is used as the fundamental ground for the social exclusion of informal African migrants. In the context of post-colonialism and post-apartheid, the conception of the state as the trustee of its population could be seen as innately woven in the political institutions as the basis for legitimization. This trusteeship is thus invoked every time the state determines to take actions that ordinarily could be seen as being against culturally upheld values or ethics. Both ways, the state succeeds in entrenching its rights to act, but also providing the justification for the population to turn the other way, metaphorically speaking and otherwise. The platform of informal migrants' experience becomes the struggle between social inclusion and social exclusion both as political distribution of resources but also of social distribution of ethics, morality or its similarity.

BUILDING INDIVIDUAL FUTURE AS A SOCIALLY EXCLUDED

Caught in a dynamic context of inclusion versus exclusion, the situation of the informal migrant demands skillful navigation of political and social vitriol. The same can be said for the South African government, as it has to navigate a highly active third sector seeking for inclusion of the informal migrant, the increasingly restive citizenry demanding economic improvements in their well-being, and certain employers that reportedly believe that foreign migrants are more hardworking than South Africans, to mention a few. Indeed, social exclusion in South Africa cannot be productively seen in the narrow light of political exclusion as have been discussed above. For if the interest is as Sen highlights "the freedom to live minimally decent lives" then, firstly, the actions of the ordinary South Africans are of paramount relevance in shaping the context in which the informal migrants daily attempt to build their future.

Secondly, the migrants' perception of what entails decent lives becomes relevant, and thirdly, the migrant evaluation of how, where and when to attempt to live decent lives cannot be disconnected from the conception of 'capability deprivation.' Below, I discuss the activities of the different actors shaping the context under the sub-section on vulnerability, I then discuss the response of the informal migrant to the context under the sub-section on hope, and finally I discuss how the informal migrant build a desired future under the section on microentrepreneurship.

VULNERABILITY

Sen highlights the complexities of social exclusion by identifying four distinctions that can be useful in understanding its nature and reach. He argues that social exclusion can be of constitutive relevance when being excluded directly creates deprivation. Social exclusion could also be of instrumental importance, if it does not directly create terrible condition for the excluded, but can lead to other deprivation through causal linkages. Furthermore, he notes that social exclusion could be either active, when the direct goal of the exclusion is to create deprivation, or passive if deprivation is created through social processes. Nevertheless, the point is to call attention to far reaches and complex nature of social exclusion. The immigration context of South

Africa and the conditions of African informal migrants is a microcosm of the complexities of social exclusion. The South Africa case becomes interesting as a large percent of its informal migrants have applied for refugee status and are either awaiting a decision or appealing against one. In this scenario, social exclusion takes many forms (in terms of either support or against) that could range from tactical, extra-legal or illegal, in the bid to protect national or migrants' interests.[23]

Firstly, post-apartheid South Africa is signatory to several international and regional regulations for fair, human rights based, and at times free mobility (within the Southern Africa Development Community (SADC) region). For example, South Africa has a bill of rights embedded in its Constitution. In addition, Article 5 of the SADC Treaty in 1992 called for "policies aimed at the progressive elimination of obstacles to the free movement of capital and labor, goods and services and of the peoples of the region generally, among members' states."[24] Secondly, South Africa is signatory to all international treaties on refugees and asylum seekers. Since 2000, the National Refugee Act that incorporates the standards of international conventions came into effect. Hence, the South African state is politically portrayed as one that promotes the discourse of constitutionality, democracy, human rights and diversity.

Thirdly, the unique context of South Africa has fostered a thriving and potent third sector or NGOs. These agents are actively working to remodel migration management in South Africa to international human rights values. CoRMSA[25] indicates that their activities progressively seek to change the migration context in ways that protect and upholds the dignity and rights of the informal migrants. Their activities are seen to contribute to the wellbeing of the informal migrants, and change South Africa's migration landscape from exclusion and control to one of survival gradually. Thus, the South African context reveals a high level of legal contestations in the practice of migration management in South Africa.

For instance, the rights of migrant workers were positively improved with the decision from a court case (Discovery health vs. Commission for Conciliation, Mediation and Arbitration (CCMA) and others, Labor Court, case JR 2877/06) involving Lanzetta an Argentinean and Discovery Health. His employer Discovery Health dismissed Lanzetta despite his work contract because his work-permit expired, citing the prohibition of an illegal immigrant by the Immigration Act. However, the court ruled that Lanzetta was still an employee under the Labor Relations Act. The decision is interpreted to apply to mean that employment contracts are valid irrespective of immigration status or the lack of it. The court ruling also strengthened the decision of the CCMA to extend its services to undocumented foreign nationals. It is important to point out that not all court decisions are favorable for the migrants.

Fourthly, the social context of South Africa is highlighted by several authors as highly hostile and prejudiced toward African migrants. Such hostilities, generally regarded as xenophobic, are characterized as "denial of rights and entitlements, expressed through prejudice and stereotypes."[26] In that context, the experience of informal African migrants paints a picture that calls attention to deprivation and exclusion in the social context—one that is substantially different from the regulations of international and regional bodies.

Several authors have called attention to the African migrants' experience of violent and often fatal xenophobia in South Africa.[27] Such xenophobic experiences include being prevented from accessing health care services, educational services for children, employment, trading, etc. For example, in an interview I conducted in Johannesburg, in 2013, informal African migrants reported that they are prevented from utilizing available health facilities in South Africa. They cited fear and experiences of discriminations and endangerments as reasons for staying away from health services.

However, the South African constitution makes provision for access to medical care for asylum seekers, as the country is a signatory to the International Bill of Human Rights. More so, Article 2 of the International Convention on Economic, Social and Cultural Rights guarantees migrants' rights to decent healthcare. In addition, section 27 of the Bill of Rights in South Africa's Constitution recognizes the rights of everyone to have access to health care services. Article 27 of South Africa's Refugee Act clarifies that like citizens, refugees have the right to access essential health services.[28] CoRMSA documents also show that South Africa's Department of Health identify with the need for basic health services to be accessible to people irrespective of their migration status. In this case, the South African government cannot be seen as actively excluding African informal migrants from accessing health care. Nonetheless, the South African government has been strongly implicated in actively creating the xenophobic social context of South Africa through its practices of immigration control and management.[29] Thus, on the one hand, the South African government is seen as not actively excluding African informal migrants from accessing health services; on the other hand, the government is seen to be actively creating a context in which the migrants are excluded.

Furthermore, Vigneswaran et al. citing the connection between the organizing principles of politics and principles of crime, argues that the discriminative, abusive and at times violent behavior of the police against informal African migrants, can be seen as representing "a collective effort by officials to shore up the state's monopoly over the legitimate means of movement and prevent other actors and organizations from encroaching on this exclusive prerogative." In that line of thoughts, it appears that while the government of South Africa is being compelled to improve the substantive inclusion of informal migrants according to international standard, other officials have assumed the responsibility to protect what they deemed as the state monopoly over both the legitimate means of movement, and of migrants' experiences in the country. Therefore, in the context of informal migration in South Africa, one can understand that vulnerability is influenced by social inclusion as well as social exclusion. That is, the social inclusion of informal migrants could create tensions and anxiety in citizens that backfires on the migrants through xenophobic discriminations and violence.

The South African case calls attention to the complexities of social exclusion in a developing country context. While it acknowledges the critical role of active social exclusion through policies, it decentralizes it, and refers us to the actual experiencing of vulnerability as central, irrespective of policies. For instance, while South Africa is seen as having a highly active third sector that fights for the rights and treatment of informal migrants according to international standard, the society is also portrayed as increasingly xenophobic and hostile to the migrants. Although it could be argued that the context of fomenting hostilities toward African migrants spurred the development of a thriving third sector, there is the suggestion that a context of highly active contestations and human rights pursuit should curtail the xenophobic hostilities. In addition, the society and officials are shown as an extension of the political, but also retaining the capacity to harbor its own agenda or interests (legally, extra-legally or illegally) which can be interpreted as self-centered or politically motivated.

In conceiving of the building of informal migrants' lives, interrogating vulnerability calls for broader perspectives that incorporate the political and the social. For instance, the social context of vulnerability calls attention to how, where and when do ordinary citizens formulate their conception of the informal migrants as the 'negatively construed' other. The focus then is not on the 'othering' but the characterizing and the evaluation of that other. From that understanding, the media for example becomes relevant, but the conception of 'media' will have to extend beyond local South African media to include a global or regional scope, if contemporary information flow is taken into consideration.

Another important aspect of the social is the relationship between ordinary citizens and the migrants. For example, prevailing informal employment relationship can create a power relationship that instigates a context of prejudice, abuse and discrimination of the lesser party. Another form of individual relationship as mentioned in literature is the personal relationship between South African females and African migrant males.[30] Steinberg has reported the hostilities of South African males toward African males on the basis of that relationship. However, there is also the suggestion of the possibility that when such relationship turn sour (as it often does) the female South African could also harbor hostilities expressed as discrimination, prejudice or xenophobia that will embrace all African migrants. Furthermore, the individual or social perception of power differentials, which could be based on the politics of nationalism, evaluation of national development within the region, or other ethnic qualifications could create basis for prejudice or xenophobia.

Quite relevantly, acknowledging the social aspect of vulnerability calls attention to the activities of the vulnerable. The role of the vulnerable (informal African migrants) could be examined either as catalytic[31] or as victims, whatever approach, it is important that the action and choice of the migrant is not blanketed.

Hope

Irrespective of experiencing vulnerability, informal African migrants continue to live in South Africa, some of them for decades. Although some authors have called attention to the temporality of the presence of the migrants in South Africa, their enduring presence suggests a hint of continuity when viewed from the perspective of individual goals and objectives. Their enduring presence and the continuity in the pursuit of personal goals and objectives can be conceptualized as hope. Snyder, a distinguished professor of clinical psychology narrates how he was introduced to the study of hope or what he referred to as "the other side of excusing," while doing research on people making excuses when faced with their error or inadequacy. His research participants informed him that the focus of the study restricted them from fully expressing themselves. The study centered on "how people want to increase the distance between themselves and their bad outcomes."

The research participants contend that they were also motivated to "decrease the distance to their positive life goals."[32] In essence then, Snyder argues that when faced with unfavorable outcomes or situations, people's reactions have two sides: they will want to take measures to reduce the experiencing of the unfavorable outcome, but the adverse outcome is not the only determinant of their reaction. Increasing access to their positive life goals is also a motivation for their action. Thus, as participants in a harsh context, the informal African migrant display hope through the actions they take to reduce the distance between themselves and the life goals.

Narrative data from my study of informal African migrants in Johannesburg in 2013, call attention to the migrants' quest to achieve better life. They indicated that it is that desire for better life that motivated the move from their home country. Their stories suggest that it is the hope to achieve better life that keeps them in the host country. Better life was used as synonym with several positive conditions and material acquisitions. The hope of the interviewees draws attention to the relevance of the future and the aspirations for the future among the vulnerable. The interviewees did not remain as informal migrants in South Africa just so that they can afford their basic daily meal, housing or clothing. Rather, they reported that they persevere in the South African context because they aspire to establish their own successful electronic business, start a construction company at home country, start international businesses, etc. In essence, they will not be satisfied with the provision or access to basic living; they imply they are seeking, a broader, stronger and more subjective acquisition of economic and social resources.

Thus, one response of the informal migrant to their harsh context is to hold on to their aspirations as a motivator and a navigator. That is, the notion of aspirations becomes relevant in the understanding of how the migrants build a future in the constraining context, creating an interesting polarization of victimhood. The relevance lies in the day-to-day decisions and choices of the migrant. Two things become relevant about the informal migrants' aspirations. Their aspirations as hope imply non-substantive achievement, and hence room for fluidity, flexibility and change. Thus, in the building of their future, the informal migrants create the image of a temporary agent, one without long-term plans.[33] Nevertheless, there is the suggestion that it is the means to achieve the plan for better life that are temporary and fluid, the hope of building a better life can be seen as more enduring and sustaining. Therefore, a conception of future building incorporates some form of deliberation, organizing, and planning into the notion of chance and opportunity.

Furthermore, the highlight of aspirations in the survival of informal migrants (i.e., in a context of struggle and harsh constraints), implies that there is the possibility of illusion, where the migrant continues to hold on to aspiration without socio-economic mobility or perceived opportunity for change. This could lead to what Czaika and Vothknect call "a hedonic treadmill," that is, increasing aspiration even when the economic returns achieved are lower or continue to fall.[34] On the contrary, there is the possibility for the situation Appadurai refers to as 'aspiration trap', when aspiration is adjusted downwards to avoid the strain and frustrations of perceived failure to achieve aspirations.[35]

In that light, the tactics of the informal migrant becomes relevant in engaging the harsh context for returns. Notwithstanding the level of productiveness of the interviewees' engagement, they evaluated their trickling returns from a broader perspective, calling attention to life chances at home country and possibility to continue to other countries with perceived better opportunities. Van Meeteren also called attention to that point, when she argued that migrants compare their present situation with the condition at their home country in the evaluation of their social mobility at host country.[36]

In the day-to-day pursuit of their aspiration, the informal migrant learns to walk with time and befriend time as a close mate. Recently, migration scholars have started to give more attention to the migrants' experiences of time especially when waiting for official decisions on their residential permits.[37] This builds on an established body of literature on the study of time. From Frank Kafka's parable Before the Law (1915) about a man that was waiting before and for the law, through Samuel Beckett's theatrical play, 'Waiting for Godot', about endlessly waiting for someone who never comes, to the several explorations of the concept of time in community, social processes, mobility, etc.[38] Although migration study was traditionally interrogated as a spatial process, some migration scholars have argued that it is as much a time process as a spatial one. In this sense, gains from the social study of time have benefited the discourse of migration, where, for example, the concept of time is discussed concerning migrants' experiences of temporality and waiting.

In their everyday practices, the informal migrant continually has to wait for customers, wait for jobs, and wait for decisions on their applications. In their narratives, they wait with expectations that in due time what they expect will come. In this way, time becomes their ally in navigating the socio-economic and political constraints that they face daily in their lives as informal migrants. For example, when they get a negative decision on their asylum application, they fill the form to reapply and ordinarily utilize the bureaucratic processing time to continue with their business and lives. Though several of the interviewees in my study bemoaned having a temporary permit for as long as three to ten years, they have utilized the years in engaging in several trading and service businesses, acquiring new income-generating skills and starting new families. Therefore, the long bureaucratic processing times for residence permits become viable opportunities for the interviewees.

In contrast, migrants' temporal expectations of the duration of stay in the host community have been argued to create ambivalence in the migrants and discourage commitments and ties to the host country.[39] More so, time has been explored from the institutional perspective, where policy makers and governments use time or length of stay as an instrument for control and categorization of migrants.[40] In this sense, bureaucratic delays in the processing of immigrants' permits are a manipulation of their time and a display of hegemonic power. According to Pierre Bourdieu, "Making people wait... delaying without destroying hope is part of the domination."[41] More recent studies of immigration control, which explored migrants' experiences of hegemonic control of time, emphasized profound feelings of uncertainty, instability, powerlessness and passivity.[42] It is worthy to note that, while migration researchers have emphasized the hegemonic control of migrants' time, scholars such as Comaroff and Comaroff, Scott, and Bourdieu[43] all stress that the dominated does not passively experience forms and systems of oppression and dominations as in the usurpation and control of migrants' time. Nevertheless, although the interviewees in my study utilized their time productively during the period of waiting for the processing of their permits, they still constantly have to deal with spatial temporalities.

For instance, they did not have a physical space they can call their own. The place of their street trading is temporal—they are constantly on the lookout for police officers that seek to arrest them and confiscate their meager wares. In addition, because their applications are being processed, they are always in danger of being deported either because they got a negative decision or because of the overzealousness of xenophobic police officers. Logically, it will be expected that such spatial temporalities should influence their experiences of time while waiting for decisions on asylum permits or the success that they seek in South Africa. Thus, the stronger the spatial temporality of the informal migrants' experiences, the less likely he or she will form ties that contradict the flexibility of temporality.

On the contrary, it can be considered that because the informal migrant engages time more as his tactical ally, or probably as a natural course of order, they develop ties that contrast their temporality. For example, several of my interviewees are in personal relationships and have children born while they have been waiting for decisions on their asylum applications. In some cases, the relationships may be with another informal migrant. When both parents are not sure of how long they must remain in South Africa before deportation, or they must rely on their informal tactics to extend their stay as long as possible.

However, time is not always productive for the informal migrants. For example, an interviewee from Ivory Coast discussed his engagement to time with an emphasis on his failure to achieve his goals despite years of being in South Africa. He expressed frustrations that he is far from achieving his personal goals for further education and employment in South Africa. He gave examples of other asylum seekers that have spent years in South Africa, and they are yet to get the refugee permit or achieve economic success. To him, the years spent in South Africa were unproductive, and he could have achieved more if those years were spent in his home country. His story raises questions about the economic difference receiving an official decision would make on the lives of the informal migrants. In a context of high unemployment rate, the rights to residence cannot guarantee access to employment and by extension economic security. That suggests that the response of the informal African migrant to the waiting period depends on the perception of, and ability to utilize, economic opportunities within the host society. Nevertheless, that could be applied more broadly to be the perception of and ability to pursue goal-related activities within the host community. For informal migrants in South Africa, not being confined to an asylum center is an opportunity to build their future. Another effect of waiting is that when an unfavorable decision is received, the apparent stability established by the informal migrant could be destabilized. For example, CoRMSA report highlights experiences of informal migrants who were unable to collect earned salaries, or work benefits because they were arrested and deported. Those experiences show that although waiting time could be productively utilized, the benefits could be severely insecure.

The above hope-aspiration approach to building futures become relevant in understanding the migrants' vulnerability and survival. While the struggles and constraints are evidenced and experienced, it does not remain the only basis for action, building their future becomes a relevant part of it. Nevertheless, it raises questions on why do the migrants see possibilities and potentialities in the dire challenging situation. The high number of struggling and unsuccessful (or not-yet-successful) migrant challenges an assumption that the few (very) affluent or economically successful migrant motivates them. One suggestion will be the potentiality or possibilities that are commonly associated with entrepreneurship as majority of the informal migrants in South Africa are engaged directly or indirectly in trade and service provision. While economist and other agents may call attention to the size of the business holding (hence Micro, Small, Medium, Large), to the actors (entrepreneurs) the emphasis is shifted from size to the profit-making process. However, this does not satisfy the puzzle of why not practice entrepreneurship at home country (if conditions are conducive, especially as it relates to violence, war and political persecution). That puzzle could call attention to the relevance of infrastructure that aids trade at the destination country, a point highlighted by the findings that 60 percent of would-be African migrants are discontent with local public services.[44]

Microentrepreneurship

In my research, economic activities form one of the central concrete pathways perceived by the interviewees as the means to their goals of a better life. Economic activities for my interviewees mainly refer to individual businesses. At the time of the study, four of the respondents were street traders selling cigarettes, candies, fruits and biscuits. The others provided services like hair cutting, hair braiding, teaching and modeling. Each of the participants informed me that they were engaged in several trading and informal service activities like house painting or roof repairs. Some of them still render several services that bring extra income aside from their primary economic activities. They all started seeking informal employment when they were unable to find formal employment, and were compelled to start their businesses. Starting new businesses required creativity on the part of some interviewees, who at times renders services without prior experience or training. They slowly started their businesses and developed the patience and skills needed to grow it from direct experience. The time and effort put into their trade and services make the activities central in their lives as informal migrants. Several studies have highlighted the economic and social relevance of entrepreneurial activities to migrants that are socially excluded in their host societies[45] and South Africa specifically. [46]

Several, authors have written on the growth of the informal sector[47] and sub-Saharan African cities have been identified as especially relevant in this phenomenon. Irrespective of the relevance of street trade[48] to the migrants, the size and seasonality of the business has made some economists, politicians and authors to dub it as 'survival business', or as "cushion to economic downturns or simple tax evasion."[49] That is, a business engagement just for the purpose of 'getting by', without the capacity to grow or lift the trader out of poverty. That negative conception of the micro businesses that make up the informal sector has contributed to it being shunned by politicians who often leave the management of the sector to local government officials in the jostle for development of urban spaces. In that trajectory, the relevance of the trade is capsuled in the use of space and the payment of tax or its twin 'formalization'. Although, more recent development of global justice, poverty alleviation and human rights have contributed to bring the sector to the focus of development inspired or disheartened agents as they jostle for the right program and project to bring succor to the depicted poor and disparate traders (see for example discussion on social protection, sustainable development, poverty eradication). On the heel of the 'neither-here-nor-there' political approach to the informal sector in sub-Saharan Africa, some authors are championing a more progressive—that is non-pathological, possibly indigenous conception of the informal sector in Africa.[50]

The substantive relevance of 'getting by' in the lives of the informal traders and service providers becomes central to the different conception of the informal sector and hence microenterprises that make up the sector. Interrogating how informal African migrants get by in South Africa through the narrative of my interviewees calls attention to a process of 'building' of individual lives. Building in this sense calls attention to the action or trade of constructing something (in this case their lives or future) as ordinarily defined in the dictionary. In essence, I understand the economic engagement of my interviewees in the informal sector of South Africa not as fragmentary, temporal or haphazard but as enduring and deliberated, though, nonetheless, unpredictable. The emphasis is to move from the migratory displacement of the informal migrant and their apparently impoverished circumstances, to the tenacity, creativity, aspiration (maybe ambition) and boldness that is often characterized as positive attributes of an entrepreneur. For instance, the case of Bola (not real name) one of my interviewees.

According to Bola's story, he was born in Lagos, Nigeria, to parents from Republic of Benin and Nigeria. While he was still in his teens the mother moved with him to Benin, and after few years, the father moved with him to Togo. He grew in Togo, mostly selling several retailed products to cars on busy highways during traffic jams. He saved some money and decided to change to selling mobile phones. With very limited funds, he traveled to Lagos, Nigeria, to buy two mobile phones (all he could afford) and, to avoid paying tax on the phones, he carefully opened the packets and kept the phones on himself as personal property. On getting to Togo, he re-packaged the phones and sold them as new phones. He did this several times and grew the business. He took loans from the bank and started importing the phones in larger quantity and supplying other cities in Togo. He reported that the business became quite successful; he opened two shops, one dedicated to mobile phones and the other electronics, and he built two houses, got married, and had two children.

Then disaster struck—on a day he received new consignment of phones and other product, his shop was robbed, everything was carted away by the robbers. His staff was arrested but after weeks, nothing came out of it and he decided to start over. He sold one of his houses to repay the loan from the bank, took new loans and started trading again. He said within months he was robbed again, this time at home, on a night before he planned to travel to Lagos for the purchase of new goods. The cash that was meant for the purchase was stolen. Devastated, he sold his remaining properties, gave his wife some money and sent her and the children to her parents. He paid back the loan from the bank and paid migrant couriers to take him to South Africa. I met him selling few bananas and roasted peanut by the roadside in Yeoville, Johannesburg, South Africa, in 2013. He said he started with selling few cigarettes, saved some money and started selling bananas and roasted peanut. Initially, he was buying the banana and roasted peanut from the nearby market, but at the time I interviewed him he was buying from the wholesale market, which is more profitable. He reported passionately that his dream is to own a big business that import electronics, and that he is pursuing that dream. I went back to Yeoville, Johannesburg, after one year, to discuss my analysis with the interviewees, but he was not there anymore. I was informed he has moved first to another African city and later to Brazil. I was given his phone number in Brazil, that he calls his friends regularly from Brazil.

It will be extremely farfetched to assume that all informal migrants who engage in street trading in Johannesburg share the same or similar story as this migrant. Yet, his story calls attention to the suggestion that from an economic perspective, this migrant displayed the qualities of an entrepreneur, but in the prevailing migration discuss, he is one more undesired 'illegal' migrant. More so, the narratives of all my interviewees, clearly calls attention to the centrality of such economic prospecting through engaging in various trade or service provision in South Africa. The relevance of their economic engagement can be measured not only in the amount of the financial trickle that they accumulate (or not) but also in the purposiveness of action, creativity and agency. This shift does not take the focus from the vulnerability of their trade, but raises questions on support to facilitate economic performance and a more human resource centered approach to migration management in South Africa specifically and sub-Saharan Africa generally.

Furthermore, an engagement with the puzzle 'why did the informal migrants start their microenterprises in the host society' raises two interesting points. Firstly, the political and social obstruction to employment in South Africa for the informal African migrant.[51] My interviewees' narratives emphasized the unwillingness of citizens to employ informal African migrants and high discrimination and abuse if employed by citizens. In addition, and high rate of unemployment in South Africa has facilitated the political prerogative to give preferential treatment to citizens in the competition for employment. Therefore, being socially and politically obstructed from formal employment created the impetus to focus on microenterprises or informal businesses as the means to desired future. Secondly, that puzzle could call attention to the relevance of infrastructure that aids microenterprises at the host country, for example, regular supply of electricity. That point was highlighted by the findings that 60 percent of would-be African migrants are considering migration because of discontent with local public services.[52]

CONCLUSION

It is a popular cliché to say that "migration is as old as the human race." In the case of Africa, the contemporary discourse of international migration within the continent raises other relevant political questions, but also social, ethical and others. For example, on the one hand, international migration within the continent is conceptually reduced to rubble if we interrogate nation-state creation via colonialism and the creation of arbitrary borders. The concept of the state assumes an oppressive, foreign and unfit lens through which to interrogate and congregate a contemporary, progressive and competitive Africa. On the other, the distinct identity, solidarity and commonality often attributed to 'Africa' as a unit, suggest colonialism and global politicking. The interest of a Nigerian, Togolese, Ghanaian, etc., building his or her future as an unwanted migrant in South Africa or other African country raises other questions apart from the global preoccupation with border control. It calls attention to the politics of 'statism' as a fixation on 'making' and 'unmaking' of all that falls within its geopolitical boundaries.

While, national borders have been engaged by politicians as fixed, the 'making' and 'unmaking' aspects of 'statism' is more dynamic and malleable, hence open to critical engagement. In that vein, the conception of unwanted migration in the African context as a discourse of border control limits a 'progressive' engagement with the borrowed connotation of the nation-state. The lives of the migrants categorized as informal migrants does not bear this preoccupation with the political limitations of national borders, especially as it relates to the 'making' or 'unmaking' of their lives. Though the physical crossing of the borders informally may not be easy or fluid, yet the conception of their future as aspirations and goals may not bare the restrictive burdens of border control.

The nation-state could choose to learn from them or criminalize (criticize) them. After years of criminalization, a new platform could be created where their dexterity, potentials and creativity could be put to more mutually profitable use. On that platform, there will be opportunities for the cooperation and collaboration of the nation-state, citizens and the migrants. In that understanding, the future of a progressive and mutually beneficial migration context rest to a large extent on the 'nation-state politics of making and unmaking. In that instance, the objective of making and unmaking will move from criminalization to cooperation with those presently categorize as informal migrants. The politics of making and unmaking could thus be extended to making micro-enterprise work as the platform for political and socio-economic cooperation. The turning point is to engage the social exclusion of informal migrant not as an end but as a fraction of the process of informal migrant-society-political engagement. There are more sides to capability deprivation of the informal migrant in a 'developing' context. Indeed, the question when faced with capability deprivation of informal migrants should extend to 'how the migrants responded, what did they do, does it work or how can it work to improve the efficiency of their displayed or newly created capabilities'.

By calling attention to the lives of unwanted African migrants in Johannesburg through their vulnerability, hope and entrepreneurial engagements, this chapter has attempted to raise awareness of the human question in the discourse of informal migration in South Africa, but also in Africa. The human question starts form the ethical conducts of ordinary citizens to the productive capacity and qualities of the informal migrants. Furthermore, it also calls attention to micro-enterprise as a possible platform for the state and informal migrants to explore a mutually beneficial relationship. The onus is on the state to exercise its power to create and facilitate such a platform. The informal migrants by their entrepreneurial response to inherent challenges in their host country have hinted of their commitment to economic exploration through trade and service provision. Indeed, Ghana's visa on arrival policy for African migrants suggests the creation of such a platform.

NOTES

1. Tolstoy, Leo. *What is Art*? Translated by A. Maude. London: Oxford University, 1975, p. 123.

2. Ibid., 121–122.

3. Ibid., 121–122.

4. Hannah Arendt, *The Human Condition*. Chicago: The University of Chicago Press. 1998.

5. Conovan, as cited in Hannah Arendt, *The Human Condition*. Chicago: The University of Chicago Press, 1998, p?

6. Saskia Sassen, *Guests and Aliens*. New York, NY, New York Press, 1999; Nigel Harris, *The New Untouchables: Immigration and the New World Worker*, London: IB Tauris, 1995; Susan Bibler Coutin, L*egalizing Moves: Salvadoran Immigrants' Struggle for U.S. Residency*. Ann Arbor: University of Michigan Press, 2000; Torpey, John. 1998. "Coming and Going: On the State Monopolization of the Legitimate 'Means of Movement'." *Sociological Theory*, Volume 16, no., 1998, pp. 241–259.

7. Notmond as translated In JohnTorpey, "Coming and Going: On the State Monopolization of the Legitimate 'Means of Movement'." *Sociological Theory*, Volume 16, no. 3, 1998, p. 239.

8. Loren Landau, "On the Politics of Exclusion and their Transcendence (A commentary)." *African Historical Review*, 2012, pp. 109–111.

9. Michael Mann, "The Autonomous Power of the State: Its Origins, Mechanisms and Results." *European Journal of Sociology/Archives Europeennes de Sociiologie*, Volume 25, no. 2, 1983, p. 60.

10. John Torpey, "Coming and Going…" p. 245.

11. Ibid., p. 245.

12. Susan Bibler Coutin, *Nations of Emigrants: Shifting boundaries of citizenship in El Salvador and the United States*. Ithaca and London: Cornell University Press, 2007; Joanne Van der Leun, *Looking for Loopholes: Processes of Incorporation of Illegal Immigrants in the Netherlands*. Amsterdam: Amsterdam University Press, 2003.

13. Darshan Vigneswaran, Araia Tesfalem, Colin Hoag, and Xolani Tshabalala, "Criminality or Monopoly? Immigration Enforcement in South Africa." *Journal of Southern African Studies*, Volume 36, no. 2, 2010, pp. 465–481.

14. Henry Schloss, "The Concept of Entrepreneurship in Economic Development." *Journal of Economic Issues*, Volume 2, 1968, pp. 228–232; Joseph Schumpeter, *Capitalism, Socialism and Democracy*. New York: Harper and Roe Publishers, 1942; Joseph Schumpeter, "The Creative Response in Economic History." *Journal of Economic History*, Volume 7, no. 2, 1947, pp. 149–159; Phillippe Aghion, "Schumpeterian Growth Theory and the Dynamics of Income Inequality." *Econometrica* Volume 70, no. 3, 2002, pp. 855–882.

15. Amartya Sen, *Resources, Values and Development*. Cambridge, MA: Harvard University Press, 2000.

16. Ibid., p. 3.

17. Ibid., p. 7.

18. Ibid.

19. Amartya Sen, "Equality of What?" In *Tanner Lectures on Human Values*, Volume 1, edited by McMurrin, Sterlin, Cambridge, MA: Cambridge University Press, and Salt Lake City: University of Utah Press, 1980; Martha Nussbaum and Amartya Sen, *The Quality of Life*. Oxford: Oxford University Press, 1993; Sudhir Anand and Martin Ravallion, "Human Development in Poor Countries: On the role of Private Incomes and Public Services." *Journal of Economic Perspectives*, 1993, pp. 133–152; Keith Griffin and J Knight, *Human Development and the International Development Strategies for the 1990s*. London: Macmillan, 1990.

20. Amartya Sen, 2000(a) Social Exclusion: Concept, Application and Scrutiny. Social Development Papers, Manila Philippines: Office of Environment and Social Development, Asian Development Bank.

21. Michael Neocosmos, From 'Foreign Natives' to 'Native Foreigners': Explaining Xenophobia in Post-Apartheid South Africa. Dakar: CODESRIA, 2006.

22. Michel Foucault, "Governmentality." In Colin Gordon, Graham Burchell and Peter Miller (Eds), *The Foucault effect: Studies in Governmentality*, Chicago, IL: University of Chicago Press, 1991, pp. 87–104; Partha Chatterjee, *The Politics of the Governed: Reflections on Popular Politics in Most of the World*. New York: Columbia University Press, 2004.

23. Amartya Sen, 2000(a) Social Exclusion.

24. Aurelia Segatti, "Migration to South Africa: Regional Challenges versus National Instruments and Interests." In *Contemporary Migration to South Africa: A Regional Development Issue*, edited by Aurelia Segatti and Loren Landau, Washington, DC: The International Bank for Reconstruction and Development/The World Bank, 2011, p. 23.

25. CORMSA: Consortium for Refugees and Asylum Seekers in South Africa report. CoRMSA's website is being revamped, hence the reports can be accessed alternatively via the following links: Accessed April–June, 2015.

26. Michael Neocosmos, *From 'Foreign Natives' to 'Native Foreigners': Explaining Xenophobia in Post-Apartheid South Africa*. Dakar: CODESRIA, 2006, p. 1.

27. Loren Landau, (Ed). *Exorcising the Demon Within: Xenophobia, Violence and Statecraft in Contemporary South Africa*. Johannesburg: Wits University Press, 2011; Kihato, Caroline W. 2011. "The City from its Margins: Rethinking urban governance through the everyday lives of migrant women in Johannesburg." *Social Dynamics*, Volume 37, no. 3, pp. 349–362; Reddy, Thiven. 2012. "The 'Cabbage and the Goat': Xenophobic violence in South Africa." *African Historical Review,* Volume 44, No. 1, pp. 3–28; Steinberg, Johnny. 2008. South Africa's Xenophobic Eruption. Pretoria, South Africa: Institute for Security Studies; Darshan Vigneswaran, Araia Tesfalem, Colin Hoag, and Xolani Tshabalala, "Criminality or Monopoly? Christal O Spel, Forthcoming. *Building Personal Lives as Informal Migrants in South Africa: Narratives of Poor African Informal Migrants in Johannesburg*. PhD Thesis, Helsinki: University of Helsinki Press.

28. Brian Williams, Eleanor Gouws, Mark Lurie, and Jonathan Crush, Spaces of Vulnerability: Migration and HIV/AIDS in South Africa. Policy Series, Cape Town: Southern African Migration Project, 2002; Sechaba Consultant and Associates, The Border Within: The Future of the Lesotho/South African International Boundary. Cape Town: Southern African Migration Project, 2002.

29. Audie Klotz, *Migration and National Identity in South Africa, 1860–2010*. New York: Cambridge University Press, 2013; Sally Peberdy, 2009. *Selecting Immigrants: National Identity and South Africa's Immigration Policies 1910–2008*. Johannesburg: Wits University Press, 2009; Jonathan Crush, (Ed.). *Beyond Control: Immigration and Human Rights in a Democratic South Africa*. Cape Town: Southern African Migration Project, 1998; Maxine Reitzes, "Immigration and Human Rights in South Africa." In Crush, Jonathan *(Ed.), Beyond Control: Immigration and Human Rights in a Democratic South Africa*, Cape Town: Queens University Press, 1998, pp. 37–54.

30. Owen Sichone, "Xenophobia and Xenophilia in South Africa: African Migrants in Cape Town." In P. Werbner, P. (Ed.), *Anthropology and the New Cosmopolitanism: Rooted, Feminist and Vernacular Perspectives*, Oxford: Berg Publisher, 2008, pp. 309–322; Johnny Steinberg, South Africa's Xenophobic Eruption.

31. Daryl Glaser, "(Dis)connections: Elite and Popular 'Common Sense' on the matter of Foreigners." In Hassim, Shireen, Kupe, Tawana, and Worby, Eric (Eds.), *Go Home or Die Here: Violence, Xenophobia and the Reinvention of Difference in South Africa*. Johannesburg: Wits University Press, 2008, pp. 53–64.

32. C.R. Snyder, (Ed.), *Handbook of Hope: Theory, Measures and Applications*. San Diego: Academic Press, 2000, pp. 5–6.

33. Jacqueline M. Hagan, *Deciding to be Legal: A Maya Community in Houston*. Philadelphia: Temple University Press, 1994.

34. Mathias Czaika and Marc Vothknecht, "Migration Aspirations: Are Migrants Trapped on A Hedonic Treadmill." *IZA Journal of Migration*, Volume 3, no. 1, 2014, p. 3.

35. Arjun Appadurai, "The Capacity to Aspire: Culture and the Terms of Recognition." In Vijayendra, Rao and Walton, Michael (Eds.), *Culture and Public Action*, California: Stanford University Press, 2004, pp. 59–84.

36. Masja Van Meeteren, *Irregular Migrants in Belgium and the Netherlands: Aspirations and Incorporation*. Amsterdam: Amsterdam University Press, 2014.

37. Andersson, Ruben, *Illegality Inc: Clandestine Migration and the Business of Bordering Europe*. Oakland: University of California Press, 2014a; Khosravi, Shahram, *Illegal Traveler: An Auto-Ethnography of Borders*. Basingstoke and New York: Palgrave Macmillan, 2010; Dhillon, Navtej, and Tarik Yousef, *Generation in Waiting: The Unfulfilled Promise of Young People in the Middle East*. Washington, DC: Brookings Institution Press, 2009.

38. Bastion, Michelle."Time and Community: A Scoping Study." *Time and Society* Volume 23, no. 2, 2014, pp. 137–166; Michelle Bastion, "The Contradictory Simultaneity of Being with Others: Exploring Concepts of Time and Community in the Work of Gloria Anzaldua." *Feminist Review*, Volume 97, 2011, pp. 151–167; Barbara Adam, *Time and Social Theory*. Cambridge, UK: Polity Press, 1994.

39. Bryan Roberts, "Socially Expected Durations and the Economic Adjustment of Immigrants." In Portes, Alejandro (Ed.), *The Economic Sociology of Immigration: Essays on Networks, Ethnicity and Entrepreneurship*. New York: Russel Sage Foundation, 1995, pp. 42–86.

40. Robin Cohen, *Frontiers of Identity: The British and the Others*. London: Longman, 1994.

41. Pierre Bourdieu, *Outline of a Theory of Practice*. Cambridge: Cambridge University Press, 1972, p. 28.

42. Richards, Naomi, and Rebecca Rotter, "Desperately Seeking Certainty? The Case of Asylum Applicants and People Planning an Assisted Suicide in Switzerland." *Sociological Research Online*, 18, no. 4 (2013): 1–16. doi:10.5153/sro.3234.

43. John L. Comaroff and Jean Comaroff, *of Revelation and Revolution, Volume 2: The Dialectics of Modernity on a South African Frontier*. Chicago, IL: University of Chicago Press, 1997; James C Scott, *Weapons of the Weak: Everyday Forms of Peasant Resistance*. New Haven and London: Yale University Press, 1985; Pierre Bourdieu, *Outline of a Theory of Practice*.

44. Africa Development Bank [AFDB]. 2015. "African Economic Outl9ook: Regional Development and Spatial Inclusion." Tunisia: AFDB, OECD, UNDP.

45. Jan Rath, (Ed.), *Immigrant Businesses: The Economic, Political and Social Environment*. New York: Palgrave, Macmillan, 2000.

46. Nina Hunter and Caroline Skinner, "Foreign Street Traders Working in Inner City Durban: Local Government Policy Challenges." *Urban Forum*, Volume 14, no. 4, 2003, pp. 301–319; Brij Maharaj and Vadi Moodley, "New African Immigration to the Durban Region." *Canadian Journal of African Studies*, 2000, pp. 149–160.

47. International Labor Organization introduced the concept of informal sector in 1972 in its Africa Mission report (Hart, 1973, 1990). The report defined informality as "way of doing things characterized by (a) ease of entry; (b) reliance on indigenous resources; (c) family ownership; (d) small scale operations; (e) labor intensive and adaptive technology; (e) skills acquired outside of the formal sector; (g) unregulated and competitive markets." Presently, two types of informal sector activities are broadly recognized (e.g., by the World Bank): Coping Strategies (Survival activities) which includes casual or temporary jobs, subsistence agriculture, etc. 2. Unofficial earning strategies (illegality in business) which includes unofficial business activities such as tax evasion, avoidance of labor or other governmental regulations. Also, included are underground activities. These conceptions of the informal sector has been widely overturned (see Lyons and Snoxell, 2005; Centeno & Portes, 2003; Lund, Nicholson & Skinner, 2000; Witt, 2000; Lund, 1998).

48. I utilize the term street trade to refer to the diverse trading and service provision that generate income for the migrants.

49. Miguel A Centeno and Alejandro Portes, The Informal Economy in the Shadow of the State. CMD Working paper 03–06 February, NJ: Princeton University, 2003.

50. Simone, AbdouMaliq, *For the City Yet to Come: Changing African Lives in Four Cities*. Durham and London: Duke University Press, 2004; AbdouMaliq Simone and Abouhani Abdelghani, *Urban Africa: Changing Contours of Survival in the City*. Dakar: CODESRIA, 2005.

51. CORMSA: Consortium for Refugees and Asylum Seekers in South Africa report.

52. Africa Development Bank [AFDB]. *African Economic Outlook*.

Chapter 12

Representation, Immigration, Experience, and Memory

A Study of Representational Dynamics of "the Other" in Post-Imperial Britain, 1947–1990s

Dollin Wilson Ovaroh-Holt

The United Kingdom embodies a history of inward and outward migration that is arguably fundamental to its existence. The arrival en masse of Huguenots to England after the French wars of religion of 1562 and 1598 and that of monarchists fleeing the French Revolution of 1789 are among many historical inflows that exemplify this tradition of incorporating foreign immigrant groups. Equally, there have been notable outward movements. According to the Ravenhill, there were emigrations from the United Kingdom to North America in the seventeenth and eighteenth centuries. Also, historical records point to a great number of people leaving Britain in the 1880s and 1900s, and more so at the outbreak of the First World War. These migrations continued, including movements into the old Commonwealth countries of Australia, Canada and New Zealand until the 1930s when economic decline in the British Empire and the United States resulted in a reversal of the trend.[1]

The centrality of migrations to the history of these inlands is underlined, according to Wallace, by the fact that descendants of the English, Welsh and Scottish were 'themselves mongrel blends of past invasions and migrations who had assimilated Irish Catholics coming en masse to Britain in the 19th century, the Jews fleeing Imperial Russia in the 1890s and from the Nazi in the 1930s and displaced persons from the Baltic Protestant states, Poland and Ukraine in 1945'.[2]

This study is however concerned with black migrations to the United Kingdom. The presence of black people is traceable to the Victorian era, but significant migrations to the United Kingdom began in the Second World War period in the context of black Caribbean people who served and worked in the British armed forces and in the ammunition industries respectively, followed by migrations from all over the new Commonwealth in the late 1940s, including those recruited at the behest of the British Government from the Caribbean to help with postwar reconstruction and fill up manpower shortfalls in the health and transport services. This amounted to an annual record of 40,000 from the mid-1950s. Also, there were people arriving in search of a better life, including those who arrived in large numbers to beat the 1962 Commonwealth Immigration Act aimed at curbing immigration. By 1961, according to Seymore-Ure, there were 336,000 overseas-born colored population in England and Wales compared to 74,500 ten years earlier.[3]

The Empire Windrush voyage of 1947 is however mythologized as symbolizing the transformations that have occurred in the United Kingdom, in the context of black Caribbean immigrants 'reconstructing new narratives of home and belongings that parallel the old ones'.[4] The arrival of the Windrush was also viewed as symbolizing, as Young and Lewis put it, a "destabilization of the psychic and cultural certainties" of white Britain.[5] After a brief period of honeymoon with the Windrush generation, many in the Conservative party, which was then in government, and a majority of the white indigenous population began to view the continuous inflow of commonwealth immigrants to the United Kingdom as a problem.[6] According to Winder, the media was complicit in stirring up resentment of black commonwealth immigrants because of their negative coverage of the Windrush:

'The Windrush was the first to be met by newsreel cameras, and the first to raise alarm in British newspapers, and the House of Commons." As Winder notes, further, "it set in motion a generation of anti-alien feelings that would drive policy for decades." Media coverage, according to Winder, was permeated with anti-immigrant themes and portrayed commonwealth immigrants as threatening the cultural certainties of white Britain.[7]

As Cox asserts also, a majority of the population viewed the presence of black commonwealth immigrants and the prospect of sharing space and neighborhoods with them as inconceivable, owing to their representations in imperial discourse as the inferior 'other', belonging to a peripheral world in the colonies. According to Cox, these negative stereotypes were ingrained in the educational system and the national psyche of metropolitan society.[8] Thus, the conceptualization of black commonwealth immigrants could not but be tainted and negatively affected by this mindset, reinforced by media coverage. The mass media, according Takeyuki, are able to "reinforce or even exacerbate these majority ethnic prejudices towards immigrants through explicitly or implicitly unfavorable coverage of them."[9] As Herman and Chomski point out, the media capitalizes on the public's anxieties and fears by sensationalizing its stories about certain groups of people, to boost circulation and maximize profits for its owners.[10]

There is the Enoch Powell's "Rivers of Blood" speech in 1968 and the Brixton disturbance of 1981. However, anthropological studies suggest that certain events or episodes affecting a group or communities linger on in their collective memories, passing from one generation to the other.[11] Equally, psychologists highlight three generally accepted classifications of memory and these are sensory, short term and long term. Studies have shown that the storage of information in people with sensory and short-term memories is not retained indefinitely. By contrast, larger quantities of information can be stored in people with long-term memory for potentially unlimited period, sometimes a whole lifespan. More specifically, the findings of a research conducted by Van Dijk shows that people are able to recall and re-tell press stories irrespective of how long ago. As Van Dijke puts it, "time is no factor where an event is massively reported, individuals can integrate the story about it into their understanding of reality and their more general knowledge about it..."[12]

SELECT LITERATURE REVIEW

The Empire Windrush, with its cargo of 417 African Caribbean passengers that docked at Tilbury in June 1948, acquired iconic status for ushering in the socio-cultural transformations that had occurred in post-imperial Britain. As Young argues, it stands for something particular in that it altered the cultural and racial landscape of imperial Britain. "It transformed the supposed cultural and racial homogeneity into a multi-cultural/multi-racial society."[13] According to Winder, it was unique in the sense that it heralded the enduring scrutiny and negative coverage that black immigrants are subjected to in the British media. The arrival of the Windrush unleashed a plethora of media discourse disseminating the myth of a mono-cultural white Britain about to be disrupted by the presence of people with alien cultures. Some newspaper editorials and commentaries propagated this myth including the alarmist notion of being 'swamped' that still permeates media coverage of arrivals since the post-independence era.[14]

What is more, many in the mainstream population were not well disposed to the idea of sharing neighborhoods with a people historically narrativized as the uncivilized, illiterate 'other'; a notion that, according to Cox, was ingrained in the national psyche and which sections of the media continued to affirm.[15] As Cottles argues, also, the host population are variously invited to construct structures of exclusion of who 'we' are against who 'we' are not, whether as 'us' and 'them', 'insider' and 'outsider'.[16]

Foregrounded in post-colonial studies along with concepts like Orientalism, 'othering' refers to the power discourse mobilized by Europe to elevate itself as the center of civilization in contrast to a constructed 'other' that is defined as 'radically different, and hence incorrigibly inferior'; providing the justification for its domination and control.[17] According to Spivak, "'other-ing' is a dialectical process because the colonizing other is established at the same as it's colonized others are produced as subjects"[18]

In Orientalism, Edward Said describes the unequal relationship between Europeans (the British, French and German colonizers) and the people of the Middle East, formerly known as Orientals, highlighting the institutionalized defense of the latter's colonization. Orientalism, according to Said, 'highlights the West's imagination and representation of the 'Orient as being culturally inferior, sensuous, despotic, mentally aberrant, inaccurate and backward', while defining itself as culturally and intellectually superior. In other words, 'the Orient is everything the west is not, and as such, in a binary opposition to each other.'[19] Europe, Said emphasizes, invented an 'Orient that is in binary opposition to it, dealing with it by making statements about, authorizing views of it, describing it, by teaching it, setting it, ruling over it: in short, …a Western style for dominating, restructuring, and having authority over it.'[20]

Conceptualizing Immigrants and the Role of the Media

According to Parekh, strangers coming to a country are conceptualized in various categories. "They can be described as foreigners, as immigrants, by their national or ethnic origins, by their religion, etc. Such descriptions are not just verbal, but evince the society's view of the outsiders' place in it and how they should be treated."[21] It can be inferred therefore that African and African Caribbean people including those born in Britain are conceptualized as the 'other', premised on the myth of ontological inferiority ascribed to their forebears in imperial discourse, and its reaffirmation in the context of negative media stereotypes.

As Dyer argues, stereotypes can be constructed around a group of people by using verbal and visual traits to represent them which 'tend to be static and unchanging.'[22] A number of studies show that commonwealth immigrants were portrayed as indolent, lesser ranking in intellect and uncivil, thus echoing the language that was the underpinning ideology for colonialism.[23] These stereotypes, according to Yarde, were recycled into 'drug-dealers', and 'muggers' in the 1980s by the press media.[24] To understand the media's role in reaffirming existing stereotypes or creating new ones, it may be worthwhile to look at its historical formation.

According to Sherwood, the late nineteenth century witnessed the publication of magazines and newspapers that were 'replete with the power of the white man and the inferiority of all races; the savagery of the black, the inscrutability and wiliness of the Oriental and the effeminacy of the Indian.' As Sherwood further states, "these themes were repeated on postcards and advertisements; in newspapers, such as *National Observer* (1888–1893) and *Daily Mail* (1896), in illustrations in magazines such as the Illustrated *London News, The Graphic* and the *Pall Mall Gazette.*"[25]

While these overtly racist themes do not feature in current media publications, certain newspapers, particularly the right-wing ones, have the potential of creating 'us' and 'them' binary between mainstream society and immigrant groups through the reinforcement of existing stereotypes, which can be detrimental to race relations. As has been mentioned earlier, Cottles points out that the host society are "variously invited to construct a sense of who 'we' are in relation to who 'we' are not, whether as 'us' and 'them', 'insider' and 'outsider', 'colonizer' and 'colonized', 'citizen' and 'foreigner', 'normal' and 'deviant', 'friend' and 'foe', the 'west' and the 'rest'. Through this means, the 'other' is marked out, "differentiated and often rendered vulnerable to discrimination."[26]

A dominant view within the pluralist school of thought is that the media is impartial and only reflects the reality on the ground. In this case as the argument goes, the media owes it to its audience to reflect the cultural otherness of immigrants and how this impinges on national cohesion. As Cottles argues, it was the justification provided for producing the following TV documentaries and shows that disparaged immigrant communities: *Special Enquiry: Has Britain A Color Bar* (1955), *Black Marries Whites* (1964), *The Negro Next Door* (1965), *People In Trouble: Mixed Marriages* (1965), *Till Death Do Us Part* (1966–74), *Fable* (1965), *A Man From the Sun* (1956), and *The Black and White Minstrels* (BBC 1958/78).[27]

Malik however debunks the notion that the media reflects reality. The kernel of his argument, which is from a Marxist perspective, is that media representations are more likely to be constructions or distortions in which immigrants, especially black people, are produced as natives, entertainers or a problem. This view seems to fit in with Allan's suggestion that 'whereas news discourse is presented by its makers as an objective, impartial translation of reality, it may instead be seen to be providing an ideological construction of realities.'[28] Negative representations is theorized within the Marxist paradigm as motivated by the imperativeness of increasing circulation in order to maximize shareholder profits, or to serve the interest of a powerful and influential elites who control and determine what is disseminated to the public.

The ideology of such newspaper outlets is, arguably, the preservation of a presumed mono-cultural Britain, and this is exemplified by the coverage of Enoch Powell's "Rivers of Blood" speech of 1968.[29] Powell's opposition to commonwealth immigration attracted huge publicity with column after column of newsprint amplifying his prophesy of bloodbath, arguably to cause panic and instigate public loathing of immigrants.[30]

Methodologies

Considering that this chapter examines the claim that African and African Caribbean immigrants are represented as 'the other' in the British media, an ethnographic field study approach was deemed suitable as it generates large amount of data and useful insights. The researcher therefore conducted 30 semistructured interviews in the homes of some interviewees, and in arranged venues with the rest, in Luton Town from December 2006 to mid-January 2007. The interviews, which took close to ninety minutes, were tape-recorded, and touched on a range of subjects including the experiences of being black and British. It particularly explored their recollections of media coverage of events that made an impact on the communities. It is instructive that without specifically probing for memories of the impact of the coverage of Enoch Powell's "Rivers of Blood" speech and the Brixton disturbance of 1981, these were spontaneously mentioned by a majority of the interviewees, especially those from the first generation.

Interviewees belonging to the second generation obviously had no experiential recollections of the first event other than stories passed down to them, but have vivid memories of newspaper coverage of the latter event. It is pertinent to mention that their recollection of these events and how they narrated it were in some cases at variance with subsequent interpretations through anniversary programs such the BBC documentary on the Windrush and other media constructions of black Britishness, as will be shown later. The interviewees were selected among people who arrived in the United Kingdom in the 1950s, 1960s and 1970s and those born in the United Kingdom in the1960s and 1970s or joined parents and families already in the United Kingdom. This formulation was geared toward reflecting the differences within the African Caribbean communities such as ethnic backgrounds, cultural orientation, patterns of, and motives for migration, including the generational divide within it.

Newspaper Analysis

A textual analysis of the accounts of the Brixton event by the *Sun*, the *Daily Mail*, the *Daily Express* and *The Times* and the *Daily Telegraph* was conducted. These newspapers were chosen because of their aversion to issues of immigration and multiculturalism.[31] The enquiry was done using a less rigorous form of content and frame analysis that scrutinized articles, opinions, commentaries and reports with the emphasis on identifying key words or labels used to describe black youths involved in the disturbance, how the stories were framed, for example, searching for repetitive usage of metaphors, phraseology, statements that evokes images of doom and threat, which key issues were highlighted and which were ignored or suppressed, spotlighting negative associations embodied in the story frames or message, and finally, the quotation of primary definers.[32]

The data or newsprints were collected from the Colindale Newspaper Library. It was narrowed down to publications on April 13–18, 1981, a period when the event was still making a significant impact in the press. This time frame yielded some dividends in the context of providing a manageable size of data for careful scrutiny.

Research Findings and Analysis: Motivations for Migrating to the United Kingdom

All of the first-generation interviewees consisting of twelve males and eight females and aged between 67 and 82 years old arrived in the United Kingdom in the 1950s and 1960s. They reported being motivated by a desire to better their lives and create opportunities for families left behind. Nearly all of these stated that the living condition in the colonies was deteriorating, owing to economic decline and there was no shortage of employment in here in the United Kingdom. As Winder argues, the economy of Montserrat, for example, was sustained more by capital remitted by its nationals back home than by income from the sale of cotton, their main export.[33]

Although oral and written evidence suggests that there were other reasons why black people migrated from the West Indies and the African continent to England, a majority of the former migrated on economic grounds. The largest number of these came from Jamaica, pushed by the economic situation of that country. There was high unemployment, especially among the youths. Forty percent of the population consisted of people below twenty-one years of age. The living standard was very low as a result, and stories of success fed back home by friends and families already in the United Kingdom attracted those who could raise the passage money to migrate.

According to seventy-six-year-old Hemingway and seventy-year-old Lewis, both male pensioners, the promptings to migrate to England became very compelling. As Hemingway puts it, "We used to hear a lot of stories about England, especially about the Midlands. There were Jobs, but no workers. Over in Jamaica, there was not so much to do. We just messed about. You know. The economic situation was, to say the least, dire. Everybody thought about England as the solution. And England needed us."

However, 70-year-old Ms. Gordon, a retired nurse, stated that her parents were doing well and wanted her to train as a teacher, work for a few years and return to Jamaica, but on realizing that her job prospects as a teacher would be constrained in the United Kingdom, as no one would employ a black teacher then, she opted for nursing, where her chance of a career was feasible, considering that the NHS was continuously recruiting. Also, she would have had a wealth of experience to take back home. As she puts it, "look I am still here after all these years. I planned to take my skills home and help my country."

According to 80-year-old Sutherland from Jamaica, peer-group pressure made him decide to migrate to the United Kingdom. He states, "I was working for the West Indies College in the 1950s and pay and condition was good. I did not have to come over to the UK for any economic reasons. However, a lot of my friends had made the trip so I was anxious that I would be left over there. You know the pressure was really strong. You got letters and all those enchanting black and white photos of England." And 78-year-old Asamoah stated as follows: "I came for further studies in 1959. I studied architecture and landscape surveying. I went back home and practiced for some years, but came back to the UK. I am still here. I have no regrets. My family is here. This is my home now."[34]

Early Experiences: First generation

Eight of the first-generation interviewees said they experienced hostilities, including direct racial insults, rude gestures, name-calling, being ignored, snubbed and given unfriendly looks. "You felt like an outcast," said Mrs. Swann, a nurse, originally from St Kitts:

> We had no racism in the Caribbean, so we didn't know how to handle the situation. When I submitted my form at the labor office, I was asked to fill it again in their presence because they did not believe I could read and write. That was the sort of racism we faced. I was really annoyed. We were taught everything about England, but England knew nothing about us.[35]

Shocking as the above experience was for Mrs. Swann, it also struck her interlocutors as surprising that she was literate. The assumption that colonial people were illiterate and primitive was rife and derives from the myths propagated about the inferiority of life in the colonies. As Said et al argue, colonialism was built on such a consciousness.[36]

More pertinently, all the respondents, without promptings, situated Enoch Powell's "Rivers of Blood" speech in 1968 as potent in that it provoked, thanks to media coverage, an escalation of hostilities toward immigrants. According to Gurnah, it exacerbated racial tension in the United Kingdom.[37] For Foot, the grandiloquence of Powell's speech was calculated to evoke public outcry.[38] To emphasize this point, the respondents stated that the speech provoked a hardening of public attitude toward black people.

The speech's aftermath is vivid in the memories of first-generation immigrants as the following comments illustrate: As Bill puts it, "There was hostility! No rooms to rent. We were barred from entering clubs. We were refused jobs that the English did not normally do. You saw signs that explicitly stated: No colored people wanted." And as 70-year-old Mrs. Cato from Barbados stated, 'Enoch Powell's racist remarks challenged our rights to be British. People looked at you with contempt.'[39]

However, not everyone attributed the resentment of immigrants to the Powell speech, or on the basis of color and cultural difference. A couple from Barbados, Mr. and Mrs. Gunter, aged 73 and 70 respectively, remembered being severally bullied by white work colleagues on the premise that their arrival and those of their communities to the United Kingdom, compounded the postwar shortages being experienced. In contrast, two interviewees stated that they had no problems with members of the white communities and cited instances of snobbery and disdainful treatments experienced from members of other West Indian and African communities. According to 79 years old Mr. Brown, originally from St Lucia: "The Africans are worse than whites. They looked down on us like we are common because they have university degrees, but then they come after our women."[40]

While this view is unrepresentative of the communities as a whole, it spotlights the divide between African and African Caribbean immigrants, the competitive intra-racial differences within the African Caribbean communities and its attendant diversity of opinions, experiences and perceptions. Reports show that some in the black Caribbean community, who had already settled, resented further influx of immigrants from the West Indies as they were overcrowding the cities, compounding the hardships being experienced and fueling racial tension. Also, West Africans were known to harbor contempt for Jamaicans for several reasons including the ease of their access to the United Kingdom, while restrictions were placed on the former. Reports on postwar immigrants in Birmingham show that some elite and sections of the media exploited these divisions in the campaign against immigration from the West Indies.

As was mentioned earlier, a significant number of Africans, as opposed to most West Indians, migrated to the United Kingdom for the purpose of acquiring academic and professional qualifications, and were either sponsored by families or awarded scholarships, and hence, were viewed as model migrants who would return to their countries of origin on accomplishing their pursuits. Viewed as such, a group's experience in the context of relations with host public may differ from others. While prejudice toward commonwealth immigrants was prevalent, experiences were contingent upon how certain groups were perceived and conceptualized by the mainstream population with the media playing a major role. The experiences of most Africans may have been ameliorated on this premise as Assamoah states below:

> I didn't experience racism or prejudice overtly. Yes, you sometimes had funny looks and the rest, but you told yourself, look, get on with it! As time went on, we gained some respect. I mean it was mutual. Treat people well and you were treated well. I think the fact that we did not rely upon state funds or do lowly jobs marked us out from the rest. The West Indians had a tough time. They were unfairly stereotyped. They had a bad press. You didn't want to be tarred with the same brush, so we kept to ourselves. But looking back now, it wasn't fair.[41]

Consequently, the relation between most first-generation black Africans and their African Caribbean counterparts was tense. West Africans, particularly, were viewed by the latter as snobbish and aloof. A commonly held view among West Indians is that black Africans collaborated in the selling and shipment of West Indians to the Caribbean as slaves. Also, Africans are said to have ingratiated themselves to the mainstream society and shied away from the struggle against racism in Britain, which West Indians claim they pioneered and fought hard for.

As part of their experiences in the United Kingdom, a majority of these interviewees, especially those who arrived in the cold season, reported being taken aback by the dreariness and gloom that enveloped the country; a far cry from the imagery of paradise and fairytale appeal ingrained by colonial education and discourse. According to Bill, it was a period when assumptions about the United Kingdom were challenged and knowledge of it reframed. As he states:

> My perspectives about England changed drastically. We were told a lot of things in school. The picture painted of England in literature and films was almost like paradise, a kind and decent society. I was shocked to see filthy and rundown places and ordinary white people sweeping the street, mopping the floor, collecting rubbish, and people getting drunk and rowdy. Back home, white people didn't clean or mop, black servants did.[42]

Second Generation

A majority of the second-generation interviewees were born in the United Kingdom. Just a few of these came to join their parents as children. It is worth noting that most of the early postwar migrants came to Britain alone. Others married upon arrival in the country; some to local British spouses. In most cases, wives, children and other relatives were re-united with husbands and fathers. As these family reunifications occurred and developed, a second generation of black Caribbean or Africans were born in Britain or arrived with their mothers as young children.[43]

Six of the second-generation respondents consisting of two males and four females reported that they experienced outright and subtle prejudice, xenophobia and bigotry. They claimed that in predominantly white neighborhoods, there was a dreadful sense of being encircled because one was always a minority. Name-callings and curious facial expressions from white schoolmates was a constant feature at the playgrounds. For instance, according to 40-year-old Miss Lewis from St Lucia who came to join her parents at the age of eight, "You had your hair touched. They touched your skin to see if the color comes off and sometimes scratched to see if I would bleed, and to see if my blood is the same color as theirs."[44]

In his memoir, *Black Gold of the Sun,* Ekow Eshun, recall that the full extent of racism and othering in the national imaginary was brought home to him in 1978 when Margaret Thatcher, the then prime minister, made a controversial statement decrying the presence of foreigners, who were swamping Britain and who would potentially alter its culture and values. Thatcher's promotion of exclusivity based on an imagined community or some shared ethnic and cultural heritage met with widespread acceptance, considering its domination in the news and media commentary locally and internationally. It also illustrates the ideologies and structures of exclusion faced by African and African Caribbean immigrant communities from political elites and the media.[45]

With regard to unpleasant attitudes harbored toward black people, there was a consensus of opinion among Jason (44), Justin (46) and Debbie (42) and Nadin (40), all of whom were born in the United Kingdom, that it was more consistent with ignorance and insensitivity to diversity, than being racially motivated. However, the rest disagreed. The point of departure being that it was motivated by racism or prejudice. All but two of these stated that they preferred the term prejudice to racism because the latter lacked conceptual clarity. Racism, according to Sharon, 'is too serious a term to use.'[46]

According to Vic, one conceptual strand underpins racism and prejudice, and that is the dislike or loathing of others for being different: 'whether it is called racism or prejudice, they're both unacceptable. The concept is about disliking certain people because they're different. You can't put a gloss on it.'[47] Jonathan argued that the term 'prejudice' is a euphemism that diminishes the perniciousness of racism. 'It should be called what it is; racism.'[48]

Remarkably, there was an agreement that attitudes toward immigrants have changed, or are changing. Vic and Jonathan however attributed such changes to the introduction of legal frameworks eradicating discrimination and promoting equal opportunities, and not the outcome of a national soul searching. This position is underpinned by the three transforming frameworks introduced from 1965 to 1976: The Race Relations Act of 1965, which established a Race Relations Board to deal with cases of discrimination and made it unlawful to discriminate in public places or on public transport. The Race Relations Act of 1968 that created the Community Relations Commission for the promotion of race relations. This Act outlawed discrimination in employment, housing, service provision and advertisements. And finally, The Race Relations Act of 1976 was developed for the purpose of converting the Race Relations Board and Community Relations Commission into the Commission for Racial Equality. The inclusion of racial disadvantage and complaints about discrimination within its purview made this Act a profoundly effective instrument for combating racism and inequality.

In addition to that, the report states that socio-economic initiatives like the Inner City Task Force, City Action Teams and the New Deal were introduced as impetus for young and upwardly mobile generation of black people to move forward in the direction of high profile success stories that have manifested in Britain's black community. Trevor Macdonald had been a news presenter on television since 1973; Lenny Henry was a popular comedian, having won a TV talent show at just 17 in 1975; and Daley Thompson had won decathlon gold at the 1980 Moscow Olympics.

Aside from cultural visibility, black people became politically active. First on a local and then on a national level as exemplified by Bernie Grant who became the first ethnic minority leader of a London Council (Haringey) and subsequently, along with Diane Abbot and Paul Boateng in 1987, made history as the first people of Caribbean and African descent to be elected members of parliament. The phenomenon of black politics took on another dimension when the entrepreneur, Val McCalla, inspired by the Brixton riots, established the first black newspaper, the *Voice*, aimed at the black community. The newspaper attracted a lot of job adverts from London Boroughs aiming to promote their diversity and became successful financially. Such was its influence in the mid-1990s in black British society that it was accused by the then Metropolitan police commissioner, Paul Condon, of inciting racial tension by its coverage of the death in custody of a young black man.

Despite this history of black achievements, which Hall refers to as 'the margin coming into representation',[49] episodes typifying racial tensions such as the 1981 Brixton riots, the murder of Stephen Lawrence in 1993 and occurrences of racial disturbance continue to problematize the notion of attitude change. This was the position vigorously asserted by Vic and Jonathan in their insistence that a sense-defying paradox is revealed when the notion of attitude change is juxtaposed against the manifest racial incidents that have occurred and continue to occur in the United Kingdom. In her assessment of post Windrush Britain, especially in the context of young black people,

Phoenix corroborates the aforementioned view that racism exists in parallel to the progress made in race relations:

> While the fiftieth anniversary of the Windrush is appropriate cause for celebration and recognition of the dynamism of British society and peoples, the children, grand-children and great grandchildren of the Windrush generation have not been engaged in a straightforward progress from exclusion and being the objects of racism to inclusion and multiculturalism and celebrations. Instead their experiences are, and have been, riven with contradictions of what Phil Cohen has termed 'multicultures' and 'multiracism.[50]

However, the views expressed above appear to be at variance with those of Jason, Justin, Debbie and Nadin as they reported not encountering racial discrimination or prejudice of any form apart from minor problems with white officialdom. They also reported having white friends with whom they get on so well. Expressing the feelings of all four, Justin stated as follows:

These respondents exemplify the dynamics of race relation in Britain, especially in the context of younger generations of black and white people. Several ethnographic reports have found that white working class young people who may have prejudices against other minority ethnic groups such as Asians or Muslims, tend to admire Afro-Caribbean subcultures owing to their 'positive masculine and class associations'. As Modood explains, "racial discrimination is not unitary in its disadvantaging because not all non-white groups are discriminated against in the same way or to the same extent."[51]

According to Modood, prejudice based on color difference is superficial in comparison to that based on cultural difference. As interactions between the different races developed, white people, Modood states, were "Not necessarily less conscious of group differences but they were far more likely to ascribe group differences on the basis of upbringing, customs, forms of socialization and self-identity than to biological hereditary." In this context, therefore, 'prejudice against Asians in general, and Muslims in particular, is much the highest of any ethnic, racial and religious group.'[52]

Representing Black Ethnic Minorities in the British Media

As Trowler counsels, a study of the representation of ethnic minority communities in the British media should avoid generalization because certain representations in parts of the tabloid press are scarcely ever found on television or the broad sheets. This difference of approach, as Trowler notes, results in accusations of bias among media organizations.[53] The BBC, for example, is viewed by some newspapers as overly liberal, metropolitan and sympathetic to issues of immigration and multiculturalism. Moreover, newspapers and the BBC are different in characters, style and perspectives. While the television media in Britain do not directly instigate anti-immigrant sentiments, they may reinforce preexisting prejudices by focusing on negative news involving people of African and African Caribbean or Asian origin. According to Braham, the news and television media in some advanced industrialized countries reinforce the majority population's prejudice toward immigrants by implicitly or explicitly portraying the latter negatively.[54]

As Trowler states, also, some media are oriented toward particular communities and represents them and their cultures in ways that differ from those of the mainstream media. The *Voice* and *Nation,* for example, are demonstrably pro-Black and have been at the forefront, following the Brixton riots, in representing black cultural life as well highlighting issues such as social deprivation, racial discrimination, unemployment and police brutality that affects these communities. The *Voice* unabashedly describes itself 'as Britain's Best Black Newspaper.' Moreover, the role of some media in combating racism is often overlooked. Programs like *This Week, Man Alive and Black in Blue* produced by Desmond Wilcox in collaboration with other journalists which exposed intolerance, bigotry, and racial prejudice in the Metropolitan police, is not given due acknowledgment.[55]

It is also worth noting that some media are able to manage a curious duality of being both fluid and static (changes and continuities) in their responses to, and coverage of, issues affecting individuals in the black ethnic minority communities. The iconic repositioning of *The Times*, the *Daily Telegraph,* the *Daily Mail* and *Daily Express* in reporting and editorializing the Stephen Lawrence murder as racially motivated, including their full reproduction of the Macpherson Report which branded the Metropolitan police as institutionally racist, is a manifestation of this phenomenon.[56] As various studies have shown, the media are able to combat as well as promote racial prejudice and thus have a considerable influence on race relations.[57]

Given the above factors, it is appropriate to analyze negative representations of black communities in the context of the ideological premises or rationale of the media responsible. As Tiffin argues, "the process of news making is not politically neutral or ideologically inert." Tiffin states further that there are factors such as news value, audience interest, profit, nationalist political agenda, organization's ethos and other priorities that constitute a 'very considerable and limiting prism through which news about immigrant communities are filtered.'[58]

According to Hebdige, the English heritage industry with a nationalist agenda are complicit in institutionalizing cultural racism in the context of setting up certain fictional values that are modeled as English or British culture which effectively exclude those perceived as 'other'.[59] According to Van Dijke, a kind of 'othering' or indirect racism is implied when sections of the media with a nationalist agenda make statements about British values because 'there is an un-stated assumption being made about non-British values.'[60] As Dijke states further, some media discourses tend to inscribe racialized stereotypes on certain minority groups.

The depiction of black people as criminals by some of the print media epitomizes racial reductionism and anti-black prejudice. Studies carried out by Dijke on the linkage of ethnicity to crime, based on a content analysis of thousands of newspaper reports from different countries, show that crime and violence are among the five most frequent stereotypes ascribed to ethnic coverage.[61] In the United Kingdom, as Trowler observes, it is not uncommon to see newspaper headlines screaming thus: 'Black Brixton Looters Jailed'[62] 'MP's Ready to Greet Dubious Immigrants.'[63]

As Yarde points out also, the media reinforces this myth by clinging on to the same old stereotypes and moral panics. 'It is repackaged according to the demon of the day and regurgitated as if the use of the same metaphors were something new. In other words, contemporary media discourse echoes the 1960s and 1970s in re-ascribing metaphors such as "floods," "tides" "deluges" of colored people including Enoch Powell's "foaming," "bloody" and "tides,"[64] or words analogous to these, to the black communities. As Yarde notes, the *Daily Mail* and *Daily Express* are most complicit in reinforcing the impression that blacks are innately conditioned to be law-breakers or criminals. In 1982, the *Daily Mail* ran a front-page story headlined, "Black Crime: The Alarming Figures." This story focused on mugging which constituted just 1 percent of all serious crime recorded. Sixteen years later, the *Daily Mail* treated its readers to a reincarnation: "Brutal Crimes of The Asylum Seekers." This was reported as having a devastating impact on crime in London, but was denied by the police. As Yarde puts it: "The same theme but a different demon."[65]

Moral Panics, Folk Devils, and Primary Definers

From time to time, according to Cohen, certain groups of people become the subject of moral panics. They are labeled as being outside the central core values of consensual society and hence posing 'a threat to societal values and interests.'[66] These panics are often allied to calls for hardening of law and order to deal with 'folk devils'. The labeling of black people as muggers and the concomitant heavy-handed policing that they faced in the 1980s is an epitome of moral panics. Mugging was presented in the media as a rapidly growing phenomenon within the black communities, but there was no official statistics to sustain this claim.

Moreover, it was not a new crime, but was labeled as such to evoke moral panic which, according to Hall, served to legitimize the expansion of punitive measures, for example, police 'mugging squads' and heavy sentences.[67]

According to Neal, the late 1970s and 1980s saw 'the emergence of arguments suggesting that young African Caribbean men were not only being criminalized culturally, but that this process had a material effect on their experiences within the criminal justice system.'[68] Furthermore, the frenzied media report that followed the discovery of HIV and AIDS sufferers in Britain, in which gay people were demonized as spreaders of the disease, which bore no concrete evidence except for the speculations of primary definers namely laboratory workers and government health ministers (given huge credence) is emblematic of moral panics.[69]

The hysteria whipped up by the media was accompanied with calls for the quarantine of those infected.[70] The media rely upon primary definers who are often powerful and influential groups within the society: government officials and corporate experts providing information that help to legitimize its definition of social reality. As Herman notes, establishment media institutions often suppress opposing views, factual evidence or experiential accounts if these do not conform to their ideological or political framework. Put succinctly, they may distort facts or create myths to conform to their presuppositions of what is reality, wanting mainstream society to collude in seeing things as they see them. As Herman states, further, they defend their uncritical dependence on primary definers on the basis that the latter are makers of the news and definers of reality.[71]

According to Chomsky and Herman, there exists a symbiotic relationship between the media and primary definers. The media (secondary definers) can amplify perceived threats to the existing cohesion of society with the backing of expert sources, providing the justification for state (police and courts: mine) intervention to eliminate such threat. Chomsky and Herman's assertions derive from a political economic perspective on the media. In this mode of thought, the media "Serves to mobilize support for the special interests that dominate the state and private activity."[72]

In *Policing the Crisis: Mugging, the State and Law and Order*, Hall et al carried out a study of newspaper hysteria over rising crime, especially mugging. Applying Cohen's concept of moral panics, they theorized that the hysteria about rising crime rate is ideologically linked to social control. According to this view, crime statistics are often distorted for political and economic ends. Moral panics over mugging could be deliberately ignited to elicit public support for 'policing the crisis'. Hall et al articulated the view that the media in collaboration with primary definers invoke moral panics to reinforce and perpetuate the consensus view. The study was underpinned by the Gramscian theory of hegemony, which holds that the media plays a vital role in the social production of news aimed at preserving the dominant ideology. According to the above perspective, sections of the British media may exploit working class fears and anxieties of black people in order to unite them with the dominant class against those labeled as 'muggers' who pose a threat to the core values of society.

As have been stated earlier, the collaboration of sections of the media in whipping up moral panics could be driven by several other factors. The desire to increase circulation or ratings, and hence, maximize shareholder profits is often a major motivation. It also serves the interests of a powerful elite or press barons with anti-immigration agenda. These are often owners of, or influential people in, news organizations who control, determine and create media content and are able to disseminate propaganda to their audience, especially about threats posed by certain groups to society.

Hall however argues, also, that media audiences do not uncritically accept textual meanings intended by editors or producers. This proposition is premised on a reception theory developed by Hall that allows for a measure of "negotiated" or "oppositional" readings of the text by the audience.' Hall's model hinges on the notion that audience/readers negotiate meaning in the media text. They take in some of the meanings embedded in the text and also translate some in their own meaning. Depending on cultural backgrounds, some audience may accept most of the media's text message, while others reject it in preference of an oppositional reading.

In Encoding/Decoding, Hall proposes the *encoding* and *decoding* of media discourse in which "The intended meaning of text located somewhere between the producer and reader is encoded by the producer in a certain way, and the reader decodes the text's message slightly differently, according to his/her personal background, and the various different situations and frames of interpretation."[73]

Analysis of Media Coverage of Events of Racial Tension

The focus on black ethnic minorities as moral panics or threat, according to Hayward, can be traced to the coverage of 1958 Nottingham and Nottinghill 'riots' in which race was represented as a problem. Permeating media and public discourse were the words 'blacks' 'problem' and 'riots'. The media singled out black youths for blame, suppressing the reality that they were protesting against a series of attacks from fascist Teddy Boys, which resulted in the murder of Kelso Cochrane. The violence perpetrated by the Teddy Boys never featured in the vocabulary of the media as was done to the black youths who were only defending themselves. As Hayward puts it, 'by their very dint of "being there," blacks were trouble-causers. They were the "other," the black intruding menace.'[74]

The coverage of these events set a historical precedent in foregrounding the narrativization of black protests as "riots," "disturbances," "unruly mob violence"; and in the context of the Brixton disturbance of 1982, as "orgies of arson," "rampaging blacks," "black tide of looters." Implicit in the media discourse of these events, according to Hayward, 'is the notion that black people 'remain invisible until and unless they are perceived as a problem. They are stereotyped and made visible only as " rioters," "looters," "scroungers," "illegal immigrants," "muggers" and a "threat."[75]

While the Nottinghill and the Brixton disturbances differ in terms of their motivations and the composition of those involved, the contents of press coverage of both events, as would be demonstrated, bear some similarities, particularly in word association and distortions. Nearly all of my respondents remembered the disturbances as a manifestation of social discontent and anger that emanated from high unemployment, poor housing, racial discrimination and disproportionate policing in the communities. The disturbances lasted for three days and were carried out predominantly by young second-generation black men born to parents who had come in the 1940s and 1950s to help rebuild postwar Britain. They fought the police, set fire to vehicles and damaged buildings. More than 300 hundred people were injured with the total cost of damage to property estimated at £7.5 million. According to Cindi John of BBC Caribbean Reports, what shocked many people was its unexpectedness and spontaneity.

On the surface, it seemed that black people were integrating into the fabric of society, but simmering beneath was accumulated tension that boiled over in Brixton. It was an expression of years of frustration and anger at racism, discrimination, poverty, powerlessness, above all, oppressive policing. The days of full employment were gone and close to half of young black men in Brixton had no job. Many black young people believed that the police discriminated against them especially with the use of the Sus law under which anybody could be stopped and searched if officers merely thought they looked suspicious. In early April 1981, the police introduced Operation Swamp in response to a relentless media campaign about increasing street crime. Stereotyped as inclined to criminality, and not conforming to the social norms and values that characterizes respectable British life, young black people became an easy target. Close to a thousand of these were stopped and searched in Brixton in six days under the Sus law, leading to a heightening of tension.

As can be argued, newspaper coverage and analysis of these socio-economic problems especially the issue of excessive policing was tokenistic as it did not constitute news value. News value, according to Trowler, derives from reporting conflicts. As Trowler points out, also, sections of the print media do not engage in 'Analyzing and reporting the underlying socio-economic causes of problems faced by minority ethnic groups," as this would not be of interest to their readers. Hartman and Husband suggest that the problems faced by black people do 'not get into the news', but the portrayal of blacks as a 'problem' fits well with journalists' ideas of what constitutes newsworthiness or news values: 'Fear, tension, conflict, "riots" among others are words which make the audience sit up and take notice' and not peace, coexistence and harmony.

Hartman and Husband however argue that in portraying black people in these images, journalists and those who make the news are only reflecting to society 'the derogatory attitudes and negative symbols concerning foreigners and blacks which are inherent in the British culture. 'Hartman and Husband, according to Trowler, partially subscribe to the pluralist school of thought that views the media as not shaping society, but that society shapes the media. Racial prejudice towards foreigners or black people, according to this view, is bequeathed to 'people brought up in a racist society.' Their judgments, feelings and perceptions of foreigners or black people are colored by 'attitudes inherited from centuries of colonialism and racism, and are hence un-trustworthy.' Media representation of race is therefore a reflection of readers' attitude; identified by editors through newspaper sales and public opinion research.[76]

The mode of accounting of the Brixton disturbance is open to a Marxist and pluralist interpretation of how the story was framed. As Howe points out, it was called "Brixton riots" by the media to convey 'the impression that it was the work of an un-educated and hysterical mob' which fits in with its audiences' perceptions of black people.[77] While Howe's point is reasonable, the Brixton event merits the description of 'riot' ascribed to it, considering its tumultuousness and sense of disorder. Besides, similar events in around the same period in Bristol and Toxteth were described as riots. What was problematic as most of my interviewees stated, is the negative association and distortions in newspaper coverage. While the media were expressing a sense of national outrage, they were at the same time arousing their readers' imaginations with images of mayhem and negative word usage.

According to Hayward, the mobilization of pejoratives to describe the event typifies the narrativization of black protests as problem. The Brixton disturbance was given a copious amount of newsprint space by sections of the media. The content and images arguably points to a mode of reporting that was designed to create moral panics on the one hand, and arouse public sympathy and support for the police on the other. It was portrayed as an attack by black youths, widely perceived as folk devils, on the police who were regarded as victims. It was arguably through this prism that sections of the print media wanted its readers to view the event.

The *Daily Mail of 13/04/81* gave it a full-blown front page, couched in images and metaphors suggestive of anarchy and desolation with the photo of an injured policewoman being led away by two male colleagues. This was arguably calculated to elicit public support for the police, and reinforce the notion that black people were an embodiment of problem. The headline read thus: '*NEW BATTLES HIT BRIXTON*'. The story which consumed six pages, with just a few inches citing the cause of the disturbance, was structured in a victim/perpetrator binary in which the police were produced as being on the receiving end of attacks from, "An army of rioting black youths who took to the streets for the third night's battle against the Metropolitan Police. 'Once again it was the weary police, fighting to maintain their control of the streets, who were under pressure young blacks emphasized time and again that their quarrel was not with the white community but with the police."[78]

The *Daily Mail's* editorials and commentaries on the event underline the view by Hartman and Husband that sections of the media relish ascribing savagery and violence to the racial 'other' because of its news worthiness.[79] Black youths were portrayed as violent-prone and possessing street-fighting capabilities including the ability to deploy improvised missiles and other lethal weapons, while white youths were positioned as merely collaborating with them, as the following lines suggest, "Crowds of young blacks gathering in groups of up to 100…and whites appearing alongside them, working with them in their street fighting tactics, had large supplies of petrol bombs and sharpened iron railings distributed to them and were being used against police and property."[80]

The *Daily Express* like the *Daily Mail* has a tradition of political partisanship and is disdainful of issues relating to multiculturalism and immigration. Its publication of 13/04/81 gave the story a full front page with the headline reading thus: 'MORE RIOTS HIT BRIXTON'. With a similar theme as *the Mail*, the *Daily Express* regaled its readers with five pages of tales of violence and mayhem. The contents of the *Daily Express*'s editorial and commentary pages, like the *Daily Mail*'s were equally hysterical and may have been aimed at amplifying the sense of threat mentioned above: "When the American race riots appeared on British television screens in the 1970s, we thought they could never happen here. Now they have, with a vengeance. Brixton is last year in Bristol writ large. Within sight of Westminster, a whole community was consumed in an orgy of rioting, looting, arson, and violence."[81]

As Hall et al pointed out, sections of the media are able to isolate certain groups of people by labeling them as folk devils who threaten the national consensus. An article in the *Daily Express* in response to the Brixton disturbances is instructive as it connotes that West Indians are an irrational group of outsiders whose violent nature are antithetical to the ethos of white Britain or profoundly un-British. The usage of the phrase 'bloody riots' in association with West Indians epitomizes the media's propensity to create a mythic nexus between violent behavior and race. The following lines are from the article being referred to in the *Daily Express* of 13/04/81:

"The local West Indian leaders have the hardest and most vital of task. They must get it across to their community that, on mainland Britain, bloody riots and 'no-go' areas will not be tolerated. The law will be upheld and order maintained—everywhere."[82]

An article in the *Sun from 13/04/*81 lends credence to the point being made. Titled *Why these blacks of Brixton hate the police*, it was written by Roy Kerridge, described as an expert on West Indian affairs. His analysis of elderly West Indians and black youths in the context of maintaining law and order was distorted and arguably colored by his, or the *Sun*'s bias. Kerridge claimed that black youths were being indoctrinated by members of the Rastafarian movement into Black Nationalism or Black Consciousness based on mystification. Having been so brain-washed, these youths, as Kerridge suggests, turn against the state and all that it represents, especially the police. The Brixton disturbance, according to this notion, is a manifestation of ideologically induced hatred for the police. Yet it was a widely acknowledged fact that the youths, including the whites among them, were protesting police maltreatment of blacks, unemployment and racism.

Kerridge was arguably manifesting Orientalism or the notion of othering by his authoritative approach to the subject, and his demonising of Rastafarians. In other words, he assumed the position of the classical Orientalist if we substitute West Indians for Orientals. As Said points out, 'Anyone who teaches, writes about, or researches the Orient is an Orientalist, and what he or she does or say is Orientalism'. The Orientalist engages the Orient from a dominant standpoint and 'deals with it by making statements about it, authorising views of it, describing it…The former dominates and the latter must be dominated.'[83] Some newspaper representation of West Indian people by 'media experts', derives from a paradigm of thought that is stamped by imperialist prejudices. The Oriental—*the other, black people, immigrants—(emphasis mine)* as Said points out, is the person represented by this mode of thinking—'a single image, a sweeping generalisation, a stereotype that crosses countless cultural and national boundaries.'[84] As Seymour-Ure argues also, the British society's way of 'thinking about coloured people, influenced by the colonial past, constitutes a built-in predisposition to accept unfavourable beliefs about them…and the mass media themselves can plausibly be claimed to share responsibility.'[85]

Blacks, according to Hayward, are an invisible group made visible by representational narratives producing them as threat, menace and barbaric.[86] Goodman asserts that to concertize the view that certain groups of people pose a threat to the social cohesion, sections of the media employ popular stereotypes or language (often coded) that they know their audience would readily relate to.[87]

As have been argued, the Brixton event occasioned an outpouring of anti-black stereotypes in the press that had the potential of deepening the existing adversarial relations between many in the mainstream population and the immigrant population. As Neal points out, the 'media may re-inscribe a familiar repertoire of racialized stereotypes...and play with white cultural anxieties and fascinations with race' when covering black protests.[88] Newspapers coverage helped shape the notion that blacks were an embodiment of problem. Arguably, this notion gains currency in the imagination of the public.

Analysis of the Coverage of Powell's Speech

The coverage of Enoch Powell's "Rivers of Blood" speech in 1968 best exemplifies the representation of race (black immigrants) as a problem.[89] After a lull in the furor that characterized immigration and race debates in Britain in the post-independence period, Enoch Powell re-ignited it with his incendiary speech. The speech was timed to coincide with the Race Relations Bill that was being debated in parliament. The speech was delivered to a modest audience of just eighty-five people in a small upstairs room in the Midlands Hotel in Birmingham. It reverberated across the world, courtesy of the intensity of media coverage.

The theme resonated powerfully with the perceptions of Britain being gripped by hordes of commonwealth immigrants who threaten its cultural essence: its very existence. Powell's argument was that the influx of immigrants was changing the character of many areas of England including his Wolverhampton constituency, the Southwest as well as much of the West Midlands and his proposed solution was the immediate reduction to 'negligible proportions' of the inflow of immigrants, followed by the introduction of voluntary repatriation programs that would encourage the resettlement of former immigrants in their countries of origin.[90]

These views were not new, as he had been calling for a halt to commonwealth immigration all along. Even the theme of a speech he had delivered earlier at Walsall was similar to that of the "Rivers of Blood." What made the latter unique was Powell's technique: his usage of adage, metaphors and anecdotes, his encapsulation of the prevailing public anxiety over increasing immigration and its news worthiness.[91] Powell quoted an anonymous constituent of his who had resolved to leave the country fearing that eventually, 'the black man will have the whip hand over the white man.' Then there was the mention of an anonymous elderly lady constituent who has become the last white person on her street, the others having been harassed and forced to leave. She has been a victim of harassment and constantly subjected to abuses by her black neighbors. First, her window was broken. Secondly, human-waste was dropped through her door-hole. Thirdly, she was constantly bullied and called names when walking on the street by black children, pejoratively described as 'charming, wide-eyed, grinning piccaninnies.'

The impact of the speech was also heightened by the fact that it had been circulated to the press beforehand and the local ATV television station had sent a crew round to record it being delivered, thus guaranteeing that suitable sound bites would appear in news bulletins. Delivered on Saturday, the speech 'received saturation coverage in the Sunday press.'[92] Three newspapers published the speech in its entirety while others, apart from the *Sunday Mirror*, gave it an exceptionally generous proportion of coverage. His panic-inducing anecdotes, phrases and statements like 'heaping up funeral pyre', 'throwing a match into gunpowder', 'the Blackman will have the whip hand over the Whiteman' were conspicuously highlighted in leading articles, arguably to reinforce the loathing of immigrants.

There was also the political component. Witness how the *Sunday Express* that is averse to immigration reported the story. Its copy of 21/04/68 was headlined: *Powell Race Blockbuster: A Crisis for Heath.* It gave the speech an elaborate coverage using a total number of 1080 words including direct and in direct quotations. Its leading article did not condemn Powell's language as the *Sunday Mirror*, *Sunday Times*, *News of the World*, *The People* and few other newspapers of that day did. According to Seymour-Ure, an article in the *Sunday Express* described him as 'controversial, brilliant, stimulating, and devastatingly original.'[93] The *Sunday Telegraph* of 21/04/68 was headlined: '*Mr. Powell Forces the Race issue*: *Emotive Speech*'. Its leading article made no mention of Powell, but its total number of words in reporting the speech, which was 1840, and 1816 for direct and indirect quotations, betrayed its endorsement, and its anti-immigration stance.

CONCLUSION

This chapter was necessitated by the believe that British media representations of black African and African Caribbean people settled in Britain is stamped by prejudice or 'othering'. As the argument goes, black people are produced as the 'other', as a problem, as a nuisance. The ascription of negative image to the black communities obscures their historical contributions to Britain, whether as fighting in the world wars or in postwar reconstruction. Moreover, the media suppresses Britain's colonialist past and its nexus to the presence of black people here. As Hall opines, 'black people have had an invisible presence for centuries in British history: they have been the hidden component in the fate and fortune of Britain as a world-imperial power'.[94]

Another area of media discourse that connotes that black people are the 'other' or outsiders is the demand for their integration into the British way of life, in the interest of national cohesion. This notion assumes that there is a homogenous form of Britishness, but British identity according to Barczewsk, has been protean as 'it adapts itself to the demands of many different audiences' and is constantly under negotiation. Barczewsk refers to nineteenth century assertion of national identity in which King Arthur and his knights are venerated as national icons by conservative elites and nostalgic romantics, while Robin Hood and his Merry Men are held as a point of reference for the working class and socialists, as illustrative of the elasticity and adaptability of British national identity.

As various studies show, the media can play a great role in combating or promoting inequality, racial prejudice and ethnic marginalization and thus have a strong influence on race relations.[95] And there have been occasions in the history of race relations in Britain when the media has demonstrated that it can be a force for good. The coverage of the Stephen Lawrence's murder and the death of Damilola Taylor are outstanding examples, and shows the media manages a curious duality of being fluid and static in its relationship to the ethnic minority communities.[96] Tsuda suggests that 'the position of the media is not so clear cut. On the one hand, it is said that it reinforces existing prejudices about immigrants, supports and disseminate dominant ideologies and collaborates with the state. On the other hand, scholars argue that the media functions as a 'watchdog that provides self-reflective commentary and actively criticizes and questions the status quo, thus becoming a serious agent for cultural, socio-political, and institutional change.'[97]

The ambivalence surrounding the impact of the media to influence public opinion or attitudes notwithstanding, it remains a powerful tool and can play a major role in promoting a positive relationship between the black communities and mainstream society. It can play a major role in articulating their problems, promoting an awareness of their contributions to Britain, so as to bring about changes to how they are perceived.

NOTES

1. See Ravenhill, *Encyclopedia Britannica* (19/12/2006); Poirier, *New Statesman*, 09/04/07.
2. Wallace, W. What Does It Mean To Be British? Identity, Values, Citizenship, 2005. p. 4.
3. Seymore-Ure, C. *Political Impact of the Mass Media*. London: Constable, 1974. p. 100.
4. Young and Lewis, 1998, p. 78.

5. Ibid, 1998. p. 78.

6. Harker, The Guardian, 24/03/07; Ian Spencer 1997; Hayward, 2006. pp. 1–2.

7. R. Winder, *Bloody Foreigners,* USA: Little Brown (2004), pp. 265–277.

8. V. Robinson, *Transcience, Settlers and Refugees: Asians in Britain.* Oxford: Clarendon Press, 1986. p. 100.

9. Takeyuki, Tsuda. "Media Images, Immigrant Reality: Ethnic Prejudice And Tradition in Japanese Media Representation of Japanese-Brazilian Migrants." (2004), p. 4.

10. Herman, Edward and S. Chomski, *Manufacturing Consent.* New York: Pantheon Books, 1988.

11. See Halbwachs, *Collective Memory,* 1980, p. 2.

12. P. Towler, *Investigating Mass Media,* second Edition. London: Collins Educational, 1996. p. 225.

13. G. Lewis, and L. Young, *Soundings, Windrush Echo.* Cambridge University Press, 1994, p. 83.

14. Winder, *Bloody Foreigner*, pp. 266–267.

15. Greenberg, Bradley S. and J.E. Brand, *Minorities and the Mass Media, Effects: 1970s-1990s,* 1994. pp. 273–274; S. Hall "Racist Ideologies and the Media." *Media Studies: A Reader,* 1996. pp. 160–168.

16. S. Cottle (ed). *Ethnic Minorities and the Media.* Buckingham: Open University Press, 2000, pp. 2–7.

17. Dehay and Chaterjee, 2004: http://www, cwrl.utexas.edu/)

18. Ashcroft, Griffiths and Tiffin H. *The Post-Colonial Studies Reader, Key Concepts.* London and New York: Rutledge 2000, p. 171.

19. E. Said, *Orientalism.* London: Penguin Books, 1978. pp. 1–28, 329–352; A. Loomba, *Colonialism/Post Colonialism.* London and New York: Rutledge, 1998. pp. 105–153.

20. E.Said. *Orientalism.* p. 3.

21. B. Parekh, *Integrating Minorities, Introduction.* London: ICA, 1986, p. 3.

22. R. Dyer, *The Matter of Images- Essays on Representation.* London: Routledge, 1993. p. 93.

23. V. Robinson, *Transcience, Settlers and Refugees: Asians in Britain.* Oxford: Clarendon Press, 1986. p. 86.

24. The *Guardian*, 19/11/01.

25. M. Sherwood, *Race & Class, A Journal for Black and Third World liberation,* volume 42 Institute of Race Relations, January and March, 2001. p. 17.

26. S. Cottle. *Ethnic Minorities,* pp. 2–7.

27. S. Malik, *The Media, An Introduction.* Cambridge: Cambridge University Press, 1986. pp. 308–328; S. Cottle. *Ethnic Minorities* 7.

28. S. Allan, *Approaches to Media Discourse.* London: Open University Press, 1998. p. 107.

29. B. Malek, *Soundings, Windrush Echo.* Cambridge: Cambridge University Press, 1998. Pp. 145–156; S. Hall, "Racist Ideologies." pp. 160–168.

30. Gurnah, *The Guardian* 22/05/01, Seymore-Ure, C. *Political Impact of The Mass Media.* London: Constable, 1978. pp. 99–113.

31. S. Neal, *The Scarman Report, the Macpherson Report and the Media, How Newspapers Respond to Race-centred Social Policy Interventions.* Cambridge University Press, 2003, p. 2.

32. D. Gould, *Writing a Media Analysis.* London: Routledge, 2004, pp. 1–8.

33. R.Winder, *Bloody Foreigners.* USA: Little Brown, 2004.

34. Asamoah oral interview.

35. Mrs Swann oral interview.

36. E. Said. Orientalism, 3.

37. Ibid p. 3.

38. P. Foot, *The Rise of Enoch Powell.* Penguin Books, 1969.

39. Cato: Oral interview. She hails from Barbados.

40. Mr Brown, originally from St Lucia. Oral interview.

41. Assamoah. Oral interview.

42. Bill, in an oral interview.

43. S.Hayward, "Blacks in Britain: Racial Discourse in UK Politics and Media." *A Review ofContemporary Media,* 2006. p. 3.

44. Miss Lewis from St Lucia came to join her parents at the age of eight in England: oral interview.

45. E. Ekow, *Black Gold of the Sun.* Hamish Hamilton: Penguin Books, 2005, pp. 68–69.

46. B. Skeggs, *Formation of Class and Gender.* London: Sage, 1997. p. 90.

47. T.A. Van Dijk, *Racism and the Press: Critical Studies in Racism and Migration.* London: Rutledge, 1991.

48. J. Gubrium and Johnson, J. "In-depth interviewing in J. Gubrium and J. Holstein (eds) In *Handbook of Interview Research, Context and Method.* Thousand Oaks: London Sage Publications, 2002).

49. Hall S. "Encoding and Decoding in the Television Discourse." In Hall, S., Hobson, D., Lowe, A. Willis, P. (ed.) *Culture, Media, Language.* London: Hutchinson, 1980.

50. Phoenix, A. *Soundings, Windrush Echo.* Cambridge University Press, 1998, p. 87.

51. May, T. "Social Research, Issues, Methods, Process," in Modood, T. *Multiculturalism and the Public Sphere, Policy Studies Institute,* Second Edition (1997).

52. Ibid., p. 96.

53. P. Towler, *Investigating Mass Media,* second Edition. London: Collins Educational, 1996, p. 207.

54. P. Braham, "How the Media Report Race." In *Culture, Society and the Media.* London, Methuen, 1982. pp. 268–286; Bradley S. Greenberg and J.E. Brand, *Minorities and the Mass Media, Effects: 1970s-1990s,* 1994. pp. 273–274; S. Hall, "Racist Ideologies and the Media." *Media Studies: A Reader,* 1996. pp. 160–68.

55. P. Towler, P. *Investigating Mass Media,* p. 207.

56. S. Neal, *The Scarman Report,* 5.

57. S. Cottle. *Ethnic Minorities,* pp. 2–7.

58. R. Tiffin, *The News from Southeast Asia* 5.

59. P.Towler, *Investigating Mass Media,* p. 209.

60. T.A.Van Dijk, *Racism and the Press.*

61. Ibid.
62. *Daily Telegraph*, 14/12/85).
63. *Daily Telegraph*, 03/12/85; P. Trowler, 1996. p. 209.
64. R. Yarde, *The Guardian*, 12/11/01.
65. Ibid.
66. S. Cohen, *Folk Devils and Moral Panics*. London; Mac Gibbon and Kee, 1972, p. 9.
67. S. Hall, *Policing the Crisis: Mugging, the State and Law and Order*. London: Macmillan Press, 1978, p. 78.
68. S. Neal *The Scarman Report,* 59.
69. J. Goodman, *Moral Panics—HIV & AIDS*. (2002), p. 1.
70. Ibid 3.
71. Edward S Hermanan and S. Chomski, *Manufacturing Consent: The Political Economy of Mass Media*. London: Vintage London, 1994. pp. 135–146.
72. Herman, Edward S. Chomski, *Manufacturing Consent*. New York: Pantheon Books, 1988. P. xi.
73. S. Hall, *Policing the Crisis*, pp. 130–135; BSource:http://www.culstock.ndirect.co.uk.
74. S. Hayward, "Blacks in Britain: Racial Discourse in UK Politics and Media." *A Review of Contemporary Media,* 2006. p. 1.
75. Ibid 2.
76. Hartman and Husband, 1974. pp. 274–279.
77. *New Statesman*, 03/04/06.
78. The Daily Mail 13/04/81.
79. Hartman and Husband, 1974. pp. 274–279.
80. Ibid.
81. *Daily Express*14/04/81.
82. Ibid.
83. E. Said, *Orientalism,* pp. 1–5.
84. Ibid.
85. Seymour-Ure quoting Hartman and husband, p. 113.
86. S. Hayward, "Blacks in Britain." pp. 2–3.
87. J. Goodman, *Moral Panics—HIV & AIDS*. (2002), p. 1.
88. S. Neal, *The Scarman Report,* 59.
89. P. Trowler, 1996, p. 214.
90. Gordon and Rosenberg, 1989. p. 45.
91. Seymour-Ure, pp. 111—117.
92. Seymour-Ure, pp. 104.
93. Seymour-Ure, p. 115.
94. S. Hall, p. 74.
95. P. Braham, pp. 268–286.
96. S. Neal, p. 59.
97. Takeyuki Tsuda, p. 3.

Chapter 13

African Immigrants and the American Experience

Sabella Ogbobode Abidde

INTRODUCTION

Africa is by no means a homogenous society. It is a continent of some fifty-four countries with multiple religions, traditions and cultural practices, and second to Asia in terms of spoken languages. For the most part, it is an agrarian society: the least unindustrialized and where more people live in tangent with nature than any other organized human society. Even so, it is not a close, dark, and hopeless society as many imagined and or proclaimed it to be.[1] But instead, it is a society that is ever changing and receptive of modernizing ideas and ideals. It is precisely for these reasons that Africans are amenable to migration, westernizing and globalizing forces.

In small and large numbers, Africans can be found in all corners of the world. As with other immigrant groups, the African population has steadily been increasing in Europe and North America. In the United States, for example, the African population has been increasing several folds, and their impact on the social, cultural economic and political landscape has been noted by many. Indeed,

> The cultural polyphony of Africans has become a noticeable aspect of the urban landscape of major metropolitan centers across the United States. Throughout America, African immigrants make significant contributions to the cultural and economic enrichment of this country. Their contributions in the areas of medicine, higher education, and engineering have been chronicled in major newspapers.[2]

This chapter, then, is about the everyday experience and reality of African immigrants living in the United States. While one cannot speak for all immigrants, it nevertheless captures the essence of what it means to be an immigrant living in one of the most modern and most industrialized of all Western societies. It's been stated and demonstrated elsewhere in this book that Africans leave the continent because of several reasons, that is, political instability, poverty, fear of persecution and inhibiting living conditions. In the last two decades, however, a significant number are leaving primarily for opportunities they believe abound abroad. In many African countries, the general condition is not healthy or enriching or conducive to personal growth and happiness. The alternative, for many Africans, therefore, is exile or self-migration.

Although conditions differ from one country to another, by and large, what we have is a continent where a sizable number of the people—especially those between the ages of 18 and 40—cannot wait to self-migrate. Nigeria is an archetypal example of a country where, if embassies assured travel visas, seventy percent or more of college students and graduates would leave of their own volition. This was the reality at the height of military authoritarianism between 1985 and 1998. And although the return to civilian rule in the summer of 1999 stabilized the country, many Nigerians still think of migrating to Europe, the oil-rich Middle East, Asia and other parts of the world. This penchant for self-migration is not likely to diminish if Nigerians—and indeed other Africans—think there is a better life and a better future outside of the continent.

THE BURDEN OF EXILE

Not minding the allure and the advantages of migration, living in exile can be awful. To leave one's family and one's society and the familiar (especially at an older age) can be disorienting. For instance, there are new skills and perhaps, a new language to be learnt, new culture to content with, and the general newness of the new society. What's more, moving from an agrarian society to an industrialized society has its drawbacks. There is, for instance, the clash of culture. In this instance, while settlement in the United States may be somewhat easy for a Nigerian, a Ghanaian or a South African, it may be somewhat difficult for a Somalian, a Mauritanian and a Malian. Much of the difficulty has to do with language and social-cultural barriers in that English-speaking Africans tend to have an easier time with the acculturation and assimilation process—as opposed to the conservative Muslim and or Anglophone countries. What's more, English-speaking African countries, are for the most part, more liberal, more open and more accommodating of Western ideas and ideals.

The burden of exile is manifested in several ways. For instance, many immigrants will come to realize that the longer they remain outside of the country of their birth, the deeper the pain and the agony. The conflict and agony is experienced mostly by the older immigrants—those in or past middle age. No matter how successful they become in their private and public lives, many do feel empty. Their successes are never fully and truly complete because, many don't have a sense of belonging in their new country. They feel foreign in a foreign land. They are conscious of their speaking accent, conscious of their mannerism and worldview, conscious of their social and religious sensibility, and conscious of the absence of the familiar.

The burden of exile is also made more painful for those who had achieved some measure of success in their homeland before migrating. For instance, if you were a "nobody" before coming to the United States, and if you are still a "nobody" after several years of sojourn, the pain of "failure" may not be much. There is usually just a sense of slight bitterness and dissatisfaction. Despite the aforesaid, many immigrants prefer to be a failure outside of their country, instead of being a failure inside of their country. We know, for instance, that poverty in Nigeria, Burkina Faso, Mali or Swaziland can be more brutal and dehumanizing than poverty in the United States. No matter how poor or dire things may be, therefore, many immigrants—even though they live in the economic and social margins—are still able to send remittances home. In many respect, poor immigrants in the United States and Canada are financially well-off than the average civil servant in many African countries. That they can help in lifting their home-based families out of searing poverty is psychologically satisfying. Many consider it a great achievement.

But for those who were "somebody" before their departure, and are now a "nobody" as immigrants, the pain is likely to be greater. This is especially true of immigrants who were professionals and had achieved a measurable level of economic success. Leaving to start afresh is a gamble—and many professionals do lose. In the first place, it takes a while to get adjusted and be accepted in professional careers. For instance, a foreign trained medical doctor, accountant, college professor or lawyer cannot begin their practice right away. Foreign trained medical doctors must, for instance, pass the United States Medical Licensing Examination sponsored by the Federation of State Medical Boards and the National Board of Medical Examiners (USMLE).[3] Securing a job at the college and university level can also be frustrating. An accomplished Nigerian author who asked for anonymity once said to this author:

> Most of the professors and successful African immigrants you see in this country are sad and depressed…especially the professors…most are angry, and are not respected by their non-Black peers. Most of these Africans are better read and smarter than many of their counterparts, but they generally are saddled with

> supporting or subservient roles; they must defer to their non-black colleagues. To make matters worse, even their students complain about their accent and mannerism, and assume they must be less qualified than other professors, especially the whites and Asians…[4]

Faced with such a situation, they are angry at their home government, angry at their colleagues, angry at their students and subordinates, and are also angry at themselves. Despite this, American colleges and universities are filled with African professors and administrators. One cannot think of a colleges or university, anywhere in the United States, without at least two Nigerian faculty members. Same can be said of universities in Canada, the United Kingdom and many other countries in Europe. One also doubts if there is a medical establishment, anywhere in the United Kingdom, Canada and the United States, without Nigerian doctors and nurses. What this means is that professional establishments in the Western world are full of Africans who prefer to practice abroad than at home. The implication is the continuation of human capital flight (sometimes referred to as brain drain).[5]

In all these places and beyond, one doubts if most of these Africans truly enjoy being there. The financial compensation may be good—great even! But many would rather be home: helping their own people and helping to advance their own countries. But here they are needed primarily for their skills and services—needed just to help develop and advance a country that is truly not theirs. How terrible it must feel to be a hired hand. They feel terrible and violated: violated by a government—their home governments—that are utterly incompetent, utterly corrupt, and utterly wayward that makes their country unlivable and in the process forcing them into exile. To be an African immigrant in the West or anywhere else is not easy. Within the international political and economic system, Africa is often an afterthought. And even at the individual level, most non-blacks do not think much of the African. Sometimes one gets the feeling that non-blacks consider Africans incapable of complex tasks: a people incapable of governing themselves without generous assistance from the Western world.

IN PURSUIT OF THE GREEN CARD

There are several ways to obtain the Alien Registration Card (otherwise known as the Green Card, or Permanent Residence Card). The card confers the legal status to live and work in the United States, and is also one of the prerequisites for obtaining US citizenship. According to the US Citizenship and Immigration Services, there are several ways through which one can obtain the card. The main categories are: through family; through a job; and through refugee or asylee status. And of course, there are other ways, including but not limited to:[6]

- Diversity Immigrant Visa Program (referred to by many as the 'Green Card Lottery')
- K Nonimmigrant (includes fiancé(e))
- Legal Immigration Family Equity Act
- Special Immigrant Juvenile Status
- Battered Spouse or Child (VAWA)
- Armed Forces Member
- Physician National Interest Waiver
- Religious Worker
- Informant (S Nonimmigrant)
- Victim of Trafficking

While legal immigrants are assured the Green Card, many others—students, those who overstayed their non-immigrant visa, the uninspected, etc.—must go through the arduous task of obtaining the card. One such way is through marriage. For many Africans, this could be one of the most frustrating, unpredictable and expensive undertaking of their young lives in the United States. Life in the United States can be unbearable without the card. The possibility of further education, securing a job, foreign travel, and unrestricted movement within the country is almost impossible without the card. To survive, many without the card must go underground to work in the informal sectors of the economy and where many are subject to abuse and exploitation. To obtain the card, therefore, an untold number do engage in fraudulent marriages and employ other extralegal means to beat the US immigration system.

RELIGIOUS BIGOTRY, RACISM, AND ETHNICITY

When some Americans think of Islam, they invariably think of terrorism and Osama bin Laden and other terrorist leaders and organizations. They forget that al-Qaeda is not Islam; and Islam does not espouse the ideas and ideals of Osama and his fellow travelers. They forget that that the Islamic State in Iraq and Syria has nothing to do with Islam—even if some of its members are committing atrocities in the name of Islam and Prophet Mohammed. And unfortunately, many Americans simply do not have a grasp—not even an elementary grasp—of the Islamic religion. Huston Smith, it was who said that "Of all the non-Western religions, Islam stands closest to the West-closest geographically, and also closest ideologically; for religiously it stands in the

Abrahamic family of religions…yet despite this mental and spatial proximity, Islam is the most difficult religion for the West to understand."[7]

This ignorance, suspicion and misperception about Islam probably accounts for why, increasingly, Muslims are being subjected to slurs and abuses and discrimination. According to Katayoun Kishihe, "The number of physical assaults against Muslims in the United States reached 9/11-era levels" in 2015. Analyzing the Pew Research Center analysis of new hate crimes statistics from the FBI, the Katayoun went on to say,

> There were 91 reported aggravated or simple assaults motivated by anti-Muslim bias in 2015, just two shy of the 93 reported in 2001. Separately, the number of anti-Muslim intimidation crimes—defined as threatening bodily harm—also rose in 2015, with 120 reported to the FBI. Again, this was the most anti-Muslim intimidation crimes reported in any year since 2001, when there were 296. Overall, the FBI reported 257 incidents of anti-Muslim hate crimes in 2015, a 67% increase from the previous year. These incidents included 301 individual crimes, 71% of which were crimes against people, as opposed to property.[8]

According to the findings of the Pew Research Center, "between 1992 and 2012, a total of about 1.7 million Muslims entered the U.S. as legal permanent residents."[9] And as of January 2016, there were about 3.3 million Muslims of all ages living in the United States. This means that Muslims made up about 1% of the total U.S. population."[10] While native-born African Americans make up a quarter of all US Muslim population, there are no data that shows how many are immigrants from Africa. Nonetheless, as with all immigrants who are Muslims, they too suffer from the hostility and hate that are directed toward the general Muslim population. To be an African and a Muslim, therefore, is to suffer double tragedies. Other than religious bigotry, there is the issue of racism and xenophobia. In the days leading to the 2016 US Presidential Election, for instance, the Republican candidate and eventual winner of the election, Mr. Donald Trump, was reported to have stoked religious, ethnic and racial bigotry by telling his listeners and supporters:

> Here in Minnesota, you've seen first-hand the problems caused by Somali refugees coming into your state without your knowledge, without your support or approval…Some of them are joining Isis and spreading their extremist views all over our country and all over the world…Everybody's reading about the disaster taking place in Minnesota…You don't even have the right to talk about it.[11]

Such hate and intolerance, directed at immigrants and other groups, is what has helped to fuel the fear, anxiety and uncertainty that has come to characterize the general American population; it is what has helped to foster the sense and feeling of nativism and xenophobic climate of recent times. More than any other immigrant groups in the United States, the Africans are especially susceptible to hate, abuse, discrimination and racism. This is primarily due to their color, speaking accent and foreignness. It is easier to pick out an African immigrant compared to those from New Zealand, Canada, or the United Kingdom. And indeed, white Americans seem to prefer immigrants from those part of the world.

Africans are generally seen as primitive, backward and uncivilizable. Long before Donald Trump's candidacy and national prominence, another presidential candidate, Patrick Buchanan, made his preference clear. In his words, "If we had to take a million immigrants in, say Zulus, next year, or Englishmen, and put them in Virginia, what group would be easier to assimilate and would cause less problems for the people of Virginia?"[12] Buchanan was a politician and public commentator who seem to hate immigrants—save those from Europe.

Even so, African immigrants have learned to cope by mostly ignoring racist and discriminatory attitude, comments and deeds by white Americans—realizing that not all whites have racist and xenophobic tendencies. The irony is that many African immigrants are also subjected to hate and discriminatory attitude from and by African Americans and blacks from Latin America and the Caribbean. The tension within the Black community—consisting continental Africans and Africans in the Diaspora—can sometimes be more depressing and overpowering than the racist attitude of the white society.[13] For many African immigrants, racism from across the color line is expected—but not from those they consider their cousins in terms of color, ancestry, history and shared experiences.

There is a second irony: the tension and suspicion within the African immigrant community (in terms of regional and ethnic differences). First, some Africans tend to, consciously or unconsciously, draw a line based on regional or colonial similarities or differences. In lager settings, for instance, West Africans tend to associate and or socialize with fellow West Africans. Otherwise, associations can be because of colonial experience and history: Anglophone (English-speaking), Francophone (French speaking), or Lusophones (Portuguese speaking). And of course, there is the northern part of the continent that is politically and geographically lumped with the Middle East.

Ethnicity, within given countries, are strengthened or made worse by colonial experiences. At the time of independence, many African countries were already struggling under the weight of the divide-and-rule policy of many colonial governments. In Nigeria, for instance, ethnic suspicious and intolerance was partly responsible for the 1966 military coups and the resultant 1967–1970 civil war. Today, the country is still reeling under ethnicity-induced animosity. Unfortunately, many Nigerian immigrants predicate their association and relationship on ethnicity. That a sizable number of Nigerians in the United States, the United Kingdom and elsewhere outside of the country would not freely and readily associate with Nigerians of whom they are not of the same ethnic group. They are *the same* only if there is a shared benefit, or they face a common danger. Or, a situation that involves national achievement at the international level.

LIFE IN AMERICA: PIPEDREAMS AND POSSIBILITIES

Despite the allure of the United States, life in America is not as rosy and as smooth as prospective immigrants think; it is not as is sometimes portrayed to those who dream of crossing the oceans, or trekking length and breadth of the Sahara Desert just to arrive the New World. For a good number of immigrants, life in America can be tough—inflicting both physical and mental pain. It can be disorienting: a series of never-ending nightmares. For the unlucky or the unrealistic, life in the United States can be likened to a whirlwind of shattered dreams or unmet expectations and in the process becoming a source of sadness, deep-seated anger and mental depression.

On the other continuum is the other America: a land of inexhaustible opportunities, the land for those who are daring and have the courage to extend frontiers. A land that rewards those who work hard and smart, who persevere and keep going even when they fail. And indeed, America has been good to millions of immigrants—immigrants who came to and could, within a reasonable time frame, attain the American dream. Whether one realizes his/her American dream or not, there are those who prefer living in America because of the sense and feeling of freedom.

RELOCATION AND THE MYTH OF RETURN

After several decades of living in the United States, it can be difficult—extremely difficult—returning to one's homeland. Relocation, under any circumstance, is not easy. This is especially so if one has spent 15 or more of his productive years in the United States. Even when well planned, reverse migration to any African country can be frustrating, energy-sapping and discouraging. This is so because several years of exile have a way of making one a stranger in one's community and country. Therefore, the early years of returning can be especially hard in terms of mannerism, worldview, social mores and cultural sensibility.

Most African countries do not have the capacity to absorb returnees. And of course, there are the problems associated with public and private infrastructure, security, and other political goods many immigrants take for granted in foreign countries: the uncertainties associated with basic human needs, that is, power, potable water, education, good roads and telecommunication, personal security, and healthcare. Nonetheless, how well and for how long one planned his/her relocation can also determine how things turn out in terms of one's place and comfort in the *new environment.* Planned or not, smooth or not, every now and then, new arrivals will get their bearings wrong. It is the price they pay for being in exile for that many years.

Of course, there is the irony many immigrants hardly speak about: the *shame of a wasted sojourn abroad.* This is the case of many immigrants who, after spending several years in the land of the United States, have nothing to show for their time abroad. No homes, no investment portfolio, no saving and none of those things that constitutes the *American dream.* Not only do they not have anything to show for their several years of sojourn, they also do not have the tangibles of success back in their homeland. For impending returnees, therefore, returning home can be a difficult, embarrassing, and expensive proposition. At the very least, it can be a complicated task.

Many African immigrants have family members who are steeped in poverty. Such people become one's responsibility. There are school and hospital bills to pay; debts to help repay; bribes to give; and family support to render. Because of the much-vaunted *African culture*, one is forced to be one's brother's keeper and in the process constraining or stunting ones economic and social growth. Despite the negativities and fear, many immigrants would like to return home. But where does one start? Fear, negativity and ambivalence aside, there is what Sulayman Nyang refers to as the *Myth of Return.* Essentially:

> All immigrants entertain the notion of leaving their home countries for countries of settlement, striking it rich, and then returning home with enough resources to live well in their countries of origin. Often, this does not happen. Instead the single immigrant marries a local woman or man and ends up with a family and children. The immigrant may then feel compelled to stay long enough to ensure those children's education and autonomy, but more often than not, the children establish their own families and what was originally meant to be short term migration becomes permanent. Due to the myth of return among the African immigrants, there is a serious gap between ideals and realities.[14]

Sulayman goes on to tell us that "most have grand ideas about what they would like to contribute to the transformation of their home countries. Because of their procrastination and ambivalence, they focus on their home countries, while neglecting to socialize their children to cope with life in their countries of origin. It is owing to this neglect that there is a growing body of young Africans who do not speak any African languages. Many thought that these languages would be acquired, as if by osmosis, through the child's interaction with members of the family. Given these challenges, it is appropriate to raise the question of socialization and the need for social and moral agency in the education of African immigrant children. There is a serious gap between the ideals of the first generation of African immigrants and the needs of the second and subsequent generations."[15]

MIGRATION AND THE FUTURE OF A CONTINENT

That the African economic, political and social space is evolving and improving is beyond debate. What is not in doubt is the fact that progress is slow, very slow. Thus, many Africans—especially the youths, are impatient and are therefore in a hurry to carve out the kind of life and living they envision for themselves. For many of them, therefore, their dreams and ambition can only be realized in faraway lands of oil-rich Middle East, Europe and North America—and increasingly in Asia. The abundance of pulling factors—in addition to globalizing phenomenon—is too alluring for millions of Africans to ignore. And of course, there are pushing factors: wars, ethnic and religious conflicts, searing poverty and unemployment, geographical and climatic factors, political instability and a political space that inhibits growth and, in some places, restricts human rights and civil liberties.

But of course, Africans are not alone. They are not unique in terms of what make self-migration appealing and lucrative. Immigrants from other parts of the world are also induced by the same or similar pull-push factors. Hence several million immigrants are on the move—crossing national borders legally and illegally to arrive at the destination of their choice. It may take a while before the number of people coming out of Africa decreases. This is primarily because of three reasons: (1) millions of young men and women in the continent have limited access to basic human needs. Thus, many are restless; (2) even as many countries in the continent make economic and political headway, the space is not elastic enough to accommodate all those who wish to stay; and (3) millions of Africans—based on their experiences—do not believe that things will improve in their lifetime.

Fifty or more years of theft and corruption, incompetence and mismanagement have taught millions of Africans to be suspicious of their government. And in many countries, the disconnection between the people and the government is so wide that it may take a lifetime to engender trust and confidence in their government and public officials. So, instead of remaining in their countries to help with the development process, millions of Africans are willing to take the risk of becoming immigrants—with the belief that they will make it, become prosperous, and then get their families (back in the continent), out of economic poverty and political misery. But as it turned out, this is not always the case. Migration, as many has come to find out, can be frustrating, painful and disappointing. And in fact, many would have been better off in their homeland.

There are no easy solutions to many of Africa's problems. One could point to the list for what many scholars and observers of Africa politics believe is responsible for the continent's underdevelopment: The Trans-Atlantic Slave Trade, colonialism, two world wars, globalization and the exploitative and overpower tendencies of Western nations. In addition, there are a dozen or so endogenous factors one could point to as contributing influences. Whatever the underdevelopment-causing factors may be—and whatever their residual effects may be—Africa is several generations away from the ideal. It is precisely for this reason that, year after year, millions of Africans will continue to look to migrations as the only avenue, or one of the few avenues, to prosperity, personal happiness and wholeness.

If there is a saving grace, a redeeming quality about migration, it is the fact that most Africans believe and practice transnational migration. It is as if, wherever they go, their hearts are bound to their country and the continent. As if they love their country and their continent, not because it is the greatest, but because Africa is theirs.[16] And so, they return for a week, a month or a year to bask in the promise and the wonder that is Africa. They return every now and then—and never truly abandoning it. The transnational nature of African immigrants is one of the factors that have helped to keep the continent going.

CONCLUSION

The movement of people within the continent—from one country to another—is ever present. But in the last two or three decades, more Africans are engaged in international migration. As they arrive in foreign countries, many are faced with social, cultural, and political problems they didn't think existed. The acculturation and assimilation process is compounded by issues relating to racism, discrimination and religious bigotry. And many are surprised to find that America is not a field of roses. They are surprised to find that it came be lonely and lonesome and frustrating. With time, many will come to realize that despite the tales and the promises they've heard time and again, not all who come to America can achieve the American dream. But no matter their lot and place within the American system, many feel grateful to be part of the system. Though they may be living in the margins, in so many ways, their conditions are far better than the condition of many of the relatives back in their homeland. Because the United States is a hopeful country, many keep trudging along. Whether they make it or not, they engage in transnational migration: living, physically and mentally, in two worlds.

NOTES

1. "Hopeless Africa." *The Economist*. May 13, 2000. Accessed October 27, 2016. http://www.economist.com/node/333429.

2. John A. Arthur. *Invisible Sojourners: African Immigrant Diaspora in the United States*. Westport, CT: Praeger, 2000.

3. "United States Medical Licensing Examination." USMLE last modified December 10, 2017. http://www.usmle.org/.

4. Private conversation. Anonymity was sought and granted.

5. Aderanti Adepoju. *International Migration Within, to and from Africa in a Globalised World*. Accra, Ghana: Sub-Saharan Publishers, 2010; and Tanner, Arno. *Emigration, brain drain and development: the case of Sub-Saharan Africa*. Helsinki: East-West Books, 2005.

6. "Green Card." US Citizenship and Immigration Services. Accessed December 10, 2016. https://www.uscis.gov/greencard.

7. Huston Smith. *The World's Religions*. San Francisco: HarperSanFrancisco, 1991.

8. Katayoun Kishi. "Anti-Muslim assaults reach 9/11-era levels, FBI data show." Pew Research Center. November 21, 2016. Accessed November 30, 2016. http://www.pewresearch.org/fact-tank/2016/11/21/anti-muslim-assaults-reach-911-era-levels-fbi-data-show/.

9. Benjamin Wormald. "The Religious Affiliation of U.S. Immigrants: Majority Christian, Rising Share of Other Faiths." Pew Research Center's Religion & Public Life Project. May 17, 2013. Accessed November 11, 2017. http://www.pewforum.org/2013/05/17/the-religious-affiliation-of-us-immigrants/#muslim.

10. Mohamed Besheer. "A new estimate of the U.S. Muslim population." Pew Research Center. January 06, 2016. Accessed October 05, 2016. http://www.pewresearch.org/fact-tank/2016/01/06/a-new-estimate-of-the-u-s-muslim-population/.

11. Ben Jacobs, and Alan Yuhas. "Somali migrants are 'disaster' for Minnesota, says Donald Trump." *The Guardian*. November 07, 2016. Accessed December 03, 2017. https://www.theguardian.com/us-news/2016/nov/06/donald-trump-minnesota-somali-migrants-isis.

12. E.J Dionne Jr. "IS BUCHANAN COURTING BIAS?" *The Washington Post*. February 29, 1992. Accessed November 10, 2016. https://www.washingtonpost.com/archive/politics/1992/02/29/is-buchanan-courting-bias/4753a57f-183b-4033-be38-4e2360e6aa00/?utm_term=.641b7f7f0084.

13. Ugboaja F. Ohaegbulam. "Continental Africans and Africans in America: The Progression of a Relationship." In *Africana Studies: A Survey of Africa And the African Diaspora*, edited by Mario Azevedo, 225–48. Durham, NC: Carolina Academic Press, 2005.

14. ———. "The African Immigrant Family in the United States of America: Challenges and Opportunities." *Ìrìnkèrindò: A Center for Islam and Public Policy*, December 2013. Accessed October 9, 2017. http://www.cippusa.com/the-african-immigrant-family-in-the-united-states-of-america-challenges-and-opportunities/.

15. Ibid.

16. Here, I have paraphrased Voltaire who said, "Our country is that spot to which our heart is bound" (Voltaire); and Seneca who said that "Men love their country, not because it is great, but because it is their own." Voltaire is the pen name for François-Marie Arouet (1694–1778). He was a French writer, philosopher and historian. Lucius Annaeus Seneca (c. 4 BC–AD 65) was a philosopher, statesman, and author.

Chapter 14

Nigerians in America

Interpersonal Relationships and the Pull of Globalization

Sabella Ogbobode Abidde

INTRODUCTION

There is not a single narrative about Africa and Africans; and for that matter, there is not a single narrative about interpersonal relationships among Africans (in and outside of the continent). And, in fact, there is not a single narrative about any group or subgroups insofar as interpersonal relationships are concerns. What this chapter offers, then, is a common thread and some safe assumptions. When it comes to Africans, therefore, anyone interested in sex and sexuality would be advised to consult Sylvia Tamale's edited work.[1] One of the seminal treatises on feminists and feminism in Africa is Gwendolyn Mikell's scholarly tome.[2] And of course, there is Oyeronke Oyewumi's work on gender studies.[3] These works, individually and collectively, illuminate and educate readers on sex and sexuality in Africa.

Whenever Africans migrate to Western societies—especially to the United States—most tend to hold on to their traditional values and social mores for as long as possible, while others speedily acculturate and or get assimilated. The speed and ease of such metamorphosis and settlement depend on several factors: What is their age and the totality of their life experiences? Are they Muslims or Christians? Are they from liberal or conservative background? Do they have college or high school education or no education at all? Are they from small towns and villages? Or are they from big cities and cosmopolitan areas and are therefore exposed to Western and globalizing factors?

While the aforesaid mentioned helps in predicting the ease of settlement, other factors are also important. These factors are domestic in nature. For instance, some states and cities in the United States are receptive to immigrants. They provide goods and services that are vital for new immigrants and which include generous welfare packages, educational needs for the children of immigrants and, most importantly, openly welcome new immigrants to their community. Minnesota, for instance, is home to a legion of Somalians and Ethiopians because of the work done by refugee and resettlements organizations in the heydays of the turmoil and war that engulfed both countries in the 1990s. The state has a global reputation for welcoming new immigrants and has been welcoming African immigrants for many years now. Also, African immigrants tend to settle in places where they already have friends and/or relatives.

EMOTIONAL CONFLICT AND CULTURAL DILEMMAS

Many African immigrants in the United States, as with immigrants from other agrarian society, suffer from emotional conflict and cultural dilemma in many areas of their lives—especially when it comes to interpersonal relationships: romance and marriage. In this instance, special attention is being paid to Nigerians. There is the *Nigerian sensibility* to romance, sex, and marriage in terms of the permissible and the public and private etiquettes that govern such connections. While the formal and informal rules may be unambiguous within Nigeria, it can be problematic in the United States. Therefore, Nigerians who migrate to the United States, for example, may be conflicted by opposing phenomena: to remain in Nigeria and if so, to what extent; or to change, to become Westernized, and if so, to what extent? Many struggles to find the balance between living the *humanistic African culture* and embracing the American culture.

How to maintain a healthy and fruitful relationship in a foreign land—without losing one's culture, core beliefs and identity and still benefit from the dominant and prevailing American way of life—is what most Nigerians continually wrestle with. Within the agrarian Nigerian society, divorce, for instance, is not prevalent. But as transplants, marital disarticulation is one of the issues they must contend with. And of course, there is the ease and informality of marriage within the American society. But for many Nigerians—more so within the older generation—there is nothing casual about marriage. As John Mbiti puts it:

> For African people, marriage is the focus of existence. It is the point where all the members of a given community meet: the departed, the living and those yet to be born. All the dimensions of time meet here, and the whole drama of history is repeated, renewed, and revitalized. Marriage is a drama in which everyone becomes an actor or actress and not just a spectator. Therefore, marriage is a duty, a requirement from the corporate society, and rhythm of life in which everyone must partake. Otherwise, he is not only abnormal but 'underhuman.' Failure to get married under normal circumstances means that the person concerned has rejected society and society rejects him in turn.[4]

Marriage can be unpredictable. We cannot, for instance tell, with any degree of certainty whether a marriage would work out or not. And just because a marriage did not end up in the divorce court, for instance, does not mean that the participants are happily wedded. In many Nigerian enclaves, even when spouses—especially the wives—are being maltreated, they are not likely to abandon their marital homes. Religious, economic, societal and cultural factors make it difficult for most women to leave. But in the United States and in many Western societies, marriages tend to have different meanings and tend to imbibe assorted colorations. Marital unions are not seen as a do-or-die *affair*. And indeed, marriages can be of different composition—with or without the possibility or desirability of offspring. And for that matter, it can be same-sex.

In the second decade of the twenty-first century, even the vaunted *African Culture* is being shaped and reshaped by globalization and modernity. This transformation is not likely to stop, but will instead become widely accepted and widely practiced. Many Nigerians are beginning to hold conversations that center around homosexuality and same-sex marriages—even if such conversations are hushed. But upon arriving in the United States, a growing number accepts such reality. And for that matter, a growing number accept and practice many of the things they would not accept and practice in Nigeria—including but not limited to having babies outside of wedlock, Las Vegas styled drive-through marriages, and elopements. For a growing number of Nigerians, marriage is no longer "the focus of existence" as John Mbiti averred in 1969.

THE AFRICAN MALE...NIGERIAN MEN

The African male is perplexing. He can be enigmatic. He can be everything and sometimes nothing. He can be sweet and loving and caring and benevolent and at the same time oppressive. His life is full of contradictions. In so many ways, he is a wounded animal because of his historical past. He was once the primary breadwinner: the head of the household. That was back in Nigeria. In the United States, the things are different because of the dynamics that governs interpersonal relationship. He may pretend that he is the head of the household, the primary bread winner. But the fact is that within five years or so marriage in the United States, or five years of migrating, he'll come to realize that the United States is a society that promotes freedom and equality. Therefore, if his wife decides and desires, she may *open the books*, making it clear she has the human and civil rights to be and to act in accordance with the legal, social and cultural mores of the society she lives in. This declaration, by some women, shocks the sensibility and the sense of self of most men.

The result has been the breakup of marriages and courtships. Thus, many big cities in the United States are replete with single mothers, or women who are in their second or third marriages; or who are simply single and or are single mothers.

Rare is the Nigerian (in the United States) who will marry a woman with children from a previous relationship or marry a woman who just went through divorce. They'd rather import a wife, or marry an "obedient" woman in the United States. In instances where this is difficult, they marry across race and color and culture. On the other hand, an increasing number of Nigerians no longer think it necessary to marry fellow Nigerians. There are three reasons for this. First, after several years of remittances to Nigeria to support their fiancée—and having to go through the tedious, unpredictable and expensive immigration process and then to have the women unilaterally declare *self-independence* or walk out of the marriage—and in severe cases, call in the government to intercede—can be injurious to the men's ego and sense of self. Consequently, many of the men no longer find marrying a fellow Nigerian appealing.

Secondly, unlike in previous generations, many Nigerian men no longer think it is necessary to marry a fellow Nigerian in order to have a stable, loving and life-long relationship. They have come to accept the fact that others from other color and races can equally provide the attributes and condition they desire in women from Nigeria. And of course, there is growing fascination with the *Other*. This fascination is brought about by the features of globalization, international travel, proximity, familiarity and education. A generation or so ago, it may have been unthinkable for an immigrant from Nigeria to marry a Korean-American, Columbian-American or a Chinese-American; but today, that's no longer the case. Across the board, interracial and multicultural marriages are on the upswing. Furthermore, there is a growing number of Nigerians who have forsaken the idea of ever returning to their homeland. This group of immigrants see themselves, first and foremost, as Americans. As citizens of the United States, therefore, marrying a Nigerian from the continent or in the diaspora, is the least of their worry. They marry whoever loves them back and who is ready to navigate the future with them.

SEX IN THE NIGERIAN ENCLAVE

In Nigeria, there is a contradiction in attitude toward sex and sexuality. For instance, a great many Nigerians are shy when it comes to public discussion about sex. They are not at all bold and open and accepting of public discussions of sex. Yet, the Nigerian music, dance and other art forms exude eroticism and sexuality. In the southern part of the country, for instance, it is not uncommon for a man to stare at a woman's bosoms or buttocks; it is not uncommon to comment about the beauty of a woman's physique; and it is also not uncommon to express sexual intentions. A generation or two ago, many of the women won't even take offense. This attitude is not about a lapse in morality or about moral decadence, or about a perversion of any sort. The southern part of the country is simply more open, more accepting and more gregarious and liberal. It is where globalization and Western more is more pronounced. But in the northern part of the country, the society is mostly conservative and reserved in attitude, pronouncement and behavior when it comes to sex and sexuality. They enjoy and engage in sexual activities as much as the south, but are given to this air of moral superiority and have the tendency to clothe most, if not everything, in religion and its conservative culture. In other words, religion and cultural factors are more pronounced there.

Until recently, sex was primarily for procreation and for the benefit and enjoyment of men. Very few men paid attention to the feelings and satisfaction of women. The women were expected to just *lay there and take it and be grateful*. And they did. But change came and came because of the impact of modernity and globalization: increased level of education; formal and informal sex education; the feminist movements and related activities; pornographic music and movies and mainstream Hollywood productions—all paved the way for the gradual liberalization of the Nigerian society.

Additionally, international travels and exposure to Western concepts and Western practices also helped in this regard. These and other ideas and ideals gradually seeped into the consciousness of the Nigerian women. As women made progress, men began to lose their grip of the social and cultural space. Since the beginning of the twenty-first century, women—especially those between the ages of 18–35—have begun to more and openly display the attitude and characteristics of their Western counterparts—independent, assertive, aggressive and competitive—and can, in most cases, go toe-to-toe with a man. It was not as this this was ever absent in the Nigerian society. No! It merely became more pervasive in the twenty-first century.

For far too long, men were dismissive of their feelings and concerns and their sexual needs. In a society where men thought it was their birthright, a sort of entitlement, to have multiple wives and sexual partners, now find that women excising their rights to as many conquests as possible. It is something else: it can be unsettling and ego-busting to the Nigerian male to know that his wife or girlfriend sometimes desire the use/aid of a vibrator or a dildo. However, the longer they remain in the United States as immigrants, the more accepting of the liberalization of sex and sexuality they will become. The good news is that the younger generation—in Nigeria and in the diaspora—do not, in most cases, have the same sexual anxiety as their parents.

NIGERIAN MEN AND THEIR FOREIGN WIVES

Increasingly, and in greater numbers, Nigerian men seems to be marrying non-Nigerian women. They are marrying, it seems, not for the primarily purpose of acquiring the Alien Registration Card (green card) but for other noble reasons. They marry, not for the curiosity, but because they are bonded and are determined to make a success of the marriage institution; they are bonded by love and faith and a commitment to one another to live their lives as one in a happy matrimony. These cross-cultural marriages have led to transformation in some men. For instance, when married to fellow Nigerians, many of these men are about control and power and they expect their wives to cook and clean and raise babies and provide sex on demand; but with the foreign wives, their attitude changes. They become partners.

WHY DO NIGERIAN MEN GO HOME TO MARRY?

Many Nigerian men living in the western world seem to believe that majority of the spinsters in Nigeria are virginal and cultured. Or at least they are deluded to believe that the women they are importing from Nigeria are different: family-oriented, dutiful and submissive— women who can cook and clean and provide sex on demand. That's the first illusion. The second illusion is this: single Nigerian females living in the United States, Canada, and Europe are spoiled, aggressive, and radical in their worldview. These men forget that just as it is dangerous and foolish to generalize about women in Nigeria, same is true of women living in western society. The fact is that one cannot tell, with any degree of quantifiable certainty, whether a woman based in Nigeria would make a better wife and partner than those based overseas.

Today, a sizable number of Nigerians who return home for a spouse do so at their own peril. Danger and deceit abound as marriages have become business ventures. Poverty, unmet needs and desperation are some of the reasons behind why the clear majority of those who are propositioned (in Nigeria) agree to say, "I do." For some, coming to America is a ticket, an investment that may yield countless returns and benefits for parents and other family members. Rare is the woman or man that would reject, say, an American-based suitor—not minding whether the suitor is financially able, educated, or a product of a good home and of good moral character. Or whether there is an iota of rapport. What matters—what really matters in many of these cases—is the destination: to escape the poverty and fetidities in Nigeria.

Across the Nigerian enclaves in many US cities, these are weekly welcoming-parties by those who went to Africa, marry and successfully petitioned for their wives to come to the United States. These types of parties, whether big or small, have become routine. The immigration process can be lengthy and frustrating—depending on the petitioner's immigration status. In the United States, at least, one could petition for his future wife by way of the Fiancé Visa provision or through outright marriage which could take upward of twenty months. And lots of money, ingenuity and perseverance! But why do African men go through this tortuous and circuitous immigration process? Why do African men go home to marry instead of marrying the women they've wined and dined and romanced right here in the United States? Most of these women are well-educated, well-read and well-traveled; they are well mannered and have proven their reliability. They have demonstrated their abilities and capabilities in all matters marital. They are women of two worlds: they know Africa and also understand the West.

Why do African men go home to marry the "unknowns" instead of marrying the proven and the reliable here in the United States? Well, it is because (1) they can; (2) most men are under the illusion that the women they knew back home are innocent, un-spoiled and virginal; (3) it is an ego-boosting exercise in that it allows them to demonstrate to their people back in Africa that they too can bring one of their own to the United States; (4) it allows some men to mask their "failures and shortcomings" since the women who are already in the United States can tell where they are on the social and economic ladder. Additionally, some men want their women to look up to them since it makes them appear more than what and who they really are (at least in the initial stages). Often, most of these marriages are not based on love or affection. Most are not even like the marriages of yester-years: a contract and a union between two families. On the part of the greenhorns, it is mostly about the need to escape the prevailing abject poverty and hopelessness that engulfed Nigeria. Many of the men involved in this marital enterprise are usually stunned—stunned and disappointed at having to contend with underachieving wives who never knew about 40-60-hour work week; women who never knew there are no currency-minting factories down the street; and not knowing that America is not what they saw in the movies and magazines, which is that America is not a world of instant riches and glamour. Not long after reality sets in, depression and identity crisis may set in. Those who can't cope then leave their husbands and marriage to go it alone believing their lots would be better without the "extra baggage."

Before the marital crisis begins, some men will plead with, cajole or trick their wives into going into the nursing profession—assuming the women were not already one. The nursing profession, they believe, is a sure avenue for making money and living the good life. Be it in Houston, Seattle, Dallas, and Miami, New York or anywhere in between, Nigerian nurses abound. They are everywhere working mostly the night and graveyard shifts, toiling day and night and away from their husbands and children just to make ends meet. With no time to smell the roses or to wonder at the beauties that surround them, they become strangers in the world they live in.

INFLUENCE OF MODERNIZATION AND GLOBALIZATION

The debate about the effects of globalization is not new. What may be new is the extent and pervasiveness of such effects. Almost three decades ago, Delores Mack, in "Husbands and Wives in Lagos: The Effects of Socioeconomic Status on the Pattern of Family Living" wrote:

> The impact of western technology upon the social fabric of traditional life is an issue of considerable concern in Nigeria and other developing countries. Much of this concern focuses upon the effects that industrialization, urbanization, and western education have upon family living, kingship ties, and sex roles. In newspapers, at social gatherings, and in public forums, the question of the changing Nigerian family is debated. Frequently, the discussions centers around preserving traditional family patterns (e.g., the polygamous nature of the African marital system, while at other times, it focuses upon the negatives effects of westernization on Nigerian traditions.[5]

Most women are no longer subservient, at least not in the way and manner we think of subservience several decades ago, when most of the women (in the United States) came from systems and traditions were the men are better educated and are at the helm of political and economic power and therefore, in most cases, are the sole economic provider. Back then, "women are to be seen and not heard."[6] They have no active voice in the running of the family and men dominate in every sphere of life.[7] But once in the United States and able to go to college, work and provide for themselves, most of these women no longer see their husbands as the sole-captain, but only as a co-captain and a co-breadwinner. This realization changes the way they relate to their husbands.

Within ten years of arriving in the United States, most of these "Nigerian wives" will succumb to the weight of a new life and a new culture. With time, these women will come to realize that they are in the land of the free and are no longer subject to the whims and growls of their men. That they need not endure the "injustice" and the subservience their mothers and grandmothers endured in the hands of their fathers and grandfathers. With education comes exposure to the American way; with employment comes economic power or economic independence; with exposure to TV and newspaper comes exposure to other facts of the American life.

Although the US Census Bureau does not provide legal separation and divorce figures for African immigrants; anecdotally, however, the assertion that more Africans are getting divorced seem to hold true. Most of these divorces occur if the husband went home to marry and petition for his wife to join him in the United States. Thus, more and more African men and women are single-handedly raising their children. This trend is common mostly in larger US cities like New York, Chicago, Los Angeles, and Houston where you there are large African population.

Globalization and modernity is having unexpected consequences within the African community in the United States. That is to say that there is a clash of traditional African culture and modernization: a clash between what was, what is and what ought to be. In a traditional African society, reasons for divorce may include (a) lack of love and affection; (b) lack of obedience on the part of the man or refusal by the man to look after the woman; (c) desertion by wife or husband; (d) sterility or infertility.[8] Today, divorce may come about simply because of "incompatible differences." Women who were mostly raised to wait on men for handouts are going out there to earn a living. Women who looked up to men now debate and take men to task. Gradually, men's position and authority is being challenged. Block by block, inch by inch, men's place and role within the home and within the greater society is being called to question. Today's men are not like their father; and today's women are not their mothers. Both sexes live in a world that is vastly different from a world that once was. When an African couple in the United States is faced with marital crisis, they usually have no one to turn to, as they are usually suspicious of Western-style therapy. According to Nwadiora:

> Traditionally, when families in Africa have problems, they seek advice from an elder within the extended family…their minister, priest, or folk healer…it is may therefore be rare for an African family to go voluntarily for therapy, unless under severe circumstances or threat…In other words, for the African psyche, the collective or the group is the ideal. For the African, the clan, the ethnic group is the basis for unity and survival.[9]

Sources of conflict include the need to make ends meet; the loneliness and isolation of life in a foreign country; the need to meet and exceed family expectations back home, which may include monthly or quarterly remittances for parents, in-laws, uncles and aunts; conflict arising from their triple identity in America (as Africans, blacks, and then being perceived as African American by the dominant white population). Although divorce is not a common phenomenon in Africa, it is not rare. In Nigeria for instance, the Native Courts were hearing thousands of divorce cases in the turn of the nineteenth century in Western Nigeria.[10]

RESISTING MODERNITY AND GLOBALIZATION

Globalization is impacting the Nigerian/African culture in ways never seen before; still we have a society, at home and abroad, where religious, anthropological and sociological behaviors are still paramount. It is for this reason that millions of Africans export their religion and culture to Western nations—especially to the United States. Religion seems to be riding on the wings of globalization and so a great many Africans still practice their religion and have, indeed, exported their religion to the United States. Even if discreetly and very small numbers, some still practice levirate and sororate marriage, and they also engage in polygyny, bridewealth, and matrilocal and patrilocal living arrangements. Though informally (and against the law), a sizable number of Nigerians living in the United States still practice polygyny.

For whatever reason, the cultural practices have remained even in the face of globalization. For instance, among the Igbos of South Eastern and the Yoruba of Western Nigeria—whether in the United States or at home—they still adhere to the traditional way of marriage whereby the groom is expected to meet some culture obligations such as paying dowry and providing the content of a "marriage list." In fact, the clear majority of Africans are bent on legitimizing their marriages and offspring and so they see to it that all cultural demands are met.

Bridewealth is an integral part of the African marriage system because the custom heightened (a) the husband's gratitude for a good wife; (b) his appreciation of the wife's dignity and worth; and (c) the wife's assurance of her husband's continued recognition and respect. In addition, bridewealth helps control both the number of women available for marriage and the rate of divorce.[11] Also, despite globalization, Africans do not commit their aged parents to hospices or to nursing home. Parents stay home to be looked after.

CONCLUSION

Globalization is having unexpected consequences within the African community in the United States. That is to say that there is a clash of traditional African culture and modernization: a clash between what was, what is and what ought to be. I have yet to come across an African man who does not complain about "our women are too much into Oprah" or that the "feminists have corrupted" African women or that "the courts have given women too much power" which have resulted in the bastardization of the home and the traditional family system. And indeed, the realization that women in the United States, as in many Western countries, have come into their own, is giving many African men sleepless nights.

Women who were mostly raised to wait on men for handouts are going out there to earn a living. Women who looked up to men now debate and take men to task. Gradually, men's position and authority is being challenged; men's place and role within the home is being called to question. Today's men are not like their father; and today's women are not like their mothers. Both sexes live in a world that is vastly different from a world that once was. The good news is that there are many more African marriages that survive and thrive than those that fail. Some men and their wives have been able to reach an understanding of how things should be, of how to conduct their matrimonial affairs; and of which American and African culture to accept or discard. They have found a balance between traditional culture and modernity. But unfortunately for some, they have not been able to withstand globalization. And so, their relationships have tended to suffer.

NOTES

1. Sylvia Tamale. *African Sexualities: A Reader*. Oxford, UK: Pambazuka Press, 2011.
2. Gwendolyn Mikell. *African Feminism: The Politics of Survival in Sub-Saharan Africa*. Philadelphia: University of Pennsylvania Press, 1997.
3. Oyèrónkẹ Oyěwùmí. *African Gender Studies: Theoretical Questions and Conceptual Issues*. Houndmills, Basingstoke, UK: Palgrave MacMillan, 2005.
4. John S. Mbiti. *African Religions & Philosophy*. New York: Praeger, 1969.
5. Delores E Mack. "Husbands and Wives in Lagos: The Effects of Socioeconomic Status on the Pattern of Family Living." *Journal of Marriage and the Family* 40, no. 4 (1978): 807–16.
6. B. Oloruntimehin. "The Struggle against Inequality: The Situation of Women and Youth." In *The State of Christian Theology in Nigeria*, edited by M. Oduyoye. Ibadan, Nigeria: Daystar Press, 1986.
7. Bartholomew Chipili. "Marriage Without Love." *Asian Journal of Theology* 15, no. 2 (October 2001): 407.
8. Luigi M. Solivetti. "Family, marriage and divorce in a Hausa community: a sociological model." *Africa* 64, no. 2 (1994): 252–71. doi:10.2307/1160983.
9. Emeka Nwadiora. "Therapy with African families." *Western Journal of Black Studies* 20, no. 3 (1996): 117–24.
10. Joseph Adebowale Atanda. "The Iseyin-Okeiho Rising of 1916: An Example of Socio-Political Conflict in Colonial Nigeria." *Journal of the Historical Society of Nigeria* 4, no. 4 (1969): 497–514; Judith Byfield. "Women, Marriage, Divorce and the Emerging Colonial State in Abeokuta (Nigeria) 1892–1904." *Canadian Journal of African Studies / Revue Canadienne des Études Africaines* 30, no. 1 (1996): 32–51; and James Lorand Matory. *Sex and the Empire that Is No More: Gender and the Politics of Metaphor in Oyo Yoruba Religion*. Minneapolis: University of Minnesota Press, 1994.
11. T.S Mwamwenda, and L. A. Monyooe. "Status of Bridewealth in an African Culture." *The Journal of Social Psychology* 137, no. 2 (1997): 269–71.

References

Abu Shouk, Ahmed I., John O. Hunwick, and R. X. O'Fahey. "A Sudanese Missionary to the United States: Satti Majid, 'Shaykh al-Islam in North America,' and his Encounter with Noble Drew Ali, Prophet of the Moorish Science Temple Movement." *Sudanic Africa, a Journal of Historical Sources* 8 (1997): 137–91.

ACBC. "Support for Migration and Border Management in Mauritania." *African Capacity Building Centre (ACBC): International Organization for Migration.* Accessed 15 August, 2016. Acbc.iom.int/where-we-work/featured-iom-projects/37-support-for-migration-and-border-management-in-mauritania.

Achebe, Chinua. *No Longer at Ease*. London: Heinemann, 1960.

"A closer look at African student mobility." A Closer Look at African Student Mobility (International Consultants for Education and Fairs). July 19, 2013. Accessed October 21, 2016. http://monitor.icef.com/2013/07/a-closer-look-at-african-student-mobility/.

Acosta, P. et al. "Do Remittances Lower Poverty Levels in Latin America?" In *Remittances and Development: Lessons from Latin America*, edited by P. Fajnzylber and J. H. López, Washington, DC: World Bank, 2008. p. 87–132.

Acosta, Yesenia D., and G. Patricia De la Cruz, *The Foreign Born from Latin America and the Caribbean: 2010*. US Department of Commerce, Economics and Statistics Administration, US Census Bureau, September 2011.

Adam, Barbara. *Time and Social Theory*. Cambridge: Polity Press, 1990.

Adams, Richard H. International Migration, emittances, and the Brain Drain. A Study of 24 Labor-Exporting Countries. The World Bank Policy Research Working Paper 3069. Retrieved November 18, 2016. http://econ.worldbank.org.

Adeola, Romola, "Preventing Xenophobia in Africa: What Must the African Union Do?" *African Human Mobility Review* 1, no. 3 (2015): 253–272.

Adepoju, Aderanti. *International Migration Within, to and from Africa in a Globalised World*. Accra, Ghana: Sub-Saharan Publishers, 2010.

———. *Migration in Africa: An Overview in the Migration Experience in Africa,* edited by Jonathan Baker and Tade Akin Aina. Sweden, UK. Nordiska Afrikainstitutet, 1995.

———. "Patterns of Migration in West Africa." In *At Home in the World?: International Migration and Development in Contemporary Ghana and West Africa,* edited by Manuh, Takiwaa. Accra: Sub-Saharan Publishers (2005): 32.

———. "South-North Migration: The African Experience," *International Migration*, 29, no. (1991): 205–21.

———. "Trends in International Migration in and from Africa." *International Migration* (2004): 59–76.

Adogame, Afe. "Contesting the ambivalences of modernity in a global context: The redeemed Christian church of god, North America." *Studies in World Christianity* 10, no. 1 (2004): 25–48.

Africa Development Bank [AFDB]. *African Economic Outl9ook: Regional Development and Spatial Inclusion*. Tunisia: AFDB, OECD, UNDP, 2015.

Agha, Asif. *Language and Social Relations*. Cambridge: Cambridge University Press, 2007.

Aghion, Philippe. "Schumpeterian Growth Theory and the Dynamics of Income Inequality." *Econometrica* 70, no. 3 (2002): 855–82.

Akinrinade, Sola, and Ogen Olukoya. "Historicising the Nigerian Diaspora: Nigerian Migrants and Homeland Relations." *Turkish Journal of Politics* 2, no. 2 (December 2011): 71–85.

Alobwed'Epie, Charles. *The Concept of Anglophone Literature*, edited by N. Lyonga, Eckhart Breitinger: Bayreuth University, 1993.

Ambroso, Guido, and Zuefle, Jeanette. "UNHCR Statistical Yearbook 2009. Trends in Displacement Protection and Solutions." The United Nations High Commission for Refugees, October 2010. Accessed October 20, 2016. http://www.unhcr.org/en-us/statistics/country/4ce532ff9/unhcr-statistical-yearbook-2009.html.

American Heritage Publishing Company. *American Heritage Dictionary of the English Language, Fifth Edition*. S.v. "Negrophobia." Retrieved July 18, 2016. http://www.thefreedictionary.com/Negrophobia.

Anand, Sudhir, and Martin Ravallion. "Human Development in Poor Countries: On the Role of Private Incomes and Public Services." *Journal of Economic Perspectives* 7, no. 1 (1993): 133–50.

Anchimbe, Eric Akad. "Anglophonism and Francophonism: The Stakes of (Official) Language Identity in Cameroon." *Alizés: Revue Angliciste de la Réunion* 25/26 (2005): 7–26.

———. Multilingualism, Postcolonialism, and Linguistic Identity: Towards a New Vision of Postcolonial Spaces. In Anchimbe (ed). *Linguistic Identity in Postcolonial Multilingual Spaces*. Newcastle: Cambridge Scholars Publishing, 2007.

Andersson, Ruben. *Illegality, Inc.: Clandestine Migration and the Business of Bordering Europe*. Oakland, CA: University of California Press, 2014.

———. "Time and the Migrant Other: European Border Controls and the Temporal Economics of Illegality." *American Anthropologist* 116, no. 4 (2014): 795–809.

Appadurai, Arjun. *Modernity at Large: Cultural Dimensions of Globalization*. London: Blackwell Publishing, 1996.

———. "The Capacity to Aspire: Culture and the Terms of Recognition." In *Culture and Public Action*, edited by Rao Vijayendra and Michael Walton. Palo Alto, CA: Stanford University Press, 2004.

Aremu, Johnson Olaosebikan and Ajayi, Adeyinka, Theresa, "Expulsion of Nigerian Immigrant Community from Ghana in 1969: Causes and Impact." *Developing Country Studies* 4, no. (2014): 176–186.

Arendt, Hannah. *The Human Condition*. Chicago: University of Chicago Press, 1998.

Arthur, John A. *Invisible Sojourners: African Immigrant Diaspora in the United States*. Westport, CT: Praeger, 2000.

Asamoah, Obed Yao. *The Political History of Ghana (1950–2013): The Experience of a Non Conformist*. Bloomington: AuthorHouse, 2014.

Ashcroft, Bill, Gareth Griffiths, and Helen Tiffin. *The Post-Colonial Studies Reader*. London: Routledge, 1995.

Awasom, Nicodemus Fru. "The Reunification Question in Cameroon History: Was the Bride an Enthusiastic or a Reluctant One?" *Africa Today* 47, no. 2 (2000): 91–119.

Awumbila, Mariama. "Linkages Between Urbanization, Rural–Urban Migration and Poverty Outcomes in Africa." World Migration Report, 2015. December 2014. Accessed October 02, 2016. https://www.iom.int/sites/default/files/our_work/ICP/MPR/WMR-2015-Background-Paper-MAwumbila.pdf.

Azikiwe, Nnamdi. *My Odyssey; An Autobiography*. New York: Praeger, 1970.

Bakewell, Oliver and Bonfiglio, Ayla, "Moving Beyond Conflict: Re-framing Mobility in the African Great Lakes Region." Working Paper for the African Great Lakes Mobility Project, Volume IMI working paper 71. Oxford: International Migration Institutes, University of Oxford, 2013,.4.

Bakewell, Oliver and De Haas, Hein. "African Migrations: Continuities, Discontinuities and Recent Transformations." In L de Haan, U Engel. and P Chabal (Eds.), *African Alternatives,* 2007. Leiden: Brill. pp. 95–118.

Bakewell, Oliver, and Gunvor Jónsson. "Migration, Mobility and the African City Synthesis report on the African Perspectives on Human Mobility Research Programme." August 2011. Accessed September 15, 2016. https://www.imi.ox.ac.uk/completed-projects/aphm/case-studies/aphm-synthesis-report.pdf/@@download.

Bakewell Oliver, Hein de Hass, and Agnieszka Kubal. "Migration Systems, Pioneers, and the Role of Agency." University of Oxford International Migration Institute Working Papers No. 48 (November 2011), 1–26.

Baldwin, John R., Sandra L. Faulkner, Michael L. Hecht, and Sheryl L. Lindsley, eds. *Redefining Culture: Perspectives Across the Disciplines*. Mahwah, NJ: Lawrence Erlbaum Associates, 2006.

Baptiste, David A., Kenneth V. Hardy and Laurie Lewis. "Family Therapy with English Caribbean Immigrant Families in the United States: Issues of Emigration, Immigration, Culture and Race." *Contemporary Family Therapy* 19, no. 3 (1997): 337–59.

Bárcena, Alicia. *Migration in Latin America and the Caribbean at the Service of Development and Human Rights*. Economic Commission for Latin America and the Caribbean (ECLAC), 2016. Retrieved December 6, 2016. http://www.cepal.org/en/articles/2016-migration-latin-america-and-caribbean-service-development-and-human-rights.

Barczewski, Stephanie L. *Myth and National Identity in Nineteenth-Century Britain: The Legends of King Arthur and Robin Hood*. Oxford: Oxford University Press, 2000.

Barker, Chris. *Global Television: An Introduction*. Oxford, UK: Blackwell Publishers, 1997.

Bastian, Michelle. "The Contradictory Simultaneity of Being with Others: Exploring Concepts of Time and Community in the Work of Gloria Anzaldúa." *Feminist Review* 97, no. 1 (2011): 151–67.

———. "Time and Community: A Scoping Study." *Time & Society* 23, no. 2 (2014): 137–66.

Batterbury, Simon. "The Sahel region; Assessing Progress Twenty-Five Years After the Great Drought." *Global Environmental Change* 11, no 1 (2001): 1–95.

Baynham, Simon. "Narco-Traffickinc in Africa: Security, Social and Economic Implications." *African Security Review* 4, no. 6 (1995): 32–38.

Beals, Ralph E., and Carmen F. Menezes. "Migrant Labour and Agricultural Output in Ghana." *Oxford Economic Papers* 22, no. 1 (March 1970): 109–27.

Bekker, Simon, "Violent Xenophobic Episodes in South Africa, 2008 and 2015." *African Human Mobility Review* 1, no. 3 (2015): 229–52.

Bell, Allan, and Peter Garrett. *Approaches to Media Discourse*. Oxford: Blackwell, 1998.

Benedict, Ruth. *Patterns of Culture*. New York: New American Library, 1949.

Benedict, Olumide H. and Wilfred I. Ukpere. "Brain Drain and African Development: Any Possible Gain from the Drain?" *African Journal of Business Management* 6, no. 7 (2011): 2421–28.

Bennett, Ian A. Bethell. "Economy, Migration, Identity: Late Capitalist Reactions against Haitians and the CSME in the Bahamas." *Wadabagei, A Journal of the Caribbean And Its Diasporas* 13, no. 2 (2010): 35–64.

Bennett, Pamela R. and Amy Lutz. "How African American is the Net Black Advantage? Differences in College Attendance Among Immigrant B1acks, Native Blacks and Whites." *Sociology of Education* 82 (2009): 70–100.

Berriane, Mohammed and De Haas, Hein. *African Migrations Research: Innovative Methods and Methodologies*. Trenton: Africa World Press, 2012.

Beukes. Anne-Marie. "The First Ten Years of Democracy: Language Policy in South Africa." Presented at the Xth Linguapax Congress on Linguistic Diversity, Sustainability and Peace: Barcelona, Spain (2004): 20–23.

Bhugra, Dinesh and Becker, Matthew A., "Migration, Cultural Bereavement and Cultural Identity." *World Psychology* 4, no. 1 (2005):18–24.

Bittle, William E., and Gilbert Geis. *The Longest Way Home; Chief Alfred C. Sam's Back-to-Africa Movement*. Detroit: Wayne State University Press, 1964.

Blommaert, Jan. "Polycentricity and Interactional Regimes in 'Global Neighbourhoods.'" *Ethnographer* 5 (2005): 220–35.

Bodvarsson, Orn B. and H. Van den Berg. *The Economics of Immigration: Theory and Policy*. New York: Springer Science Business and Media, 2013.

Bordeau, Jamie. Xenophobia*: The Violence of Fear and Hate*. New York: Rosen Publishing Group (2010): 1–64.

Borjas, George J. "Self-Selection and the Economics of Migration." Accessed 4 August, 2016. http://cream-migration.org/files/G_Borjas_Self-Selection_SOLE_June_10.pdf.

Bourdieu, Pierre. *Outline of a Theory of Practice*. Cambridge, UK: Cambridge University Press, 1972.

Bourdieu, Pierre. *Pascalian Meditations*. Stanford, CA: Stanford University Press, 2000.

Braham, Peter. "How the Media Report Race." In *Culture, Society, and the Media*, edited by Michael Gurevitch, Tony Bennett, James Curran, and Janet Woollacott, 269–86. London: Methuen, 1982.

Breton, R. Isajiw, W.W., Kalbach, W.E., and Reitz, J.G. *Ethnic Identity and Equality*. Toronto: Toronto University Press, 1990.

"Brotherhood of the Cross and Star. Christ Universal Spiritual School of Practical Christianity." Accessed January 11, 2011. http://www.ooo-bcs.org/.

Bryant, Jennings, and Dolf Zillmann. *Media Effects: Advances in Theory and Research*. Hillsdale, NJ: Erlbaum, 1994.

Brzozowski, Jan. "International Migration and Economic Development." *Estudos Avançados* 26, no. 75 (2012): 137–56.

Bureau of the Census, 1990. "Ethnic Profiles for State CPH-L-136: 1993: The Foreign Born Population in the United States 1990." In Rumbaut, Rubén G., Origins and Destinies: Immigration to the United States Since World War II, *Sociological Forum* 9, no. 4 (Dec.,1994): 596.

Burns, Avery, "Feeling the Pinch: Kenya, Al-Shabaab, and East Africa's Refugee Crisis," *Refuge Canada's Journal for Refugees* 27, no. 1 (2010): 5–15.

Cabieses, Baltica, HelenaTunstall, Kate E. Pickett, and Jasmine Gideon. "Changing Patterns of Migration in Latin America: How can Research Develop Intelligence for Public Health?" *Rev Panam Salud Publica* 34, no.1 (2013): 68–74.

Cameron, Deborah. "Identity, Difference and Power: Locating Social Relations in Talk." In *Working with Spoken Discourse*, edited by Deborah Cameron, 161–79. London: Sage, 2001.

Canagarajah, Suresh. "Constructing Hybrid Postcolonial Subjects: Codeswitching in Jaffna Classrooms." In *Voices of Authority: Education and Linguistic Difference*, edited by M. Heller and M. Martin-Jones, 113–212. London: Ablex Publishing, 2001.

Canagarajah, Suresh and Jerskey, Maria. "Meeting the Needs of Advanced Multilingual Writers." In *The Sage Handbook of Writing Development,* edited by Roger Beard, Debra Myhill, Jeni Riley and Martin Nystrand, 472–88. London: Routledge, 2009.

Capps, Randy, Kristen McCabe, and Michael Fix. "Diverse Streams: African Migration to the United States." April 2012. Accessed September 11, 2016. http://www.migrationpolicy.org/research/CBI-african-migration-united-states.

———. *New Streams: Black African Migration to the United States*. Washington, DC: Migration Policy Institute, 2011.

Cardinall, W.A. *The Gold Coas,* (Accra, 1931), cited in T. Antwi-Bosiakoh, "Understanding Migration Motivations in West Africa: The Case of Nigerians in Ghana," *Legon Journal of Sociology* 3, no. 2 (2009): 6.

CARICOM, "The CARICOM Single Market and Economy (CSME)" Secretariat Address: Turkeyen, Greater Georgetown, Guyana, South America, 2001–2016. Retrieved July 11. 2016. http://caricom.org/our-work/the-caricom-single-market-and-economy-csme/.

Carling, Jorgen, "Unauthorized Migration from Africa to Spain." *International Migration* 45, no. 4 (2007): 3–37.

Carney, George O. "Culture: a working definition." In *Fast Food, Stock Cars and Rock-n-Roll: Place and Space in American Pop Culture,* edited by G.O. Carney, 1–14. Lanham, MD: Rowman & Littlefield, 1995.

Castles, Stephen, Hein De Haas and Mark J. Miller. *The Age of Migration: International Population Movements in the Modern World*. Houndmills, Basingstoke, Hampshire: Palgrave Macmillan Higher Education, 2014.

Castles, Stephen, and Mark J. Miller. "The Age of Migration: International Population Movements in the Modern World," in Douglas S. Massey, *Patterns and Processes of International Migration in the 21st Century*, Paper prepared for Conference on

African Migration in Comparative Perspective, Johannesburg, South Africa, 4–7 June, 2003, 7.

Centeno, Miguel A, and Alejandro Portes. "The Informal Economy in the Shadow of the State." CMD Working paper 03-06 February, NJ: Princeton University., 2003.

Centre for Human Rights. 2009. *The Nature of South Africa's Legal Obligations to Combat Xenophobia.* Pretoria: Centre for Human Rights. Retrieved July 8, 2016. https://www.africaportal.org/dspace/articles/nature-south-africas-legal-obligations-combat-xenophobia.

Chatterjee, Partha. *The Politics of the Governed: Reflections on Popular Politics in most of the World.* New York: Columbia University Press, 2004.

ChildStats.gov: Forum on Child and Family Statistics. "FAM4 Children of at least one Foreign Born Parent: Percentage of Children Ages 0-17 by Nativity of Child and Parents, Parent's Education, Poverty Status, and Other Characteristics, Selected Years 1994–2014." Accessed June 15, 2016. http://www.childstats.gov/americaschildren/family4.asp.

Child Trends Data Bank. "Appendix 1—Of Children Younger than 18, Number and Percentage who are Immigrants, and Percentage of Immigrants and Non-Immigrants with Selected Characteristics: Selected Years, 1994–2014." Accessed September 29, 2016. http://www.childtrends.org/wp-content/uploads/2012/07/110_appendix1.pdf.

Chisu, Teresa Ko. "From Whiteness to Diversity: Crossing the Racial Threshold in Bicentennial Argentina." *Ethnic and Racial Studies* 37, no. 14 (2014): 2529–46.

Chrishti, Muzaffar and Stephen Yale-Loehr. The Immigration Act of 1990: Unfinished Business a Quarter-century later. *Policy Briefs*, Washington, DC: MPI (Migration Policy Institute), 2016.

Chuku, Gloria. *Ethnicities, Nationalities, and Cross-cultural Representations in Africa and the Diaspora*. Durham, NC: Carolina Academic Press, 2015.

Clemens, Michael. "Does Development Reduce Migration?" CGD Working Paper 359. Washington, DC: *Center for Global Development.* http://www.cgdev.org/publication/does-development-reduce-migration-working-paper- 359. (Accessed October 16, 2016).

CODESRIA. The Council for the Development of Social Science Research in Africa. www.codesria.org (Accessed Aug 26, 2016).

Coe, Cati. "Child circulation and West African Migration." *Movement, Mobilities and Journeys* 6 (2016): 389–407.

Cohen, Stanley. *Folk Devils and Moral Panics:The Creation of the Mods and Rockers.* London: MacGibbon and Kee Ltd, 1972.

Cohen, Robin, ed. *The Cambridge Survey of World Migration*, New York: Cambridge University Press, 1995.

Collier, P. *Exodus: How Migration is Changing our World.* Oxford: Oxford University Press, 2013.

Comaroff, John L., and Jean Comaroff. *Of Revelation and Revolution, Volume 2: The Dialectics of Modernity on a South African Frontier.* University of Chicago Press, 1997.

Condon, Patrick. "Minnesota Leads Nation in Somali Immigrants, Minneapolis Public Radio." October 31, 2008. http://minnesota.publicradio.org/display/web/2006/02/17/somalipop/.

Corm, Georges. "Labor Migration in the Middle East and North Africa A View from the Region." Accessed October 09, 2016. http://siteresources.worldbank.org/INT-MENA/Resources/SF_background-3.pdf.

Cottle, Simon. *Ethnic Minorities and the Media: Changing Cultural Boundaries*. Buckingham: Open University Press, 2000.

Council on Hemispheric Affairs. "Barbadian First Policy Flogs Guyanese in Barbados," August 5, 2009. Retrieved July 12, 2016. http://www.coha.org /barbadian-first-policy-flogs-guyanese-in-barbados/

Coutin, Susan Bibler. *Nations of Emigrants: Shifting Boundaries of Citizenship in El Salvador and the United States*. Ithaca, NY: Cornell University Press, 2007.

———. *Legalizing Moves: Salvadoran Immigrants' Struggle for U.S. Residency*. Ann Arbor, MI: University of Michigan Press, 2005.

Cross, Catherine, Gelderblom, Derik, Roux, Niel, and Mafukidze, Jonathan. Eds. *Views on Migration in Sub-Sahara Africa. Proceedings of an African Migration Alliance Workshop*. Cape Town: HSRC Press, 2006.

Crush, Jonathan. *Beyond Control: Immigration and Human Rights in a Democratic South Africa*. Cape Town: IDASA—Canada, 1998.

———. *The Border Within: The Future of the Lesotho-South African International Boundary*. Cape Town: Idasa, 2002.

———. Crush, Jonathan, South-North Migration: South Africa's Two Diasporas: Engagement and Disengagement, Southern African Migration Programme (SAMP), 2011.

Czaika, Mathias, and Marc Vothknecht. "Migration and Aspirations—Are Migrants Trapped on a Hedonic Treadmill?" *IZA Journal of Migration* 3, no. 1 (2014): 1.

Davidson, Basil. *The Black Man's Burden: Africa and the Curse of the Nation-State*. New York: Times Books, 1992.

Davis, Darién, J., Latin America: Afro-Descendants, State of the World's Minorities 2006, Accessed July 27, 2016. www.refworld.org/pdfid/4795b32e1f.pdf.

De Haas, Hein. *Irregular Migration from West Africa to the Maghreb and the European Union: An Overview of Recent Trends*. Publication. Geneva: International Organization for Migration, 2011.

Dhillon, Navtej, and Tarik Yousef. *Generation in Waiting: The Unfulfilled Promise of Young People in the Middle East*. Washington, DC: Brookings Institution Press, 2009.

Dijk, Teun A. *Racism and the Press: Critical Studies in Racism and Migration*. London: Routledge, 1991.

Diouf-Kamara, Sylviane. "The Senegalese in New York: A Model Minority?" translated by Richard Philcox, in *Black Renaissance/Renaissance Noir* 2 (Summer-Fall 1997): 95–115.

Djamba, Yanyi K., "African Immigrants in the United States: A Socio-Demographic Profile in Comparison to Native Blacks." *Journal of Asian and African Studies* 34 (1999): 210–15.

Dosumu-Johnson, T. *Reflections of an African Nationalist*. New York: Vantage Press, 1980.

Doyle, Michael and David Straus. *How to Make Meetings Work!: The New Interaction Method*. Chicago: Playboy Press, 1993.

Duffield, Ian. "Duse Mohamed Ali and the Development of Pan-Africanism, 1866-1945." Ph.D. dissertation, Edinburgh University, 1971.

Dung, Elijah. J and Paul Erhunmwunsee. "Pan-Africanism and the African Diaspora: A Geographic Perspective." *In Pan-Africanism In Modern Times: Challenges, Concerns and Constraints,* edited by Olayiola Abegunrin and Sabella O. Abidde, 81–98. Lanham, Boulder, New York, London: Lexington Books, 2016.

Durant, Jorge and Massey, Douglas, S. "New World Orders: Continuities and Changes in Latin American Migration." T*he Annals of the American Academy of Political and Social Science* 630, no. 1 (2010): 20–52.

Dyer, Richard. *The Matter of Images: Essays on Representation*. London: Routledge, 2002.

Ebbe, O. N., "Drug Trafficking, Money Laundering, and Political-Criminal Nexus in Africa," *Paper presented at the Annual Meeting of the American Sociological Association, Atlanta Hilton Hotel, Atlanta, GA Online* (16 August 2003). Accessed October 23, 2008. http://www.allacademic.com/meta/p107613_index.html.

Echu, George. The Language Question in Cameroon. Yaoundé. [Online]; Available, Accessed April 4, 2006. htt://www.linguistik-online.de/18 04/echu.html, (2004).

———. Multilingualism as a Resource: The Lexical Appropriation of Cameroon Indigenous Languages by English and French. Echu. Yaoundé, (2003a): 1–14. Accessed June 28, 2008. http://www.inst.at/trans/13Nr/echu13.htm.

———. "Coping with Multilingualism: Trends in Evolution of Language Policy in Cameroon," 2003b. Accessed September 7, 2007. http:///web.fu- berlin.de/phin/phin25/p25t2.htm.

Eisenbruch, M., "From Post-Traumatic Stress Disorder to Cultural Bereavement: Diagnosis of Southeast Asian Refugees." *Social Science and Medicine* 33 (1991): 673–80.

Ekundare, R. Olufemi. *An Economic History of Nigeria, 1860–1960*. New York: Africana Pub., 1973.

Ellis, Elizabeth. "Multilingualism: The Unmarked Case." *Estudios de Sociolingüística* 7, no. 2 (2006):173–96.

Erdmann, Susan. "A Third Space: Discursive Realizations of Immigrant Identity." *Language and Intercultural Communication* 15, no. 4 (2015): 475–93.

Erhunmwunsee, Paul, Sunita George, David Iyegha and Paul Tribble. *Fundamentals of World Geography,* 2nd ed. Boston, MA: Pearson Publishing, 2009.

Eshun, Ekow. *Black Gold of the Sun: Searching for Home in England and Africa*. London: Hamish Hamilton, 2005.

Esses, Victoria. "Siege Mentality." *New Scientist Magazine*. March 7, 2015.

"EU Relations with Mali." *European Union External Action*. Accessed August 20, 2016. eeas.europa.eu/mali/index_en.htm.

Ewart, Andrea M., "CSME: The CARICOM Single Market and Economy." www.developtradelaw.com2013, 2013. Retrieved July 10, 2016. http://developtradelaw.net/wp-content/uploads/2013/03/CSME.pdf

Falola, Toyin. *The African Diaspora: Slavery, Modernity, and Globalization*. Rochester: University of Rochester Press, 2013.

Falola, Toyin, and Aribidesi Adisa. Usman. *Movements, Borders, and Identities in Africa*. Rochester, NY: University of Rochester Press, 2009.

Fanon, Frantz. *Black Skin, White Masks*. London: Pluto Press, 1986.

Feliciano, Cynthia. "Education and Ethnic Identity Formation Among Children of Latin American and Caribbean Immigrants." *Sociological Perspectives* 52, no. 2 (2009): 135–58.

Ferdjani, Hannane. "African Students in China: An Exploration of Increasing Numbers and Their Motivations in Beijing." *Centre For Chinese Studies,* Stellenbosch, South Africa, 2012.

Feuk, Rut, Perrault, Nadine and Delamónica, Enrique*, Children and International and the Caribbean Migration in Latin America.* ECLAC, United Nations, UNICEF. Challenges, Newsletter on Progress Towards the Millennium Development Goals from a Child Rights Perspective. November 11, 2010.

Findley, Sally E. "Mali: Seeking Opportunity Abroad." *Migration Policy Institute* (1 September, 2004). Accessed 19 August 2016. www.migrationpolicy.org/article/mali-seeking-opportunity-abroad.

Fiona, Mc Laughlin, ed. *Languages of Urban Africa.* London and New York: Continuum International Publishing Group, 2009.

Flahaux, Marie-Laurence, and Hein De Haas. "African Migration: Trends, Patterns, Drivers." *Comparative Migration Studies* 4, no. 1 (January 22, 2016). Retrieved https://link.springer.com/content/pdf/10.1186%2Fs40878-015-0015-6.pdf

Foot, Paul. *The Rise of Enoch Powell: An Examination of Enoch Powell's Attitude to Immigration and Race*. Baltimore: Penguin Books, 1969.

Foucault, Michel. "Governmentality." In t*he Foucault Effect: Studies in Governmentality*, edited by Colin Gordon, Graham Burchell, and Peter Miller, 87–104. Chicago: University of Chicago Press, 1991.

———. The Order of Discourse. Inaugural Lecture at the College de France Given 2 December, 1971. Accessed February 2, 2016. http://ssi.sagepub.com/content/10/2/7.citation.

———. *The Order of Things: An Archaeology of the Human Sciences*. New York: Vintage Books, 1970.

Freddy Kasseri, "Migrants Are Dying out Here." October 09, 2008. Accessed October 11, 2016. http://www.irinnews.org/report/80836/niger-freddy-kasseri-migrants-are-dying-out-here.

Freeman, Lance. "Does Spatial Assimilation Work for Black Immigrants in the US?" *Urban Studies* 39, no. 11 (2002): 1983–2003.

Friedberg, Rachel M and Jennifer Hunt. "The Impact of Immigrants on Host Country Wages, Employment and Growth." *Journal of Economic Perspectives* 9, no. 2 (1995): 23–44.

Frsa, Koko Adomdza, "Understanding Afrophobia, Afrophobism and Institutional Afrophobia." *Afrophobia Challenge* 2010, Retrieved July 18, 2016.http://afrophobia.webs.com/understandingafrophobia.htm.

Frum, David. "Why Britain Left." *The Atlantic* (24 June 2016). Accessed September 26, 2016.http://www.theatlantic.com/international/archive/2016/06/brexit-eu/488597/.

Gambino, Christine P., Edward N. Trevelyan, and John Thomas Fitzwater. *The Foreign Born Population from Africa: 2008–2012*. US Department of Commerce, Economics and Statistics Administration, US Census Bureau, October 2014.

Gemenne, François, Caroline Zickgraf, and Dina Lonesco. "The State of Environmental Migration 2015 A Review of 2014." 2015. Accessed October 29, 2016. https://publications.iom.int/system/files/pdf/state_environmental_migration_2014_0_0.pdf.

Georgiou, Myria. "Consuming Ethnic Media, Constructing Ethnic Identities, Shaping Communities: The Case Study of Greek Cypriots in London." In *Race/Gender/*

Media: Considering Diversity Across Audiences, Content, and Producers. edited by Rebecca Ann Lind, 52–60. Boston: Allyn & Bacon, 2004.

Gibson, Campbell J. and Emily Lennon. "Historical Census Statistics on the Foreign-born Population of the United States: 1850–1990." from US Bureau of the Census, Population Division (February 1999). Accessed October 31, 2008.http://www.census.gov/population/www/documentation/twps0029/twps0029.html

Gibson, John, and David McKenzie. The Economic Consequences of "Brain Drain" of the Best and Brightest: Microeconomic Evidence from Five Countries. *World Bank Policy Research Working Paper* 5394, Washington, DC: World Bank, 2010.

Girvan, Norman. "Caribbean Xenophobia: Where will it End?" *Caribbean Political Economy*, May 26, 2007. (np). Retrieved July 12, 2016.http://www.normangirvan.info/caribbean-xenophobia-where-will-it-end-norman-girvan/.

———. "Reinventing the CSME." Address to The Caribbean Association of Judicial Officers 3rd Biennial Conference, Accra Beach Hotel, Bridgetown, Barbados, September 27, 2013. Retrieved July 12, 2016. http://www.normangirvan.info/.

Giuliano, P., Ruiz-Arranz, M. "Remittances, Financial Development and Growth." *Journal of Development Economics* 90 (2009): 144–52.

Glaser, Daryl, Shireen Hassim, Kupe, and Eric Worby. "(Dis)connections: Elite and Popular 'Common Sense' on the matter of Foreigners." In *Go Home or Die Here: Violence, Xenophobia and the Reinvention of Difference in South Africa*. Johannesburg: Wits University Press, 2008.

Gocking, Roger S. *The History of Ghana*. Westport: Greenwood Publishing Group, 2005.

González, Alvarado Iván and Sánchez, Hilda**.** Trends in the Region—Migration in Latin America and the Caribbean: A View from the ICFTU/ORIT, n.d. Retrieved August 20, 2016. library.fes.de/pdf-files/gurn/00084.pdf. 101–108.

Goodman, Joel. "Moral Panic: HIV and AIDS." July 2007. Accessed July 2007. http://www.joelgoodman.co.uk/files/pdfs/moralpanic.pdf.

Gordon, Paul, and David Rosenberg. *Daily Racism: The Press and Black People in Britain*. London: Runnymede Trust, 1989.

Gould, Douglas. "Writing a Media Analysis." October 2004. Accessed May 2007. http://www.issuelab.org/resources/1337/1337.pdf.

Grant, Richard. *Africa: Geographies of Change*. Oxford, New York: Oxford University Press, 2015.

Greenwood, Michael J. "Internal Migration in Developed Countries." In *Handbook of Population and Family Economics,* edited by Mark Rosenzweig and Oded Stark, 647–720. Amsterdam: Elsevier Publishers, 1997.

Grieco, Elizabeth. *The African Foreign Born in the United States*. Migration Policy Institute—Migration Information Source: US in Focus (September 2004). Accessed November 1, 2008. http://www.migrationinformation.org/Usfocus/display.cfm?ID=250

Grieco, Elizabeth M., Yesenia D. Acosta, G. Patricia de la Cruz, Christine Gambino, Thomas Gryn, Luke J. Larsen, Edward N. Trevelyan, and Nathan P. Walters. *The Foreign-Born Population in the United States: 2010*. US Department of Commerce, Economics and Statistics Administration, US Census Bureau, May 2012.

Griffin, Keith B., and John B. Knight. *Human Development and the International Development Strategy for the 1990s*. Houndmills, Basingstoke, Hampshire: Macmillan in association with the United Nations, 1990.

Griffiths, Melanie. *Frenzied, Decelerating and Suspended: The Temporal Uncertainties of Failed Asylum Seekers and Immigration Detainees*. Oxford: Centre on Migration, Policy and Society (COMPAS), University of Oxford, 2013.

Grigolini, S. "When Houses Provide More Than Shelter. Analyzing the Uses of Remittances within their Sociocultural Context." In *Migration And Economy. Global and Local Dynamics*, edited by L. Trager. Oxford: Altamira Press, 2005.

Grinberg, León, and Rebeca Grinberg. *Psychoanalytic Perspectives on Migration and Exile*. New Haven: Yale University Press, 1989.

Gumperz, John J. *Discourse Strategies*. Cambridge: Cambridge University Press, 1982.

Haas, Hein de. "Migration and Development: A Theoretical Perspective." *International Migration Review* 44, no. 1 (Spring 2010): 227–64.

———. Migration Transitions: A Theoretical and Empirical Inquiry into the Developmental Drivers of International Migration. In: XXVI IUSSP International Population Conference. Marrakech, Morocco. 2 October 2009, 1–49.

———. "Migration and Development: A Theoretical Perspective." *International Migration Institute Working Papers*, University of Oxford, no. 9, 2008, 1–61.

Haas, Marie-Laurence Flahaux and Hein De. 2016. "African Migration: Trends, Patterns, Drivers." *Comparative Migration Studies* 4, no.1 Accessed October 9, 2017. https://comparativemigrationstudies.springeropen.com/track/pdf/10.1186/s40878-015-0015-6?site=comparativemigrationstudies.springeropen.com.

Habeeb, William Mark. *Civil Wars in Africa*. Philadelphia: Mason Crest, 2014.

Haddad, Y. Y. ed. *Muslims in the West: From Sojourners to Citizens*. New York: Oxford University Press, 2002.

Hagan, Jacqueline Maria. *Deciding to be Legal: A Maya Community in Houston*. Philadelphia: Temple University Press, 1994.

Halbwachs, Maurice. *The Collective Memory*. New York: Harper & Row, 1980.

Hall, John R. "The Time of History and the History of Times." *History and Theory* 19, no. 2 (1980): 113–31.

Hall, Stuart. "Encoding and Decoding in the Television Discourse." In *Culture, Media, Language*, edited by Stuart Hall, Dorothy Hobson, Andrew Lowe, and Paul Willis, 128–38. London: Hutchinson, 1980.

———. *Policing the Crisis: Mugging, the State, and Law and Order*. London: Macmillan, 1978.

———."Racist Ideologies and the Media." In *Media Studies a Reader -- 3rd Edition*, edited by Sue T. Thornham, Caroline Bassett, and Paul Marris, 271–82. New York: New York University Press, 2000.

Harris, Nigel. *The New Untouchables: Immigration and the New World Worker*. London: I.B. Tauris, 1995.

Hart, Keith. "Informal Income Opportunities and Urban Employment in Ghana." *The Journal of Modern African Studies* 11, no. 1 (1973): 61–89.

Hayward, Susan. "Blacks in Britain: Racial Discourse in UK Politics and Media." *Jump Cut: A Review of Contemporary Media* 41 (1997, 2006): 49–58.

Hecht, M. L., R. J. Jackson II, and M. J. Pitts. "Culture," In *Intergroup Communication: Multiple Perspectives*, edited by H. Giles and J. Hardwood, 21–42. New York: Peter Lang, 2005.

Heller, Monica. *Bilingualism: A Social Approach*. New York: Palgrave Macmillan, 2007.

Herman, Edward S., and Noam Chomsky. *Manufacturing Consent: The Political Economy of the Mass Media*. New York: Pantheon Books, 1988.

Higgins, Christina. *English as a Local Language: Post-Colonial Identities and Multilingual Practices*. Bristol, UK: Multilingual Matters, 2009.

Higuchi, Naoto, Brazilian Migration to Japan: Trends, Modalities and Impact. Expert Group Meeting on International Migration and Development in Latin America and the Caribbean Population Division Department of Economic and Social Affairs. United Nations Secretariat Mexico City, 30 November—2 December 2005, 2006.

Hill, Brandon. "Negrophobia: Michael Brown, Eric Garner, and America's Fear of Black People." *TIME*, August 29, 2014. Accessed July 18, 2016. http://time.com/3207307/negrophobia-michael-brown-eric-garner-and-americas-fear-of-black-people/.

Hoffman, Alecia Dionne. "The Influence of China's Foreign Aid Policies on the Political Economy of Nigeria, 1979-2010." PhD diss. Clark Atlanta University, 2015.

Hooper, James. "A Destination Too Far? Modeling Destination Accessibility and Distance Decay in Tourism." *GeoJournal* 80, no. 1 (2015): 33–46.

Hornbeck, J.F., "CARICOM: Challenges and Opportunities for Caribbean Economic Integration," CRS Report for Congress, Congressional Research Service, January 7, 2008. pp. 1–23. Retrieved July 10, 2016. http://www.sice.oas.org/TPD/CAR_EU/Studies/CRSCARICOM_Challenges_e.pdf.

Horowitz, Donald. L. *The Deadly Ethnic Riot*, Berkeley, CA. California University Press, 2001.

Hseih, H.F. and Sarah, E. Shannon. "Three Approaches to Qualitative Content Analysis." *Qualitative Health Research* 15, no. 9 (2005): 277–1288.

Huddleston, Thomas, Jan Niesson, Eadaoin Ni Chaoimh, and Emile White. *Migration Integration Policy Index III*. Brussels, Belgium: British Council and Migration Policy Group, 2011. Accessed 20 August, 2016. http://www.mipex.eu/sites/default/files/downloads/migrant_integration_policy_index_mipexiii_2011.pdf.

"Humiliated Abroad, Rejected at Home: Pathetic, Painful World of Nigeria's Deportees—Punch Newspapers." *Punch Newspapers*. April 30, 2016. Accessed August 16, 2016. http://punchng.com/humiliated-abroad-rejected-home-pathetic-painful-world-nigerias-deportees/.

Hunter, Nina, and Caroline Skinner. "Foreign Street Traders Working in Inner City Durban: Local Government Policy Challenges." *Urban Forum* 14, no. 4 (2003): 301–19.

"Immigration in Mauritania." *International Organization for Migration*. Accessed 15 August, 2016. http://www/iomdakar.org/profiles/print/21.

International Federation of Red Cross and Red Crescent Societies. "Drought in the Horn of Africa: Preventing the Next Disaster." 2011. Accessed September 7, 2016. http://www.ifrc.org/PageFiles/90410/1203800-Drought%20in%20the%20Horn%20of%20Africa-Preventing%20the%20next%20disaster-EN-LR.pdf.

International Labor Organization, "*International Migration, Racism, Discrimination and Xenophobia*." International Organization for Migration and Office of the United Nations High Commissioner for Human Rights, 2001.

International Monetary Fund. "Regional Economic Outlook: Sub-Saharan Africa." *World Economic and Financial Surveys*, Washington, DC: IMF, 2008.

International Organization for Migration and The UN Migration Agency. "Dignified, Orderly and Safe Migration for The Benefit of All." IOMSNAPSHOT. September 2016. Accessed October 2016. https://www.iom.int/sites/default/files/about-iom/iom_snapshot_a5_en.pdf.

International Organization for Migration (IOM). "Mapping of Nigerian Health and Education Professionals in the United States of America. Accessed September 19, 2016. https://publications.iom.int/system/files/pdf/mapping_of_nigerians_in_the_us.pdf.

"IOM-Japan Project Implemented in Mauritania and Mali." *IOM Quarterly Newsletter: IOM Mauritania*. No. 1 (June 16, 2015). Accessed 15 August 2016. acbc.iom.int/news/iom-japan-project-implemented-mauritania-and-mali.

"IOM Mauritania." *International Organization for Migration*. Accessed 15 August 2016. http://www.iom.int/sites/default/files/country/docs/mauritania/IOM-Mauritania_Newsletter-June-August-2015-EN.pdf.

"IOM Niger Assists 30th Convoy of Repatriated Migrants from Algeria." *International Organization for Migration* (18 March, 2016). Accessed 20 August, 2016. www.iom.int/news/iom-niger-assists-30th-convoy-repatriated-migrants-algeria.

John, Cindi. "The Legacy of the Brixton Riots." *BBC News*. April 05, 2006. Accessed January 20, 2007. http://news.bbc.co.uk/2/hi/uk_news/4854556.stm.

Johnson, John M. "In-Depth Interviewing." In *Handbook of Interview Research, Context and Method*, edited by Jaber F. Gubrium and James A. Holstein. London: Sage Publications, 2002.

Jones, Adele, Jacqueline Sharpe, and Michele Sogren. "Children's Experiences of Separation from Parents as a Consequence of Migration." *Caribbean Journal of Social Work* 3 (2004): 89–109.

Kabbani, Rana. *Imperial Fictions: Europe's Myths of Orient*. London: Pandora, 1994.

Kamwangamalu, M. Nkonko. "Ethnicity and Language Crossing in Post-Apartheid South Africa." *International Journal of Social Language*, 152, (2001): 86–95.

Kao, Grace. "Parental Influences on the Educational Outcomes of Immigrant Youth." *The International Migration Review* 38, no. 2 (2004): 427–49.

Kay, Diana, "The Resettlement of Displaced Persons in Europe, 1946-1951." In *The Cambridge Survey of World Migration*, edited by Robin Cohen, 154–58. Cambridge: Cambridge University Press, 1995.

Kent, Mary M. "Immigration and America's Black Population." *Population Bulletin* 62, no. 4 (2007): 2–16.

Kersting, Norbert, "New Nationalism and Xenophobia in Africa—a New Inclination?" *Africa Spectrum* 1 (2009): 7–18.

Khosravi, Shahram. *'Illegal' Traveler: An Auto-Ethnography of Borders*. Basingstoke: Palgrave Macmillan, 2010.

Kigotho, Wachira. "A Profile of Sub-Saharan African Students in America ..." September 18, 2015. Accessed September 19, 2016. http://www.universityworldnews.com/article.php?story=20150917132859939.

Kihato, Caroline Wanjiku. "The City from its Margins: Rethinking Urban Governance through the Everyday Lives of Migrant Women in Johannesburg." *Social Dynamics* 37, no. 3 (2011): 349–62.

King, Kenneth. "James E.K. Aggrey: Collaborator, Nationalist, Pan African." *Canadian Journal of African Studies* 3, no. 3 (Fall 1970): 511–30.

Klein, Naomi. *The Shock Doctrine: The Rise of Disaster Capitalism*. New York: Metropolitan Books/Henry Holt, 2007.

Klotz, Audie. *Migration and National Identity in South Africa, 1860–2010*. New York: Cambridge University Press, 2013.

Kluckhohn, C., and W. H. Kelly. "The Concept of Culture." In *The Science of Man in the World Crisis*, edited by Ralph Linton, 78–106. New York: Columbia University Press, 1945.

Kluckhohn, Clyde. *Mirror for Man: The Relation of the Anthropology to Modern Life*. New York: Whittlesey House, 1949.

Knight, Alan, "Populism and Neo-Populism in Latin America, Especially Mexico," *Journal of Latin American Studies* 30, no. 2 (1998): 223–48.

Kohnert, Dirk. "African Migration to Europe: Obscured Responsibilities and Common Misconceptions." May 2007. https://www.giga-hamburg.de/en/system/files/publications/wp49_kohnert.pdf.

Kroeber, Alfred L., and Clyde Kluckhohn. *Culture A Critical Review of Concepts and Definitions*. New York: Vintage Books, 1952.

Kayira, Legson. *I Will Try*. New York: Doubleday, 1965.

Labonté, Ronald, David Sanders, Thubelihle Mathole, Jonathan Crush, Abel Chikanda, Yoswa Dambisya, Vivien Runnels, Corinne Packer, Adrian Mackenzie, Gail Tomblin Murphy, and Ivy Lynn Bourgeault. "Health Worker Migration from South Africa: Causes, Consequences and Policy Responses." *Human Resources for Health* 13, no. 92 (2015). https://human-resources-health.biomedcentral.com/track/pdf/10.1186/s12960-015-0093-4?site=human-resources-health.biomedcentral.com.

Landale, Nancy S., Kevin JA Thomas, and Jennifer Van Hook. "The Living Arrangements of Children of Immigrants." *The Future of Children/Center for the Future of Children, the David and Lucile Packard Foundation* 21, no. 1 (2011): 43–70.

Landau, Loren B. *Exorcising the Demon Within: Xenophobia, Violence and Statecraft in Contemporary South Africa*. Johannesburg: Wits University Press, 2011.

———. "Immigration and the State of Exception: Security and Sovereignty in East and Southern Africa," *Millennium: Journal of International Studies* 34, no. 2 (2005): 325–48.

———. "On the Politics of Exclusion and their Transcendence (a commentary)." *African Historical Review* 44, no. 1 (2012): 109–11.

Langley, J. Ayodele. *Panafricanism and Nationalism in West Africa, 1900–45*, Oxford: Clarenden Press, 1973.

Lashley, Myrna. "The Unrecognized Social Stressors of Migration and Reunification in Caribbean Families." *Transcultural Psychiatry* 37, no. 2 (2000): 203–17.

Lee, June H.H. and Guadagno, Lorenzo. "World Migration Report: Migrants and Cities: New Partnerships to Manage Mobility." International Organization for

Migration (IOM). Last modified October 9, 2017. http://publications.iom.int/system/files/wmr2015_en.pdf.

Lee, Woojin, Roemer, John, and Van der Straeten, Karine. "Racism, Xenophobia, and Redistribution." *Journal of the European Economic Association* 4, no. 2/3 (2006). Papers and Proceedings of the Twentieth Annual Congress of the European Economic Association, 2006. (Apr-May, 2006), 446–54.

Lessault, David and Marie-Laurence Flahaux. "Regards Statistiques sur L'histoire de L'émigration Internationale au Sénégal [Statistical Views on the History of International Migration from Senegal]." *Revue Européenne des Migrations Internationales* 29, no.4 (2013): 59–88.

Lewis, Gail, and Lola Young. *Windrush Echoes: Issue 10.* London: Lawrence & Wishart Ltd, 1998.

Leun, Joanne Van der. *Looking For Loopholes: Processes of Incorporation of Illegal Immigrants in the Netherlands.* Amsterdam: Amsterdam University Press, 2003.

Lewin-Epstein, Noah and Levanon, Asaf, "National Identity and Xenophobia in an Ethnically Divided Society," in Koenig, Matthias. Editor, *"National Identity and Attitudes Towards Migrants- Findings from the ISSP", International Journal on Multicultural Societies* 7, no. 2, (2005): pp. 90–118. UNESCO.

Livingstone, Livingstone, James Curran, and Michael G. Gurevitch. "Audience Reception." In *Mass Media and Society*. London: Rutledge, 1996.

Logan, John R and Glenn Deane. "Black Diversity in Metropolitan America." *Lewis Mumford Center for Comparative Urban and Regional Research.* Univ. of Albany 2003: 1–13.

Lohrmann, R. "Irregular Migration: A Rising Issue in Developing Countries." *International Migration* 25, no. 3 (1987): 253–66.

Lollock, L. (2001), *The Foreign-Born Population in the United States. Population Characteristics*, U.S. Census Bureau (www.census.gov), 2001.

Loomba, Ania. *Colonialismo/postcolonialismo*. Roma: Meltemi, 2000.

Lund, F. J. *Women Street Traders in Urban South Africa: A Synthesis of Selected Research Findings.* Durban: School of Development Studies, University of Natal, 1998.

Lund, F. J., Jillian Nicholson, and Caroline Skinner. *Street Trading*. Durban: University of Natal, School of Development Studies, 2000.

Lyons, Michal, and Simon Snoxell. "Sustainable Urban Livelihoods and Marketplace Social Capital: Crisis and Strategy in Petty Trade." *Urban Studies* 42, no. 8 (2005): 1301–20.

Mabogunje, Akin L. "Systems Approach to a Theory of Rural-Urban Migration." *Geographical Analysis* 2, no. 1 (January 1970): 1–18.

Macaulay, Ronald. Is Sociolinguistics Lacking in Style? *Cuadernos de Filologia Inglesa R* (1999): 9–33.

Macionis, John, J., *"Society: the Basics"*, 14th ed. USA. Pearson Education Inc. 2016.

Maharaj, Brij, and Vadi Moodley. "New African Immigration to the Durban Region." *Canadian Journal of African Studies* 34, no. 1 (2000): 149–60.

Mai, M. Magdaline. *An Analysis of the Effects of Space and Territoriality on Language Use: A Sociolinguistic Analysis of a Multilingual Population in the Diaspora.* Mannheim: LAP LAMBERT Publishing. 2012.

———. Negotiation of Identities and Language Practices Among Cameroonian Immigrants in Cape Town. Unpublished PhD thesis, University of the Western Cape, Cape Town, 2011.

Mann, Michael. "The Autonomous Power of the State: Its Origins, Mechanisms and Results." *European Journal of Sociology / Archives Européennes de Sociologie* / Europäisches *Archiv für Soziologie* 25, no. 02 (1984): 185–213.

Mariano Jr., Bernardo. "African Migration Trends: Key Facts and Figures." African-European Parliamentary Dialogue on Migration and Development. October 03, 2014. Accessed October 10, 2016. http://a-dtap.awepa.org/wp-content/uploads/2014/10/2-Oct-2014-Migration-trends-in-Africa-for-AWEPA-conference.pdf.

Martínez, Pizarro, Jorge. International Migration in Latin América and the Caribbean: A Summary View of Trends and Patterns. Santiago, Chile: Economic Commission for Latin America and Center for Latin American Research in Demography; 2005.

Martínez Pizarro, Jorge—Cano Christiny, María Verónica—Soffia Contrucci, Magdalena. Trends and Patterns of Latin American and Caribbean Migration to 2010 and Challenges for a Regional Agenda. United Nations Economic Commission for Latin America and the Caribbean. (2014) Retrieved December 6, 2016. http://www.cepal.org/es/publicaciones/37218-tendencias-patrones-la-migracion-latinoamericana-caribena-2010-desafios-agenda

Massey, Douglas S., "Patterns and Processes of International Migration in the 21st Century." Conference on African Migration in Comparative Perspective, Johannesburg, South Africa, 4–7 June, 2003, 1–41.

Massey, Douglass S., Joaquin Arango, Graeme Hugo et.al. "Theories of International Migration: A Review and Appraisal." *Population and Development Review.* 19, no. 3 (September 1993): 431–66.

May, Tim. "Social Research: Issues, Methods and Process." 1997. http://www.mheducation.co.uk/openup/chapters/0335206123.pdf.

Mberu, Blessing U., and Roland Pongou. "Nigeria: Multiple Forms of Mobility in Africa's Demographic Giant." April 16, 2014. Accessed September 16, 2017. http://www.migrationpolicy.org/article/nigeria-multiple-forms-mobility-africas-demographic-giant.

McCabe, Kristen, "African Immigrants in the United States." Migration Policy Institute, July 21, 2011. Retrieved http://www.migrationpolicy.org/article/african-immigrants-united-states.

Meeteren, Masja Van. *Irregular Migrants in Belgium and the Netherlands: Aspirations and Incorporation.* Amsterdam: Amsterdam University Press, 2014.

"Migration Facts Algeria." *Robert Schuman Center for Advanced Studies: Migration Policy Centre* (April 2013). Accessed 20 August, 2016. Migrationpolicycentre.eu/docs/facts_sheet/Factsheet%20Algeria.pdf.

"Migration Patterns, Trends and Policy Issues in Africa." December 2010. Accessed October 17, 2017. https://www.afdb.org/fileadmin/uploads/afdb/Documents/Procurement/Project-related-Procurement/WORKING%20119%20word%20document%20AA.PDF.

Migration Policy Institute. "Frequently Requested Statistics on Immigrants and Immigration in the United States." Accessed September 29, 2016. http://www.

migrationpolicy.org/article/frequently-requested-statistics-immigrants-and-immigration-united-states#Children with Immigrant Parents.

"Migration Processes, Familial Characteristics, and Schooling Dropout among Black Youths." *Demography* 49, no. 2 (2012), 477–98.

Mikell, Gwendolyn. *African Feminism: The Politics of Survival in Sub-Saharan Africa*. Philadelphia: University of Pennsylvania Press, 1997.

Mitchell, Natasha, and Julia Bryan. "School-Family-Community Partnerships: Strategies For School Counselors Working with Caribbean Immigrant Families." *Professional School Counseling* 10, no. 4 (2007): 399–409.

Mörner, Magnus, and Harold Sims. *Adventurers and Proletarians, The Story of Migrants in Latin America*. Pittsburgh, PA: University of Pittsburgh Press, 1985.

Moya, Josè C. "Immigration in Latin America," Accessed August 18, 2016.

———. "Migration." In *Encyclopedia of Latin American History and Culture*. 2nd ed., edited by Jay Kinsbruner. New York: Charles Scribner's Son, 2008.

MPC Team. "MPC Migration Profile." *MPC Migration Policy Centre*. Accessed 15 August 2016. www.migrationpolicycentre.eu/docs/migration_profiles/Mauritania.pdf.

Muruthi, Bertranna, J. Maria Bermúdez, Kevin R. Bush, Megan McCoy, and Morgan A. Stinson. "Afro-Caribbean Mothers in the US: An Exploratory Study from a Transnational Feminist Perspective." *Women & Therapy* 39, nos. 3–4 (2016): 413–31.

Myers, N. "Environmental Refugees: An Emergent Security Issue." *Organization for Security and Cooperation in Europe* (2005). Accessed September 28, 2016. http://www.osce.org/eea/14851.

Navara, Geoffrey S. "How Adolescent Children of African Jamaican Immigrants Living in Canada Perceive and Negotiate Their Roles Within a Matrifocal Family." *Family Process* 48, no. 3 (2009): 441–58.

Navjot, Lamba K., Marie Mulder and Lori Wilkinson. *Immigrants and Ethnic Minorities on the Praries: A Statistical Compedium*. Edmonton, AB: Prairie Centre of Excellence for Research on Immigration and Integration, 2000.

Ndi, Emmanuel Yenshu Vubo and Humphrey Ngala. "Cross-border Migrations, Regional International and Conviviality in the Gulf of Guinea: Reality and Prospects" In *Environment, Agriculture and Cross-border Migration,* edited by Emmanuel Yenshu Vubo. Dakar: CODESRIA, 2015.

Neal, Ronald V. "Merchants of Death Target Africa," *Africa Recovery* 12, no. 1 (August 1998): p. 7.

Neal, Sarah. "The Scarman Report, the Macpherson Report and the Media: How Newspapers Respond to Race-centered Social Policy Interventions." *Journal of Social Policy* 32, no. 1 (2003): 55–74. doi:10.1017/s004727940200689x.

Neamtu, Ioana Daniela, *The Impact of International Migration on Source Countries A Cross Country Analysis*, Master thesis, Retrieved December 6, 2016 www.dagliano.unimi.it/media/Cattaneo_Cristina.pdf.

Neocosmos, Michael. From "'Foreign Natives' to 'Native Foreigners' Explaining Xenophobia in Post-Apartheid South Africa, Citizenship and Nationalism, Identity and Politics." Dakar, CODESRIA, 2010.

———. "Re-thinking Politics in Today: Elements of a critique of political liberalism in Southern Africa." Durban, South Africa: Center for Civil Society, 2005.

Ngefac, Aloysius. "Linguistic Choices in Postcolonial Multilingual Cameroon University of Yaounde I." *Nordic Journal of African* Studies 19 no. 3 (2010): 149–64.

"Nigeria: The Madness of Foreign Education." Nigeria: The Madness of Foreign Education. February 12, 2016. Accessed October 14, 2016. http://allafrica.com/stories/201602151753.html.

Nyamnjoh,Francis B. *Insiders and Outsiders: Citizenship and Xenophobia in Contemporary Southern Africa.* London: Zed Books, 2006.

———. "Racism, Ethnicity and the Media in Africa: Reflections Inspired by Studies of Xenophobia in Cameroon and South Africa." *Africa Spectrum* 1 (2010): 57–93.

Nkrumah, K. *Ghana: The Autobiography of Kwame Nkrumah.* New York: International Publishers, 1957.

Nkulu, Kiluba L. *Serving the Common Good: A Postcolonial African Perspective on Higher Education.* New York: P. Lang, 2005.

Norwegian Refugee Council. "Displacements Due to Natural Hazard-Induced Disasters." *Internal Displacement Monitoring Center* (iDMC), Global Estimates for 2009 and 2010. Geneva: NRC (Norwegian Refugee Council), 2011.

Nussbaum, Martha Craven, and Amartya Sen. *The Quality of Life.* Oxford: Clarendon Press, 1993.

Nyang, Sulayman S. "Growth of Islam in America," *The Saudi Gazette,* October 19, 1983.

———. "The African Immigrant Family in the United States of America: Challenges and Opportunities." *Ìrìnkèrindò: A Journal Of African Migration* no. 5 (December 2011): 150. Accessed October 9, 2017. http://www.cippusa.com/the-african-immigrant-family-in-the-united-states-of-america-challenges-and-opportunities/.

O'Connor, Catherine and Sarah, Michaels. "When is Dialogue Dialogic?" *Human Development* 50 (2007): 275–285.

Okeke, Godwin S. M. "The Uprooted Emigrant: The Impact of Brain Drain, Brain Gain, and Brain Circulation on Africa's Development." In *Trans-Atlantic Migration: The Paradoxes of Exile,* edited by Toyin Falola and Niyi Afolabi, 119–40. New York: Routledge, 2008.

Okome, Mojubaolu. O. "Spinning an African Academy into the World Wide Web: the Liberatory and Democratic Potential of African Scholarship in Cyberspace." CODESRIA-ASC Conference Series 2006: *The Bridging the North-South Divide in Scholarly Communication on Africa: Threats and Opportunities in the Digital Era.* University of Leiden, the Netherlands, 6–8 September 2006. Accessed October 10, 2008. http://www.ascleiden.nl/Pdf/elecpublconfokome.pdf.

Olukoshi, Adebayo. "The Impact of IMF-World Bank Program in Nigeria." In *The IMF, the World Bank and the African Debt: The Economic Impact*, edited by Bade Onimode. London: Zed Books, 1989.

Omoniyi, Tope. "Hierarchy of Identities." In *Sociolinguistics of Identity. Australian Review of Applied Linguistics,* edited by T. Omoniyi and G. White, 32, no. 1 (2006): 195–208.

Onuoha, Freedom. "Boko Haram and the Evolving Salafi Jihadist Threat in Nigeria." In *Boko Haram: Islamism, Politics, Security and the State in Nigeria*, by Marc-Antoine Pérouse de Montclos, 158–191. Boston: Leiden: African Studies Centre, 2014.

Organization of American States (OAS), "Third Report of the Continuous Reporting System on International Migration in the Americas (SICREMI) 2015," Department of Social Inclusion. Migration and Development Program (MIDE). Continuous Reporting System on International Migration in the Americas (SICREMI). IV. Series. Retrieved August 22, 2016, https://www.google.com/url?url=https://www.oas.org/docs/publications/SICREMI-2015-.

O'Rourke, Kevin H.O and Sinnott, Richard, "The Determinants of Individual Attitudes towards Immigration," *European Journal of Political Economy* 22 (2006): 838–61.

Orozco, Manuel. "Globalization and Migration: The Impact of Family Remittances in Latin America." *Latin American Politics and Society* 44, no. 2 (2012): 41–66.

Oyěwùmí, Oyèrónkẹ́. *African Gender Studies: Theoretical Questions and Conceptual Issues*. Houndmills, Basingstoke, England: Palgrave MacMillan, 2005.

Parekh, Bhikhu. "Integrating Minorities." London: Institute of Contemporary Arts, 2001.

Parsons, Talcott, Edward Shils, Kaspar D. Naegele, and Jesse R. Pitts, eds. *Theories of Society: Foundations of Modern Sociological Theory*. New York: The Free Press of Glencoe, Inc., (1962): 963–93.

Paulino, Edward. "Anti-Haitianism, Historical Memory, and the Potential for Genocidal Violence in the Dominican Republic," *Genocide Studies and Prevention: An International Journal* 1, no. 3 (2006): 264–288. Article 5. Available at: http://scholarcommons.usf.edu/gsp/vol1/iss3/5

Pavlenko, Aneta and Blackledge, Adrian, eds. *Negotiation of Identities in Multilingual Contexts*. Toronto: Multilingual Matters, 2004.

Peberdy, Sally. *Selecting Immigrants: National Identity and South Africa's Immigration Policies, 1910–2008*. Johannesburg: Wits University Press, 2009.

Pedraza, Lisdey Espinoza. "Brain Drain. Social and Political Effects in Latin American Countries." *Revista Grafía* 10, no. 2 (2013): 29–48.

Peil, Margaret. "Ghanaian Migrants Abroad." *African Affairs* 94 (1995): 345–67.

Pennycook, Alastair. *Language as a Local Practice*. New York: Routledge 2010.

Peth, Simon A. What is Translocality? A Refined Understanding of Place and Space in a Globalized World. 2014. Accessed November 9, 2015. http://transre.org/en/blog/what-trans locality/.

Pew Research Center. "The Global Divide on Homosexuality: Greater Acceptance in More Secular and Affluent Countries." (4 June 2013). Accessed August 6, 2016. http://www.pewglobal.org/2013/06/04/the-global-divide-on-homosexuality/.

Pizarro, Jorge Martínez and Miguel, Villa. "International Migration in Latin America and the Caribbean: A Summary View of Trends and Patterns," United Nations Expert Group Meeting on International Migration and Development, Population Division Department of Economic and Social Affairs United Nations Secretariat. New York, 6–8 July 2005, 1-20.

Pottinger, Audrey M. "Children's Experience of Loss by Parental Migration in Inner City Jamaica." *American Journal of Orthopsychiatry* 75, no. 4 (2005): 485–96.

Pottinger, Audrey M. "Report on Pilot Project on Loss and Violence in Students from Inner City Communities and a School-Based Intervention Programme." Paper presented at a Meeting of the Ministry of Education, Kingston, Jamaica, July 2003.

Pottinger, Audrey M., Angela Gordon Stair, and Sharon Williams Brown. "A Counselling Framework for Caribbean Children and Families who Have Experienced Migratory Separation and Reunion." *International Journal for the Advancement of Counselling* 30, no. 1 (2008): 15–24.

Price, Janet, and Margrit Shildrick. *Feminist Theory and the Body: A Reader*. New York: Routledge, 1999.

Ranis, Gustav. "Arthur Lewis' Contribution to Development Thinking and Policy." *Yale University Economic Growth Center Discussion Paper n. 891* (August 2004). Accessed 5 August, 2016. http://ssrn.com/abstract=583302.

Ranis, Gustav and John H.C. Fei. "A Theory of Economic Development." *The American Economic Review* 51, no. 4 (September 1961): 533–65. JSTOR 1812785.

Rashad, A. *Islam, Black Nationalism & Slavery. A Detailed History*. Beltsville, MD: Writer's Inc., 1995.

Rath, Jan. *Immigrant Businesses: The Economic, Political, and Social Environment*. New York: Palgrave Macmillan, 2000.

Ratha, Dilip and Shaw, William. "Causes of South-South Migration and Its Socioeconomic Effects." *Migration Information Source*, October 27, 2007. http://www.migrationpolicy.org/article/causes-south-south-migration-and-its-socioeconomic-effects.

Ratha, Dilip, et al. *Migration and Remittances Recent Developments and Outlook*. Migration and Development Brief 26, Global Knowledge Partnership on Migration and Development, (KNOMAD), April 2016.

Ravenstein, E. G. "The laws of Migration." *Journal of the Royal Statistical Society* 52, no. 2 (June 1889): 241–305.

Reddy, Thiven. "The 'Cabbage and the Goat': Xenophobic Violence in South Africa." *African Historical Review* 44, no. 1 (2012): 3–28.

Reitzes, Maxine. "Immigration and Human Rights in South Africa." In *Beyond Control: Immigration and Human Rights in a Democratic South Africa*, edited by Jonathan Crush, 37–54. Cape Town: Queens University Press, 1998.

Ricca, Sergio. *International Migration in Africa Legal and Administrative Aspects*. International Labour Office, Geneva, Switzerland, 1989.

Rice, Andrew. "Mission from Africa," *The New York Times*, April 8, 2009. Accessed January 17, 2011.http://www.nytimes.com/2009/04/12/magazine/12churcheshttp://www.nytimes.com/2009/04/12/magazine/12churches-t.html?pagewanted=allt.html?pagewanted=all.

Richards, Naomi, and Rebecca Rotter. "Desperately Seeking Certainty? The Case of Asylum Applicants and People Planning an Assisted Suicide in Switzerland." *Sociological Research Online* 18, no. 4 (2013). 1–16. doi:10.5153/sro.3234.

Rizzo, J. "A Shrinking Lake and A Rising Insurgency Migratory Responses to Environmental Degradation and Violence in The Lake Chad Basin." In *The State of Environmental Migration 2015*, edited by François Gemenne, Caroline Zickgraf, and Dina Lonesco. Geneva, Switzerland: International Organization For Migration, 2015.

Roberts, Bryan, ed. "Socially Expected Durations and the Economic Adjustment of Immigrants." In *The Economic Sociology of Immigration: Essays on Networks, Ethnicity and entrepreneurship*, edited by Alejandro Portes, 42–86. New York: Russel Sage Foundation, 1995.

Robinson, Vaughan. *Transients, Settlers, and Refugees: Asians in Britain*. Oxford: Clarendon Press, 1986.

Robinson, Bashir. A. and J. Gregory Robinson. "Estimates of Emigration of the Foreign-Born Population: 1980–1990," *US Bureau of the Census Population Division Working Paper No. 9*, (December 1994). Accessed October 31, 2008. http://www.census.gov/population/www/documentation/twps0009/twps0009.html

Roediger, David R. *The Wages of Whiteness: Race and the Making of the American Working Class*. London: Verso, 1991.

Roitman, Janet, John Comaroff, and Jean Comaroff. "The Ethics of Illegality in the Chad Basins." In *Law and Disorder in the Postcolony*, 247–72. Chicago: University of Chicago Press, 2006.

Rong, Xue Lan, and Frank Brown. "The Effects of Immigrant Generation and Ethnicity on Educational Attainment Among Young African and Caribbean Blacks in the United States." *Harvard Educational Review* 71, no. 3 (2001): 536–66.

Rowntree, Lester, Martin Lewis, Marie Price, and William Wyckoff. *Globalization and Diversity: Geography of a Changing World*, 5th edition. New Jersey: Upper Saddle River, Prentice Hall, 2015.

Rumbaut, Rubén G. "Origins and Destinies: Immigration to the United States Since World War II." *Sociological Forum* 9, no. 4 (Dec.1994): 583–621.

Rwamatwara, Egide. "Forced Migration in Africa: a Challenge to Development." *Stichproben. Wiener Zeitschrift für kritische Afrikastudien* 8, no. 5 (2005): 173–191.

Rydgren, Jens. "Meso-level Reasons for Racism and Xenophobia: Some Converging and Diverging Effects of Radical Right Populism in France and Sweden," *European Journal of Social Theory* 6, no. 1 (2003): 45–68.

Said, Edward W. *Culture and Imperialism*. New York: Knopf, 1993.

———. *Orientalism*. New York: Vintage Books, 1979

———. *Reflections on Exile and Other Essays*. Cambridge, MA: Harvard University Press, 2000.

Sassen, Saskia. *Guests and aliens*. New York: New Press, 1999.

Schloss, Henry H. "The Concept of Entrepreneurship in Economic Development." *Journal of Economic Issues* 2, no. 2 (1968): 228–32.

Schoumaker, Bruno, Marie-Laurence Flahaux, Djamila Schans, Cris Beauchemin, Valentina Mazzucato, and Paper Sakho. "Changing Patterns of African Migration: A Comparative Analysis." In *Migration between Africa and Europe: Trends, Factors and Effects,* edited by C. Beauchemin. New York: Springer-Verlag and INED Population Studies Series, 2015.

Schumpeter, Joseph A. *Capitalism, Socialism, and Democracy*. New York: Harper, 1950.

Schumpeter, Joseph A. "The Creative Response in Economic History." *The Journal of Economic History* 7, no. 2 (1947): 149–59.

Scott, James C. *Weapons of the Weak: Everyday Forms of Peasant Resistance*. New Haven: Yale University Press, 1985.

Searcey, Ian. "Immigration archive: Ugandan Asians in Leicester (1972)" *4 News*, Wednesday April 24, 2013. Retrieved July 8, 2016.http://www.channel4.com/news/immigration-archive-ugandan-asians-in-leicester-1972.

Segatti, Aurelia. "Migration to South Africa: Regional Challenges versus National Instruments and Interests." In *Contemporary Migration to South Africa: A regional development issue*, edited by Aurelia Segatti and Loren Landau, 9–29. Washington, DC: The International Bank for Reconstruction and Development/ The World Bank., 2011.

Semple, Kirk. "A Somali Influx Unsettles Latino Meatpackers," from *New York Times* (15 October 2008). Accessed November 1, 2008. http://www.nytimes.com/2008/10/16/us/16immig.html?ref=us

Sen, Amartya. *Development as Freedom*. New York: Knopf, 1999.

Sen, Amartya. "Equality of What." In *Tanner Lectures on Human Values, Vol. 1*, edited by Sterlin McMurrin. Salt Lake City: University of Utah Press, 1980.

Sen, Amartya. *Resources, Values, and Development*. Cambridge, MA: Harvard University Press, 1997.

Sen, Amartya. *Social Exclusion: Concept, Application, and Scrutiny*. Manila, Philippines: Office of Environment and Social Development, Asian Development Bank, 2000.

Seymour-Ure, Colin. *The Political Impact of Mass Media*. London: Constable, 1974

Sherwood, Marika. "Race, Empire and Education: Teaching Racism." *Race & Class* 42, no. 3 (2001): 1–28.

Shimeles, Abebe. "Migration Patterns, Trends and Policy Issues in Africa." Working Paper Series. December 2010.

Short, John Rennie. *Human Geography: A Short Introduction*. Oxford, NY: Oxford University Press, 2015.

Sichone, Sichone. "Xenophobia and Xenophilia in South Africa: African Migrants in Cape Town." In *Anthropology and the new Cosmopolitanism: Rooted, Feminist and Vernacular Perspectives*, by Werbner, 309–22. New York: Bloomsbury Academic, 2009.

Simmel, Georg, "The Stranger," From Kurt Wolff (Trans.) *The Sociology of Georg Simmel*. New York: Free Press (1950): 402–408.

Simone, AbdouMaliq M. *For the City Yet to Come: Changing African Life in Four Cities*. Durham: Duke University Press, 2004.

Simone, AbdouMaliq M., and Abdelghani Abouhani. *Urban Africa: changing contours of survival in the city*. London: Zed Books in association with CODESRIA, Dakar, Senegal, 2005.

Sjaastad, Larry A. "The Cost and Returns of Human Migration." *Journal of Political Economy* 7, no. 5 (October 1962): 80–93.

Skeggs, Beverley. *Formations of Class and Gender: Becoming Respectable*. London: SAGE, 1997.

Smith, Andrea, Richard N. Lalonde, and Simone Johnson. "Serial Migration and its Implications for the Parent-Child Relationship: A Retrospective Analysis of the Experiences of the Children of Caribbean Immigrants." *Cultural Diversity and Ethnic Minority Psychology* 10, no. 2 (2004): 107–22.

Smith, Matthew. *Bringing Peace to the Workplace*. Leona St: Oakland, 1986.

Smith, Rowland. *Exile and Tradition: Studies in African and Caribbean Literature*. New York: Africana Pub. Co., 1976.

Snyder, Charles R. *Handbook of Hope: Theory, Measures and Applications*. London: Academic Press, 2000.

Sobibo, Kwanele, Wet, Phillip, de, and Zwane, Thuletho. 'Township Politics Fuel the Attacks on Outsiders," *Mail & Guardian,* 30 January 2015. (Johannesburg). Retrieved July 6, 2016. http://mg.co.za/article/2015-01-29-township-politics-fuel-the-attacks-on-outsiders July 5, 2016.

Solimano, Andrés. "Global Migration and International Development in Unstable Times. International Center for Globalization and Development," Working paper No. 25, June, 2016, 1-35. Retrieved December 3, 2016 www.Ciglob.org.

———. ed, *The International Mobility of Talent: Types, Causes and Development Impact*. New York: Oxford University Press, 2008.

Spatafora, N. "Worker's Remittances and Development." *World Economic Outlook*, Washington, DC: IMF, April 2005, Chapter 2.

Spel, Christal O. "Building Personal Lives as Informal Migrants in South Africa: Narratives of Poor African Informal Migrants in Johannesburg." PhD Thesis, Helsinki: University of Helsinki Press, Forthcoming.

Spencer, Ian R. G. *British Immigration Policy since 1939: The Making of Multi-Racial Britain*. London: Routledge, 1997.

———."The Open Door, Labour Needs and British Immigration Policy, 1945–55." *Immigrants & Minorities* 15, no. 1 (1996): 22–41.

Stanford Encyclopedia of Philosophy. 2015. "Immigration". *Stanford Center for the Study of Language and Information (*CSLI), Stanford University (2015). Accessed August 14, 2016. htpps://plato.stanford.edu.

Stebleton, Michael J. "Career Counseling with African Immigrant College Students: Theoretical Approaches and Implications for Practice." *The Career Development Quarterly* 55, no. 4 (2007): 290–312.

Steinberg, Johnny. "South Africa's Xenophobic Eruption." Institute for Security Studies, Pretoria: South Africa: 2008.

Streiff-Fenart, Jocelyne and Aurelia Segatti eds. *The Challenge of the Threshold: Border Closures and Migration Movements in Africa.* Plymouth, UK: Lexington Books, 2014.

SULAIR: Africa South of the Sahara. *Topics: Education: African Brain Drain.* The Board of Trustees of the Leland Stanford Junior University, 1994–2010. Accessed October 31, 2008. http://www-sul.stanford.edu/depts/ssrg/africa/africaneducation/africa-brainhttp://www-sul.stanford.edu/depts/ssrg/africa/africaneducation/africa-brain-drain.htmldrain.html.

Sword, Keith, "The Repatriation of Soviet Citizens at The End of The Second World War." In *The Cambridge Survey of World Migration*, edited by Robin Cohen, 323–26. Cambridge: Cambridge University Press, Cambridge, 1995.

Takyi, Baffour. "The Making of the Second Diaspora: On the Recent African Immigrant Community in the United States of America." *The Journal of Black Studies* 26, no. 1 (2002): 32–43.

Tamale, Sylvia. *African Sexualities: A Reader*. Oxford, UK: Pambazuka Press, 2011.

Tanner, Arno. *Emigration, Brain Drain and Development: The Case of Sub-Saharan Africa*. Helsinki: East-West Books, 2005.

Taylor, Edward J. "International Migration, Remittances and Development: Myths and Facts." *International Migration* 37, no.1 (1999): 63–88.

Tebeje, Ainalem. "Brain Drain and Capacity Building in Africa," from International Development Research Centre: Science for Humanity (22 February 2005).

Accessed October 31, 2008. http://www.idrc.ca/en/ev-71249-201-1-DO_TOPIC.html.

———. "Brain Drain and Capacity building in Africa." International Development Resource Center (IDRC). Retrieved December 3, 2016 https://www.idrc.ca/en/article/brain-drain-and-capacity-building-africa.

Terminski, Bogumil. "Towards Recognition and Protection of Forced Environmental Migrants in the Public International Law: Refugee or IDPs Umbrella." *Policy Studies Organization Summit Proceedings*. Washington: Policy Studies Organization, 2011.

The 1983–1985 Ethiopian famine, Hazards and Vulnerability Research Institute, Department of Geography, University of South Carolina, Columbia, South Carolina. Accessed October 19, 2016. http://webra.cas.sc.edu/hvri/feature/oct2013.dom.aspx.

Thomas, Kevin T.A. "Parental Characteristics and the Schooling Progress of the Children of Immigrant and U.S.-Born Blacks." *Demography* 46, no. 3 (2009): 513–34.

Thomas, Kevin J. A. "What Explains the Increasing Trend in African Emigration to the U.S.?" *The International Migration Review* 45, no. 1 (2011): 3–28.

Tienda, Marta and Susan Sanchez. "Latin American Immigration to the United States." *Daedalus* 142,no. 3 (2013): 48–64.

Tiffen, Rodney. *The News from Southeast Asia: The Sociology of Newsmaking*. Singapore: Institute of Southeast Asian Studies, 1978.

Tignor, Robert L., Jeremy Adelman, Peter Brown, Benjamin Elman, and Stephen Kotkin. *Worlds Together, Worlds Apart: A History of the World: Beginnings through the Fifteenth Century*. 4th ed. Vol. 1. New York: W. W. Norton & Company, 2013.

Tilly, Charles. "War Making and State Making as Organized Crime." In *Bringing the State Back in*, edited by Peter B. Evans, Dietrich Rueschemeyer, and Theda Skocpol, 169–91. Cambridge, MA: Cambridge University Press, 1985.

Tillman, Kathryn H. "Coresident Sibling Composition and the Academic Ability, Expectations, and Performance of Youth." *Sociological Perspectives* 51, no. 4 (2008): 679–711.

Todaro, Michael P. *Economic Development in the Third World*. London: Longman Publishers, 1989.

———. "Migration and Economic Development: A Review of Theory, Evidence, Methodology, and Research Priorities." Occasional Paper 18 (Institute for Development Studies University of Nairobi, 1976). Accessed 12 August, 2016.Mobile.opendocs.ids.ac.uk/opendocs/handle/1233456789/791.

———. "A Model of Labor Migration and Urban Unemployment in Less Developed Countries." *American Economic Review* 59, no. 1 (1969): 138–48.

Tolstoy, Leo, and Aylmer MAUDE. *What is Art? ... Translated ... With an Introduction by A. Maude*. London: Oxford University Press, 1975.

Torpey, John. "Coming and Going: On the State Monopolization of the Legitimate "Means of Movement"." *Sociological Theory* 16, no. 3 (1998): 239–59.

Tromp, Emsley D. "The Caribbean Marketplace Succeeding in a Globalizing World," Address delivered by President of the Bank van de Nederlandse Antillen On the Occasion of the 2007 TOG Partners' Conference Willemstad, Curacao (2007): pp. 1–8.

Trowler, Paul. *Investigating Mass Media*. London: Collins Educational, 1996.

Tsuda, Takekuji, "Media Images, Immigrant Reality: Ethnic Prejudice and Tradition in Japanese Media Representations of Japanese-Brazilian Return Migrants," CCIS: Center for Comparative Immigration Studies. University of California, San Diego (2004): 1–30.

Tyler, Imogen. "'Welcome to Britain': The Cultural Politics of Asylum." *European Journal of Cultural Studies* 9, no. 2 (2006): 185–202.

Tylor, Edward Burnett. *Primitive Culture*. London: Murray, 1871.

Uganda Human Rights Commission. "*The 12th Annual Report of the Uganda Human Rights Commission to the Parliament of the Republic of Uganda,*" Uganda Human Rights Commission, 2009. Retrieved July 5, 2016. http://www.google.com/url?url=http://www.rwi.lu.se/NHRIDB/Africa/Uganda/2009%2520Annual%2520Report.pdf&rct=j&frm=1&q=&esrc=s&sa=U&ved=0ahUKEwihu5nz_uTNAhVJHh4KHSHOB6MQFggUMAA&usg=AFQjCNEYoitqBugylMz_q77ASqGYscuZ4A.

United Nations Children's Fund. "Uprooted: The Growing Crisis for Refugee and Migrant Children," *Division of Data, Research and Policy*. New York: UNICEF, 3 United Nations Plaza, 2016.

United Nations. "Trends in International Migrantstock: The 2013 Revision—Migrants by Age and Sex." United Nations Department of Economic and Social Affairs Population Division, December 2013. Accessed October 2016. http://www.un.org/en/development/desa/population/publications/pdf/migration/migrant-stock-age-2013.pdf

UN. Department of Economic and Social Affairs, International Migration Report 2015. United Nations New York, 2016. Retrieved December 3, 2016. www.un.org/.../population/migration/.../migrationreport/.../MigrationReport2015_Highlights.pdf.

United Nations, Department of Economic and Social Affairs. "Trends in International Migrant Stock: Migrants by Destination and Origin." (United Nations database, POP/DB/MIG/Stock/Rev.2013). New York: United Nations, 2013.

United Nations, Department of Economic and Social Affairs. "Trends in International Migrant Stock: Migrants by Destination and Origin." (*United Nations database, POP/DB/MIG/Stock/Rev.*2015), New York: United Nations, 2015.

United Nations Economic Commission for Africa. "Free Movement of Persons, Residence and Establishment (Protocol A/P 1/5/79)." *ECOWAS*. http://documenation.ecowas.int/download/en/legal_documentation/pro-tocols/PROTOCOL%20RELATING%20TO%20%FREE%20MOVEMENT%20OF%20PERSONS.pdf. Accessed 20 August 2016.

United Nations. "Human Development Report 2009: Overcoming Barriers, Human Mobility and Development." 2009. Accessed October 10, 2016. http://hdr.undp.org/en/content/human-development-report-2009.

UN Migration Agency. "Global Migration Flows (IN)." *The International Organization for Migration*. Accessed 15 August 2016. www.iom.int/countries/algeria.

UN Migration Agency. "Global Migration Flows (IN)." *The International Organization for Migration*. Accessed 19 August 2016. www.iom.int/countries/mali.

UN Migration Agency. "Global Migration Flows (IN)." *The International Organization for Migration*. Accessed 15 August, 2016. www.iom.int/countries/mauritania.

UN Migration Agency. "Global Migration Flows (OUT)." *The International Organization for Migration.* Accessed 15 August, 2016. www.iom.int/countries/algeria.

UN Migration Agency. "Global Migration Flows (OUT)." *The International Organization for Migration.* Accessed 19 August 2016. www.iom.int/countries/mali.

UN Migration Agency. "Global Migration Flows (OUT)." *The International Organization for Migration.* Accessed 15 August, 2016. www.iom.int/countries/mauritania.

United Nations, United Nations Recommendations on Statistics of International Migration, Revision 1 *in International Migration Flows to and From Selected Countries: The 2015 Revision Cd-Rom Documentation*, United Nations Economic and Social Affairs, Population Division, December, 2015.

UNESCO, UNESCO Science Report 2010. *The Current Status of Science Around the World.* Retrieved December 1, 2016 www.unesco.org/new/.../HQ/.../SC_Facts-Figures_USR10_EN.pdf.

United States Census Bureau. "African-Born Population in U.S. Roughly Doubled Every Decade Since 1970." Accessed September 29, 2016. http://www.census.gov/newsroom/press-releases/2014/cb14-184.html.

United States Department of Health and Human Services, Centers for Disease Control and Prevention, & National Center for Emerging and Zoonotic Infectious Diseases. "Congolese Refugee Health Profile." August 29, 2014. Accessed September 19, 2016. https://www.cdc.gov/immigrantrefugeehealth/profiles/congolese/index.html.

United States Department of Homeland Security. *Yearbook of immigration Statistics.* (2004–2007). Accessed October 31, 2008. http://www.dhs.gov/ximgtn/statistics/publications/yearbook.shtm.

United States Department of State. *2015 Trafficking in Human Persons Report.* Accessed 15 August, 2016. www.state.gov/documents/organizations/258880.pdf.

———. *2015 Trafficking in Human Persons Report.* Accessed 15 August, 2016. www.state.gov/documents/organizations/258878.pdf.

"United States Medical Licensing Examination." United States Medical Licensing Examination Accessed December 10, 2017. http://www.usmle.org/.

United Nations. "World Migration in Figures." A joint contribution by UN-DESA and the OECD. October 03, 2013. Accessed September 19, 2016. https://www.oecd.org/els/mig/World-Migration-in-Figures.pdf.

Van Moppes, David. "The African Migration Movement: Routes to Europe." The Working Papers on Migration and Development, Report No. 5. Nijmegen, The Netherlands: Research Group on Migration and Development, Radboud University.

Vigneswaran, Darshan, Tesfalem Araia, Colin Hoag, and Xolani Tshabalala. "Criminality or Monopoly? Informal Immigration Enforcement in South Africa." *Journal of Southern African Studies* 36, no. 2 (2010): 465–81.

Vigouroux, Cecile. "There Are no Whites in South Africa': Territoriality, Language and Identity Among Francophone Africans in Cape Town." 16 Passage Gatbois, Paris, *Language and Communication* 25 (2005): 237–55.

———. "The Smuggling of La Francophonie: Francophone Africans in Anglophone Cape Town (South Africa)" *Language in Society* 37(2008):415–34.

Wallerstein, Immanuel, *World-Systems Analysis: An Introduction 1.* Durham, NC: Duke University Press Books 2004.

———. "*1972: Asians Given 90 days to Leave Uganda*," *BBC News*, On This Day 1950-2005, Retrieved July 5, 2016. http://news.bbc.co.uk/onthisday/hi/dates/stories/august/7/newsid_2492000/2492333.stm.

———. "*CARICOM Single Market and Economy (CSME)*", KnowledgeWalk Institute, last modified July 10. 2016. http://www.caribbeanelections.com/education/integration/csme.asp.

———. "Trinidad Denies Racial Profiling Following Deportation of African Nationals", *Caribbean 360*, December 10, 2014. Retrieved July 12, 2016. http://www.caribbean360.com/news/trinidad-denies-racial-profiling-following-deportation-african-nationals.

———. "US Group Condemns Trinidad's Deportation of Africans", Jamaica Observer, Friday, December 12, 2014. Retrieved July 12, 2016.http://www.jamaicaobserver.com/news/US-group-condemns-Trinidad-s-deportation-of-Africans.

———. "The Dominican Republic's discrimination against Haitians." *The Washington Post*, November 7, 2013. Retrieved July 27, 2016. https://www.washingtonpost.com/opinions/the-dominican-republics-discrimination-against-haitians/2013/11/07/9066d436-4236-11e3-a751-f032898f2dbc_story.html.

Wardhaugh, Ronald. *An Introduction to Sociolinguistics*. Oxford: Basil Blackwell Limited, 1992.

Weissbord, Robert G. *Ebony Kinship: Africa, Africans, and the Afro-American*. Westport, Connecticut: Greenwoord Press, 1973.

Welsh, Tierney and Teresa, Sneed. 2014. "What is Driving Homophobia in Africa?" *U.S. News and World Report*. (16 October 2014) http://www.usnews.com/news/articles/2014/10/16/how-anti-lgbt-legislation-in-uganda-nigeria-and-gambia-is-shaping-africa (Accessed Sep 8, 2016).

Wendt, Alexander. "Anarchy is What States make of It." In *International Politics: Enduring Concepts and Contemporary Issues*, 12th ed., edited by Robert Art and Robert Jervis, 59–66. New York: Pearson Longman Publishers, 2015.

Williams, Brian, Eleanor Gouws, Mark Lurie, and Jonathan Crush. *Spaces of Vulnerability: Migration and HIV/AIDS in South Africa*. Cape Town: Idasa, 2002.

Williams, Raymond. *Keywords: A Vocabulary of Culture and Society*. New York: Oxford University Press, 1976.

Winder, Robert. *Bloody Foreigners: The Story of Immigration to Britain*. London: Abacus, 2005.

Winthrop, Robert H. *Dictionary of Concepts in Cultural Anthropology*. New York: Greenwood Press, 1991.

Witt, Harald. "Formal and Informal Economy Linkages in the Fruit and Vegetable Sector." Durban's Technical Task Team for the Informal Economy Research report, Durban, 2000.

Wodak, Ruth. *Disorders of Discourse*. Longman: University of Michigan, 1996.

World Bank. "Global Economic Prospects: Economic implications of Remittances and Migration." Washington, DC: World Bank, 2006. Age of migration website – www.age-of-migration.com.

———. Regional and International Migration in the Caribbean and its Impact on Sustainable Development Compendium on Recent Research on Migration in the

Caribbean. Caribbean Expert Group Meeting on Migration, Human Rights and Development in the Caribbean 14–15 September 2005 28 October 2005, Port of Spain, Trinidad and Tobago.

———. "The ICD "Experience Africa" Program. The African Diaspora. Introduction to the African Diaspora Across the world." nd. Retrieved December 6, 2016http://www.experience-africa.de/index.php?en_the-african-diaspora.

———. "Countries in Latin America and the Caribbean, Worldometers." Retrieved August 22, 2016. http://www.worldometers.info/geography/how-many-countries-in-latin-america/.

———. "Migration and Families, International Dialogue on Migration (IDM), 2014: Human Mobility and Development: Emerging Trends and New Opportunities for Partnerships Intersessional Workshop," October 7–8, 2014. International Organization for Migration (IOM), Background paper. P. 2.

World Bank Group. "Migration and Remittance Data[XLS]." Accessed 15 August, 2016. http://www.worldbank.org/en/topic/migrationremittancesdiasporaissues/brief/migration-remittances-data.

Yearwood, Edilma L. ""Growing Up" Children: Current Child-Rearing Practices Among Immigrant Jamaican Families." *Journal of Child and Adolescent* Psychiatric *Nursing* 14, no. 1 (2001): 7–17.

Young, Robert. "Franglais or Camfran." Accessed April 21, 2008. http://158.130.17.5/~myl/languagelog/archives/004225.html

Zelinsky, Wilbur. "The Hypothesis of the Mobility Transition." *Geographical Review* 61, no. 2 (1971): 219–49.

Zlotnik, Hania. "International Migration in Africa: An Analysis Based on Estimates of the Migrant Stock." September 01, 2004. Accessed October 19, 2016. http://www.migrationpolicy.org/article/international-migration-africa-analysis-based-estimates-migrant-stock.

Index

About the Editors

Sabella Ogbobode Abidde is an Associate Professor of Political Science, and a member of the graduate faculty at Alabama State University Montgomery, Alabama. He obtained his PhD from Howard University in Washington D.C. with a disciplinary focus on World Affairs and a minor in Public Policy and Development Studies. While at Howard, he was a Sasakawa Young Leaders Fellowship Fund (SYLFF) fellow. And from 2011–2014, he was a columnist for Nigeria's newspaper of record, the *Punch*. He is the author, most recently, of *Nigeria's Niger Delta: Militancy, Amnesty and the Post-Amnesty Environment*. Lanham, MD: Lexington Books, 2017. And he coedited, with Olayiwola Abegunrin, *Pan-Africanism in Modern Times: Challenges, Concerns and Constraints*. Lanham, Maryland: Lexington Books, 2016. His areas of teaching and research include African politics and institutions, state violence and terrorism, comparative politics, oil and environmental politics and trans-national issues.

Brenda Ingrid Gill is a mixed-method prepared family sociologists and an Associate Professor of Sociology in the Department of Criminal Justice and Social Sciences at Alabama State University Montgomery, Alabama. She received a PhD from Wayne State University, Detroit Michigan. Her research focus, mostly international, includes: multiculturalism, diversity, family, media, and violence (family and school). Her work includes two chapters on Pan-Africanism: Pan-Africanism in Latin America and the Caribbean: Past, Present, and Future, and Pan-Africanism and Women: Projections and Speculations for the Future in *Pan-Africanism in Modern Times: Challenges, Concerns and Constraints,* edited by Olayiwola Abegunrin and Sabella Abidde (Lexington Book, 2016). A previous chapter on multiculturalism from an international perspective published in Voices of Diversity (2009), which explores experiences, challenges, similarities, and differences with diversity and multiculturalism in several countries.

About the Contributors

Alecia D. Hoffman teaches political science at Alabama State University in Montgomery. She earned her PhD in political science from Clark Atlanta University. Her research interests include Sino-African relations, international relations, and South-South cooperation.

Brenda Ingrid Gill is an associate professor of sociology in the Department of Criminal Justice and Social Sciences at Alabama State University, Montgomery, Alabama.

Bruce Ormond Grant is an independent scholar and a noted blogger for The Village—an organ of The Congressional Black Caucus Foundation, Washington DC. He holds a PhD in African Studies and Research from Howard University in Washington, DC.

Christal Oghogho Spel is currently an advanced doctoral candidate of social and public policy at the University Of Helsinki, Finland. She holds a master's degree in Development and International Cooperation from the University of Jyvaskyla, Finland.

Dollin Wilson Ovaroh-Holt graduated from the Universities of East London and Bedfordshire with postgraduate degrees in Forced Migration and Refugee Studies (MA), International Human Rights Law (LLM) and Media Representation (MA by Research).

Elisha Jasper Dung is an associate professor of geography in the Department of Criminal Justice and Social Sciences at Alabama State University. He holds an MA degree in geography from the University of Northern Iowa and a PhD in Geography from Oklahoma State University.

George K. Danns is a professor of sociology at the University of North Georgia. He has a PhD in sociology from the State University of New York at Stony Brook and was awarded a Ford Foundation Fellowship for Doctoral Research in Latin America and the Caribbean.

Leonard Sitji Bombom is a lecturer in the Department of Geography and Planning, University of Jos, Nigeria. His MA is from the University of Northern Iowa, Cedar Falls, and his Ph.D. from Oklahoma State University–Stillwater Oklahoma.

Magdaline Mbong Mai completed an MA in applied linguistics and a PhD in sociolinguistics, all at the University of the Western Cape. She is currently a Postdoctoral Research Fellow at the University of Johannesburg in the Department of Communication Studies.

Olayinka Oyegbile is an award-winning journalist who has won many journalism fellowships—including the Knight Journalism Fellowship at the Centers for Disease Control and Prevention (Atlanta, Georgia). He is currently the deputy editor of The Nation on Sunday in Nigeria.

Paul O. Erhunmwunsee is a professor of geography and the Chair of the Department of Criminal Justice and Social Sciences at Alabama State University. He holds an MS in engineering and a PhD in geography both from the University of Wisconsin, Milwaukee.

Sabella Ogbobode Abidde is an associate professor of political science in the Department of History and Political Science at Alabama State University Montgomery, Alabama.

Sasha Drummond-Lewis received her PhD in sociology from Wayne State University in Detroit, Michigan. She is currently an assistant professor of sociology in the Department of Sociology, Anthropology, and Criminal Justice at the University of Michigan-Flint.

Sulayman S. Nyang was a professor and Chair of the Department of African Studies, Howard University in Washington, DC. He has written extensively on Islamic, African and Middle Eastern affairs, and has served as consultant to several national and international agencies.